Fourth Edition

Professional Selling

A Trust-Based Approach

Thomas N. Ingram
Colorado State University

Raymond W. LaForge
University of Louisville

Ramon A. Avila
Ball State University

Charles H. Schwepker Jr.
University of Central Missouri

Michael R. Williams
Illinois State University

THOMSON

SOUTH-WESTERN

Australia · Brazil · Canada · Mexico · Singapore · Spain · United Kingdom · United States

THOMSON

SOUTH-WESTERN

Professional Selling: A Trust-Based Approach, Fourth Edition
Thomas N. Ingram, Raymond W. LaForge, Ramon A. Avila, Charles H. Schwepker, Jr., Michael R. Williams

VP/Editorial Director:
Jack W. Calhoun

Publisher:
Neil Marquardt

Developmental Editor:
Michael Guendelsberger

Editorial Assistant:
Clara Kuhlman

Marketing Manager:
Nicole C. Moore

Marketing Coordinator:
Sarah Rose

Marketing Communications Manager:
Sarah Greber

Content Project Manager:
Patrick Cosgrove

Manager, Editorial Media:
John Barans

Technology Project Manager:
Pam Wallace

Senior Manufacturing Coordinator:
Diane Gibbons

Production House:
International Typesetting and
Composition

Printer:
West Eagan, MN

Art Director:
Stacy Shirley

Internal Designer:
Lou Ann Thesing

Cover Designer:
Lou Ann Thesing

Cover Illustration:
Ted Knapke

Library of Congress Control Number:
2006908739

For more information about our
products, contact us at:
**Thomson Learning Academic
Resource Center
1-800-423-0563**

**Thomson Higher Education
5191 Natorp Boulevard
Mason, OH 45040
USA**

BRIEF CONTENTS

CONTENTS

The fourth edition of *Professional Selling: A Trust-Based Approach* is intended to continue to provide students and professors with comprehensive coverage of contemporary professional selling in an interesting and challenging manner. We integrate the most recent sales research and leading personal selling practice into our effective and time-tested pedagogical format. The major professional selling topics are organized into ten modules and presented in a logical sequence from the perspective of a professional salesperson. The ten-module format makes it easy for professors to cover the modules in a semester or quarter and have plenty of time for role plays and other experiential exercises. This makes it possible for students to learn the important concepts and processes from the text and then apply them in various types of active-learning activities.

The most exciting aspect of the fourth edition of *Professional Selling: A Trust-Based Approach* is the new trust-based sales process. The official definition of marketing was recently revised with a focus on creating, communicating, and delivering value, and managing customer relationships. We think this new definition has important implications for professional selling, since salespeople play a key role in value creation, communication, and delivery, and in managing customer relationships. In addition, most sales processes imply that salespeople deliver a sales presentation that is largely a monologue. Yet, most successful sales interactions are an active dialogue between the buyer and seller. Thus, our new trust-based sales process emphasizes creating, communicating, and delivering value; initiating, developing, and enhancing customer relationships; and collaborative sales dialogue throughout the entire process. This new model is presented in Module 1 and emphasized in the remaining modules. We have changed the names of several modules to reflect the focus on value, relationships, and dialogue. Our new trust-based sales process has been tested in our classes and students really like it. It helps to overcome the negative stereotypes many students have about personal selling. Students seem to embrace a concept of professional selling based on value, relationships, and dialogue. We are delighted with student response to our new sales process model.

STRENGTHS OF THIS EDITION

We have maintained what has worked well in previous editions, revised all modules to incorporate the latest developments in sales thought and practice, and added new content and pedagogy. The key strengths of the fourth edition of *Professional Selling: A Trust-Based Approach* are:

- The new trust-based sales process as the major organizing framework for the entire text. The overall model is presented in Module 1 and all remaining modules are linked to it. This provides a coherent, organized framework for the text and for a professional selling class.
- One of the ways we present leading professional selling practice is through comments made in each module from our Professional Selling Panel. We have added several new sales professionals to this panel. These sales professionals represent a variety

of different industries. They share what they and their companies are doing now. These "Professional Selling in the 21st Century" boxes give students an accurate picture of the "real world" of professional selling in today's business environment.

- The Opening Vignettes for all modules are new. The purpose of these vignettes is to engage students by generating interest in the material to be covered in a module. These vignettes typically present well-known firms and their up-to-date professional selling practices.
- Numerous role plays are in every module. An icon in the margin indicates each role play. The role plays are normally tied to the "Ethical Dilemma" boxes, exercises in the "Building Professional Selling Skills" section at the end of each module, and the short cases in the "Making Professional Selling Decisions" section at the end of each module. Each role play provides the characters, the scene, specific directions, and questions to guide a discussion of completed roles plays. We use these role plays in our classes and students learn a great deal from participating and discussing them.
- At the end of the text we provide a complete section of "Experiential Exercises." These exercises are in addition to those found at the end of each module. The "Experiential Exercises" are numbered to reflect the appropriate module for the exercise. We have tried to provide a large number of different types of exercises so that professors can find ones that meet their needs the best.
- The video package was developed specifically for the text. Therefore, it demonstrates and teaches the specific concepts and skills covered in the text. Experienced actors present clear examples of important concepts and skills. An off-camera spokesperson provides narrative explanations and asks a variety of questions for students to think about and answer. We have found the video package to be an effective learning aid in our professional selling classes.

We are excited about the fourth edition of *Professional Selling: A Trust-Based Approach*. We have used the text successfully in our professional selling classes. Students find the book to be readable and interesting, like the many examples and active-learning exercises, and many indicate they are going to keep the book to use in their career. Most students complete the course with a more favorable attitude toward professional selling and many decide to pursue sales jobs and careers. The positive impact that *Professional Selling: A Trust-Based Approach* has had on students over the years is a source of immense satisfaction for us.

MODULE PEDAGOGY

The following pedagogical format is used for each module to facilitate the student learning process.

Objectives. Specific learning objectives for the module are stated in behavioral terms so that students will know what they should be able to do after the module has been covered.

Opening Vignettes. All modules are introduced by an opening vignette that typically consists of a recent, real-world company example addressing many of the key points to be discussed in the module. These opening vignettes are intended to generate student interest in the topics to be covered and to illustrate the practicality of the module coverage.

Key Words. Key words are highlighted in bold type throughout each module and summarized in "Understanding Professional Selling Terms" at the end of the module to alert students to their importance.

Boxed Inserts. Each module contains two boxed inserts titled "Professional Selling in the 21st Century." The comments in these boxes are provided by members of our Professional Selling Panel and were developed specifically for our text.

Figure Captions. Every figure in the text includes a summarizing caption designed to make the figure understandable without reference to the module discussion.

Module Summaries. A module summary recaps the key points covered in the module by restating and answering questions presented in the learning objectives at the beginning of the module.

Developing Professional Selling Knowledge. Ten discussion questions are presented at the end of each module to review key concepts covered in the module. Some of the questions require students to summarize what has been covered, while others are designed to be more thought provoking and extend beyond module coverage.

Building Professional Selling Skills. Application exercises are supplied for each module, requiring students to apply what has been learned in the module to specific personal selling situations. Many of these exercises allow students to record responses directly in the book. This encourages active learning in a workbook format.

Making Professional Selling Decisions. Each module concludes with two short cases. Most of these cases represent realistic and interesting professional selling situations. Many are designed so that students can role play their solutions.

SUPPLEMENTS

Instructor's Resource CD (IRCD)

The Instructor's Resource CD delivers all the traditional instructor support materials in one handy place: a CD. Electronic files are included on the CD for the complete Instructor's Manual, Test Bank, computerized Test Bank and computerized Test Bank software (ExamView), and chapter-by-chapter PowerPoint presentation files that can be used to enhance in-class lectures.

- *Instructor's Manual*
  The Instructor's Manual for the fourth edition of *Professional Selling: A Trust-Based Approach* contains many helpful teaching suggestions and solutions to text exercises to help instructors successfully integrate all of the materials offered with this text into their class. Each module includes the following materials designed to meet the instructor's needs.

  - Learning objectives
  - Module outline and summary
  - Ideas for student involvement
  - Possible answers to review sections in the text, "Developing Professional Selling Knowledge" and "Building Professional Selling Skills"
  - Ideas for how to incorporate the "Role Play" exercises found in the text into the classroom setting, as well as suggestions for grading the "Role Plays"
  - Suggestions on how to effectively integrate the video package into the classroom discussion

  The Instructor's Manual files are located on the IRCD in Microsoft Word format.

- *Test Bank*
  The revised and updated Test Bank includes a variety of multiple choice and true/false questions, which emphasize the important concepts presented in each chapter. The Test Bank questions vary in levels of difficulty so that each instructor can tailor his or her testing to meet his or her specific needs. The Test Bank files are located on the IRCD in Microsoft Word format.

- *ExamView (Computerized) Test Bank*
  The Test Bank is also available on the IRCD in computerized format (ExamView), allowing instructors to select problems at random by level of difficulty or type,

customize or add test questions, and scramble questions to create numerous versions of the same test.

- *PowerPoint Presentation Slides*
  Created by Scott Inks of Ball State University, this package brings classroom lectures and discussions to life with the Microsoft PowerPoint presentation tool. Extremely professor friendly and organized by chapter, these chapter-by-chapter presentations outline chapter content. The eye-appealing and easy-to-read slides are tailored specifically to the *Professional Selling* text from the Ingram author team. The PowerPoint presentation slides are available on the IRCD and as downloadable files on the text support site (www.thomsonedu.com/marketing/imgram).

Web Site

Visit the text Web site at www.thomsonedu.com/marketing/ingram to find instructor's support materials as well as study resources that will help students practice and apply the concepts they have learned in class.

- **Student Resources**
  - Online quizzes for each chapter are available on the Web site for those students who would like additional study materials. After each quiz is submitted, automatic feedback tells the students how they scored and what the correct answers are to the questions they missed. Students are then able to e-mail their results directly to the their instructor if desired.
  - Crossword quizzing of glossary terms and definitions arranged by chapter is also available for extra review of key terms found in the text.
  - Students can download the PowerPoint presentation slides from the Web site.
- **Instructor Resources**
  - Downloadable Instructor's Manual files are available in Microsoft Word format and Adobe Acrobat format.
  - Downloadable PowerPoint presentation files are available in Microsoft PowerPoint format.

Videos

In response to many requests for contemporary, relevant, and up-to-date videos, the authors and a team of experienced selling educators have updated the video package specifically designed for *Professional Selling: A Trust-Based Approach, Fourth Edition*. The videos illustrate the concepts and skills of relationship and consultative selling. Each video has been developed to accurately and effectively demonstrate and teach specific selling concepts. Experienced actors provide clear examples and an off-camera spokesperson provides a narrative explanation and reinforcement. Students are asked to consider and answer a variety of teaching-related questions.

ACKNOWLEDGMENTS

The writing of a book is a long and arduous task that requires the dedicated efforts of many individuals. The contributions of these individuals are greatly appreciated and deserve special recognition. We are especially grateful for the efforts of the reviewers who continue to help us make this a great text.

A substantial amount of credit for this book should go to all of the wonderful people at Thomson South-Western. Their expertise, support, and constant encouragement turned an extremely difficult task into a very enjoyable one. We would like to recognize specifically the tremendous efforts of the following professionals and friends: Neil Marquardt, Mike Guendelsberger, Patrick Cosgrove, Clara Kuhlman, Sarah Rose, and Stacy Shirley. Without their efforts the fourth edition would not have been possible. We also wish to thank the many individuals with whom we did not have direct contact but who assisted in the development and production of this book.

We are also very appreciative of the support provided by our colleagues at Colorado State University, the University of Louisville, Central Missouri State University, Ball State University, and Illinois State University. We also wish to extend a special thanks to Scott A. Inks of Ball State University.

Thomas A. Ingram
Raymond W. LaForge
Ramon A. Avila
Charles H. Schwepker, Jr.
Michael R. Williams.

MODULE FORMAT

Professional Selling: A Trust-Based Approach was written for students. Therefore, its aim is to provide comprehensive coverage of professional selling in a manner that you will find interesting and readable. Each module blends recent research results with current professional selling practice in a format designed to facilitate learning.

At the beginning of each module, "Objectives" highlight the basic material that the student should expect to learn. These learning objectives are helpful in reviewing modules for future study. An opening vignette then illustrates many of the important ideas to be covered in the module, using examples of companies in various industries to illustrate the diversity and complexity of professional selling. Most of the companies described in the vignettes are well known, and most of the situations represent recent actions by these firms.

Key words in the body of each module are printed in bold letters, and figures and exhibits are used liberally to illustrate and amplify the discussion in the text. Every figure contains an explanation so that it can be understood without reference to the text.

Each module contains two boxed inserts entitled **Professional Selling in the 21st Century**. The examples in both boxes have been provided specifically for this textbook by sales executives from various companies whom we recruited to serve as a **Professional Selling Panel**. To ensure that the textbook includes the latest practices from leading sales organizations, each executive was asked to provide specific examples of "best practices" in their company. Backgrounds of each executive are provided at the end of this section.

Salespeople are confronted with various ethical issues when performing their job activities. Many of these ethical issues are addressed in **An Ethical Dilemma** boxes that appear throughout the modules. You will be presented with realistic ethical situations faced by salespeople and you will be asked to recommend appropriate courses of action.

A module summary is geared to the learning objectives presented at the beginning of the module. **Understanding Professional Selling Terms** lists the key words that appear in bold throughout the module. **Developing Professional Selling Knowledge** presents ten questions to help you develop an understanding of important professional selling issues and relationships. **Building Professional Selling Skills** consists of three exercises in which you can apply the professional selling knowledge learned in the module. **Making Professional Selling Decisions** includes two interesting case situations that allow you to make important professional selling decisions. If you understand professional selling terms, develop professional selling knowledge, and build professional selling skills, you will be prepared to make successful professional selling decisions. Opportunities for student role plays are identified with this icon:

ROLE PLAY

PROFESSIONAL SELLING PANEL

Tom Avila's title of sales engineer for Davis and Davis has him representing approximately 20 different companies in protected territories in the process-control industry. Based in Denver, Colorado, Tom holds a B.S. in business with a focus in finance, management, and marketing from Ball State University.

Darrell Beaty is manager of business development for Ontario Systems. In his position, he provides leadership and direction to members of the business development group. The primary responsibility of the group is to build strong relationships with strategic clients and assist with strategic goals of Ontario Systems. Darrell attended Ball State University.

Greg Burchett is a district sales manager for Wallace Computer Services in Ft. Wayne, Indiana. He supervises four salespeople who sell commercial printing and supplies to businesses and organizational customers. Greg has a B.S. in marketing from Indiana University, Bloomington.

Kari Darding is a manager at Wells Fargo Financial. Kari and her sales team utilize the trust-based, collaborative selling process to provide a diverse array of financial products designed to meet the specific needs of each individual customer. Kari graduated from Illinois State University with a degree in marketing.

Kim Davenport is a senior district sales manager for Shering-Plough Labs. He manages 16 pharmaceutical sales representatives in Arizona and New Mexico. Kim holds a B.S. in marketing and general business administration from Ball State University.

John Haack is the senior vice president of sales and marketing for Ball Foster Glass. He has held various sales and marketing management positions in the packaging industry throughout his career. John holds a B.S. in business from Ball State University.

Jerry Heffel started with The Southwestern Company as a college student salesperson in 1965, and has been president of the company since 1980. He is responsible for current profitability and setting the future direction for the company. Jerry has a B.A. in history from Oklahoma State University, and an M.B.A. from the University of Oklahoma.

Jamie Howard is the vice president of Chicago-based Active Solutions where he has direct responsibility for managing the organization's sales and marketing programs and personnel. Jamie has achieved a solid record of sales success in the highly competitive contract furniture industry, including a host of national and regional top performance awards. He provides his sales force with the benefits of his exceptional knowledge and expertise in trust-based selling. Widely known for his proficiency in sales training and development, Jamie regularly gives his time to work with university sales classes and mentor up-and-coming sales professionals. Jamie holds a B.S. in business with a major in marketing from Illinois State University.

John Klich is a financial representative and college unit director for Northwestern Mutual Financial Network. Based in Schaumburg, Illinois, John has established a successful career in life insurance, investments, and financial planning. He is also active in and responsible for the development of career agents and manages a top-ranked college internship program.

Steve Kehoe, CFP, CLU, is president of Kehoe Financial Services LLC in Cincinnati, Ohio. Steve provides financial services to more than 1,300 clients. He has a B.S. from Ball State University and a Master's of Science from Indiana University.

David Laube is the securities principal at the Bloomington, Illinois office of GCG Financial. David has built a successful sales and sales management career over the past 20 years by helping his clients solve complicated financial problems with innovative and customized solutions. He actively works with his diverse base of clients, mentors, and coaches his sales team, serves on the boards of two universities, and has been a qualifying member of the Million Dollar Round Table since 1998. In addition to his professional designations of Chartered Life Underwriter (CLU), Certified Funds Specialist (CFS), and Chartered Financial Consultant (ChFC), David holds an M.A. in communication from the University of Iowa and a B.A. in English/speech from the University of Northern Iowa. He is also a graduate of the Purdue College of Management at Purdue University and the Leadership Forum from the American College in Bryn Mawr, Pennsylvania.

John K. Marcum, CFM, is vice president, senior financial advisor, for Merrill Lynch in Indianapolis, Indiana. John has a B.S. from Ball State University.

Jim Micklos is a Senior Account Manager with Motivation Excellence, Inc., Schaumburg, Illinois. Jim has more than 30 years sales experience. He started his career with the Belden Corporation. Jim has a B.S. in business from Ball State University.

L.A. Mitchell is sales planner of business management for Lucent Technologies. She works with the sales team as a strategic financial partner with the sales directors, which involves financial analysis, forecasting, and the identification of sales opportunities. L.A. has a B.S.B.A. in marketing and an M.S. in marketing from Colorado State University.

Kelly Osterling is a sales representative with R R. Donnelly in Indianapolis, Indiana. She has recently been responsible for strategic sales planning in her region. Kelly has a B.S. in marketing from Ball State University.

Cole Proper is the director of business development at AFFINA—the Customer Relationship Company where he manages the sales and marketing of AFFINA's suite of outsourced contact center services to *Fortune 500*, midsize, and government organizations. Cole attributes his consistent record of sales success to his focus on creating unique, value added solutions for business clients. Cole is a graduate of Illinois State University where he majored in marketing.

Steve Roe is a sales representative for King Systems (Medical Supplies) Indianapolis, Indiana. He has over 30 years of sales experience. Steve has a B.S. in Business from Ball State University.

Aaron Simmons is an agent for State Farm Insurance. He has succeeded in establishing and building a highly successful insurance and financial services business. With full responsibility for all sales and marketing strategies and activities related to his central-Illinois-based agency, Aaron works closely with a wide variety of consumer as well as business clients. Prior to joining State Farm, Aaron was a top performing salesperson and district manager with Wallace. His combined experiences in sales and marketing provide him with a rich background of valuable business experience, which he readily shares with others in training programs and university-level classes. Aaron is a graduate of Illinois State University.

Adam Spangler is an investment representative for Edward D. Jones & Co. His sales office is located in central Illinois where he has developed a strong 100-plus client base consisting of individuals, families, and businesses. He manages over $9,000,000 in assets. Adam holds a B.S. in business with a major in marketing from Illinois State University.

Missy Harbit Rust is an executive sales representative for Glaxo Wellcome, Inc. Her pharmaceutical accounts territory is in central Indiana. Missy attended Ball State University and has a B.S. in marketing and fashion merchandising.

Stephanie Urich is an area manager for Hormel Foods Corporation. Her unit is responsible for food service sales to institutional customers in the Chicago area. Stephanie has a B.S. in marketing from Ball State University.

David Waugh is a national account executive with Confio Software in Boulder, Colorado. In a short period of twelve years, David has established a solid record of success in sales and marketing roles for companies such as ADP, Platinum Technology, and IBM. David graduated from Illinois State University as a marketing major with a concentration in personal selling and sales management.

Dave Wheat is an area manager for TransWestern Publishing in Muncie, Indiana. He has held various sales and marketing positions throughout his career. Dave has a B.S. in marketing from Ball State University.

Jon Young is a National Account Manager with Ontario Systems Corporation, Muncie, Indiana. He is responsible for the western half of the United States. Jon has a B.S. and MBA from Ball State University.

Thomas N. Ingram (Ph.D., Georgia State University) is professor of marketing and First Bank Professor of Business Administrations at Colorado State University. Before commencing his academic career, he worked in sales, product management, and sales management with Exxon and Mobil. Tom is a recipient of the Marketing Educator of the Year award given by Sales and Marketing Executives International (SMEI). He was honored as the first recipient of the Mu Kappa Tau National Marketing Honor Society recognition award for Outstanding Scholarly Contributions to the Sales Discipline. On several occasions, he has been recognized at the university and college level for outstanding teaching. Tom has served as the editor of the *Journal of Personal Selling & Sales Management*, chair of the SMEI Accreditation Institute, and as a member of the Board of Directors of SMEI. He is the former editor of the *Journal of Marketing Theory & Practice*. Tom's primary research is in personal selling and sales management. His work has appeared in the *Journal of Marketing, Journal of Marketing Research, Journal of Personal Selling & Sales Management*, and the *Journal of the Academy of Marketing Science*, among others. He is the coauthor of one of the "Ten Most Influential Articles of the 20th Century" as designated by the Sales and Sales Management Special Interest Group of the American Marketing Association.

Raymond W. (Buddy) LaForge is the Brown-Forman Professor of Marketing at the University of Louisville. He is the founding executive editor of the *Marketing Education Review*, founding executive editor of the Sales Educator Network, has served as associate editor for the Sales Education and Training section of the *Journal of Personal Selling & Sales Management*, has coauthored *Marketing: Principles & Perspectives, Sales Management: Analysis and Decision Making, Professional Selling: A Trust-Based Approach, The Professional Selling Skills Workbook*, and coedited *Emerging Trends in Sales Thought and Practice*. His research is published in many journals including the *Journal of Marketing, Journal of Marketing Research, Decision Sciences, Journal of the Academy of Marketing Science*, and the *Journal of Personal Selling & Sales Management*. Buddy has served as vice president/marketing for the Academy of Business Education, vice president of marketing, teaching, and conferences for the American Marketing Association Academic Council, chair of the American Marketing Association Sales Interest Group, and on the Direct Selling Education Foundation Board of Directors and Academic Program Committee, DuPont Corporate Marketing Faculty Advisory Team for the Sales Enhancement Process, Family Business Center Advisory Board, and Strategic Planning Committee for the National Conference on Sales Management. He currently serves as vice chair for awards and recognition for the AMA Sales SIG and administers the AMA Sales SIG/DSEF Sales Dissertation Grants.

Charles H. Schwepker, Jr. (Ph.D., University of Memphis) is Professor of Marketing at the University of Central Missouri. He has experience in wholesale and retail sales. His primary research interests are in sales management, personal selling, and marketing ethics. His articles have appeared in the *Journal of the Academy of Marketing Science*, the *Journal of Business Research*, the *Journal of Public Policy and*

Marketing, Journal of Personal Selling & Sales Management, Journal of Service Research, and the *Journal of Business Ethics*, among other journals, various national and regional proceedings, and books including *Marketing Communications Classics* and *Environmental Marketing*. He has received both teaching and research awards, including the James Comer Award for best contribution to selling and sales management theory awarded by the *Journal of Personal Selling & Sales Management* and two "Outstanding Paper" awards at the National Conference in Sales Management, among others. He is on the editorial review boards of the *Journal of Personal Selling & Sales Management, Journal of Marketing Theory & Practice, Journal of Business & Industrial Marketing, Journal of Relationship Marketing, Journal of Selling and Major Account Management*, and the *Southern Business Review*, and has twice won awards for outstanding reviewer. He is a coauthor of *Sales Management: Analysis and Decision Making*.

Ramon A. Avila (Ph.D., Virginia Tech University) is the George and Frances Ball Distinguished Professor of Marketing at Ball State University. Before coming to Ball State, he worked in sales with the Burroughs Corporation. He has held two visiting professorships at the University of Hawaii and another at the Kelley School of Business at Indiana University. In 2003, Ramon earned Ball State's Outstanding Faculty Award. In April 2002, Ramon received a Leavey Award. This award was given for innovation in the classroom with his advanced selling class. Ramon was presented the 1999 Mu Kappa Tau's Outstanding Contributor to the Sales Profession. He is only the third recipient of this award. Ramon has also received the University's Outstanding Service award, the University's Outstanding Junior Faculty award, the College of Business Professor of the Year, and the Dean's Teaching award every year since its inception in 1987. Ramon also sits on five editorial review boards. Ramon's primary research is in personal selling and sales management. His work has appeared in the *Journal of Marketing Research, Journal of Personal Selling & Sales Management, The Journal of Management, Industrial Marketing Management, The Marketing Management Journal*, and the *Journal of Marketing Theory & Practice*, among others. He is the coauthor of *The Professional Selling Skills Workbook*.

Michael R. Williams (Ph.D., Oklahoma State University) is professor of marketing and director of the Professional Sales Institute at Illinois State University. Prior to his academic career, Mike established a successful 30-plus year career in industrial sales, market research, and sales management and continues to consult and work with a wide range of business organizations. He has co-authored *The Professional Selling Skills Workbook, Sales Management: Analysis and Decision Making*, and a variety of executive monographs and white-papers on sales performance topics. Mike's research has been published in many different national and international journals including the *Journal of Personal Selling & Sales Management, International Journal of Purchasing and Materials Management, Journal of Business and Industrial Marketing, Quality Management Journal*, and *Journal of Industrial Technology*. His work has also received numerous honors, including Outstanding Article for the Year in *Journal of Business and Industrial Marketing*, the AACSB's Leadership in Innovative Business Education Award, and the Marketing Science Institute's Alden G. Clayton Competition. In 2004, Mike was honored with the Mu Kappa Tau Marketing Society recognition award for Outstanding Scholarly Contributor to the Sales Discipline. He has also been honored with numerous university, college, and corporate teaching and research awards including Old Republic Research Scholar, the presentation of a seminar at Oxford's Braesnose College, Who's Who in American Education, and Who's Who in America. Mike has and continues to serve in leadership roles as an advisor and board member for sales and sales management associations and organizations including the University Sales Center Alliance, National Conference in Sales and Sales Management, and Vector Marketing.

KEY TO SALES SUCCESS: TALK *WITH* THE CUSTOMER, NOT *AT* THE CUSTOMER

For decades, salespeople have focused on honing their messages into persuasive presentations referred to as sales "pitches." In today's world of professional selling, the emphasis is changing, with astute salespeople striving for collaborative dialogue with the customer. This involves more conversation to discuss the customer's situation and needs openly before the salesperson makes a purchase recommendation. Reaction Design, a California-based company, uses this approach in selling chemical reaction and chemical process simulation software to corporate, government, and academic clients. Geoff Rogers, vice president of sales for Reaction Design, says that salespeople are understandably enthusiastic about their products, which creates a tendency to overpower their customers with one-way presentations. According to Rogers, this short-circuits the customer's involvement in the buying process and is largely ineffective.

An effective alternative is to focus presentations on defining the customer's needs, explaining the value the customer can receive from the sales organization, and ultimately having the customer verify the value they can receive. This approach makes the purchase decision a joint agreement rather than a pure purchase decision. Rogers says that formal presentations still have a role in his sales organization, but establishing a productive sales dialogue is by far the more effective way to gain customers.

Establishing dialogue through collaborative conversations with customers is also used with good results by Harden & Associates, a major broker of employee benefit services and insurance in Florida. According to Dan Dieterle, a senior vice president and top producer in the company, the focus has changed from a product-based sale to a consultative approach that emphasizes defining customer objectives. Dieterle says this gives the customer more control over the buying process. His customers apparently prefer this approach, as the company has doubled in size over the past five years and successfully converts 80 percent of its prospects into customers.

Source: From "Simple Is In," by Theodore B. Kinni from *Selling Power* (June 2006): 23–25.

EVOLUTION OF PERSONAL SELLING

The successful professional salesperson of today and the future is likely a better listener than a talker, is more oriented toward developing long-term relationships with customers than placing an emphasis on high-pressure, short-term sales techniques, and has the skills and patience to endure lengthy, complex sales processes. Like the salespeople in the opening vignette, today's salesperson strives to deliver relevant presentations based on unique customer needs, and meeting those customer needs requires teamwork between salespeople and others in the organization. For more on teamwork, see "Professional Selling in the 21st Century: The Importance of Teamwork in Sales."

Personal selling is an important part of **marketing**, which is usually a separate organizational function that creates, communicates, and delivers value to customers and manages customer relationships in ways that benefit both the organization and its

Objectives

After completing this module, you should be able to

1 Describe the evolution of personal selling from ancient times to the modern era.

2 Explain the contributions of personal selling to society, business firms, and customers.

3 Distinguish between transaction-focused traditional selling and trust-based relationship selling.

4 Discuss five alternative approaches to personal selling.

5 Describe the three primary roles fulfilled by consultative salespeople.

6 Understand the sales process as a series of interrelated steps.

PROFESSIONAL SELLING IN THE 21ST CENTURY

The Importance of Teamwork in Sales

Jerry Heffel, president of the Southwestern Company, offers his perspective on teamwork:

Sometimes the salesperson is referred to as the lead car in the business train. But just having a lead car doesn't make a train. For this reason, a salesperson who is effective long term is also an effective team player—he or she realizes they need coordinated involvement from many different parts of the organization in order to serve the customer. At the same time, whenever they see themselves as part of the customer's team, and that they are both striving for the same outcome, they become an indispensable part of the value chain for that customer. Southwestern's sales training philosophy stresses this team aspect: We tell our salespeople that they are the gas and oil of the free enterprise system, but they also need the tires, the car body, the drive train, and what's in the trunk to get anywhere significant.

stakeholders.[1] Personal selling also involves creating, communicating, and delivering customer value, and **trust-based professional selling** (a form of personal selling) focuses primarily on interpersonal communication between buyers and sellers to initiate, develop and enhance customer relationships. It requires that salespeople earn customer trust and that their selling strategy meets customer needs and delivers value.

The interpersonal communications dimension sets personal selling apart from other marketing communications such as advertising and sales promotion, which are directed at mass markets. Personal selling is also distinguished from direct marketing and electronic marketing in that salespeople are talking with buyers before, during, and after the sale. This allows a high degree of immediate customer feedback, which becomes a strong advantage of personal selling over most other forms of marketing communications.

Although advertising is far more visible to the general public, personal selling is actually the most important part of marketing communications for most businesses. This is particularly true in firms that engage in business-to-business marketing, where more money is spent on personal selling than on advertising, sales promotion, publicity, or public relations. In this book, we typically describe personal selling in this business-to-business context, in which a salesperson or sales team interacts with one or more individuals from another organization.

As personal selling continues to evolve, it is more important than ever that salespeople focus on delivering customer value while initiating, developing, and enhancing customer relationships. What constitutes value will likely vary from one customer to the next depending on the customer's situation, needs, and priorities, but **customer value** will always be determined by customers' perception of what they get in exchange for what they have to give up. In the simplest situations, customers buy a product in exchange for money. In most situations, however, customers define value in a more complex manner, by addressing questions such as:

- Does the salesperson do a good job in helping me make or save money?
- Is this salesperson dependable?
- Does this salesperson help me achieve my strategic priorities?
- Is the salesperson's company easy to work with, i.e., hassle-free?
- Does the salesperson enlist others in his or her organization when needed to create value for me?
- Does the sales representative understand my business and my industry?

Another important development in personal selling is the recognition that customers want to be heard loud and clear when expressing what they want from suppliers and their salespeople. In days gone by, as illustrated in the opening vignette, personal selling often consisted of delivering a message or making a pitch. That approach was typically associated with a "product push" strategy in which customers were pressured to buy without much appreciation for their real needs. Today' sales organizations are far more interested in establishing a productive dialogue with customers than in simply pitching products that customers may or may not want or need. In our highly competitive world, professional buyers have little tolerance for aggressive, pushy sales people.

Sales dialogue refers to the series of conversations between buyers and sellers that take place over time in an attempt to build relationships. The purposes of these conversations are to:

- determine if a prospective customer should be targeted for further sales attention.
- clarify the prospective customer's situation and buying processes.
- discover the prospective customer's unique needs and requirements.
- determine the prospective customer's strategic priorities.
- communicate how the sales organization can create and deliver customer value.
- negotiate a business deal and earn a commitment from the customer.
- make the customer aware of additional opportunities to increase the value received.
- assess sales organization and salesperson performance so that customer value is continuously improved.

As you can see, sales dialogue is far more than idle chitchat. The business conversations that constitute the dialogue are customer-focused and have a clear purpose; otherwise there would be a high probability of wasting both the customer's and the salesperson's time, which no one can afford in today's business environment. Whether the sales dialogue features a question-and-answer format, a conversation dominated by the buyer conveying information and requirements, or a formal sales presentation in which the salesperson responds to buyer feedback throughout, the key idea is that both parties participate in and benefit from the process.

Throughout this course, you learn about new technologies and techniques that have contributed to the evolution of the practice of personal selling. This module provides an overview of personal selling, affording insight into the operating rationale of today's salespeople and sales managers. It also describes different approaches to personal selling and presents the sales process as a series of interrelated steps. The appendix at the end of the module discusses several important aspects of sales careers, including types of selling jobs and characteristics and skills needed for sales success. In the highly competitive, complex environment of the world business community, personal selling and sales management have never played more critical roles.

Origins of Personal Selling

Ancient Greek history documents selling as an exchange activity, and the term *salesman* appears in the writings of Plato.[2] However, true salespeople, those who earned a living only by selling, did not exist in any sizable number until the Industrial Revolution in England, from the mid-eighteenth century to the mid-nineteenth century. Prior to this time, traders, merchants, and artisans filled the selling function. These predecessors of contemporary marketers were generally viewed with contempt because deception was often used in the sale of goods.[3]

In the latter phase of the Middle Ages, the first door-to-door salesperson appeared in the form of the peddler. Peddlers collected produce from local farmers, sold it to townspeople, and, in turn, bought manufactured goods in town for subsequent sale in rural areas.[4] Like many other early salespeople, they performed other important marketing functions—in this case, purchasing, assembling, sorting, and redistributing of goods.

Industrial Revolution Era

As the Industrial Revolution began to blossom in the middle of the eighteenth century, the economic justification for salespeople gained momentum. Local economies were no longer self-sufficient, and as intercity and international trade began to flourish, economies of scale in production spurred the growth of mass markets in geographically dispersed areas. The continual need to reach new customers in these dispersed markets called for an increasing number of salespeople.

It is interesting to note the job activities of the first wave of salespeople in the era of the Industrial Revolution. The following quotation describes a salesperson who served the customer in conjunction with a producer:

> Thus, a salesman representing the producing firm, armed with samples of the firm's products, could bring the latter to the attention of a large number of potential customers—whether buying for sale to others or for their own production requirements—who might not, without the salesman's visit, have learnt of the product's existence, and give them the opportunity of examining and discussing it without having to go out of their way to do so . . . . Even if the salesman did not succeed in obtaining an order, he frequently picked up valuable information on the state of the market, sometimes the very reasons for refusal . . . . This information could be very useful to the producer.[5]

Post–Industrial Revolution Era

By the early 1800s, personal selling was well-established in England but just beginning to develop in the United States.[6] This situation changed noticeably after 1850, and by the latter part of the century, salespeople were a well-established part of business practice in the United States. For example, one wholesaler in the Detroit area reported sending out 400 traveling salespeople in the 1880s.[7]

At the dawning of the twentieth century, an exciting time in the economic history of the United States, it became apparent that marketing, especially advertising and personal selling, would play a crucial role in the rapid transition of the economy from an agrarian base to one of mass production and efficient transportation.

Glimpses of the lives of salespeople in the early 1900s, gained from literature of that period, reveal an adventuresome, aggressive, and valuable group of employees often working on the frontier of new markets. Already, however, the independent maverick salespeople who had blazed the early trails to new markets were beginning to disappear. One clear indication that selling was becoming a more structured activity was the development of a **canned sales presentation** by John H. Patterson of the National Cash Register Company (NCR). This presentation, a virtual script to guide NCR salespeople on how to sell cash registers, was based on the premise that salespeople are not "born, but rather they are made."[8]

Sales historians noted the changes occurring in personal selling in the early twentieth century. Charles W. Hoyt, author of one of the first textbooks on sales management, chronicled this transition in 1912, noting two types of salespeople:

> The old kind of salesman is the "big me" species . . . . He works for himself and, so far as possible, according to his own ideas . . . . There is another type of salesman. He is the new kind. At present he is in the minority, but he works for the fastest growing and most successful houses of the day. He works for the house, and the house works for him. He welcomes and uses every bit of help the house sends to him.[9]

Hoyt's observations about the "old" and the "new" salesperson summed up the changing role of personal selling. The managements of firms in the United States were beginning to understand the tremendous potential of personal selling and, simultaneously, the need to shape the growth of the sales function. In particular, a widespread interest arose in how to reduce the cost of sales. According to Hoyt, this did not mean hiring lower-cost salespeople, but instead called for "distributing much larger quantities of goods with less motion."[10]

War and Depression Era

The 30-year span from 1915 to 1945 was marked by three overwhelming events—two world wars and the Great Depression in the United States. Because economic activity concentrated on the war efforts, new sales methods did not develop quickly during those periods. During the Great Depression, however, business firms, starved for sales volume, often employed aggressive salespeople to produce badly needed revenue. Then, with renewed prosperity in the post–World War II era, salespeople emerged as important employees for an increasing number of firms that were beginning to realize the benefits of research-based integrated marketing programs.

Professionalism: The Modern Era

In the middle 1940s, personal selling became more professional. Not only did buyers begin to demand more from salespeople, but they also grew intolerant of high-pressure, fast-talking salespeople, preferring instead a well-informed, customer-oriented salesperson. In 1947, the *Harvard Business Review* published "Low-Pressure Selling,"[11] a classic article followed by many others that called for salespeople to increase the effectiveness of their sales efforts by improving their professional demeanor.

An emphasis on **sales professionalism** is the keynote of the current era. The term has varied meanings, but in this context we use it to mean a customer-oriented approach that uses truthful, nonmanipulative tactics to satisfy the long-term needs of both the customer and the selling firm. The effective salesperson of today is no longer a mere presenter of information but now must stand equipped to respond to a variety of customer needs before, during, and after the sale. In addition, salespeople must be able to work effectively with others in their organizations to meet or exceed customer expectations.

In examining the status of sales as a true profession, one study found that sales meets four of the six criteria that define professions, and that progress is still needed on the other two dimensions.[12] This study concluded that sales meets the criterion of operating from a substantial knowledge base that has been developed by academics, corporate trainers and executives, and professional organizations. Sales also meets the criterion of making a significant contribution to society, which is discussed in the next section of this module. Third, through professional organizations such as the Strategic Account Management Association (SAMA) and through a common sales vocabulary such as that found in textbooks and training materials, sales meets the professional criterion of having a defined culture and organization of colleagues. Fourth, sales does have a unique set of professional skills, though these skills vary depending on the specific nature of a given sales position.

Two areas in the study indicated that sales needs additional progress to be viewed as a profession on a par with law, medicine, and other long-recognized professions. The first area has to do with how much autonomy salespeople have to make decisions and the amount of public trust granted to salespeople. While many business-to-business salespeople have considerable decision-making autonomy, others have very little. Public trust could be improved by a widely accepted certification program such as the CPA designation for accountants. At present, however, very few salespeople have professional certification credentials. While many salespeople do have considerable autonomy, public trust in certification programs is modest; thus the results are mixed as to whether the sales profession meets this professional criterion.

The final area where sales needs to improve is to adhere to a uniform ethical code. While many companies have ethical codes and some professional organizations have ethical codes for salespeople, there is no universal code of ethics with a mechanism for dealing with violators. Until such a code is developed and widely accepted in business, some members of society will not view sales as a true profession.

Whether or not sales is viewed as a true profession, comparable to law and medicine, salespeople can benefit tremendously by embracing high ethical standards, participating in professional organizations, and working from a continually evolving knowledge base. In so doing, they will not only be more effective, they will also help advance sales as a true profession.

Future evolution is inevitable as tomorrow's professional salesperson responds to a more complex, dynamic environment. Also, increased sophistication of buyers and

EXHIBIT 1.1 Continued Evolution of Personal Selling

Change	Salesforce Response
Intensified competition	More emphasis on developing and maintaining trust-based, long-term customer relationships More focus on creating and delivering customer value
More emphasis on improving sales productivity	Increased use of technology (e.g., laptop computers, electronic mail, databases, customer relationship management software) Increased use of lower-cost-per-contact methods (e.g., telemarketing for some customers) More emphasis on profitability (e.g., gross margin) objectives
Fragmentation of traditional customer bases	Sales specialists for specific customer types Multiple sales channels (e.g., major accounts programs, telemarketing, electronic networks) Globalization of sales efforts
Customers dictating quality standards and inventory/shipping procedures to be met by vendors	Team selling Salesforce compensation sometimes based on customer satisfaction and team performance More emphasis on sales dialogues rather than sales pitches
Demand for in-depth, specialized knowledge as an input to purchase decisions	Team selling More emphasis on customer-oriented sales training

of new technologies will demand more from the next generation of salespeople. Exhibit 1.1 summarizes some of the likely events of the future.[13]

CONTRIBUTIONS OF PERSONAL SELLING

As mentioned earlier in this module, more money is spent on personal selling than on any other form of marketing communications. Salespeople are usually well-compensated, and salesforces of major companies often number in the thousands. For example, Microsoft has 16,000 salespeople, American Express has 23,000, and Pepsico has 36,000.[14]

We now take a look at how this investment is justified by reviewing the contributions of personal selling to society in general, to the employing firm, and to customers.

Salespeople and Society

Salespeople contribute to their nations' economic growth in two basic ways. They act as stimuli for economic transactions, and they further the diffusion of innovation.

Salespeople as Economic Stimuli

Salespeople are expected to stimulate action in the business world—hence the term **economic stimuli**. In a fluctuating economy, salespeople make invaluable contributions by assisting in recovery cycles and by helping to sustain periods of relative prosperity. As the world economic system deals with issues such as increased globalization of business, more emphasis on customer satisfaction, and building competitiveness through quality improvement programs, it is expected that salespeople will be recognized as a key force in executing the appropriate strategies and tactics necessary for survival and growth.

Salespeople and Diffusion of Innovation

Salespeople play a critical role in the **diffusion of innovation**, the process whereby new products, services, and ideas are distributed to the members of society. Consumers who are likely to be early adopters of an innovation often rely on salespeople as a primary source of information. Frequently, well-informed, specialized salespeople provide useful information to potential consumers who then purchase from a lower-cost outlet. The role of salespeople in the diffusion of industrial products and services is particularly crucial. Imagine trying to purchase a companywide computer system without the assistance of a competent salesperson or sales team!

While acting as an agent of innovation, the salesperson invariably encounters a strong resistance to change in the latter stages of the diffusion process. The status quo seems to be extremely satisfactory to many parties, even though, in the long run, change is necessary for continued progress or survival. By encouraging the adoption of innovative products and services, salespeople may indeed be making a positive contribution to society.

Salespeople and the Employing Firm

Because salespeople are in direct contact with the all-important customer, they can make valuable contributions to their employers. Salespeople contribute to their firms as revenue producers, as sources of market research and feedback, and as candidates for management positions.

Salespeople as Revenue Producers

Salespeople occupy the somewhat unique role of **revenue producers** in their firms. Consequently, they usually feel the brunt of that pressure along with the management of the firm. Although accountants and financial staff are concerned with profitability in bottom-line terms, salespeople are constantly reminded of their responsibility to achieve a healthy "top line" on the profit and loss statement. This should not suggest that salespeople are concerned only with sales revenue and not with overall profitability. Indeed, salespeople are increasingly responsible for improving profitability, not only by producing sales revenues, but also by improving the productivity of their actions.

Market Research and Feedback

Because salespeople spend so much time in direct contact with their customers, it is only logical that they would play an important role in market research and in providing feedback to their firms. For example, entertainment and home products retailer Best Buy relies heavily on feedback from its sales associates in what it calls a customer-centricity initiative, which places the customer at the center of its marketing strategy. Feedback from sales associates helps Best Buy offer tailored products to specific customer segments, design appealing in-store merchandising formats, increase sales volume for in-home services, and improve the effectiveness of customer-support call centers. Results of the customer-centricity program have been so positive that Best Buy is rapidly increasing the number of participating stores as it tries to fend off Wal-Mart and other major competitors.[15]

Some would argue that salespeople are not trained as market researchers, or that salespeople's time could be better used than in research and feedback activities. Many firms, however, refute this argument by finding numerous ways to capitalize on the salesforce as a reservoir of ideas. It is not an exaggeration to say that many firms have concluded that they cannot afford to operate in the absence of salesforce feedback and research.

Salespeople as Future Managers

In recent years, marketing and sales personnel have been in strong demand for upper management positions. Recognizing the need for a top management trained in sales,

Terry Kelly, sales representative for EFAX, a computer software company, has just concluded a sales call with Landnet, one of his distributors. During the call, purchasing agent Linda Meyer mentioned that Ron Hawkins, Landnet's top salesperson, had suddenly resigned and moved out of the state. Meyer said that this unexpected resignation could not have come at a worse time, as several key customer contracts were pending renewal, and Landnet had no candidates to replace Hawkins. On his way to his next sales call with Netserve, his largest distributor, Kelly debated whether or not he should share the news of Hawkins' resignation. After all, the buyer at Netserve viewed Kelly as a great source of market information, and Kelly figured that the Netserve buyer would hear the news anyway before the day was over. What should Kelly do?

many firms use the sales job as an entry-level position that provides a foundation for future assignments. As progressive firms continue to emphasize customer orientation as a basic operating concept, it is only natural that salespeople who have learned how to meet customer needs will be good candidates for management jobs.

Salespeople and the Customer

Given the increasing importance of building trust with customers and an emphasis on establishing and maintaining long-term relationships, it is imperative that salespeople be honest and candid with customers. Salespeople must also be able to demonstrate knowledge of their products and services, especially as they compare competitive offerings. Customers also expect salespeople to be knowledgeable about market opportunities and relevant business trends that may affect a customer's business. There has been a long-standing expectation that salespeople need to be the key contact for the buyer, who expects that they will coordinate activities within the selling firm to deliver maximum value to the customer.

The overall conclusion is that buyers expect salespeople to contribute to the success of the buyer's firm. Buyers value the information furnished by salespeople, and expect salespeople to act in a highly professional manner.[16] See "An Ethical Dilemma" for a scenario in which the salesperson must think about where to draw the line in sharing information with customers.

As salespeople serve their customers, they simultaneously serve their employers and society. When the interests of these parties conflict, the salesperson can be caught in the middle. By learning to resolve these conflicts as a routine part of their jobs, salespeople further contribute to developing a business system based on progress through problem solving. Sales ethics will be discussed in detail in Module 2.

CLASSIFICATION OF PERSONAL SELLING APPROACHES

In this section, we take a closer look at alternative approaches to personal selling that professionals may choose from to best interact with their customers. Some of these approaches are simple. Other approaches are more sophisticated and require that the salesperson play a strategic role to use them successfully. More than three decades ago, four basic approaches to personal selling were identified: stimulus response, mental states, need satisfaction, and problem solving.[17] Since that time, another approach to personal selling, termed **consultative selling**, has gained popularity. All five approaches to selling are practiced today. Furthermore, many salespeople use elements of more than one approach in their own hybrids of personal selling.

As a prelude to our discussion of approaches to personal selling, an expansion of two key points is in order. Recall that personal selling differs from other forms of marketing communications because it is a personal communication delivered by employees or agents of the sales organization. Because the personal element is present, salespeople have the opportunity to alter their sales messages and behaviors during a sales presentation or as they encounter unique sales situations and customers. This is referred to as **adaptive selling**. Because salespeople often encounter buyers with different personalities, communications styles, needs, and goals, adaptive selling is an important concept.

A second point is that personal selling is moving from transaction-based methods to relationship-based methods. Rather than trying to maximize sales in the short run, relationship-based selling approaches focus on solving customer problems, providing opportunities, and adding value to the customer's business over an extended period. Exhibit 1.2 illustrates how transaction-based selling differs from relationship-based selling. We now explore one element of Exhibit 1.2 in detail—personal selling approaches.

Comparison of Transaction-Focused Traditional Selling with Trust-Based Relationship Selling   EXHIBIT 1.2

	Transaction-Focused Traditional Selling	Trust-Based Relationship Selling
Typical skills required	Selling skills	Selling skills Information gathering Listening and questioning Strategic problem solving Creating and demonstrating unique, value-added solutions Teambuilding and teamwork
Primary perspective	The salesperson and the selling firm	The customer and the customer's customers
Personal selling approaches	Stimulus response, mental states	Need satisfaction, problem solving, consultative
Desired outcome	Closed sales, order volume	Trust, joint planning, mutual benefits, enhance profits
Role of salesperson	Make calls and close sales	Business consultant and long-term ally Key player in the customer's business
Nature of communication	One-way, from salesperson to customer Pushing products	Two-way and collaborative Strive for dialogue with the customer
Degree of salesperson's involvement in customer's decision-making process	Isolated from customer's decision-making process	Actively involved in customer's decision-making process
Knowledge required	Own company's products Competition Applications Account strategies Costs Opportunities	Own company's products and resources Competition Applications Account strategies Costs Opportunities General business and industry knowledge and insight Customer's products, competition, and customers
Post-sale follow-up	Little or none: move on to conquer next customer	Continued follow-through to: • Ensure customer satisfaction • Keep customer informed • Add customer value • Manage opportunities

Stimulus Response Selling

Of the five views of personal selling, **stimulus response selling** is the simplest. The theoretical background for this approach originated in early experiments with animal behavior. The key idea is that various stimuli can elicit predictable responses. Salespeople furnish the stimuli from a repertoire of words and actions designed to produce the desired response. This approach to selling is illustrated in Figure 1.1.

An example of the stimulus response view of selling would be **continued affirmation**, a method in which a series of questions or statements furnished by the salesperson is designed to condition the prospective buyer to answering "yes" time after time, until, it is hoped, he or she will be inclined to say "yes" to the entire sales proposition. This method is often used by telemarketing personnel, who rely on comprehensive sales scripts read or delivered from memory.

Stimulus response sales strategies, particularly when implemented with a canned sales presentation, have some advantages for the seller. The sales message can be structured in a logical order. Questions and objections from the buyer can usually be anticipated and addressed before they are magnified during buyer–seller interaction. Inexperienced salespeople can rely on stimulus response sales methods in some settings, and this may eventually contribute to sales expertise.

The limitations of stimulus response methods, however, can be severe, especially if the salesperson is dealing with a professional buyer. Most buyers like to take an active role in sales dialogue, and the stimulus response approach calls for the salesperson to dominate the flow of conversation. The lack of flexibility in this approach is also a disadvantage, as buyer responses and unforeseen interruptions may neutralize or damage the effectiveness of the stimuli.

Considering the net effects of this method's advantages and disadvantages, it appears most suitable for relatively unimportant purchase decisions, when time is severely constrained and when professional buyers are not the prospects. As consumers in general become more sophisticated, this approach will become more problematic.

Mental States Selling

Mental states selling, or the *formula approach* to personal selling, assumes that the buying process for most buyers is essentially identical and that buyers can be led through certain mental states, or steps, in the buying process. These mental states are typically referred to as **AIDA** (attention, interest, desire, and action).

FIGURE 1.1   **Stimulus Response Approach to Selling**

Salesperson Provides Stimuli:	Buyer Responses Sought:	Continue Process Until Purchase Decision
Statements Questions Actions Audio/Visual Aids Demonstrations	Favorable Reactions and Eventual Purchase	

The salesperson attempts to gain favorable responses from the customer by providing stimuli, or cues, to influence the buyer. After the customer has been properly conditioned, the salesperson tries to secure a positive purchase decision.

Rachel Duke sells advertising for her college newspaper. One of her potential clients is contemplating buying an ad for an upcoming special issue featuring bars and restaurants. Over the past two weeks, Duke has tried unsuccessfully to get a commitment from the restaurant owner to place an ad. Her sales manager has suggested that Rachel call the prospect and tell him that there is only one remaining ad space in the special issue, and that she must have an immediate answer to ensure that the prospect's ad will appear in the special issue. The sales manager said, "Rachel, this guy is stalling. You've got to move him to action, and this technique will do the trick." Duke was troubled by her manager's advice, since the special issue had plenty of ad space remaining. If you were Duke, would you follow her sales manager's advice? Why or why not?

Appropriate sales messages provide a transition from one mental state to the next.

Like stimulus response selling, the mental states approach relies on a highly structured sales presentation. The salesperson does most of the talking, as feedback from the prospect could be disruptive to the flow of the presentation.

A positive feature of this method is that it forces the salesperson to plan the sales presentation prior to calling on the customer. It also helps the salesperson recognize that timing is an important element in the purchase decision process and that careful listening is necessary to determine which stage the buyer is in at any given point.

A problem with the mental states method is that it is difficult to determine which state a prospect is in. Sometimes a prospect is spanning two mental states or moving back and forth between two states during the sales presentation. Consequently, the heavy guidance structure the salesperson implements may be inappropriate, confusing, and even counterproductive to sales effectiveness. We should also note that this method is not customer oriented. Although the salesperson tailors the presentation to each customer somewhat, this is done by noting customer mental states rather than needs. See "An Ethical Dilemma" for a situation in which the salesperson is contemplating the movement of the prospect into the "action" stage.

The mental states method is illustrated in Exhibit 1.3.[18] Note that this version includes "conviction" as an intermediate stage between interest and desire. Such minor variations are commonplace in different renditions of this approach to selling.

Mental States View of Selling   EXHIBIT 1.3

Mental State	Sales Step	Critical Sales Task
Curiosity	Attention	Get prospects excited, then you get them to like you.
Interest	Interest	Interview: needs and wants
Conviction	Conviction	"What's in it for me?" Product—"Will it do what I want it to do?" Price—"Is it worth it?" "The hassle of change" "Cheaper elsewhere" Peers—"What will others think of it?" Priority—"Do I need it now?" (sense of urgency)
Desire	Desire	Overcome their stall.
Action	Close	Alternate choice close: which, not if!

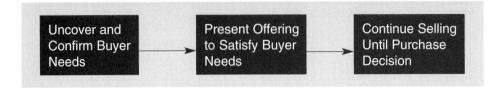

FIGURE 1.2   Need Satisfaction Approach to Selling

| Uncover and Confirm Buyer Needs | → | Present Offering to Satisfy Buyer Needs | → | Continue Selling Until Purchase Decision |

The salesperson attempts to uncover customer needs that are related to the product or service offering. This may require extensive questioning in the early stages of the sales process. After confirming the buyer's needs, the salesperson proceeds with a presentation based on how the offering can meet those needs.

Need Satisfaction Selling

Need satisfaction selling is based on the notion that the customer is buying to satisfy a particular need or set of needs. This approach is shown in Figure 1.2. It is the salesperson's task to identify the need to be met, then to help the buyer meet the need. Unlike the mental states and stimulus response methods, this method focuses on the customer rather than on the salesperson. The salesperson uses a questioning, probing tactic to uncover important buyer needs. Customer responses dominate the early portion of the sales interaction, and only after relevant needs have been established does the salesperson begin to relate how his or her offering can satisfy these needs.

Customers seem to appreciate this selling method and are often willing to spend considerable time in preliminary meetings to define needs prior to a sales presentation or written sales proposal. Also, this method avoids the defensiveness that arises in some prospects when a salesperson rushes to the persuasive part of the sales message without adequate attention to the buyer's needs.

Problem-Solving Selling

Problem-solving selling is an extension of need satisfaction selling. It goes beyond identifying needs to developing alternative solutions for satisfying these needs. The problem-solving approach to selling is depicted in Figure 1.3. Sometimes even competitors' offerings are included as alternatives in the purchase decision.

The problem-solving approach typically requires educating the customer about the full impact of the existing problem and clearly communicating how the solution delivers significant customer value. This is true even in cases where the solution seems

FIGURE 1.3   Problem-Solving Approach to Selling

| Define Problem | → | Generate Alternative Solutions | → | Evaluate Alternative Solutions | → | Continue Selling Until Purchase Decision |

The salesperson defines a customer problem that may be solved by various alternatives. Then an offering is made that represents at least one of these alternatives. All alternatives are carefully evaluated before a purchase decision is made.

to be an obviously beneficial course of action for the buyer. For example, SoftSwitching Technologies' Dynamic Sag Corrector (DySC) practically eliminates expensive power-related downtime in manufacturing processes. Competitive products are expensive and hard to maintain. Yet the company found that DySC did not sell because buyers were used to having downtime in manufacturing and were not sure DySC would be a solution.[19] To be successful in problem-solution selling, salespeople must be able to get the buyer to agree that a problem exists and that solving it is worth the time and effort required.

The problem-solving approach to selling can take a lot of time. In some cases, the selling company cannot afford this much time with each prospective customer. In other cases, the customers may be unwilling to spend the time. Insurance salespeople, for example, report this customer response. The problem-solving approach appears to be most successful in technical industrial sales situations, in which the parties involved are usually oriented toward scientific reasoning and processes and thus find this approach to sales amenable.

Consultative Selling

Consultative selling is the process of helping customers reach their strategic goals by using the products, services, and expertise of the sales organization.[20] Notice that this method focuses on achieving strategic goals of customers, not just meeting needs or solving problems. Salespeople confirm their customers' strategic goals, then work collaboratively with customers to achieve those goals.

In consultative selling, salespeople fulfill three primary roles: strategic orchestrator, business consultant, and long-term ally. As a **strategic orchestrator**, the salesperson arranges the use of the sales organization's resources in an effort to satisfy the customer. This usually calls for involving other individuals in the sales organization. For example, the salesperson may need expert advice from production or logistics personnel to fully address a customer problem or opportunity. In the **business consultant** role, the salesperson uses internal and external (outside the sales organization) sources to become an expert on the customer's business. This role also includes an educational element—that is, salespeople educate their customers on products they offer and how these products compare with competitive offerings. As a **long-term ally**, the salesperson supports the customer, even when an immediate sale is not expected.

Yellow Book USA, the largest independent yellow pages company with 600 directories in the Unites States and the United Kingdom, uses consultative selling to satisfy the needs of a wide variety of small businesses. Typically, Yellow Book's customers operate on a very tight budget and need to know the return on their expenditures. It is also common for small business owners to wear many hats, serving as the sales manager, buyer, and budget director. To be successful, Yellow Book's salespeople must be able to understand and explain the value of their advertising in the context of the customer's overall business strategy and be able to furnish details of the expected and actual return on investment from their advertising. Accordingly, Yellow Book incorporates these topics into its sales training program.[21] For more on consultative selling, see "Professional Selling in the 21st Century: Consultative Selling."

SALES PROCESS

The nonselling activities on which most salespeople spend a majority of their time are essential for the successful execution of the most important part of the salesperson's job, the **sales process**. The sales process has traditionally been described as a series of interrelated steps beginning with locating qualified prospective customers. From there, the salesperson plans the sales presentation, makes an appointment to see the customer, completes the sale, and performs post-sale activities.

Consultative Selling

L. A. Mitchell, sales planner for Lucent Technologies, comments on the increasing use of consultative selling.

Professional selling is becoming much more of a consultative process than in years past. The pace of business has accelerated, and it is hard for individual buyers to be experts on everything they buy. That's where consultative selling comes in. When buyers know they have a problem, but don't know how to solve it, our salespeople can offer a tailored solution. The solution must fit within the buyer's allotted budget, and it must be consistent with the goals and strategies within the buying organization. Consultative salespeople must also be on the scene after the sale to be sure that any necessary training and service issues are handled to the client's satisfaction. With consultative selling, making the sale is important, but the real focus is on providing expertise which enables clients to improve company operations and productivity.

As you should recall from the earlier discussion of the continued evolution of personal selling (refer to Exhibit 1.1), the sales process is increasingly being viewed as a relationship management process, as depicted in Figure 1.4. In this conceptualization of the sales process, salespeople strive to attain lasting relationships with their customers. The basis for such relationships may vary, but the element of trust between the customer and the salesperson is an essential part of enduring relationships. To earn the trust of customers, salespeople should be customer oriented, honest and dependable. They must also be competent and able to display an appropriate level of expertise to their customers. Finally, the trust-building process is

FIGURE 1.4   Trust-Based Sales Process

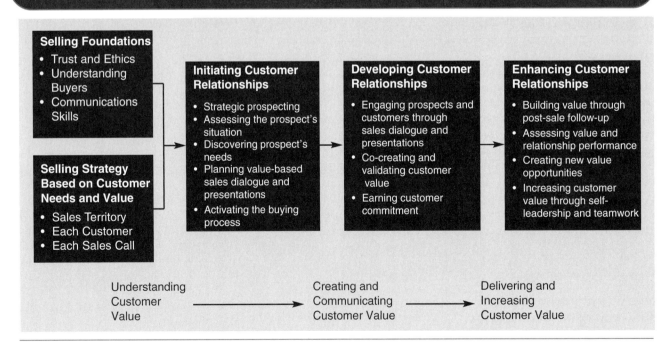

The three major phases of the sales process are initiating, developing, and enhancing customer relationships. Salespeople must possess certain attributes to earn the trust of their customers and be able to adapt their selling strategies to different situations. Throughout the sales process, salespeople should focus on customer value, first by understanding what it is, then by working with customers to create value, communicate value, and continually increase customer value.

facilitated if salespeople are compatible with their customers, that is if they get along with and work well with each other.[22] These attributes are reflected by Blake Conrad, who sells medical supplies for Centurion Specialty Care. Conrad, based in Denver, says:

> You simply cannot have productive relationships with your customers unless they trust you. I work really hard to show customers that I care about their bottom line, and I would never sell them something they don't really need. If I don't have an answer for them on the spot, I make every effort to get the answer and get back to them the same day. Customers appreciate the fact that I do what I say and follow up on all the details. To me, being customer oriented and dependable is just part of my job. It makes selling a lot more fun when your customers trust you, and—guess what—I sell more to customers who trust me.[23]

Another important element of achieving sound relationships with customers is to recognize that individual customers and their particular needs must be addressed with appropriate selling strategies and tactics. In selling, we discuss strategy at four levels: corporate, business unit, marketing department, and the overall sales function. An individual salesperson is strongly guided by strategy at these higher levels in the organization but must also develop selling strategies and tactics to fit the sales territory, each customer, and ultimately, each sales call. Our coverage in this text focuses on developing sales strategies for individual customers and specific sales calls.

When studying the sales process, we should note that there are countless versions of the process in terms of number of steps and the names of the steps. If, however, you were to examine popular trade books on selling and training manuals used by corporations, you would find that the various depictions of the sales process are actually more alike than truly unique. The sales process shown in Figure 1.4 is comparable to most versions of the sales process, with the exception of those versions that advocate high-pressure methods centering on how to get the customer to "say yes" rather than focusing on meeting the customer's true needs. Our version of the sales process suggests that salespeople must have certain attributes to inspire trust in their customers and that salespeople should adapt their selling strategy to fit the situation.

Another point that should be stressed is that the sales process is broken into steps to facilitate discussion and sales training, not to suggest discrete lines between the steps. The steps are actually highly interrelated and, in some instances, may overlap. Further, the stepwise flow of Figure 1.4 does not imply a strict sequence of events. Salespeople may move back and forth in the process with a given customer, sometimes shifting from step to step several times in the same sales encounter. Finally, claiming a new customer typically will require multiple sales calls.

The remainder of this book explores the sales process shown in Figure 1.4. Part I, comprised of Modules 2–4, covers the Foundations of Professional Selling. Module 2 discusses the important topics of building trust and sales ethics. Module 3 provides in-depth coverage of buyer behavior, while Module 4 focuses on the communications skills necessary for sales success. Part II, Initiating Customer Relationships, opens with strategic prospecting in Module 5. Module 6 covers planning value-based sales dialogue and presentations as well as initiating contact with the customer. Developing Customer Relationships is treated in Part III. Module 7 discusses issues that arise during sales dialogues and presentations, while Module 8 discusses how salespeople can validate customer value and earn customer commitment. Part IV, Enhancing Customer Relationships, focuses on how salespeople add customer value through follow-up in Module 9, and through self-leadership and teamwork in Module 10. To learn more about careers in professional selling, please see Appendix 1 at the end of Module 1.

SUMMARY

1. **Describe the evolution of personal selling from ancient times to the modern era.** The history of personal selling can be traced as far back as ancient Greece. The Industrial Revolution enhanced the importance of salespeople, and personal selling as we know it today had its roots in the early twentieth century. The current era of sales professionalism represents a further evolution.

2. **Explain the contributions of personal selling to society, business firms, and customers.** Salespeople contribute to society by acting as stimuli in the economic process and by assisting in the diffusion of innovation. They contribute to their employers by producing revenue, performing research and feedback activities, and comprising a pool of future managers. They contribute to customers by providing timely knowledge to assist in solving problems.

3. **Distinguish between transaction-focused traditional selling and trust-based relationship selling.** As summarized in Exhibit 1.2, trust-based selling focuses more on the customer than does transaction-focused selling. The salesperson will act as a consultant to the customer in trust-based selling, whereas transaction-based selling concentrates more on making sales calls and on closing sales. There is far more emphasis on post-sales follow-up with relationship selling than with transaction selling, and salespeople must have a broader range of skills to practice relationship selling.

4. **Discuss five alternative approaches to personal selling.** Alternative approaches to personal selling include stimulus response, mental states, need satisfaction, problem solving, and the consultative approach. Stimulus response selling often uses the same sales presentation for all customers. The mental states approach prescribes that the salesperson lead the buyer through stages in the buying process. Need satisfaction selling focuses on relating benefits of the seller's products or services to the buyer's particular situation. Problem-solving selling extends need satisfaction by concentrating on various alternatives available to the buyer. Consultative selling focuses on helping customers achieve strategic goals, not just meeting needs or solving problems. In consultative selling, salespersons fulfill three primary roles: strategic orchestrator, business consultant, and long-term ally to the customer.

5. **Describe the three primary roles fulfilled by consultative salespeople.** The three roles are strategic orchestrator, business consultant, and long-term ally. As a strategic orchestrator, salespeople coordinate the use of the sales organization's resources to satisfy the customer. As a business consultant, the salesperson becomes an expert on the customer's business and educates the customer on how his or her products can benefit the customer. The consultative salesperson acts as a long-term ally to the customer, acting in the customer's best interest even when an immediate sale is not expected.

6. **Discuss the sales process as a series of interrelated steps.** As presented in Figure 1.4, the sales process involves initiating, developing, and enhancing customer relationships. Salespeople must possess certain attributes to earn the trust of their customers and be able to adapt their selling strategies to different situations. Throughout the sales process, salespeople should focus on customer value, first by understanding what customer value is to the customer, then by working to create, communicate, and continually increase that value. Salespeople initiate customer relationships through strategic prospecting, assessing the prospect's situation, planning value-based sales dialogue, and activating the buying process. Relationships are then further developed through engaging prospects in a true

dialogue to earn commitment from those prospects. Salespeople enhance customer relationships by following up after the sale, taking a leadership role, and sometimes working as part of a team to constantly increase the value received by the customer. The details of the sales process are covered in Modules 5–10 in this book.

UNDERSTANDING SALES MANAGEMENT TERMS

marketing
trust-based professional selling
customer value
sales dialogue
canned sales presentation
sales professionalism
economic stimuli
diffusion of innovation
revenue producers
adaptive selling
stimulus response selling

continued affirmation
mental states selling
AIDA
need satisfaction selling
problem-solving selling
consultative selling
strategic orchestrator
business consultant
long-term ally
sales process

DEVELOPING PROFESSIONAL SELLING KNOWLEDGE

1. What factors will influence the continued evolution of personal selling?

2. How do salespeople contribute to our society? Are there negative aspects of personal selling from a societal perspective?

3. What are the primary contributions made by salespeople to their employers?

4. Most businesses would have a difficult time surviving without the benefits of the salespeople who call on them. Do you agree?

5. How are need satisfaction and problem-solving selling related? How do they differ?

6. How does the consultative selling approach differ from problem-solving and need satisfaction selling? Explain the three key roles of consultative salespersons.

7. When do you think stimulus response selling would be most effective?

8. How important is teamwork between the customer and the sales organization in practicing consultative selling? How does teamwork within the sales organization factor into consultative selling?

9. Is adaptive selling as important in domestic markets as it is in international markets?

10. Discuss the final step of the sales process (enhancing customer relationships) as related to the continuing evolution of personal selling.

BUILDING PROFESSIONAL SELLING SKILLS

1. **Situation:** Assume you are a salesperson for a packaging manufacturing company that supplies retail stores with custom-imprinted shopping bags. The company has manufacturing facilities in Texas, Georgia, New York, and California. There are five functional areas in the company: marketing (includes sales), production, finance and accounting, customer service and shipping, and human resources. You work out of the California plant, which serves the United States west of

ROLE PLAY

the Rocky Mountains. Within the marketing department, your key contact is the product manager who routinely interacts with individuals from production, customer service, and shipping to coordinate production runs with promised delivery dates. The product manager has no direct authority over any of the personnel in production or customer service and shipping. For the following situations, explain how you would try to gain the cooperation of the right people to meet customer needs. It is important that you achieve customer satisfaction but not at the expense of profitability.

Scenario A: A large customer unexpectedly runs out of shopping bags and is requesting a shipment within 72 hours. Normal lead time for existing customers is 10 working days. Production is fully booked, that is, there is no idle capacity in the California plant.

Scenario B: A long-time customer buys three sizes of shopping bags, all shipped in identical corrugated boxes. The smallest bags are packed 500 to a box, the medium-sized bags 250 to a box, and the largest 100 to a box. Black-and-white labels on one end of the corrugated boxes denote bag sizes. The customer wants labels in three different colors to denote bag size. According to the customer, store employees could then tell at a glance if stock for a particular size was running low and thus place prompt requests for reorders. Currently, the black-and-white labels are applied by a machine as part of the manufacturing process. The color labels would have to be custom produced and hand-fed into the labeling machine, whereas existing labels are printed inexpensively in large quantities and fed automatically into the labeling machine.

2. Your knowledge of selling can help you get started in a sales career. Landing a job is like making a major sale in that your knowledge, skills, and attitudes must meet the needs of the employer. One way to match up with employer needs is to use the feature-advantage-benefit (FAB) approach to assess yourself relative to employer needs. In selling, a feature is a factual statement about the product or service, for example, "at 10 pounds, it is the lightest electrical motor in its performance category." An advantage describes how the product can be used or help the customer, for example, "it is light enough to be used in portable applications." The benefit is the favorable outcome the customer will experience from the advantage, for example, "your customers no longer will have to come to the repair center for assistance, as service reps will be able to use portable repair kits in the field." To translate this method to the job search, think of yourself as the "product." Select an appropriate company and discover what they are looking for in sales job applicants. You can use classified ads, the college placement

The FAB Job-Search Matrix (Example)

A Need	B Feature	C Advantage	D Benefit
Employer or Problem	Student		Employer
"This job requires …"	"I have …"	"This means …"	"You will …"
frequent sales presentations to individuals and groups	taken 10 classes that required presentations	I require limited or no training in making presentations	save on the cost of training; you have ability and confidence to be productive early

(List additional needs, features, advantages, and benefits.)

center, personal contacts, or other sources to find a sales position that you are interested in. Using the following example as a starting point, complete an FAB worksheet that shows how you are qualified for the job. In a real job search, this information could be translated to your résumé or cover letter requesting an interview.

3. Many industry observers believe that entrepreneurs must have strong selling skills to succeed. At a minimum, entrepreneurs should understand the sales process well enough to direct the sales efforts of others. To better understand the linkages between entrepreneurship and selling, visit the *Inc* magazine Web site at **http://www.inc.com**. From the home page, click on the "Sales" link under the "Resource Centers" menu. Check under the "Departments" menu for "How-To Guides" and "Articles by Topic" to identify material related to this module. Write a brief report summarizing your findings.

MAKING PROFESSIONAL SELLING DECISIONS

Case 1.1: Biomod, Inc.
Background

Biomod, Inc., a California-based manufacturer of educational models of the human body, has been in business since the mid-1960s. The company's products, sold primarily to middle schools in the United States, are available in plastic or as computer images. Accompanying products include lesson plans for teachers, and workbooks and computer programs for students. Biomod has enjoyed healthy sales increases in recent years, as schools increasingly integrated computer-assisted instruction into their curricula. Five years ago, Biomod began selling consumer versions of its models through selected specialty educational toy stores and recently began selling on its own Web site. In addition, Biomod is also selling on the Web through Hypermart.com and Ed-Toys. Further, Biomod has had discussions with Toys "Я" Us, and the giant retailer seems eager to stock Biomod products.

Current Situation

Biomod has employed Zack Wilson, a recent graduate of San Diego State University, for the past six months. He has become familiar with all aspects of marketing the Biomod product line and is now the sales representative for electronic retailing accounts. Wilson is truly excited about his job, as he sees the explosive growth potential for selling Biomod products on the Internet. His first big success came when he convinced Hypermart.com to sell Biomod products. After all, Hypermart has the reputation in most circles as the premier electronic retailer. Thirty days after his initial sales to Hypermart, Wilson was thrilled to land Ed-Toys as his second electronic retailer.

No doubt about it, Zack Wilson was on a roll. Securing commitments from Hypermart and Ed-Toys within a month was almost too good to be true. In fact, there was only one problem facing Wilson. Hypermart had begun discounting the Biomod product line as much as 20 percent off suggested retail, and Ed-Toys was unhappy with the intense price competition. The following conversation had just taken place between Wilson and Ed-Toys buyer Andrea Haughton:

Haughton: Zack, your line looked really promising to us at suggested retail prices, but meeting Hypermart's pricing sucks the profit right out of the equation. Are you selling Hypermart at a lower price than us?

Wilson: Absolutely not! Hypermart just decided to promote our line with the discounts.

Haughton: So the discounts are just a temporary promotion? When will Hypermart stop discounting?

Wilson: Well, I don't really know. What I mean by that is that Hypermart often discounts, but in the case of the Biomod line, I've got to believe it's just a temporary thing.

Haughton: Why do you think so?

Wilson: Because they haven't asked me for a lower price. Like you, they can't be making much of a profit after the discounts.

Haughton: Well, Zack, we need to stop the bleeding! I can't go on meeting their prices. If they're not making money either, maybe it's time you get them to stop the discounting. Can you talk with them about getting up to suggested retail?

Wilson: Andrea, you know I can't dictate retail selling prices to them any more than I could to you.

Haughton: Nor am I suggesting you try to dictate prices. I am simply suggesting that you let them know that if they choose to go back to suggested retail, we will surely follow. If we can't sell at suggested retail, we will have little choice but to stop selling the Biomod line. I'm sure you can appreciate the fact that we have profit expectations for every line we sell. At 20 percent off, Zack, the Biomod line just doesn't cut it for us.

Wilson: O.K., I will see what I can do.

Later in the day, Wilson checked his e-mail and found a disturbing message from Barbara Moore, a Biomod sales representative for the retail store division. Moore's message informed Wilson that one of her key retailers had visited the Hypermart Web site and was extremely upset to see the heavy discounting on the Biomod line. Moore claimed that she was in danger of losing her account and that she feared a widespread outcry from other specialty stores as word of the Hypermart discounting would quickly spread. Moore strongly urged Wilson to do what he could to get Hypermart back to suggested retail. Wilson noted that Moore had copied both her sales manager and Rebecca Stanley, Wilson's sales manager, with her e-mail message.

The following day, Wilson called on Warren Bryant, Hypermart's buyer for the Biomod line. He conveyed to Bryant that Ed-Toys and some of the store retailers were upset with the discounting. Bryant shrugged off the news, commenting only that "it's a dog-eat-dog" world and that price competition was part of the game. Wilson asked Bryant if he was happy with the profit margins on the Biomod line, and Bryant responded that he was more concerned with growing Hypermart's market share than with profit margins. He told Wilson, "Our game plan is grab a dominant share, then worry about margins." At this point, Bryant gave Wilson something else to think about:

Bryant: Hey, Zack, I noticed you guys are selling the same products on your own Web site as the ones we're selling on ours.

Wilson: True, what's the problem?

Bryant: Well, I just read in the trade press where Home Depot told their vendors that they don't buy from their (Home Depot's) competitors and that they view vendor Web sites as competitors to their retail business. Maybe we feel the same way. We sell on the Web, and if you do too, then you're really a competitor for us.

Wilson: Warren, you know that we only do a little volume on the Web. Our site is really more of an information site.

Bryant: But you do offer an alternative to other electronic retailers and us by selling on your own site. And by the way, don't your store retailers oppose your selling on the Web?

Wilson: At this point, most of them are small retailers, and frankly speaking, they view you as more of a threat than us selling on our own site. Besides, our store division salesforce is working on a software package that will enable our store retailers to easily set up their own Web sites over the next six months or so.

Bryant: Unbelievable! What you're saying is that another division in your company is creating even more Web-based competition for me! I thought we had a real future together, but I've got to do some heavy-duty thinking on that. Thanks, Zack, but I'm really busy and need to move on to some other priorities this afternoon. Call me if you have any new thoughts on where we go from here.

Wilson left Hypermart and began the hour-long drive back to the office. "Good thing I've a little time to think about this situation," he thought as he drove along. "I need to talk with Rebecca Stanley just as soon as I get to the office."

Questions

1. How do you think Wilson got into this dilemma?
2. If you were Rebecca Stanley, Wilson's sales manager, what would you advise Wilson to do?

Situation: Read Case 1.1.

Characters: Zack Wilson, Biomod   **ROLE PLAY**
sales representative; Rebecca Stanley, Biomod sales manager.

Scene 1:   *Location*—Stanley's office.
Action—Wilson explains to Stanley what has occurred with the Ed-Toys and Hypermart accounts. Rather than telling Wilson how to deal with Hypermart and Ed-Toys from this point forward, Stanley directs Wilson to devise his own strategy. Rebecca then tells Wilson that she would like to visit both accounts with him within a week, and that she would like to review his strategy for Hypermart and Ed-Toys within 48 hours.

Upon completion of the role play, address the following questions:

1. Is Stanley justified in telling Wilson to devise his own strategy rather than giving him specific direction at this time? What are the advantages and disadvantages of her approach?
2. How could this situation have been prevented?

Scene 2:   *Location*—Stanley's office. *Action*— Wilson presents his strategy to Stanley.

Upon completion of the role play, address the following questions:

1. What are the strengths and weaknesses of Wilson's interaction with Ed-Toys and Hypermart?
2. What further suggestions can you make for dealing with Hypermart and Ed-Toys?

Case 1.2: Plastico, Inc.
Background

Plastico, Inc., located in New York, is a manufacturer of plastic components. The company is noted for producing high-quality products. Its salesforce calls on large accounts, such as refrigerator manufacturers who might need large quantities of custommade products, such as door liners. Recent increases in new-home sales over the past several years have fueled refrigerator sales and, subsequently, sales at Plastico. Moreover, federal regulations requiring that dishwasher liners be made of plastic, rather than porcelain, have enhanced Plastico's sales.

Current Situation

Sharon Stone had recently been assigned to the central Michigan territory. Although this was her first sales job, she felt confident and was eager to begin. She had taken a sales course in college and had just completed the company's training program. The company stressed the use of an organized sales presentation in which the salesperson organizes the key points into a planned sequence that allows for adaptive behavior by the salesperson as the presentation progresses. She was familiar with this approach because she had studied it in her college sales course.

Stone's first call was at a small refrigerator manufacturer in Ann Arbor. She had called the day before to set up an appointment with materials purchasing manager David Kline at 9:00 A.M. On the morning of her meeting, Stone was running behind schedule because of an alarm clock malfunction. As a result, she ended up in traffic she did not anticipate and did not arrive for her appointment until 9:10 A.M. When she informed the receptionist she had an appointment with Kline, she was told he was in another meeting. He did agree, however, to see Stone when his meeting was finished, which would be about 9:45 A.M. Stone was upset Kline would not wait 10 minutes for her and let the receptionist know it.

At 9:50 A.M. Stone was introducing herself to Kline. She noticed his office was filled with University of Michigan memorabilia. She remembered from her training that the first thing to do was build rapport with the prospect. Thus she asked Kline if he went to the University of Michigan. This got the ball rolling quickly. Kline had graduated from Michigan and was a big fan of the basketball and football teams. He was more than happy to talk about them. Stone was excited; she knew this would help her build rapport. After about 25 minutes of football and basketball chit-chat, Stone figured it was time to get down to business.

After finally getting Kline off the subject of sports, Stone began to discuss the benefits of her product. She figured if she did not control the conversation Kline would revert to discussing sports. She went on and on about the material compounds comprising Plastico plastics, as well as the processes used to develop plastic liners. She explained the customizing process, the product's durability, Plastico's ability to provide door liners in any color, and her company's return and credit policies. After nearly 25 minutes, she finally asked Kline if he had any questions.

Kline asked her if she had any product samples with her. Stone had to apologize—in all the confusion this morning she ran off and left the samples at home. Then Kline asked her about the company's turnaround time from order to delivery. Knowing quick turnaround was important to Kline, and feeling this prospect may be slipping away, she told him it was about four weeks, although she knew it was really closer to five. However, she thought, if Kline ordered from them and it took a little longer, she could always blame it on production. When the

issue of price emerged, Stone was not able to clearly justify in Kline's mind why Plastico was slightly higher than the competition. She thought that she had clearly explained the benefits of the product and that it should be obvious that Plastico is a better choice.

Finally, Kline told Stone he would have to excuse himself. He had a meeting to attend on the other side of town. He thanked her for coming by and told her he would consider her offer. Stone thanked Kline for his time and departed. As she reflected on her first call she wondered where she went wrong. She thought she would jot down some notes about her call to discuss with her sales manager later.

Questions

1. What problems do you see with Stone's first sales call?
2. If you were Stone's sales manager, what would you recommend she do to improve her chances of succeeding?

ROLE PLAY

Situation:	Read Case 1.2.
Characters:	Sharon Stone, Plastico sales representative.
Scene:	*Location*—Plastico's Michigan office during a weekly sales meeting shortly after her sales call with David Kline. *Action*—Stone reviews her sales call with Kline with other Plastico sales representatives and their sales manager. This is a regular feature of the weekly meetings, with the idea being that all sales representatives can learn from the experiences of others. Stone has decided to compare her call with Kline to some of the material from her sales training with Plastico. This material, which contrasts transaction-focused selling with trust-based relationship selling, is shown in Exhibit 1.2. Her review will analyze whether she did or did not practice trust-based relationship selling during her call with Kline.

Upon completion of the role play, address the following questions:

1. Is Stone's review of her sales call accurate?
2. What steps should Stone take to begin to develop a strong relationship with Kline?

This appendix is designed to give an in-depth look at sales careers. We first discuss characteristics of sales careers, then describe several different types of personal selling jobs. The appendix concludes with a discussion of the skills and qualifications necessary for success in sales careers.

CHARACTERISTICS OF SALES CAREERS

Although individual opinions will vary, the ideal career for most individuals offers a bright future, including good opportunities for financial rewards and job advancement. As you read the following sections on the characteristics of sales careers, you might think about what you expect from a career and whether your expectations could be met in a sales career. The characteristics to be discussed are

- job security
- advancement opportunities
- immediate feedback
- prestige
- job variety
- independence
- compensation

Job Security

Salespeople are revenue producers and thus enjoy relatively good job security compared with other occupational groups. Certainly, individual job security depends on individual performance, but in general, salespeople are usually the last group to be negatively affected by personnel cutbacks.

Competent salespeople also have some degree of job security based on the universality of their basic sales skills. In many cases, salespeople are able to successfully move to another employer, maybe even change industries, because sales skills are largely transferable. For salespeople working in declining or stagnant industries, this is heartening news.

There looks to be a fairly strong demand for salespeople within the 2004–2005 time period. Overall U.S. job growth is expected to be approximately 13 percent in that time, which represents above average opportunities in technical sales, advertising, real estate, some services sectors, and in sales management positions. (See Exhibit 1A.1.)[1] Even life insurance, where expected overall job growth is less than average in 2004–2014, offers strong opportunities for those with college degrees.[2]

Advancement Opportunities

As the business world continues to become more competitive, the advancement opportunities for salespeople will continue to be an attractive dimension of sales careers. In highly competitive markets, individuals and companies that are successful in determining and meeting customer needs will be rewarded with opportunities for advancement. One reason that many successful salespeople ultimately find their way into top management is that they display some of the key attributes required for success in executive

EXHIBIT 1A.1 Occupational Outlook for Salespeople

Job Type	2004 Employment	Projected Growth 2004–2012 Percentage
Manufacturers and Wholesalers (nontechnical)	1,453,625	12.9
Manufacturers and Wholesalers (technical)	397,421	14.4
Advertising Sales Representatives	154,370	16.3
Real Estate Agents	348,358	14.7
Insurance Agents	399,652	6.6
Securities, Commodities, and Financial Services	280,906	11.5
Other Services	380,476	18.7
Retail	4,256,138	17.3
Sales Engineers	73,617	14.0
Sales Managers	336,514	19.7

positions. According to the U.S. Bureau of Labor, top executives must have highly developed personal skills, be able to communicate clearly and persuasively, and have high levels of self-confidence, motivation, business judgment, and determination.[3]

Immediate Feedback

Salespeople receive constant, immediate feedback on their job performance. Usually, the results of their efforts can be plainly observed by both salespeople and their sales managers—a source of motivation and job satisfaction. On a daily basis, salespeople receive direct feedback from their customers, and this can be stimulating, challenging, and productive. The opportunity to react immediately to customer feedback during sales presentations is a strong benefit of adaptive selling, and distinguishes selling from other forms of marketing communications such as advertising and public relations. The spontaneity and creativity involved in reacting to immediate feedback is one dimension of selling that makes it such an interesting job.

Prestige

Traditionally, sales has not been a prestigious occupation in the eyes of the general public. There is some evidence that as the general public learns more about the activities and qualifications of professional salespeople, the image of salespeople, and thus the prestige of selling, is improving. An analysis of the popular press (excluding business publications) reveals that there are more positive than negative mentions of news-making salespeople. In a positive light, salespeople are frequently seen as knowledgeable, well-trained, educated, and capable of solving customer problems. The negative aspects of salespeople's image often center on deception and high-pressure techniques.[4]

Another study indicates that salespeople historically have been depicted in movies and television programs more often than not in a negative light.[5] Even so, the struggling, down-and-out huckster as depicted by Willy Loman in Arthur Miller's 1949 classic *Death of a Salesman* is hardly typical of the professional salesperson of today and the future. Professional salespeople destroy such unfavorable stereotypes, and they would not jeopardize customer relationships by using high-pressure sales techniques to force a premature sale.[6] These perceptions are especially true in the business world, where encounters with professional salespeople are commonplace.

Job Variety

Salespeople rarely vegetate due to boredom. Their jobs are multifaceted and dynamic. For a person seeking the comfort of a well-established routine, sales might not be a good career choice. In sales, day-to-day variation on the job is the norm. Customers change, new products and services are developed, and competition introduces new elements at a rapid pace.

The opportunity to become immersed in the job and bring creativity to bear is demonstrated by General Mills, whose salesforce has been named one of the best in America. According to John Maschuzik, vice president of sales in the western United States, salespeople's customization of promotional efforts for their customers is crucial to the company's success. Maschuzik says that General Mills gives their salespeople a lot of latitude and the opportunity to be creative in spending retail promotion money.[7]

Independence

Sales jobs often allow independence of action. This independence is frequently a by-product of decentralized sales operations in which salespeople live and work away from headquarters, therefore working from their homes and making their own plans for extensive travel.

Independence of action and freedom to make decisions are usually presented as advantages that sales positions have over tightly supervised jobs. College students who prefer sales careers rate freedom to make decisions second only to salary as an important job consideration.[8] Despite its appeal, however, independence does present some problems. New recruits working from their homes may find the lack of a company office somewhat disorienting. They may need an office environment to relate to, especially if their past work experience provided regular contact in an office environment.

The independence of action traditionally enjoyed by salespeople is being scrutinized by sales managers more heavily now than in the past. The emphasis on sales productivity, accomplished in part through cost containment, is encouraging sales managers to take a more active role in dictating travel plans and sales call schedules.

Compensation

Compensation is generally thought to be a strong advantage of sales careers. Pay is closely tied to performance, especially if commissions and bonuses are part of the pay package.

Starting salaries for inexperienced salespersons with a college degree typically average $40,000. Between the extremes of the highly experienced salesperson and the inexperienced recruit, an average salesperson earns approximately $50,000–$70,000 per year. More experienced salespeople, including those who deal with large customers, often earn in the $85,000–$135,000 range. Top salespeople can earn hundreds of thousands of dollars annually, with some exceeding a million dollars in annual earnings.

CLASSIFICATION OF PERSONAL SELLING JOBS

Because there are so many unique sales jobs, the term *salesperson* is not by itself very descriptive. A salesperson could be a flower vendor at a busy downtown intersection or the sales executive negotiating the sale of Boeing aircraft to the People's Republic of China.

We briefly discuss six types of personal selling jobs:

- sales support
- new business

- existing business
- inside sales (nonretail)
- direct-to-consumer sales
- combination sales jobs

Sales Support

Sales support personnel are not usually involved in the direct solicitation of purchase orders. Rather, their primary responsibility is dissemination of information and performance of other activities designed to stimulate sales. They might concentrate at the end-user level or another level in the channel of distribution to support the overall sales effort. They may report to another salesperson, who is responsible for direct handling of purchase orders, or to the sales manager. There are two well-known categories of support salespeople: missionary or detail salespeople and technical support salespeople.

Missionary salespeople usually work for a manufacturer but may also be found working for brokers and manufacturing representatives, especially in the grocery industry. There are strong similarities between sales missionaries and religious missionaries. Like their counterparts, sales missionaries are expected to "spread the word" with the purpose of conversion—to customer status. Once converted, the customer receives reinforcing messages, new information, and the benefit of the missionary's activities to strengthen the relationship between buyer and seller.

In the pharmaceutical industry, the **detailer** is a fixture. Detailers working at the physician level furnish valuable information regarding the capabilities and limitations of medications in an attempt to get the physician to prescribe their product. Another sales representative from the same pharmaceutical company will sell the medication to the wholesaler or pharmacist, but it is the detailer's job to support the direct sales effort by calling on physicians.

Technical specialists are sometimes considered to be sales support personnel. These **technical support salespeople** may assist in design and specification processes, installation of equipment, training of the customer's employees, and follow-up service of a technical nature. They are sometimes part of a sales team that includes another salesperson who specializes in identifying and satisfying customer needs by recommending the appropriate product or service.

New Business

New business is generated for the selling firm by adding new customers or introducing new products to the marketplace. Two types of new-business salespeople are pioneers and order-getters.

Pioneers, as the term suggests, are constantly involved with either new products, new customers, or both. Their task requires creative selling and the ability to counter the resistance to change that will likely be present in prospective customers. Pioneers are well-represented in the sale of business franchises, in which the sales representatives travel from city to city seeking new franchisees.

Order-getters are salespeople who actively seek orders, usually in a highly competitive environment. Although all pioneers are also order-getters, the reverse is not true. An order-getter may serve existing customers on an ongoing basis, whereas the pioneer moves on to new customers as soon as possible. Order-getters may seek new business by selling an existing customer additional items from the product line. A well-known tactic is to establish a relationship with a customer by selling a single product from the line, then to follow up with subsequent sales calls for other items from the product line.

Most corporations emphasize sales growth, and salespeople operating as pioneers and order-getters are at the heart of sales growth objectives. The pressure to perform in these roles is fairly intense; the results are highly visible. For these reasons, the new-business salesperson is often among the elite in any company's salesforce.

Existing Business

In direct contrast to new-business salespeople, other salespeople's primary responsibility is to maintain relationships with existing customers. Salespeople who specialize in maintaining existing business include **order-takers**. These salespeople frequently work for wholesalers and, as the term *order-taker* implies, they are not too involved in creative selling. Route salespeople who work an established customer base, taking routine reorders of stock items, are order-takers. They sometimes follow a pioneer salesperson and take over the account after the pioneer has made the initial sale.

These salespeople are no less valuable to their firms than the new-business salespeople, but creative selling skills are less important to this category of sales personnel. Their strengths tend to be reliability and competence in assuring customer convenience. Customers grow to depend on the services provided by this type of salesperson. As most markets are becoming more competitive, the role of existing-business salespeople is sometimes critical to prevent erosion of the customer base.

Many firms, believing that it is easier to protect and maintain profitable customers than it is to find replacement customers, are reinforcing sales efforts to existing customers. For example, Frito-Lay uses 18,000 route service salespeople to call on retail customers at least three times weekly. Larger customers see their Frito-Lay representative on a daily basis. These salespeople spend a lot of their time educating customers about the profitability of Frito-Lay's snack foods, which leads to increased sales for both the retailer and for Frito-Lay.

Inside Sales

In this text, **inside sales** refers to nonretail salespeople who remain in their employer's place of business while dealing with customers. The inside-sales operation has received considerable attention in recent years, not only as a supplementary sales tactic, but also as an alternative to field selling.

Inside sales can be conducted on an active or passive sales basis. Active inside sales include the solicitation of entire orders, either as part of a telemarketing operation or when customers walk into the seller's facilities. Passive inside sales imply the acceptance, rather than solicitation, of customer orders, although it is common practice for these transactions to include add-on sales attempts. We should note that customer service personnel sometimes function as inside-sales personnel as an ongoing part of their jobs.

Direct-to-Consumer Sales

Direct-to-consumer salespeople are the most numerous type. There are approximately 4.3 million retail salespeople in this country and perhaps another million selling real estate, insurance, and securities directly to consumers. Add to this figure another several million selling direct to the consumer for such companies as Tupperware, Mary Kay, and Avon.

This diverse category of salespeople ranges from the part-time, often temporary salesperson in a retail store to the highly educated, professionally trained stockbroker on Wall Street. As a general statement, the more challenging direct-to-consumer sales positions are those involving the sale of intangible services such as insurance and financial services.

Combination Sales Jobs

Now that we have reviewed some of the basic types of sales jobs, let us consider the salesperson who performs multiple types of sales jobs within the framework of a single position. We use the case of the territory manager's position with GlaxoSmith Kline Consumer Healthcare (GSK) to illustrate the **combination sales job** concept. GSK, whose products include Aqua-Fresh toothpaste, markets a wide range of consumer healthcare goods to food, drug, variety, and mass merchandisers. The territory manager's job blends responsibilities for developing new business, maintaining and stimulating existing business, and performing sales support activities.

During a typical day in the field, the GSK territory manager is involved in sales support activities such as merchandising and in-store promotion at the individual retail store level. Maintaining contact and goodwill with store personnel is another routine sales support activity. The territory manager also makes sales calls on chain headquarters personnel to handle existing business and to seek new business. And it is the territory manager who introduces new GSK products in the marketplace.

QUALIFICATIONS AND SKILLS REQUIRED FOR SUCCESS BY SALESPERSONS

Because there are so many different types of jobs in sales, it is rather difficult to generalize about the qualifications and skills needed for success. This list would have to vary according to the details of a given job. Even then, it is reasonable to believe that for any given job, different persons with different skills could be successful. These conclusions have been reached after decades of research that has tried to correlate sales performance with physical traits, mental abilities, personality characteristics, and the experience and background of the salesperson.

Success in sales is increasingly being thought of in terms of a strategic team effort, rather than the characteristics of individual salespersons. For example, three studies of more than 200 companies that employ 25,000 salespersons in the United States and Australia found that being customer-oriented and cooperating as a team player were critical to salespersons' success.[9]

Being careful not to suggest that sales success is solely a function of individual traits, let us consider some of the skills and qualifications that are thought to be especially critical for success in most sales jobs. Five factors that seem to be particularly important for success in sales are empathy, ego drive, ego strength, verbal communication skills, and enthusiasm. These factors have been selected after reviewing three primary sources of information:

- a study of more than 750,000 salespeople in 15,000 companies (Greenberg and Greenberg)[10]
- two reviews of four decades of research on factors related to sales success (Comer and Dubinsky; and Brown, Leigh, and Haygood)[11]
- surveys of sales executives[12]

Empathy

In a sales context, **empathy** (the ability to see things as others would see them) includes being able to read cues furnished by the customer to better determine the customer's viewpoint. According to Spiro and Weitz, empathy is crucial for successful interaction between a buyer and a seller.[13] An empathetic salesperson is presumably in a better position to tailor the sales presentation to the customer during the planning stages. More important, empathetic salespeople can adjust to feedback during the presentation.

The research of Greenberg and Greenberg found empathy to be a significant predictor of sales success. This finding was partially supported in the review by Comer and Dubinsky, who found empathy to be an important factor in consumer and insurance sales but not in retail or industrial sales. Supporting the importance of empathy in sales success is a multi-industry study of 215 sales managers by Marshall, Goebel, and Moncrief.[14] These researchers found empathy to be among the top 25 percent of skills and personal attributes thought to be important determinants of sales success. Even though some studies do not find direct links between salesperson empathy and success, empathy is generally accepted as an important trait for successful salespeople.

As relationship selling grows in importance, empathy logically will become even more important for sales success.

Ego Drive

In a sales context, **ego drive** (an indication of the degree of determination a person has to achieve goals and overcome obstacles in striving for success) is manifested as an inner need to persuade others in order to achieve personal gratification. Greenberg and Greenberg point out the complementary relationship between empathy and ego drive that is necessary for sales success. The salesperson who is extremely empathetic but lacks ego drive may have problems in taking active steps to confirm a sale. However, a salesperson with more ego drive than empathy may ignore the customer's viewpoint in an ill-advised, overly anxious attempt to gain commitment from the customer.

Ego Strength

The degree to which a person is able to achieve an approximation of inner drives is **ego strength.** Salespeople with high levels of ego strength are likely to be self-assured and self-accepting. Salespeople with healthy egos are better equipped to deal with the possibility of rejection throughout the sales process. They are probably less likely to experience sales call reluctance and are resilient enough to overcome the disappointment of inevitable lost sales.

Salespeople with strong ego drives who are well-equipped to do their jobs will likely be high in **self-efficacy**; that is, they will strongly believe that they can be successful on the job. In situations in which their initial efforts meet resistance, rejection, or failure, salespeople high in self-efficacy are likely to persist in pursuing their goals. In complex sales involving large dollar amounts and a long sales cycle (the time from first customer contact to eventual sale), it is crucial to continue working toward a distant goal despite the very real possibility of setbacks along the way. For example, airplane manufacturers hoping to land contracts with the airlines typically pursue such contracts for several years before a buying decision is made. For those who persevere, however, the payoff can be well worth the extended effort.

Interpersonal Communication Skills

Interpersonal communication skills, including listening and questioning, are essential for sales success. An in-depth study of 300 sales executives, salespeople, and customers of 24 major sales companies in North America, Europe, and Japan found that effective salespeople are constantly seeking ways to improve communication skills that enable them to develop, explain, and implement customer solutions. The companies in the study are some of the best in the world at professional selling: Sony, Xerox, American Airlines, Fuji, and Scott paper.[15]

Another major study across several industries found that three communications skills in particular were among the top 10 percent of success factors for professional salespeople.[16] The highest-rated success factor in this study was listening skills, with ability to adapt presentations according to the situation and verbal communications skills following close behind.

To meet customer needs, salespeople must be able to solicit opinions, listen effectively, and confirm customer needs and concerns. They must be capable of probing customer expectations with open- and closed-ended questions and responding in a flexible manner to individual personalities and different business cultures in ways that demonstrate respect for differences.[17] This requires adaptable, socially intelligent salespeople, especially when dealing with multicultural customers.[18]

The importance of communication skills has been recognized by sales managers, recruiters, and sales researchers. These skills can be continually refined throughout a sales career, a positive factor from both a personal and a career development perspective.

Enthusiasm

When sales executives and recruiters discuss qualifications for sales positions, they invariably include **enthusiasm**. They are usually referring to dual dimensions of enthusiasm—an enthusiastic attitude in a general sense and a special enthusiasm for selling. On-campus recruiters have mentioned that they seek students who are well beyond "interested in sales" to the point of truly being enthusiastic about career opportunities in sales. Recruiters are somewhat weary of "selling sales" as a viable career, and they welcome the job applicant who displays genuine enthusiasm for the field.

Comments on Qualifications and Skills

The qualifications and skills needed for sales success are different today from those required for success two decades ago. As the popularity of relationship selling grows, the skills necessary for sales success will evolve to meet the needs of the marketplace. For example, Greenberg and Greenberg's research has identified what they call an "emerging factor" for sales success, a strong motivation to provide service to the customer. They contrast this **service motivation** with ego drive by noting that, although ego drive relates to persuading others, service motivation comes from desiring the approval of others. For example, a salesperson may be extremely gratified to please a customer through superior postsale service. Greenberg and Greenberg conclude that most salespeople will need both service motivation and ego drive to succeed, although they note that extremely high levels of both attributes are not likely to exist in the same individual. Nonetheless, there is a growing interest in bringing service concepts and practices into the world of professional selling. While it may be difficult to recruit salespeople who are high on the service dimension, it is certainly feasible to provide appropriate training and to reinforce the desired service behaviors through sales management practices. Without significant emphasis on servicing existing customers, a company is not truly practicing relationship selling.[19]

Our discussion of factors related to sales success is necessarily brief, as a fully descriptive treatment of the topic must be tied to a given sales position. Veteran sales managers and recruiters can often specify with amazing precision what qualifications and skills are needed to succeed in a given sales job. These assessments are usually based on a mixture of objective and subjective judgments.

Professional selling offers virtually unlimited career opportunities for the right person. Many of the skills and qualifications necessary for success in selling are also important for success as an entrepreneur or as a leader in a corporate setting. For those interested in learning more about sales careers, consult these sources: *Sales & Marketing Management* magazine at **http://salesandmarketing.com**; *Selling Power* magazine at **http://sellingpower.com**; and Sales and Marketing Executives International, a professional organization, at **http://www.smei.org**.

UNDERSTANDING SALES MANAGEMENT TERMS

sales support personnel
missionary salespeople
detailer
technical support salespeople
pioneers
order-getters
order-takers
inside sales

combination sales job
empathy
ego drive
ego strength
self-efficacy
interpersonal communications skills
enthusiasm
service motivation

The Foundations of Professional Selling

The three modules in Part One provide the important foundations for successful professional selling. In Module 2 we will discuss building trust with customers and sales ethics. Trust between the buyer and seller is essential for long-term, mutually beneficial relationships. Ethical sales behavior is an important ingredient in the trust-building process.

Module 3 provides in-depth coverage of buyer behavior in business markets. Business buyers and buyers for other types of organizations are often quite sophisticated in their purchasing practices. In contrast to most consumer purchases, most business purchase situations are more complex, demanding well-planned and well-executed sales communications.

In Module 4, we focus on the communications skills necessary for sales success. In particular, questioning and listening are covered in-depth. The SPIN and ADAPT questioning methods are presented as important tools for determining buyer needs and advancing the sale.

DEVELOPING TRUST AND MUTUAL RESPECT WITH CLIENTS

Motivation Excellence Inc. (MEI) is a full-service performance improvement company that specializes in highly creative and results-oriented incentive systems. Their incentive planning process is focused on exceeding clients' sales and marketing goals and providing those clients with a solid return on investment. The ability of their sales team and executive management to develop client relationships on a rock-solid foundation of mutual respect, trust, and confidence has been critical to MEI's long-term success.

The company was founded by Greg Lewis in 1985 and is dedicated to the highest standards of integrity, mutual respect, and trust and to creating an environment that provides unparalleled client service while building client relationships into long-lasting partnerships. Their mission statement clearly defines the criticality of developing trust and mutual respect with clients, suppliers, and their employees.

MEI develops custom solutions to address their clients' sales and marketing challenges, which requires the gathering of highly confidential and extremely market-sensitive information in order to be effective in developing the structure of incentive programs.

Jim Micklos (senior account executive with MEI) spends anywhere from several months to several years developing the respect of his clients and prospects. He knows it can take five to ten or more touches (sales calls) to gain the credibility he needs to do business with a client. Once this credibility is established, Micklos utilizes two key documents to obtain the critical information required. First is the two-sided Mutual Confidentiality Agreement that was specifically written to protect both the client's and MEI's confidential information. Second is a list of Program Design Questions that details the sales, profit margin, market share, go-to-market strategies, etc., that provide the fundamental data to build the foundation for the incentive program. The companies MEI works with have to be very comfortable to pass on this type of sensitive information.

Simply stated, building trust and securing clients' confidence are critical to MEI's success.

The performance improvement process includes targeted mailings to clients' personnel, highlighting their award-earning opportunities. The reward for superior performance may include deluxe travel to well-known resorts throughout the world as well as a selection of high quality, brand name merchandise from MEI's catalogue of awards.

During the award redemption and fulfillment process, MEI lives by the intent of their mission statement. Client contacts may be tempted to ask for free or discounted personal travel benefits and/or sample merchandise items, but the company is unwilling to arrange such benefits. It lives by the ethical standards articulated by the founder and detailed in the mission statement.

MEI's focus on exceeding client expectations by providing unsurpassed client service and delivering programs with extraordinary ROIs is reflected in their client retention rate in excess of 95 percent in an industry where 55 to 60 percent is the norm. It all starts with developing the mutual respect and trust required to obtain the data that enables development of their custom solutions.

Objectives

After completing this module, you should be able to

1 Explain the importance of trust.

2 Discuss the distinguishing characteristics of trust-based selling.

3 Discuss how to earn trust.

4 Explain how knowledge bases help build trust and relationships.

5 Understand the importance of sales ethics.

6 Discuss three important areas of unethical behavior.

Mutual respect, trust, confidence, and ethical behavior cannot be overemphasized in today's business environment. MEI's success is a result of client relationships built on that foundation.

Source: Interview with Jim Micklos, Motivation Excellence Inc., July 20, 2006.

Trust reflects the extent of the buyer's confidence that it can rely on the salesperson's integrity. That being said, it is important to note that trust means different things to different people. According to John Newman,[1] vice president of Integrated Supply Chains Segment at A. T. Kearney, trust is defined in many ways. Buyers define trust with such terms as **openness**, **dependability**, **candor**, **honesty**, **confidentiality**, **security**, **reliability**, **fairness**, and **predictability**, as well as other things. For example, in the Kearney study, one manufacturer related trust to credibility and said, "What trust boils down to, in a nutshell, is credibility, and when you say you are going to do something, you do it, and the whole organization has to be behind that decision." Another manufacturer related trust to confidentiality in that "they were afraid that the sales guys were going around and telling account B what account A is doing" and identified this as a violation of trust. Another company related trust to openness in that "we have to share information that traditionally is not shared." One president told how his engineers were sharing manufacturing secrets with their suppliers that would have cost the engineers their jobs if they had held the discussion prior to the past five years.[2]

A salesperson has to determine what trust means to each of his or her buyers, as shown in Figure 2.1. If it is confidentiality, then the salesperson must demonstrate how his or her company handles sensitive information. If credibility is the concern, then the salesperson must demonstrate over time that all promises will be kept. Therefore, trust is whatever it means to the buyer, and it is the salesperson's job through questioning to determine what trust attributes are critical to relationship building for a specific buyer.

In this module, we first discuss the meaning of trust in the sales context. Next we explore the importance of trust to salespeople. This is followed by a discussion of how to earn trust and what knowledge bases a salesperson can use to build trust in buyer–seller relationships. Finally, the importance of sales ethics in building trust is reviewed.

FIGURE 2.1   **Trust Builders**

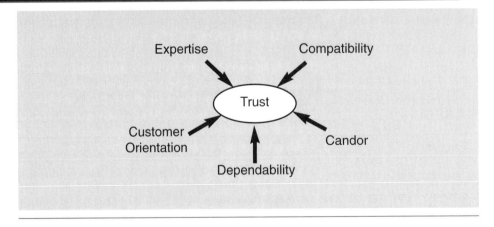

Trust means different things to different people. Trust can be developed by using any of the trust builders. It is the salesperson's job through questioning to determine what trust attributes are critical to relationship building for a specific buyer.

A N   E T H I C A L   D I L E M M A

Jasmine Alexander, account manager for a large copy company, had been calling on the purchasing department of the local college. She thought the purchasing agent Tom Smith, was receptive, but she was not sure he was passing on her literature to the copy center. She had asked several times if she could call directly on the copy center but was told no.

Several weeks later while attending a party, she met the director of the copy center, Terry Wolf, and they talked about their respective jobs. Alexander was invited by Wolf to stop by and look over the center. She gladly accepted. A few days later Alexander received a message from Smith not to call on the college anymore. Did Alexander do anything wrong? How would you have handled the situation?

What Is Trust?

"The essence of trust is that the industrial buyer believes that he can rely on what the salesperson says or promises to do in a situation where the buyer is dependent upon the salesperson's honesty and reliability."[3] One of the keys to a long-term relationship with any client is to create a basis of trust between the sales representative and the client organization.[4]

Thus, gaining credibility in the trust area is essential in order to be seen as a reliable salesperson. Long-term sales success in any industry will generally be built on the concept of referral, and trust plays an important role. Clients obviously seek a salesperson they can trust. The problem is, depending on the industry and the situation, they may have had bad experiences that have lowered their hopes of ever finding a trustworthy partner. "An Ethical Dilemma" illustrates how easy it is for a salesperson to lose the trust of a buyer even when it is an innocent misunderstanding. Consultative salespeople are in a unique position to capitalize on building credibility with customers who place a high value on trust. Because customers are looking for a trustworthy partner with whom to do business but may have difficulty trusting most salespeople, this equates to an opportunity for the salesperson.

The "trust" described here is beyond the typical transaction-oriented trust schema. Issues—such as, Will the product arrive as promised? Will the right product actually be in stock and be shipped on time? Will the invoice contain the agreed-on price? Can the salesperson be found if something goes wrong?—are only initial concerns. In relationship selling, trust is based on a larger set of factors due to the expanded intimacy and longer-term nature of the relationship. The intimacy of this relationship will result in the sharing of information by both parties that could be damaging should either side leak it or use it against the partner.

Trust answers the questions:

1. Do you know what you are talking about?—competence; expertise
2. Will you recommend what is best for me?—customer orientation
3. Are you truthful?—honesty; candor
4. Can you and your company back up your promises?—dependability
5. Will you safeguard confidential information that I share with you?—customer orientation; dependability

"Trust" is an integral part of the relationship between customers and suppliers and results in increased long-term revenues and profits.[5]

WHY IS TRUST IMPORTANT?

In today's increasingly competitive marketplace, buyers typically find themselves inundated with choices regarding both products and suppliers. In this virtual buyers' market, traditional selling methods that focused on closing the sale have been found to be inefficient and often counterproductive to the organization's larger, longer-term marketing strategy. In this new competitive environment, buyers are demanding unique solutions to their problems—product solutions that are customized on the basis of their particular problems and needs. Additionally, the adversarial, win-lose characteristics so customary in traditional selling are fading fast. In their place, longer-term buyer–seller relationships are evolving as the preferred form of doing business. Although buyers are finding it more effective and efficient to do *more* business with *fewer* suppliers, sellers are finding it more effective to develop a continuing stream of business from the right customers.

This shift toward relationship selling has altered both the roles played by salespeople and the activities and skills they exercise in carrying out these roles—the selling process itself. Today's more contemporary selling process is embedded within the relationship marketing paradigm. As such, it emphasizes the initiation and nurturing of long-term buyer–seller relationships based on mutual trust and value-added benefits. As Jim Micklos of MEI pointed out in the opening vignette, it can take from five to ten or more sales calls to establish the trust needed to do business with a prospect. The level of problem-solving activity common to relationship selling requires deliberate and purposeful collaboration between both parties. These joint efforts are directed at creating unique solutions based on an enhanced knowledge and understanding of the customer's needs and the supplier's capabilities so that both parties derive mutual benefits. The nature of this integrative, win-win, and collaborative negotiation relies on augmented communication and interpersonal skills that nurture and sustain the reciprocal trust that allows all parties to fully share information and work together as a strategic problem-solving team.

The skills and activities inherent to relationship selling can be classified according to their purpose as (1) initiation of the relationship (Modules 5 and 6); (2) development of the relationship (Modules 7 and 8); and (3) enhancement of the relationship (Modules 9 and 10). As the activities comprising the selling process have changed, so too have the relative importance and degree of selling effort devoted to each stage of the process.

HOW TO EARN TRUST

Trust is critically important to any relationship. Several variables are critical in helping salespeople earn a buyer's trust, such as expertise, dependability, candor, customer orientation, and compatibility. Each is briefly discussed as to its importance.

Expertise

Inexperience is a difficult thing for a young salesperson to overcome. Most recent college graduates will not have the **expertise** to be immediately successful, especially in industrial sales. Companies spend billions of dollars to train new recruits in the hope of speeding up the expertise variable. Training to gain knowledge on company products and programs, industry, competition, and general market conditions are typical subjects covered in most sales training programs. Young salespeople can shadow more experienced salespeople to learn what it takes to be successful. They must also go the extra yard to prove to their customers their dedication to service. For example, Missy Rust, of GlaxoSmithKline, had recently spent a few minutes with an anesthesiologist discussing a new product, a neuromuscular blocker. A few days later, the physician called her at 1 A.M. to discuss a patient whom he thought was a good candidate for this drug. He was unsure of the correct dosage and needed Rust's expertise in this matter. Rust immediately drove to the hospital and was in the operating room for more than four hours observing the surgery and answering the doctor's questions about this new drug.[6]

Another factor to consider is that many organizations have recently been downsized, thus dramatically cutting the purchasing area in terms of both personnel and support resources. As a result, buyers are having to do more with less and, as such, are thirsty for expertise, be it current insights into their own operations, financial situation, industry trends, or tactical skills in effectively identifying emerging cost cutting and revenue opportunities in their business. Of course, expertise will be even more critical with certain buyers who are technical, detail-driven, and/or just uninformed in a certain area.

Salespeople should be striving to help their clients meet their goals. As an example, individuals or business owners can go online and trade stocks for themselves, but if they think someone else (e.g., financial planner, securities company) is more knowledgeable and brings more expertise to the table, then they will use him or her.

Today's buyers will respond positively to any attempts to assist them in their efforts to reach bottom-line objectives, be it revenue growth, profitability, or financial or strategic objectives. Thus, "expertise" will take on an even more important role in the customer's assessment of the seller's credibility. For some buyers, especially those with economic or financial responsibilities (e.g., CFO, treasurer, owner-manager), a representative's ability to "contribute" to the bottom line will dominate the perception of a seller's credibility. This is a very important consideration for salespeople, given their pivotal strategy of penetrating accounts at the economic buyer level. Salespeople are seeking to convince clients that they are (1) actively dedicated to the task of positively influencing their bottom-line objectives and (2) capable of providing assistance, counsel, and advice that will positively affect the ability to reach objectives.[7] This is easier said than done because salespeople frequently do not understand the long-term financial objectives of their client.[8]

Buyers today want recommendations and solutions, not just options. Salespeople must be prepared to help their clients meet their goals by adding value.

Buyers are continually asking themselves: Does the salesperson have the ability, knowledge, and resources to meet his or her prospective customers' expectations? Not only are salespeople selling their knowledge but the entire organization and the support that they bring to the buyer. Does the salesperson display a technical command of products and applications (i.e., is he or she accurate, complete, objective)? During one sales call, a buyer asked about a specific new product that the company was promoting in its advertising. The salesperson responded that the product was launched before he was trained on it. This not only cast doubts on the salesperson's ability but also on the company for failing to train the salesperson.

Expertise also deals with the salesperson's skill, knowledge, time, and resources to do what is promised and what the buyer wants. Small customers must think that they are being treated as well as larger customers and have access to the same resources.

Salespeople must exhibit knowledge generally exceeding that of their customer, not just in terms of the products and services they are selling but in terms of the full scope of the customer's financial and business operations (e.g., products, programs, competitors, customers, vendors). They must bring skills to the table, be it discovery, problem solving, program and systems development, financial management, or planning. These skills must complement those of the customer and offer insight into the best practices in the customer's industry. It is not enough to be an expert. This expertise must translate into observable results and **contributions** for the buyer.

Dependability

Dependability centers on the predictability of the salesperson's actions. Buyers have been heard to say, "I can always depend on her. She always does what she says she is going to do." Salespeople must remember what promises they make to a customer or prospect. Once a promise is made, the buyer expects that promise to be honored. The buyer should not have to call the salesperson to remind him or her of the promise. The salesperson should take notes during all sales calls for later review. It is harder to forget to do something if it is written down. A salesperson is trying to establish that his or her actions fit a pattern of prior dependable behavior. That is, the salesperson refuses to promise what he or she cannot deliver. The salesperson must also demonstrate an ability to handle confidential information. Buyers and sellers are depending on each other to guard secrets carefully and keep confidential information confidential! "An Ethical Dilemma" demonstrates the importance of trust and the issue of confidentiality.

Candor

Candor deals with the honesty of the spoken word. One sales manager was overheard telling his salesforce "whatever it takes to get the order." One of the salespeople replied, "Are you telling us to stretch the truth if it helps us get the order?" The manager replied, "Of course!" The trustworthy salesperson understands doing "anything to get an order" will ultimately damage the buyer–seller relationship.

Salespeople have more than words to win over the support of the buyer; they have other sales aids such as testimonials, third-party endorsements, trade publications, and consumer reports. The salesperson must be just as careful to guarantee that the proof is credible. It takes only one misleading (even slightly) event to lose all credibility.

Customer Orientation

Customer orientation means placing as much emphasis on the customer's interests as your own. An important facet of customer orientation is that salespeople work to satisfy the long-term needs of their customers rather than their own short-term goals.

A salesperson who has a customer orientation gives fair and balanced presentations. This includes covering both the pros and cons of the recommended product. The pharmaceutical industry has done a good job understanding this principle, as many firms require their salespeople to describe at least one side effect of their drug for each benefit given. This is done not only because of the legal consideration but also to demonstrate to the physician expertise and trustworthiness. Traditional salespeople often ignored negative aspects of a product, which can turn off many buyers. A customer orientation should also include clear statements of benefits and not overpower the buyer with information overload.

Salespeople with a customer orientation really turn into advisors; that is, they advise rather than "sell." It is critical not to push a product that the buyer does not need to meet a short-term goal. Kim Davenport of Shering-Plough (see "Professional Selling in the 21st Century: Being in Sync with Your Customers") states, "It is critically important to have a customer orientation. The ultimate goal of any relationship is to transform the personal relationship into a business relationship."[9]

Being in Sync with Your Customers

Kim Davenport, district manager with Shering-Plough Pharmaceutical Company, discusses his philosophy in building relationships. It is critically important that his field reps have the ability to initiate relationships, manage relationships, and transform relationships into long-term partnerships. His salespeople call on physicians and their staff with the ultimate goal of not only building long-term relationships but also increasing the sales in each of their accounts.

I tell my reps, if you are uncomfortable forming a new relationship with a physician, how will you ever be able to connect with receptionists, office managers, nurses, and nurse practitioners, and others in the practice? This takes a real knack of trying to get to know a lot of different personalities who perform different functions in the office. Anyone of these individuals can be of equal importance for us to get our foot in the door and gain new business.

Salespeople must truly care about the partnership, and they must be willing to "go to bat" for the client when the need arises. A warehouse fire left one company without any space to store inventory. The salesperson worked out same-day delivery until the warehouse was rebuilt. This left a lasting impression on the buyer. They knew that if they ever needed any help, their salesperson would come through for them.

Salespeople must be fully committed to representing the customer's interests. Although most salespeople are quick to "talk the talk" about their absolute allegiance to their customer's interests, when it comes to "walking the walk" for their customer on such issues as pricing, production flexibility, and design changes, many lack the commitment and/or skills necessary to support the interests of their clients.

To be an effective salesperson and gain access to a customer's business at a partnership level, the client must feel comfortable with the idea that the salesperson is motivated and capable of representing his or her interests. Exhibit 2.1 looks at some of the questions salespeople need to answer satisfactorily to gain the buyer's trust and confidence.

Compatibility/Likability

Customers generally like to deal with sales representatives whom they know, they like, and they can feel a bond with. Doug Lingo of Hoechst Marion Roussel Pharmaceutical states that his best friends are his physicians. He goes to Indiana University and Indiana Pacer basketball games with them, he has gone camping with the physicians and their families, and he even had a family vacation shared with one of

---

Questions that Salespeople Need to Satisfactorily Answer to Gain a Buyer's Trust   **EXHIBIT 2.1**

Expertise: Does the salesperson know what he or she needs to know? Does the salesperson and his or her company have the ability and resources to get the job done right?

Dependability: Can I rely on the salesperson? Does the salesperson keep promises?

Candor: Is the salesperson honest in his or her spoken word? Is the salesperson's presentation fair and balanced?

Customer Orientation: Does the salesperson truly care about the partnership? Will the salesperson go to bat for the customer (i.e., wrong order, late delivery)?

Compatibility: Will the buyer like doing business with the salesperson? Will the buyer like doing business with the salesperson's company?

his physicians. He goes on to state that "compatibility" is critical to his success as a salesperson.[10]

Some salespeople are too quick to minimize the importance of rapport building in this era of the economic buyer. It also may be true that today's buyers are not as prone to spend time discussing personal issues in sales calls as they might have been 10 or 15 years ago. Salespeople today have to be more creative and resourceful when attempting to build rapport. It is not unusual for a pharmaceutical salesperson to take a lunch for the entire staff into a physician's office. These lunches can be for as many as 20 to 40 persons. The salesperson now has time to discuss his or her products over lunch to a captive audience.

Salespeople have to be aware that their buyers are under considerable time pressure and that some will find it difficult to dedicate time to issues outside of the business. However, remember that buyers are human and do value compatibility, some more, some less.

Compatibility and **likability** are important to establishing a relationship with key gatekeepers (e.g., receptionists and secretaries). First impressions are important, and a salesperson's ability to find commonalities with these individuals can go a long way in building much-needed allies within the buying organization. Likeability is admittedly an emotional factor that is difficult to pin down, yet a powerful force in some buyer–seller relationships.

If a salesperson has done a good job of demonstrating the other trust-building characteristics, then compatibility can be used to enhance trust building. Buyers do not necessarily trust everyone they like, but on the other hand, it is difficult to trust someone they do not like.

KNOWLEDGE BASES HELP BUILD TRUST AND RELATIONSHIPS

The more the salesperson knows, the easier it is to build trust and gain the confidence of the buyer. Buyers have certain expectations of the salesperson and the knowledge that he or she brings to the table. As outlined in Figure 2.2, salespeople may draw

FIGURE 2.2	Knowledge Bases

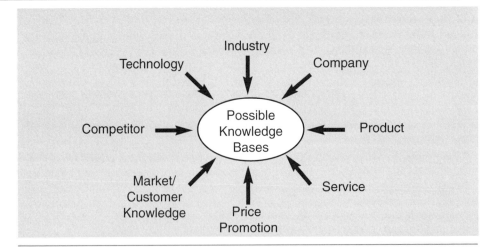

The more the salesperson knows, the easier it is to build trust and gain the confidence of the buyer. Buyers have certain expectations of the salesperson and the knowledge that he or she brings to the table. Most knowledge is gained from the sales training programs and on-the-job training.

Topics Generally Covered during Initial Sales Training Programs   EXHIBIT 2.2

- Industry history
- Company history and policies
- Product
  - promotion
  - price
- Market
  - line of business (*know your customer*)
  - manufacturing
  - wholesaling
  - financial
  - government
  - medical, etc.
- Competitive knowledge
- Selling techniques
- Initiating customer relationship
  - prospecting
  - precall
  - approaching the customer
- Developing customer relationships
  - sales presentation delivery
  - handling sales resistance
- Enhancing customer relationships
  - follow-up
  - customer service

from several knowledge bases. Most knowledge is gained from the sales training program and on-the-job training.

Sales training will generally concentrate on knowledge of the industry and company history, company policies, products, promotion, prices, market knowledge of customers, **competitor knowledge**, and basic selling techniques. Exhibit 2.2 summarizes topics generally covered during initial sales training programs.

Industry and Company Knowledge

Salespeople may be asked what they know about their company and industry. Every industry and company has a history. The personal computer industry has a short history of 20 years, fax technology even shorter. Other industries have been around for centuries. Some industries change so quickly, such as the pharmaceutical industry through multiple mergers, that it is critical for the salesperson to know his or her industry to keep physicians informed on new companies, drugs, and procedures. Many buyers are too busy to stay informed and count on their salespeople to help them make sound decisions.

Salespeople should be familiar with their own company's operation and policies. Buyers may ask the salesperson questions such as: How long has your company been in the market? How many people does the company employ? Does the company have a local, regional, national, or international customer base? Who started the company? Who is the president? CEO? What is their market share? What is their market share on this particular product? Salespeople who could not answer such questions would not inspire the trust of the buyer.

Each company initiates policies to ensure consistent decisions are made throughout the organization. An organization implements policies to control factors such as price, guarantees, warranties, and how much money can be spent per week taking clients out to lunch. Knowing the company's policies prevents misunderstanding.

For example, if a representative says yes to a customer's request to return goods 60 days after receipt when company policy is 30 days, the shipping department might refuse to accept the returned merchandise. The salesperson looks incompetent to both sales management and the customer. If the customer is not allowed to return the goods to the factory, the angry customer probably will never buy from the salesperson again.

Salespeople must understand their company policies. This includes being familiar with the company's formal structure and key personnel. It is important to work as a team with all company personnel. This helps build team spirit and a willingness to cooperate when a salesperson needs help in meeting a customer's need. It is difficult to provide outstanding service when the sales department is not on good terms with shipping and delivery, for instance.

Product Knowledge

Product knowledge includes detailed information on the manufacture of a product and knowing whether the company has up-to-date production methods. What materials are used when making the products? What quality control procedures are involved? Who are the design engineers?

Salespeople representing their company are expected to be experts on the products they sell. The fastest way to win the respect of a buyer is to be perceived as being an expert. If the buyer truly feels the salesperson knows what he or she is talking about, then the buyer will be more willing to discuss the salesperson's solution to the buyer's problems or opportunities.

The salesperson must know what his or her product can and cannot do. Just knowing product features is insufficient.

Service

The effective salesperson must be ready to address **service issues** such as:

- Does the company service its products or does the company send them to a third party?
- Does the company service its products locally or send them off to another state for service?
- Does the price include service or will there be a service charge when service is needed?
- What does the service agreement include? Shipping? Labor? Or none of these?
- How long does the service generally take? Same day? Within a week? Will a loaner be provided until the product is fixed?
- Are there any conditions that make service not available? After five years? Damage from flood? fire?

Buyers need to be comfortable with answers to these questions, and a good salesperson will make sure they are answered appropriately.

Darrell Beaty from Ontario Systems in Muncie, Indiana, spends quite a bit of time discussing service with each of his prospects.[11] His company sells collection software (i.e., receivables) that requires support from his field engineers. Ontario Systems also has an 800 support group that takes calls 24 hours a day, seven days a week. Why is this important to Beaty? One of his major competitors also has 800 support, but only 8–5, Monday through Friday. Beaty knows that he has service superiority. Salespeople who can offer the better service have an advantage for generating new business and taking away business from the competition. The salesperson's service mission is to provide added value for the customer. It is important for the salesperson to understand what service dimensions are a concern to the buyer.

For instance, delivery, installation, training, field maintenance, and investing are all issues that a salesperson may be prepared to talk about. Buyers, however, may only be concerned with inventory because their present supplier runs out of stock frequently.

| Service Superiority | EXHIBIT 2.3 |

Dimension	Potential Superiority
1. Delivery	Can our company demonstrate speed? Deliver more often?
2. Inventory	Can we meet the demands of our customers at all times?
3. Training	Do we offer training? At our site? At our customer's?
4. Field maintenance	Do we go to the field to fix our products? Do our customers have to bring their equipment to us to fix?
5. Credit and financial consideration	Do we grant credit? Do we help finance?
6. Installation	Do we send a team to your site for start-up?
7. Guarantees and warranties	What are our guarantees? How long? What do we cover?
8. Others	Do we offer anything unique that our competition does not?

Exhibit 2.3 reviews service dimensions in which a salesperson could demonstrate service superiority. Additions may be made depending on specific customer demands.

Promotion and Price

Promotion and **price knowledge** are other knowledge tools that the salesperson must understand. The ability to use this knowledge often makes the difference between a well-informed buyer who is ready to make a decision and another buyer who is reluctant to move the sales process forward. Hershey Foods Corporation supports its retailers with heavy promotions during Halloween, Christmas, and Easter. The promotional programs must be explained properly so the buyer can place the correct order size during the promotion. How many dollars are to be spent? Is it a national program? Is this a co-op program? What will it cost the buyer? If these questions are answered properly, the buyer will be more at ease and ready to make a purchase.

Price can be another area that makes a buyer hesitant if not properly explained. Knowledge of pricing policies is important because the salesperson often is responsible for quoting price and offering discounts. As a representative of the selling firm, these quotes legally bind a company to their completion.

Salespeople need complete understanding of their companies' pricing policies. Does the company sell its products for a set price or can the salesperson negotiate? Can the salesperson give additional discounts to get a potential client whom the company has been after for years? Does the company allow trade-ins?

Market and Customer Knowledge

Market and **customer knowledge** is critical to the success of today's salesperson. Some companies today, because of their size, send their salesforce out to call on all customer types. Larger companies typically break their customers into distinct markets. Computer manufacturers may break out their customer types by markets (i.e., salespeople sell to a particular line of business). For instance, the salesperson may only sell to manufacturers, wholesalers, financial institutions, government, education, or medical companies. This allows the salesperson to become an expert in a line of business. For a salesperson to be effective, the salesperson must learn what the client needs, what benefits the client is seeking, and how the salesperson's products satisfy the buyers' specific needs. Buyers are not interested in factual knowledge unless it relates to fulfilling their specific needs. Having the salesforce learn one line of business well allows the salesperson to concentrate on the needs of a specific market. The salesperson can become an expert in one line of business

Do What You Say You Are Going to Do!

Jon Young, national account manager for Ontario Systems Corporation, discusses his philosophy on why buyers buy from whom they do.

I've been in the sales business for over 25 years now, and I know what my buyers want. They want me to do what I say I am going to do! I have learned to measure my words carefully. It is easy to agree with the prospect or buyer when they ask for something, just to get an order signed. The trouble comes in when it is time to make it happen, and we can't. Then my company and I look bad. It can cost us the order down the road or, at the very least, a lot of ill will that takes a long time to make right.

The cornerstone of my selling philosophy is trust and expertise. I have to know what I am talking about— but, equally important, my customers and prospects have to trust what I am saying. Sometimes it is better to give up business to a competitor than to over-promise and under-deliver. Clients and prospects talk to their friends when you do a good job for them. They also tell their friends when you screw up and don't keep your promises. As I said before, I measure my words carefully. I want to be able to keep every promise I make during the time frame the customer expects the promise to come true. I live by this golden rule of keeping promises, and it does pay huge dividends in the long run.

more quickly than if he or she had to know how the entire marketplace used the salesperson's products.

Information about customers is gathered over time and from very different sources. A salesperson can use trade associations, credit agencies, trade magazines, trade directories, newspapers, and the World Wide Web as valuable resources. The AT&T Toll-free Internet Directory has directories on people, business, and Web sites. Using the Web to do an initial search on a company can tell a salesperson about what products a company makes, what markets they serve, and so on. A salesperson must use his or her time wisely when gathering information. Jon Young, national account manager for Ontario Systems Corporation, (see "Professional Selling in the 21st Century: Do What You Say You Are Going to Do!") states, "I have to know what I am talking about—but, equally important, my customers and prospects have to trust what I am saying."

Competitor Knowledge

Salespeople will probably be asked how their product stands up against the competition. The buyer may ask, Who are your competitors in our marketplace? How big are you compared with your competitors? How do your company's prices compare with others in your industry? How does your product quality compare with the industry norm? These are important questions that every salesperson must be prepared to answer. Salespeople must have knowledge of their competitor's strengths and weaknesses to better understand their own products' position when comparing. A good salesperson must adjust his or her selling strategy depending on whom he or she is selling against.

Salespeople must be able to deliver complete comparative product information in a sales presentation. Comparisons of competitors' products for a customer's decision are critical especially when your features and benefits are superior to those of the competition.

It is important that salespeople distinguish their products from the competition. The ultimate question a buyer asks is, Why should I use your product over the one I am presently using? A salesperson must have competitive knowledge to answer this question. What are the competitor's relative strengths and weaknesses? What weaknesses make this competitor vulnerable? Once the salesperson can determine the competitor's limitations, the salesperson can demonstrate the superiority of his or her product. A salesperson must answer the questions, How are you different from the competition? How are you better than the competition? A salesperson must be able to determine his or her differential competitive advantage.

	Using Technology to Build Bridges to Customers **EXHIBIT 2.4**
Technology	**Bridge**
World Wide Web	Price updates can be placed on the Web for customers to access. New product information can be made available to customers and prospects.
E-mail	Buyer and salesperson can virtually communicate 24 hours a day. Mass communications can be sent out to all customers and prospects.
Pagers	Buyers with an emergency have immediate access to their salesperson by having them paged.
Facsimile	Nonelectronic documents can be transmitted 24 hours a day. Fax on demand.
Cell Phones	Buyer and seller have immediate access to each other.
Voice-mail	Salesperson and buyer can leave messages for each other and save time and effort.

Technology Knowledge

Salespeople must use technology to their advantage. Twenty years ago, salespeople had to know where a reliable pay phone was located in each of the cities they visited. Many opportunities were missed because salespeople could not reach prospects while they were in the field. Today's salesperson has the luxury of cell phones, facsimile technology, the World Wide Web, pagers, voice-mail, and e-mail. Salespeople should communicate in the manner preferred by their prospects and clients. Some clients use e-mail extensively and want to use e-mail over phone conversations. Some buyers like to fax orders in and would rather not meet the salesperson face to face. A good salesperson must recognize these preferences and act accordingly. Each of these can either be a bridge to the customer or an obstacle. Salespeople should be building bridges to all their prospects and customers by using technology appropriately (see Exhibit 2.4). If a pager number is on a salesperson's business card, then the salesperson must return pages within a reasonable period of time. Likewise, if a facsimile number is given to prospects, then the fax machine must be turned on at all times and working properly.

Probably the most oversold form of technology is voice-mail. Many companies have gone to this method of communication hoping to free secretaries and making it easier to leave messages for the salesperson. The difficulty arises when a customer wants to talk to a salesperson and can get only a recording. Sometimes, the voice-mail is full and it is impossible to leave a message. It is also possible to use voice-mail to screen calls, and many buyers and salespeople complain that it is virtually impossible to make contact when their counterpart refuses to return their call.

Technology can be a friend or a foe of a salesperson. If used properly, technology can build bridges to prospects and clients and develop relationships. If technology is not used properly, then a salesperson can find him- or herself alienating the customers and turn a potential resource into a reason for a prospect not to do business with the salesperson.

SALES ETHICS

Ethics refers to right and wrong conduct of individuals and institutions of which they are a part. Personal ethics and formal codes of conduct provide a basis for deciding what is right or wrong in a given situation. Ethical standards for a profession are based on society's standards, and most industries have developed a code of behaviors that are compatible with society's standards. Professions in this country owe much of their public regard to standards of conduct established by professional organizations. Reflecting this, the American Marketing Association has adopted a code of ethics, which appears in Exhibit 2.5.[12]

EXHIBIT 2.5 The American Marketing Association's Code of Ethics

Code of Ethics
Members of the American Marketing Association (AMA) are committed to ethical professional conduct. They have joined together in subscribing to this Code of Ethics embracing the following topics.

Responsibilities of the Marketer
Marketers must accept responsibility for the consequences of their activities and make every effort to ensure that their decisions, recommendations, and actions function to identify, serve, and satisfy all relevant publics: customers, organizations, and society.

Marketers' professional conduct must be guided by:

1. The basic rule of professional ethics: not knowingly to do harm.
2. The adherence to all applicable laws and regulations.
3. The accurate representation of their education, training, and experience.
4. The active support, practice, and promotion of this Code of Ethics.

Honesty and Fairness
Marketers shall uphold and advance the integrity, honor, and dignity of the marketing profession by:

1. Being honest in serving consumers, clients, employees, suppliers, distributors, and the public.
2. Not knowingly participating in a conflict of interest without prior notice to all parties involved.
3. Establishing equitable fee schedules, including the payment or receipt of usual, customary, and/or legal compensation for marketing exchanges.

Rights and Duties of Parties in the Marketing Exchange Process
Participants in the marketing exchange process should be able to expect that:

1. Products and services offered are safe and fit for their intended uses.
2. Communications about offered products and services are not deceptive.
3. All parties intend to discharge their obligations, financial and otherwise, in good faith.
4. Appropriate internal methods exist for equitable adjustment and/or redress of grievances concerning purchases.

It is understood that the above would include, *but is not limited to*, the following responsibilities of the marketer.

In the area of product development and management:
- Disclosure of all substantial risks associated with product or service usage.
- Identification of any product component substitution that might materially change the product or impact on the buyer's purchase decision.
- Identification of extra cost-added features.

In the area of promotions:
- Avoidance of false and misleading advertising.
- Rejection of high-pressure manipulations or misleading sales tactics.
- Avoidance of sales promotions that use deception or manipulation.

In the area of distribution:
- Not manipulating the availability of a product for purpose of exploitation.
- Not using coercion in the marketing channel.
- Not exerting undue influence over the reseller's choice to handle a product.

In the area of pricing:
- Not engaging in price fixing.
- Not practicing predatory pricing.
- Disclosing the full price associated with any purchase.

In the area of marketing research:
- Prohibiting selling or fund-raising under the guise of conducting research.
- Maintaining research integrity by avoiding misrepresentation and omission of pertinent research data.
- Treating outside clients and suppliers fairly.

Organizational Relationships
Marketers should be aware of how their behavior may influence or impact on the behavior of others in organizational relationships. They should not demand, encourage, or apply coercion to obtain unethical behavior in their relationships with others, such as employees, suppliers, or customers.

1. Apply confidentiality and anonymity in professional relationships with regard to privileged information.
2. Meet their obligations and responsibilities in contracts and mutual agreements in a timely manner.
3. Avoid taking the work of others, in whole, or in part, and representing this work as their own or directly benefiting from it without compensation or consent of the originator or owner.
4. Avoid manipulation to take advantage of situations to maximize personal welfare in a way that unfairly deprives or damages the organization of others.

Any AMA member found to be in violation of any provision of this Code of Ethics may have his or her Association membership suspended or revoked.

What Types of Sales Behaviors Are Unethical?	**EXHIBIT 2.6**

According to a survey of 327 customers, salespeople are acting unethically if they:

1. Show concern for own interest, not clients'
2. Pass the blame for something they did wrong
3. Take advantage of the poor or uneducated
4. Accept favors from customers so the seller feels obliged to bend policies
5. Sell products/services that people don't need
6. Give answers when they don't really know answers
7. Pose as market researcher when doing phone sales
8. Sell dangerous or hazardous products
9. Withhold information
10. Exaggerate benefits of product
11. Lie about availability to make sale
12. Lie to competitors
13. Falsify product testimonials

Salespeople are constantly involved with ethical issues. A sales manager encourages his or her salesforce to pad their expense account in lieu of a raise. A salesperson sells a product or service to a customer that the buyer does not need. A salesperson exaggerates the benefits of a product to get a sale. The list can go on and on.

Recall that sales professionalism requires a truthful, customer-oriented approach. Customers are increasingly intolerant of nonprofessional, unethical practices. Sales ethics is closely related to trust. Deceptive practices, illegal activities, and non-customer-oriented behavior have to be attempted only once for a buyer to lose trust in his or her salesperson. Research has identified some of the sales practices deemed unethical as shown in Exhibit 2.6.[13]

Image of Salespeople

Sales and Marketing Executives International (SMEI) has been concerned with the image of salespeople and has developed a code of ethics as a set of principles that outline the minimum requirements for professional conduct. SMEI has developed a 20- to 30-hour certification process that declares that a salesperson shall support and preserve the highest standards of professional conduct in all areas of sales and in all relationships in the sales process. Exhibit 2.7[14] is the SMEI Code of Ethics that pledges a salesperson will adhere to these standards.

A sales professional deserves and receives a high level of respect on the job. Buyers who do not interact with professional salespeople on a regular basis may believe in the negative stereotype of the salesperson as a pushy, shifty, not-to-be-trusted sort. Where does this stereotype come from? Some salespeople are not professional in their approach, and this contributes to the negative stereotype. In the past, television programs, movies, and even Broadway productions have fostered the negative image of salespeople. During the 1960s and 1970s, the popular press also contributed to the negative image of salespeople. A study of how salespeople are portrayed in the popular press found that salespeople are often associated with deceptive, illegal, and non-customer-oriented behavior.[15] Three of the more important areas of unethical behavior, deceptive practices, illegal activities, and non-customer-oriented behavior, are discussed.

Deceptive Practices

Buyers have been known to be turned off by all salespeople because a few are unscrupulous and are even scam artists. This is unfortunate because all salespeople (good and bad) pay the price for this behavior. Unfortunately, some salespeople do use quota pressure as an excuse to be deceptive. The salesperson has the choice to either

EXHIBIT 2.7   SMEI Certified Professional Salesperson® Code of Ethics

The SMEI Certified Professional Salesperson (SCPS) Code of Ethics is a set of principles that outline minimum requirements for professional conduct. Those who attain SCPS status should consider these principles as more than just rules to follow. They are guiding standards above which the salesperson should rise.

An SCPS shall support and preserve the highest standards of professional conduct in all areas of sales and in all relationships in the sales process. Toward this end an SCPS pledges and commits to these standards in all activities under this code.

As an SCPS I pledge to the following individuals and parties:

I. With respect to **The Customer**, I will:

Maintain honesty and integrity in my relationship with all customers and prospective customers.

Accurately represent my product or service in order to place the customer or prospective customer in a position to make a decision consistent with the principle of mutuality of benefit and profit to the buyer and seller.

Continually keep abreast and increase the knowledge of my product(s), service(s), and industry in which I work. This is necessary to better serve those who place their trust in me.

II. With respect to **The Company** and other parties whom I represent, I will:

Use their resources that are at my disposal and will be utilized only for legitimate business purposes.

Respect and protect proprietary and confidential information entrusted to me by my company.

Not engage in any activities that will either jeopardize or conflict with the interests of my company. Activities that may be or which may appear to be illegal or unethical will be strictly avoided. To this effect I will not participate in activities that are illegal or unethical.

III. With respect to **The Competition**, regarding those organizations and individuals that I compete with in the marketplace, I will:

Only obtain competitive information through legal and ethical methods.

Only portray my competitors, and their products and services in a manner which is honest, truthful, and based on accurate information that can or has been substantiated.

IV. With respect to **The Community** and society which provide me with my livelihood, I will:

Engage in business and selling practices which contribute to a positive relationship with the communities in which I and my company have presence.

Support public policy objectives consistent with maintaining and protecting the environment and community.

Participate in community activities and associations which provide for the betterment of the community and society.

I AM COMMITTED to the letter and spirit of this code. The reputation of salespeople depends upon me as well as others who engage in the profession of selling. My adherence to these standards will strengthen the reputation and integrity for which we strive as professional salespeople.

I understand that failure to consistently act according to the above standards and principles could result in the forfeiture of the privilege of using the SCPS designation.

Candidate's Signature

_____

Signature   Date

ignore the trust-building approach and persuade the customer to buy or go to the next sales meeting and catch the wrath of his or her sales manager for being under quota. Salespeople giving answers when they do not know, exaggerating product benefits, and withholding information may appear to only shade the truth, but when it causes harm to the buyer, the salesperson has jeopardized future dealings with the buyer.

Illegal Activities

Misusing company assets has been a long-standing problem for many sales organizations. Using the company car for personal use, charging expenses that did not occur, and selling samples for income are examples of misusing company assets. Some of these violations of company property also constitute violations of the Internal Revenue Service (IRS) law and are offenses that could lead to jail or heavy fines.

Bribes are another area that causes some salespeople to run afoul of the law. A competitor may be offering bribes; this, in turn, puts pressure on the salesperson's company to respond with bribes of its own. It is difficult for a salesperson to see potential sales going to the competition. Salespeople offering bribes on their own can be punished. Companies that engage in bribery may find themselves being prosecuted and fined. Rockwell International and Lockheed made illegal payments to foreign customers and had to suffer the humiliation of the bad publicity and the fines.

Another area of legal concern that involves the salesforce is product liability. Salespeople can create product liabilities for a company in three ways: **express warranty**, **misrepresentation**, and **negligence**. A salesperson can create a product warranty or guarantee that obligates the selling organization even if they do not intend to give the warranty. Express warranties are created by any affirmation of fact or promise, any description, or any sample or model that a salesperson uses, which is made part of the basis of the bargain.

Basis of the bargain is taken to mean that the buyer relied on the seller's statements in making the purchase decision. If a salesperson tells a prospect that a machine will turn out 50 units per hour, a legal obligation has been created for the firm to supply a machine that will accomplish this. Misrepresentation by a salesperson can also lead to product liability even if the salesperson makes a false claim thinking it is true. The burden of accuracy is on the seller. Salespeople are required by law to exercise "reasonable care" in formulating claims. If a salesperson asserts that a given drug is safe without exercising reasonable care to see that this claim is accurate, the salesperson has been negligent. Negligence is a basis for product liability on the part of the seller.

Although these tactics may increase sales in the short run, salespeople ruin their trust relationship with their customer and company. Given the legal restrictions that relate to selling practices, a salesperson, as well as the selling organization, should exercise care in developing sales presentations.

Non-Customer-Oriented Behavior

Most of today's sales organizations emphasize trust-building behaviors and are customer-oriented. Unfortunately, there are a few salespeople and companies today that concentrate on short-term goals and allow outmoded sales tactics to be practiced. Most buyers will not buy from salespeople who are pushy and practice the hard sell. Too much is at stake to fall for the fast-talking, high-pressure salesperson. Buyers have been through their own training, and they understand the importance of developing a long-term relationship with their suppliers. Exhibit 2.8 summarizes these practices.

How Are Companies Dealing with Sales Ethics?

Many companies spend time covering ethics in their training programs. These programs should cover topics such as the appropriateness of gift giving, the use of

EXHIBIT 2.8 **Areas of Unethical Behavior**

Deceptive Practices	Illegal Activities
Deceive	Defraud
Hustle	Con
Scam	Misuse company assets
Exaggerate	
Withhold bluff	

Non-Customer-Oriented Behavior

Pushy

Hard sell

Fast talking

High pressure

expense accounts, and dealing with a prospect's unethical demands. Each company will have its own policies on gift giving. John Huff of Shering-Plough states, "Just a few years ago, I could spend my expense account on Indiana Pacers tickets or a golf outing with doctors. That is not the case today. There is a lot of gray area concerning gift giving by salespeople to their business and prospects. The pharmaceutical industry has policed itself so now gift giving has all but been eliminated. I must know the rules of my company and industry."[16] Receiving Christmas gifts is another area that must be explained during training. Some buyers are not allowed to accept gifts from salespeople.

Another important training area is the use of expense accounts. Salespeople should be trained in how to fill out the expense account form and what is acceptable for submission. Some companies allow personal mileage to be included; others do not. If guidelines are established, then there is less of a chance for a misunderstanding by the salesperson.

Sometimes unethical behavior is not initiated by the salesperson but by the buyer. Salespeople must be trained in dealing with prospects who make unethical demands. Buyers can be under pressure from their company to stay within budget or to move up the timetable on an order. A buyer may ask a salesperson to move him or her up on the order list in exchange for more business down the road. One pharmacist set up a deal with a salesperson to buy samples illegally. The trust-based salesperson has to shut down any short-term gain for long-term success. A salesperson's career is over if the word circulates that he or she cannot be trusted.

A salesperson must also be concerned with our legal system and that of other countries. It cannot be an excuse for today's well-trained salesperson to say he or she did not know that a law was being broken. When in doubt the salesperson must check out all state and local laws. In addition, there are industry-specific rules and regulations to be considered. Exhibit 2.9 covers a number of legal reminders.

A salesperson has his or her reputation to tarnish only once. In this day and age of mass communication (phone, e-mail, Web sites), it is easy for a buyer to get the word out that a salesperson is acting unethically and end that salesperson's career.

Legal Reminders EXHIBIT 2.9

For salespeople:

1. Use factual data rather than general statements of praise during the sales presentation. Avoid misrepresentation.
2. Thoroughly educate customers before the sale on the product's specifications, capabilities, and limitations.
3. Do not overstep authority, as the salesperson's actions can be binding to the selling firm.
4. Avoid discussing these topics with competitors: prices, profit margins, discounts, terms of sale, bids or intent to bid, sales territories or markets to be served, rejection or termination of customers.
5. Do not use one product as bait for selling another product.
6. Do not try to force the customer to buy only from your organization.
7. Offer the same price and support to buyers who purchase under the same set of circumstances.
8. Do not tamper with a competitor's product.
9. Do not disparage a competitor's product without specific evidence of your contentions.
10. Avoid promises that will be difficult or impossible to honor.

For the sales organization:

1. Review sales presentations and claims for possible legal problems.
2. Make the salesforce aware of potential conflicts with the law.
3. Carefully screen any independent sales agents used by the organization.
4. With technical products and services make sure the sales presentation fully explains the capabilities and dangers of products and service.

SUMMARY

1. **Discuss the distinguishing characteristics of trust-based selling**. Trust means different things to different buyers. It can be defined as confidentiality, openness, dependability, candor, honesty, confidence, security, reliability, fairness, and predictability. It is the salesperson's job to determine what trust means to each of his or her buyers. Salespeople must question their buyers as to what trust attributes are their greatest concerns.

2. **Explain the importance of trust**. In today's increasingly competitive marketplace, buyers typically find themselves inundated with choices regarding both products and suppliers. Buyers are demanding unique solutions to their problems, which are customized on the basis of their specific needs. This shift toward relationship selling has altered both the roles played by salespeople and the activities and skills they exercise in carrying out these roles—the selling process itself. Today's more contemporary selling process is embedded within the relationship marketing paradigm. As such, it emphasizes the initiation and nurturing of long-term buyer–seller relationships based on mutual trust and value-added benefits. The level of problem-solving activity common to relationship selling requires deliberate and purposeful collaboration between both parties. These joint efforts are directed at creating unique solutions based on an enhanced knowledge and understanding of the customer's needs and the supplier's capabilities so that both parties derive mutual benefits.

3. **Discuss how to earn trust**. Buyers are constantly asking themselves whether the salesperson truly cares about them. Salespeople can answer this question for the buyer by demonstrating trust-building activities. Trust can be earned by demonstrating expertise, dependability, candor, customer orientation, competence, and compatibility.

4. **Explain how knowledge bases help build trust and relationships**. Salespeople do not have much time to make a first impression. If a salesperson can demonstrate expertise in the buyer's industry, company, marketplace, competitive knowledge, and so on, then the buyer will more likely be willing to listen to the salesperson if he or she brings valued experience to the buyer.

5. **Understand the importance of sales ethics**. Salespeople are constantly involved with ethical issues. A sales manager encourages his or her salesforce to pad their expense account in lieu of a raise. A salesperson sells a product or service to a customer that the buyer does not need. A salesperson exaggerates the benefits of a product to get a sale. The list can go on and on. How a salesperson handles these situations will go a long way in determining the salesperson's credibility. One wrong decision can end a salesperson's career.

6. **Explain three important areas of unethical behavior**. Three of the more popular areas of unethical behavior are deceptive practices, illegal activities, and non-customer-oriented behavior.
   - Deceptive practices: Salespeople giving answers they do not know, exaggerating product benefits, and withholding information may appear to only shade the truth, but when it causes harm to the buyer, the salesperson has jeopardized future dealings with the buyer.
   - Illegal activities: Misusing company assets has been a long-standing problem for many sales organizations. Using the company car for personal use, charging expenses that did not occur, and selling samples for income are examples of misusing company assets. Some of these violations discovered by company probing also constitute violations of the Internal Revenue Service (IRS) law and are offenses that could lead to jail or heavy fines.
   - Non-customer-oriented behavior: Most buyers will not buy from salespeople who are pushy and practice the hard sell. Too much is at stake to fall for the fast-talking, high-pressure salesperson.

UNDERSTANDING PROFESSIONAL SELLING TERMS

trust	industry knowledge
openness	company knowledge
dependability	product knowledge
candor	service issues
honesty	service knowledge
confidentiality	promotion knowledge
security	price knowledge
reliability	market knowledge
fairness	customer knowledge
predictability	technology knowledge
expertise	ethics
contribution	express warranty
customer orientation	misrepresentation
compatibility/likability	negligence
competitor knowledge	basis of the bargain

DEVELOPING PROFESSIONAL SELLING KNOWLEDGE

1. What is the essence of trust for a salesperson?
2. If trust means different things to different buyers, how is a salesperson to determine what trust means for each buyer?

3. Why is trust important to a salesperson?

4. How might a salesperson go about earning trust?

5. What does it mean for a salesperson to have a customer orientation?

6. How would you rank the five trust-builders in order of importance?

7. Explain why expertise is such an important relationship builder.

8. How do knowledge bases help build trust and relationships?

9. Do you think certain knowledge bases are more important than others? Why?

10. What are the three areas of unethical behavior? Discuss each.

BUILDING PROFESSIONAL SELLING SKILLS

1. Relationship selling is directed toward achieving mutually satisfying results between buyer and seller that sustain and enhance future interactions. In the past several years, there has been a growing recognition that adversarial, "me-against-you" buyer–seller relationships are often nonproductive for both parties. The director of Xerox's training university in Leesburg, Virginia, says the biggest change in its sales training in the past decade is that "we spend a lot more time on what the customer thinks is important."

   Competition has intensified, technology has advanced, and pressure to improve productivity has soared. Given these changes in the marketplace, many firms are cutting down on the number of approved vendors. People are busier than ever, and there is no time for the misinformation and posturing often associated with the old style of selling. In a nutshell, it is increasingly productive to work closely with customers.

   Relationship selling requires a different set of skills and attitudes than is true for transaction-oriented selling. Questioning and listening become more important than talking. High-pressure sales approaches and gimmicky closing methods are taboo in relationship selling. Personality matters but not as much as appealing to the buyer's rational side in an interesting, well-illustrated, concise manner.

   To initiate, develop, and enhance customer relationships, salespeople must demonstrate their trustworthiness. As detailed in the introduction to this module, research has identified at least five characteristics of trust-building salespeople:

   1. **Expertise**—The ability, knowledge, and resources to meet customer expectations.
   2. **Dependability**—The predictability of your actions.
   3. **Candor**—Honesty of the spoken word.
   4. **Customer orientation**—Placing as much emphasis on the customer's interest as your own.
   5. **Compatibility**—Rooted in each party's perception of "having something in common" with the other. Admittedly, an emotional factor, difficult to pin down, yet a powerful force in some buyer–seller relationships.

   What are your ideas about how you can improve your trust-building behavior as you interact with customers? Use the following worksheet as a guide to how you might use each of the trust builders.

   Ideas for Action (Trust-Building Worksheet)

   1. Expertise

   _____

   _____

   _____

   _____

   _____

   _____

2. Dependability

_____
_____
_____
_____
_____
_____

3. Candor

_____
_____
_____
_____
_____

4. Customer Orientation

_____
_____
_____
_____
_____
_____

5. Compatibility

_____
_____
_____
_____
_____
_____

6. Others

_____
_____
_____
_____
_____

2. Sales professionalism requires a truthful, customer-oriented approach. Customers are increasingly intolerant of nonprofessional, unethical sales practices. Assess the following actions a salesperson might take with regard to their legality, ethicality, and professionalism.

Please circle your response for each category.

1. Shows concern for his or her own interests, not that of the client.

    legal/illegal   ethical/unethical   professional/unprofessional

2. Passes the blame for something he or she did wrong.

    legal/illegal   ethical/unethical   professional/unprofessional

3. Takes advantage of the poor and uneducated.

    legal/illegal   ethical/unethical   professional/unprofessional

4. Accepts favors from customers so that the seller feels obliged to bend policies.

   legal/illegal   ethical/unethical   professional/unprofessional

5. Sells products or services that people do not need.

   legal/illegal   ethical/unethical   professional/unprofessional

6. Gives answers when he or she does not really know answers.

   legal/illegal   ethical/unethical   professional/unprofessional

7. Poses as market researcher when doing phone sales.

   legal/illegal   ethical/unethical   professional/unprofessional

8. Sells dangerous or hazardous products.

   legal/illegal   ethical/unethical   professional/unprofessional

9. Withholds information.

   legal/illegal   ethical/unethical   professional/unprofessional

10. Exaggerates benefits of product.

    legal/illegal   ethical/unethical   professional/unprofessional

11. Lies about availability of product to make the sale.

    legal/illegal   ethical/unethical   professional/unprofessional

12. Lies to competitors.

    legal/illegal   ethical/unethical   professional/unprofessional

13. Falsifies product testimonials.

    legal/illegal   ethical/unethical   professional/unprofessional

3. **Situation:**   Read the Ethical Dilemma on page 35.

   Characters: Jasmine Alexander, account manager; Tom Smith, purchasing manager, Terry Wolf, copy center director.

   Scene 1:   *Location*—Party attended by Alexander and copy center manager, Wolf.

   Action—Copy center manager asks Alexander to stop by and look over the copy center.

ROLE PLAY

Role play this conversation and how Alexander might have handled things differently.

   Scene 2:   *Location*—Telephone call from the purchasing manager Smith to Alexander.

   Action: Purchasing manager makes telephone call to Alexander.

Role play the phone conversation where the purchasing manager asks Alexander not to call on his company anymore.

Upon completion of the role play, address the following question:

3a. Alexander suspected her literature was not getting from Smith to Wolf. Why not go for broke and take the visit with Wolf? Something good might have happened.

4. **Situation:**   Read the Ethical Dilemma on page 38.

   Characters: Jesse Powell, sales representative; Tom Stafford, restaurant owner; Desk Clerk

   Scene 1:   *Location*—Powell is sitting at his desk.

   Action—Powell takes a call from Stafford.

ROLE PLAY

Role play the conversation between Stafford and Powell where Stafford asks Powell not to call on him anymore.

   Scene 2:   *Location*—Two to three weeks later Powell sees Stafford at a restaurant waiting in line.

   Action—Powell initiates a conversation with Stafford.

Role play how Powell might handle Stafford's call from a few weeks ago.

Upon completion of the role play, address the following question:

4a. What are the dangers of discussing confidential information in public?

5. Conveying trust is an important part of a salesperson's job. It is critical to treat all customers fairly. Ethics plays a role in every salesperson's daily activities. The problem is what appears to be ethical to one person is not to another. Salespoeple must deal with ethical dilemmas every day. Take a look at the following Web sites and research the topic of sales ethics. Look at company Web sites and see if they put any special emphasis on ethics or sales ethics.

   Web Site Information
   http://www.business-ethics.com
   http://www.ibe.org.uk
   http://ecampus.bentley.edu
   http://www.societyforbusinessethics.org
   http://www.ethics.org
   http://www.theecoa.org
   http://www.ethicscenter.com
   http://www.csrnews.com
   http://www.bsr.org
   http://www.bus.duq.edu
   http://www.ethics.harvard.edu
   http://www.lilly.com

6. Go to http://www.ethics.org. Place your cursor on "Resources." Next, click on "Articles." Under "Organizational Ethics," click on "Business." After reviewing the articles, which ones have sales implications? What are the sales implications?

7. Type http://www.ibe.org.uk. Place your cursor on "Publications." Click on "Summary." Go to and read the article, "Taking the Temperature: Ethical Supply Chain Management." What message does this article have for salespeople? What are the ethical challenges facing supply chain management?

MAKING PROFESSIONAL SELLING DECISIONS

Case 2.1: Schmidt Business Forms
Background

Congratulations! As a new salesperson for Schmidt Business Forms, you have just completed training and have been assigned the southwest territory. Schmidt Business Forms designs and manufactures a full line of both stock and customized forms for use in all types of business. Operating throughout the United States and Canada, Schmidt is recognized as one of the three leaders in the industry.

Current Situation

Doctors' General Hospital was once a major account in your territory. Over this past year, virtually all the hospital's forms business has been switched from Schmidt to one of your main competitors. Due to the large volume and many types of forms used, Doctors' has placed the purchasing responsibility for all forms in the hands of Jim Adams in the purchasing department. An experienced professional purchasing agent, Adams has been in this position for several years and has purchased significant volumes of forms from Schmidt in the past. In the course of calling on Adams at his office in the hospital, you have learned that Doctors' dropping Schmidt as a forms source did not happen overnight. Although the loss of this account was not related to any single problem, you have learned that the switch to your competitor was basically due to a combination of events that resulted in a loss of trust in Schmidt. Several shipments did not arrive as promised, causing major problems for both billing and admissions. Even though the final proof copies were correct, a newly designed, multipart computer form was found to be short one of its pages. This required emergency room staff to take time and use a copier (located one floor up) until the forms could be rerun and delivered two weeks later. The final straw concerned an admissions form that Schmidt had been supplying the hospital for more than three years. For some reason, a new shipment of the admissions forms was the wrong size and would not fit into patient files without being folded. In each event, the prior salesperson worked with Adams to get the problems resolved and the correct forms delivered. Discounts were also given to help offset the inconvenience incurred. Nevertheless, Schmidt has lost the account, the previous salesperson has quit the company, and you have inherited the challenge of winning back Adams and Doctors' General Hospital.

Questions

1. Put yourself in the role of the salesperson for Schmidt Business Forms in the selling situation just described and review the *trust-building behaviors* presented in this module. Using the following worksheet as a guide, discuss and give examples of how you might use each of the *trust builders* to re-establish a relationship with Jim Adams and win back the Doctors' General Hospital account.

Trust-Building Worksheet

1. Expertise:

_____
_____
_____
_____
_____
_____
_____
_____
_____

2. Dependability:

_____
_____
_____
_____
_____
_____
_____

3. Candor:

_____
_____
_____
_____
_____
_____
_____
_____

4. Customer Orientation:

_____
_____
_____
_____
_____
_____
_____
_____
_____
_____

5. Compatibility:

_____

_____

_____

_____

_____

_____

_____

_____

_____

_____

Situation:	Read Case 2.1.
Characters:	Salesperson, Schmidt Business Forms; Jim Adams, purchasing agent, Doctors' Hospital
Scene:	*Location*—Jim Adams' office. *Action*—Salesperson stops in to see Adams.

ROLE PLAY

Role play your first sales call with Adams now that you have all the information on why they switched suppliers.

Upon completion of the role play, address the following questions:

1. Should a salesperson have a strategy to go after lost customers? How might this be done?
2. It is easy to pass on the blame to the former salesperson, delivery, and production people. Discuss the pros and cons of this strategy.

Case 2.2: Sales Ethics: A Case Study[17]
Background

Packaging Systems, Incorporated (PSI), a wholly owned subsidiary of an international oil company, is a major supplier of polyethylene film to various industrial and agricultural markets. In the past, a primary product has been a shredded film that is used for soil erosion control by farmers and commercial landscapers.

In recent years, PSI has become a major supplier in the pallet overwrap market. In this application, film is used to secure a product or products to a pallet for shipping. Compared with PSI's other markets, growth and profits in the pallet overwrap market have been outstanding. The bright prospects for the pallet overwrap market coupled with the stagnation of the shredded film market has led PSI management to make the following decisions: (1) limit production output and marketing activities of shredded film and (2) expand production output and marketing emphasis of pallet overwrap film.

The PSI salesforce was informed of the shift in emphasis in a memo from Bill Chandler, the sales manager for industrial and agricultural products (see Exhibit 2.10).

Current Situation

Jeff Braxton is the PSI sales representative in the Chicago area. He had given Chandler's memo a lot of thought before he reluctantly began to implement his sales manager's suggestions. During his weekly phone call to Chandler, Braxton had voiced some of his objections.

Chandler: So, Jeff, how is the shredded film cutback and pallet overwrap expansion coming along in Chicago?

Braxton: O.K., I guess, but personally, I have some problems with it.

Chandler: For example?

Braxton: Some of the shredded film accounts are refusing to roll over and play dead. They are saying that we can't cut them off, and a couple have been pretty hostile. They're talking lawsuit, Bill.

Chandler: That's out of your area of concern, Jeff. Let attorneys worry about that. Besides, I doubt many will sue when they consider the legal and financial resources of our parent company.

Braxton: Whatever you say, Bill. The other thing that bothers me is the written guarantee to provide pallet overwrap film. Seems to me that there could be shortages, strikes, or fires that could prevent us from following through on the promise to supply film.

Chandler: Highly unlikely, Jeff. You are worrying too much. You're new to the game. Do yourself a favor and follow my suggestions.

Braxton: Well, you're the boss . . .

In the past 30 days, several events had complicated the PSI strategy. An explosion and resulting fire had destroyed all the pallet overwrap production equipment and inventory in one of the PSI plants. A terrorist group had declared its responsibility for the explosion. PSI sales representatives were instructed to tell their accounts that the damage was minimal and that supply and service levels would not be affected. PSI management hoped to use production from the other four plants to cover the loss until rebuilding could be completed.

Fifteen days after the crippling fire, PSI received another severe blow. A trade dispute with several oil-producing nations erupted. This caused almost immediate raw material shortages for all PSI products. The matter was now becoming unpleasant for PSI. Braxton's phone call earlier in the day

Memorandum   EXHIBIT 2.10

To: Industrial/Agricultural Salesforce
From: Bill Chandler
Subject: Shredded Film Cutback/Pallet Overwrap Expansion

Effective immediately, we will be putting more emphasis on pallet overwrap film production and marketing. To allow this expansion, we will be cutting back our sales of shredded film by approximately 30 percent. I suggest you terminate your relationship with your marginal customers to accomplish the 30 percent reduction in shredded film. Now is the time to weed out customers who are:

1. Bad credit risks or slow to pay their bills;
2. Located more than 500 miles from any of our five manufacturing plants;
3. Low-volume buyers;
4. Low-loyalty customers, that is, they also buy from competitors.

To help the push in pallet overwrap film, we plan to approach high-potential target accounts with these tactics:

1. We will guarantee source of supply in writing: This should be attractive because most buyers are nervous about the availability of anything made from petroleum-based raw materials.
2. We will designate target accounts as national accounts; this is basically to stroke their corporate ego; we do not plan a real national accounts program.
3. We will designate selling teams to close the target accounts; the team will be made up of one sales representative, a member of management, and technical support personnel; once the accounts are closed, the sales representative will have responsibility for maintaining the account.

I will be talking with each of you in the near future to finalize plans for your respective territory.

Regards,

Bill

was the first of many bearing bad news for Chandler.

Braxton: Everybody out here is either hostile or not speaking at all. The grapevine is buzzing and practically all of our accounts know about the cover-up on the fire. Maybe that's what is making them take such a hard line on their guaranteed source of supply deal. The consensus is that we guaranteed the source of supply in writing and did not cite exceptions such as fires and trade disputes. Their message to me is, "You get the product, or we sue. We don't care where you get it, even if you have to buy from one of your competitors and resell it to us, and remember we want the competitive price you

promised. Anything short of this, and we'll never buy from you again."

Questions

1. An ethical issue exists when there is a question of whether an action is right or wrong. List the issues that, in your opinion, are ethical issues in this case.

2. In terms of the SCPS Code of Ethics (Exhibit 2.7), how would you evaluate Braxton's actions?

3. In terms of the SCPS Code of Ethics (Exhibit 2.7), how would you evaluate Chandler's actions?

4. How should the affected customers now be treated to minimize the damage to both PSI and to the customers?

UNDERSTANDING YOUR BUYERS IS THE KEY TO SALES SUCCESS

Cole Proper is a director of business development at AFFINA —The Customer Relationship Company, which provides a suite of outsourced contact center services to Fortune 500, mid-size, and government organizations. AFFINA's services include customer service support, inbound sales and order taking, fulfillment, research, and marketing. Proper works primarily with companies in telecommunications, consumer electronics, packaged goods, and consumer products. He credits his success in business development to his uncompromising commitment to understanding his buyers' situations, buying processes, needs, and expectations. In addition to his commitment to the customer, Proper has an extensive knowledge of AFFINA's capabilities, which is critical for developing unique solutions that differentiate his company's services from others and maximize value for the customer.

Proper is accustomed to selling to large buying teams and working through a sales cycle that often lasts from six to eighteen months. His customers' buying teams include managers, directors, vice presidents, (CXO)-level sponsors, and procurement departments—each with their own established goals and concepts. Understanding all of them is critical. While a CXO may evaluate outsourcing as a cost reduction opportunity, a service vice president is likely to focus on improving customer satisfaction and loyalty. While this example is not exclusive, Proper emphasizes that salespeople must understand the goals of each decision maker in order to provide optimal solutions.

In 2004, Proper introduced AFFINA to the director of customer service for a growing prepaid wireless telecommunications company. During the first meeting with the prospect, it became clear that the company was interested in evaluating outsourcing as a possible solution to an immediate problem associated with its rapid expansion. To service its growing customer base, the wireless company needed to increase its support staff but lacked the required space. This was a critical issue, but Proper began by learning about the organization's goals beyond the current capacity crisis. During the needs analysis process, it was clear that AFFINA was well positioned to assist the prospective company in achieving its strategic initiatives and growth plans.

Proper began exploring all aspects of the wireless business—its current contact center operation, retail network, marketing strategy, growth obstacles, etc. Through many meetings with various departments, he learned about the company's philosophy of providing outstanding customer service to differentiate it from its competitors. He also became aware of the challenges it faced in the growing market. It was soon clear that AFFINA could assist the wireless company in a number of ways: in lowering its operating expenses through process enhancements and efficiencies of scale, by offering an effective methodology for measuring the company's customer satisfaction and retailer effectiveness, and simultaneously resolving the issue of capacity.

The following eight months at the wireless company, however, saw a volatile sales cycle characterized by overwhelming organizational change and conceptual differences.

Source: Personal interview with Cole Proper, July 19, 2006.

Objectives

After completing this module, you should be able to

1 Categorize primary types of buyers.

2 Discuss the distinguishing characteristics of business markets.

3 List the different steps in the business-to-business buying process.

4 Discuss the different types of buyer needs.

5 Describe how buyers evaluate suppliers and alternative sales offerings by using the multiattribute model of evaluation.

6 Explain the two-factor model that buyers use to evaluate the performance of sales offerings and develop satisfaction.

7 Explain the different types of purchasing decisions.

8 Describe the four communication styles and how salespeople must adapt and flex their own styles to maximize communication.

9 Explain the concept of buying teams and specify the different member roles.

The first two months were spent developing the solution and working toward acceptance. Then, the wireless company implemented a major reorganization. The senior leadership team that had been supporting the AFFINA project either moved on or began new assignments. A new chief operating officer (COO) joined the company, and the chief financial officer (CFO) joined the buying team—a team that was totally different from the one Proper had established a relationship with and one with different conceptual views for a successful partnership. Nevertheless, AFFINA's solution was compelling, so Proper was excited to meet the new decision makers and learn about their interests. When new decision makers enter the buying process, everything that has worked to get you to the present has to be reconsidered.

The new COO was focused on stabilizing existing customer relationships, learning how to best serve the evolving market, and strengthening the retail distribution network. His conceptual views merged nicely with AFFINA's capabilities and proposed solution. However, the Information Technology (IT) staff and CFO were making changes internally that threatened the proposed IT infrastructure and pricing models. Through a series of meetings, Proper was able to uncover the goals of each decision maker and overcome all obstacles. The solution was revised, and an agreement was executed. It was evident in the end, that flexing to various communication styles and meeting the challenges associated with organizational change were invaluable.

Proper's selling experience underscores that the sales process is often disrupted—unexpectedly and beyond the control of the salesperson. Many times the reasons for disruption are not risks identified by the sales team. This illustrates the critical importance of understanding your buyers and being flexible when opportunities shift direction. As Proper discovered, the same problems are likely to exist within a company even if a new buying team is introduced. To be successful in implementing your solution, focus on understanding the reasons why each decision maker wants resolution. You must understand the personal goals as well as the organizational goals that will be achieved once the challenges are eliminated.

Following a discussion on different types of buyers, this module develops a model of the buying process and the corresponding roles of the salesperson. Buyer activities characteristic to each step of the purchase decision process are explained and related to salesperson activities for effectively interacting with buyers. This is followed by an explanation of different types of purchasing decisions to which salespeople must respond. The influence of individual communication styles on selling effectiveness is also discussed. The growing incidence of multiple buying influences and buying teams is then demonstrated, along with their impact on selling strategy. Finally, emergent trends such as relationship strategies, supply-chain management, target pricing, and the growing importance of information and technology are discussed from the perspective of the salesperson.

TYPES OF BUYERS

Salespeople work and interact with many different types of buyers. These buyer types range from heavy industry and manufacturing operations to consumers making a purchase for their own use. These variants of customer types arise out of the unique buying situations they occupy. As a result, one type of buyer will have needs, motivations, and buying behavior that are very different from another type of buyer. Consider the different buying situations and the resulting needs of a corporate buyer for Foot Locker compared with the athletic equipment buyer for a major university or Joe Smith, attorney at law and weekend warrior in the local YMCA's basketball league. As illustrated in Exhibit 3.1, each of these buyers may be looking for athletic shoes, but their buying needs are very different. To maximize selling effectiveness, salespeople must understand the type of buyer with whom they are working and respond to their specific needs, wants, and expectations.

Different Needs of Different Athletic Shoe Buyers **EXHIBIT 3.1**		
	Buyer for Foot Locker Shoe Stores	**University Athletic Equipment Buyer**	**Joe Smith—YMCA Weekend Warrior**
Functional Needs	• Has the features customers want • Well constructed—minimizes returns • Offers point-of-sale displays for store use • Competitive pricing	• Individualized sole texture for different player performance needs • Perfect fit and size for each team member • Custom match with university colors • Size of supplier's payment to coach and school for using their shoes	• Offers the leading edge in shoe features • Prominent brand logo • Highest-priced shoes in the store
Situational Needs	• Can supply stores across North America • Ability to ship to individual stores on a just-in-time basis • Offers 90-day trade credit	• Ability to deliver on time • Provide supplier personnel for team fittings • Make contract payments to university and coach at beginning of season	• Right size in stock, ready to carry out • Takes Visa and MasterCard
Social Needs	• Invitation for buying team to attend trade show and supplier-sponsored reception	• Sponsor and distribute shoes at annual team shoe night to build enthusiasm • Include team and athletes in supplier brand promotions	• Offers user-group newsletter to upscale customers • Periodic mailings for new products and incentives to purchase
Psychological Needs	• Assurance that shoes will sell at retail • Brand name with strong market appeal • Option to return unsold goods for credit	• Brand name consistent with players' self-images • The entire team will accept and be enthusiastic toward product decision • Belief that the overall contract is best for the university, team, and coaches	• Reinforces customer's self-image as an innovator • Product will deliver the promised performance • One of only a few people having purchased this style of shoe
Knowledge Needs	• Level of quality—how the shoe is constructed • How the new features impact performance • What makes the shoe unique and superior to competitive offerings • Product training and materials for sales staff	• What makes the shoe unique and superior to competitive offerings • Supporting information and assurance that the contracted payments to university and coaches are superior to competitive offerings	• What makes the shoe unique and superior to competitive offerings • Assurance that everybody on the court will not be wearing the same shoe

The most common categorization of buyers splits them into either (1) **consumer markets** or (2) **business markets**. Consumers purchase goods and services for their own use or consumption and are highly influenced by peer group behavior, aesthetics, and personal taste. Business markets are composed of firms, institutions, and governments. These members of the business market acquire goods and services to use as inputs into their own manufacturing process (i.e., raw materials, component parts, and capital equipment), for use in their day-to-day operations (i.e., office supplies, professional services, insurance), or for resale to their own customers. Business customers tend to stress overall value as the cornerstone for purchase decisions.

Distinguishing Characteristics of Business Markets

Although there are similarities between consumer and business buying behaviors, business markets tend to be much more complex and possess several characteristics that are in sharp contrast to those of the consumer market. These distinguishing characteristics are described in the following sections.

Concentrated Demand

Business markets typically exhibit high levels of concentration in which a small number of large buyers account for most of the purchases. The fact that business buyers tend to be larger in size but fewer in numbers can greatly impact a salesperson's selling plans and performance. For example, a salesperson selling high-grade industrial silicon for use in manufacturing computer chips will find that his or her fate rests on acquiring and nurturing the business of one or more of the four or five dominant chip makers around the world.

Derived Demand

Derived demand denotes that the demand in business markets is closely associated with the demand for consumer goods. When the consumer demand for new cars and trucks increases, the demand for rolled steel also goes up. Of course, when the demand for consumer products goes down, so goes the related demand in business markets. The most effective salespeople identify and monitor the consumer markets that are related to their business customers so they can better anticipate shifts in demand and assist their buyers in staying ahead of the demand shifts rather than being caught with too much, too little, or even with the wrong inventory. Republic Gypsum's salespeople accurately forecast a boom in residential construction and the pressure it would put on the supply of sheetrock wallboard. Working closely with their key customers, order quantities and shipping dates were revised to prevent those customers from being caught with inadequate inventories to supply the expanded demand. This gave those customers a significant competitive advantage over their competitors who were surprised and suddenly out of stock.

Higher Levels of Demand Fluctuation

Closely related to the derived demand characteristic, the demand for goods and services in the business market is more volatile than that of the consumer market. In economics, this is referred to as the **acceleration principle**. As demand increases (or decreases) in the consumer market, the business market reacts by accelerating the buildup (or reduction) of inventories and increasing (or decreasing) plant capacity. A good example would be the rapidly growing demand for tri-mode wireless phones with advanced capabilities such as voice-activated dialing and vision-enabled access to the Internet and Web with enhanced full-color screens. In response to higher consumer demand, wholesalers and retailers are increasing their inventories of these advanced phones while decreasing the number of single-mode voice-only devices they carry. In response, manufacturers have shifted their production away from the voice-only wireless phones to increase their production of the more advanced Internet-capable models. Salespeople are the source of valuable information and knowledge enabling their customers to anticipate these fluctuations and assisting them in developing more effective marketing strategies. As a result, both the buying and selling organizations realize mutual positive benefits.

Purchasing Professionals

Buyers in the business markets are trained as purchasing agents. The process of identifying suppliers and sourcing goods and services is their job. This results in a more professional and rational approach to purchasing. As a result, salespeople must possess increased levels of knowledge and expertise to provide customers with a richer and more detailed assortment of application, performance, and technical data.

Salespeople Have Become Sources of Advantage for the Customer

John Sullivan is the senior management consultant for Prime Resource Group where he works with a list of global accounts in improving sales performance. Sullivan has an extensive background in sales and sales management and offers his reflections on the evolution of personal selling.

The salesperson's role in Era 1 would best be described as that of a persuader. Training was focused exclusively on three areas: presenting, handling objections, and closing. The agenda was to get the customer to do what the salesperson wanted the customer to do. Era 1 was replaced by an emphasis on a new set of skills and a more enlightened win–win perspective of the salesperson's role.

This was Era 2 and emphasized questioning, listening, and building a relationship with the customer. Communication was directed toward developing an understanding of the customer's needs. The salesperson's role was that of a problem solver—to understand the customer's needs and close the gap with his or her product as the solution. Era 2 has continued to evolve, and today more than ever before salespeople have become a source of business advantage for the customer. One point of view regarding this business advantage is that the salesperson becomes a consultant to the customer where they apply their business acumen and understanding of the customer's business situation to create a solution that the customer truly values. Often, this is a solution that the customer has never experienced and would never think of asking for.

Multiple Buying Influences

Reflecting the increased complexity of many business purchases, groups of individuals within the buying firm often work together as a buying team or center. As a result, salespeople often work simultaneously with several individuals during a sales call and even different sets of buyers during different sales calls. Buying team members come from different areas of expertise and play different roles in the purchasing process. To be effective, the salesperson must first identify, then understand and respond to, the role and key buying motives of each member.

Close Buyer–Seller Relationships

The smaller customer base and increased usage of supply chain management, characterized by buyers becoming highly involved in organizing and administering logistical processes and actively managing a reduced set of suppliers, has resulted in buyers and sellers becoming much more interdependent than ever before. This increased interdependence and desire to reduce risk of the unknown has led to an emphasis on developing long-term buyer–seller relationships characterized by increased levels of buyer–seller interaction and higher levels of service expectations by buyers. "Professional Selling in the 21st Century: Salespeople Have Become Sources of Advantage for the Customer"[1] describes the shift in selling models to that of a consultant serving as a source of business advantage for the customer. This shift requires salespeople to change their focus from quickly selling the buyer and closing the current transaction and, in its place, adapt a longer-term perspective emphasizing continuing multiple exchanges into the future. This perspective often includes making multiple sales calls to develop a better understanding of the buyer's needs and then responding to those needs with a sales offering that solves the buyer's needs and enhances the buyer–seller relationship in favor of future interactions.

THE BUYING PROCESS

Buyers in both the consumer and business marketplace undergo a conscious and logical process in making purchase decisions. As depicted in Figure 3.1, the sequential

FIGURE 3.1   Comparison of Buying Decision Process Phases and Corresponding Steps in the Selling Process

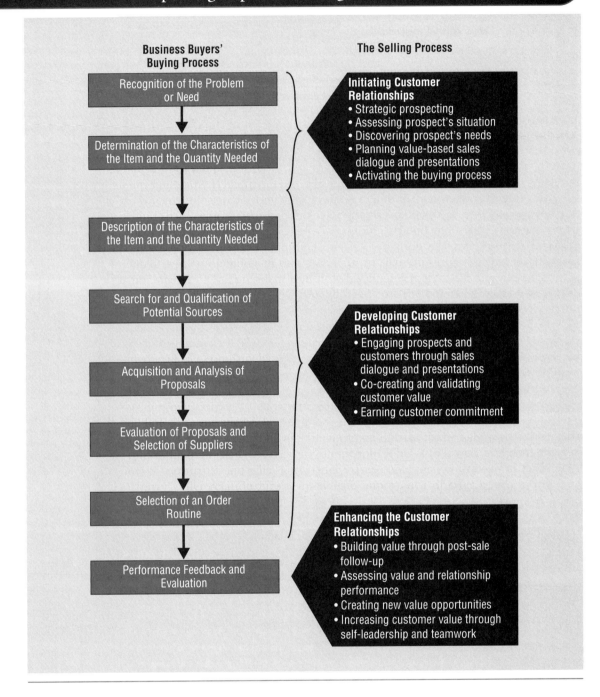

and interrelated phases of the **business buyers' purchase process** begin with (1) *recognition of the problem or need*, (2) *determination of the characteristics of the item and the quantity needed*, (3) *description of the characteristics of the item and quantity needed*, (4) *search for and qualification of potential sources*, (5) *acquisition and analysis of proposals*, (6) *evaluation of proposals and selection of suppliers*, (7) *selection of an order routine*, and (8) *performance feedback and evaluation*.

Depending upon the nature of the buying organization and the buying situation, the buying process may be highly formalized or simply a rough approximation of what actually occurs. The decision process employed by General Motors for the acquisition of a new organization-wide computer system will be highly formalized and purposefully reflect each of the previously described decision phases. Compared to General Motors, the decision process of Bloomington Bookkeeping, a single office and four-person operation, could be expected to use a less formalized approach in working through their buying decision process for a computer system. In the decision to replenish stock office supplies, both of the organizations are likely to use a much less formalized routine—but still, a routine that reflects the different decision phases.

As further illustrated by Figure 3.1, there is a close correspondence between the phases of the buyer's decision process and the selling activities of the salesperson. It is important that salespeople understand and make use of the interrelationships between the phases of the buying process and selling activities. Effective use of these interrelationships offers salespeople numerous opportunities to interact with buyers in a way that guides the shaping of product specifications and the selection of sources while facilitating the purchase decision.

Phase One—Recognition of the Problem or Need: The Needs Gap

Needs are the result of a gap between buyers' **desired states** and their **actual states**. Consequently, need recognition results from an individual cognitively and emotionally processing information relevant to his or her actual state of being and comparing it to the desired state of being. As illustrated in Figure 3.2, any perceived difference, or **needs gap**, between these two states activates the motivation or drive to fill the gap and reach the desired state. For example, the SnowRunner Company's daily production capacity is limited to 1,000 molded skimobile body housings. Their research indicates that increasing capacity to 1,250 units per day would result in significant reductions in per-unit costs and allow them to enter additional geographic markets—both moves that would have significant and positive impacts on financial performance. The perceived need to expand production activates a corresponding motivation to search for information regarding alternative solutions and acquire the capability to increase production by 250 units.

However, if there is no gap, then there is no need and no active buying motive. It is common for salespeople to find themselves working with buyers who, for one reason or another, do not perceive a needs gap to be present. It is possible that they do not have the right information or lack a full understanding of the situation and the existence of options better than their current state. It is also possible that their understanding of the actual state might be incomplete or mistaken. For

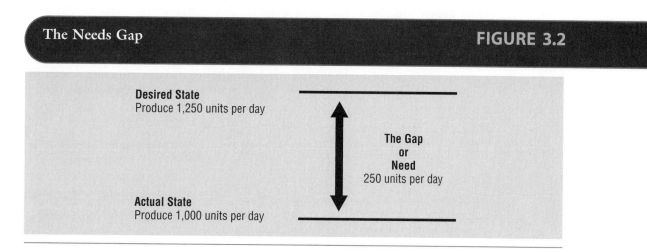

The Needs Gap   **FIGURE 3.2**

Desired State
Produce 1,250 units per day

**The Gap
or
Need**
250 units per day

Actual State
Produce 1,000 units per day

The needs gap is the difference between the buyer's perceived desired state and the buyer's perceived actual state.

AN ETHICAL DILEMMA

Shannon Weis recently accepted a position as a financial representative with a brand name insurance and financial services organization and has completed her licensing requirements as well as the company's three month training program. She has transitioned into the field where she will be working with Eric Wilkins, her coach and mentor. Wilkins is a senior salesperson with the company and has earned a reputation as a high volume producer. Wilkins and Weis have just returned to the field office after spending the day calling on new prospects and working through the company's fact-finder guide—a questioning sequence designed to collect the necessary information for profiling prospective customers and discovering their needs for insurance and financial services. As the two settled into the day's office routine, Weis asked Wilkins to show her how to assess the customer information so it would provide her with an understanding of the customer's needs and expectations. She was eager to learn how to create a unique package of services that would provide the best value for the customer. In response to Weis' request, Wilkins explained that ". . . it is not necessary to detail the customer's needs. It's much more effective in terms of getting the sale to simply go through the information and find the right pieces that will illustrate to the customer why they need the package we want to sell them. That will allow you to sell the services that carry the highest sales commissions." He continued, "It might not be the optimum package for the customer, but it won't hurt them. As long as you use some of the customer's information and feed it back to them, they will think you have customized the package just for them and make the purchase. That way they are happy, and you get the bigger commission with a lot less effort—that's a real win–win, right?"

What do you think about Wilkins' preferred way of using customer information to make the sale? What problems might result from Wilkins' selling methods?

---

example, SnowRunner's buyers might not understand the cost reduction possibilities and increased market potential that could result from increased capacity. As a result, they perceive no need to increase production—the desired state is the same as their actual state. Similarly, the buyers might be functioning with incomplete information regarding the company's actual state of reduced production capacity due to SnowRunner's existing molding machines requiring increased downtime for maintenance. Properly realized, this lowering of the actual state would result in a needs gap. Successful salespeople position themselves to assist buyers in identifying and understanding needs as a result of their broader expertise and knowledge regarding product use and application. Salespeople can also use sales conversations to present buyers with information and opportunities that effectively raise the desired state, generate a need, and trigger the purchase decision process. Top-performing salespeople understand the importance of assisting their buyers in forming realistic perceptions of the actual state and the desired state. In this manner, the salesperson can continue to serve as a nonmanipulative consultant to the buyer while affecting buying motives that yield mutual benefits to all parties. However, it should be noted that the persuasive power of assisting the buyer in determining and comparing desired and actual states can also be misused and lead to unethical and manipulative selling behaviors such as those exhibited in "An Ethical Dilemma."

Types of Buyer Needs

The total number of potential customer needs is infinite and sometimes difficult for salespeople to grasp and understand on a customer-by-customer basis. Consequently, many salespeople find it helpful to group customer needs into one of five basic types or categories that focus on the buying situation and the benefits to be provided by the product or service being chosen.[2] These five general types of buyer needs are described as follows:

- **Situational needs** are the specific needs that are contingent on, and often a result of, conditions related to the specific environment, time, and place (e.g., emergency car repair while traveling out of town, a piece of customized production equipment to fulfill a customer's specific situational requirements, or providing for quick initial shipment to meet a buyer's out-of-stock status).
- **Functional needs** represent the need for a specific core task or function to be performed—the functional purpose of a specific product or service. The need for a sales offering to do what it is supposed to do (e.g., alcohol disinfects, switches open and close to control some flow, the flow control valve is accurate and reliable).
- **Social needs** comprise the need for acceptance from and association with others—a desire to belong to some reference group. For example, a product or service might be associated with some specific and desired affinity group or segment (e.g., Polo clothing is associated with upper-income, successful people; ISO 9000 Certification is associated with high-quality vendors; leading e-commerce Web sites include discussion groups to build a sense of community).
- **Psychological needs** reflect the desire for feelings of assurance and risk reduction, as well as positive emotions and feelings such as success, joy, excitement, and stimulation (e.g., a Mont Blanc pen generates a feeling of success; effective training programs create a sense of self-control and determination; selection and use of well-known, high-quality brands provides assurance to buyers and organizations alike).
- **Knowledge needs** represent the desire for personal development, information, and knowledge to increase thought and understanding as to how and why things happen (e.g., product information, newsletters, brochures, along with training and user support group meetings/conferences provide current information on products and topics of interest).

Categorizing buyer needs by type can assist the salesperson in bringing order to what could otherwise be a confusing and endless mix of needs and expectations. Organizing the buyer's different needs into their basic types can help salespeople in several ways. First, as illustrated by Exhibit 3.1 and the example worksheet in Exhibit 3.2, the basic types can serve as a checklist or work sheet to ensure that no significant problems or needs have been overlooked in the process of needs discovery. Organizing what at first might appear to be different needs and problems into their common types also helps the salesperson to better understand the nature of the buyer's needs along with the interrelationships and commonalities between them. In turn, this enhanced understanding and the framework of basic types combine to serve as a guide for salespeople in generating and then demonstrating value-added solutions in response to the specific needs of the buyer.

As previously discussed, the specific circumstances or types of solution benefits that a buyer is seeking should determine a salesperson's strategy for working with that buyer. Consequently, it should be noted that the needs of business buyers tend to be more complex than consumers' needs. Like consumers, organizational buyers are people and are influenced by the same functional, social, psychological, knowledge, and situational experiences and forces that affect and shape individual needs. However, in addition to those individual needs, organizational buyers must also satisfy the needs and requirements of the organization for which they work. As depicted by Figure 3.3, these organizational needs overlay and interact with the needs of the individual. To maximize selling effectiveness in the organizational or business-to-business market, salespeople must generate solutions addressing both the individual and organizational needs of business buyers.

Phase Two—Determination of the Characteristics of the Item and the Quantity Needed

Coincident to recognizing a need or problem is the motivation and drive to resolve it by undertaking a search for additional information leading to possible solutions.

EXHIBIT 3.2 Example Work Sheet for Organizing Buyer Needs and Benefit-Based Solutions

Primary Buyer: **Bart Waits**
Buying Organization: **SouthWest Metal Stampings**
Primary Industry: **Stamped Metal Parts and Subcomponents**

Basic Type of Need	Buyer's Specific Needs
Buyer's Situational Needs	• Requires an 18 percent increase in production to meet increased sales • On-hand inventory will not meet production/delivery schedule • Tight cash flow pending initial deliveries and receipt of payment
Buyer's Functional Needs	• Equipment to provide effective and efficient increase in production • Expedited delivery and installation in six weeks or less • Equipment financing extending payments beyond initial receipts
Buyer's Social Needs	• Expansion in production transforms them into Top 10 in industry • Belonging to user group of companies using this equipment • Feeling that they are an important customer of the supplier
Buyer's Knowledge Needs	• Confidence that selected equipment will meet needs and do the job • Assurance that seller can complete installation in six weeks • Saving face—to believe borrowing for equipment is common • Evidence that this is the right choice • Understanding new technology used by the selected equipment • Training program for production employees and maintenance staff

FIGURE 3.3   Complex Mix of Business Buyer Needs

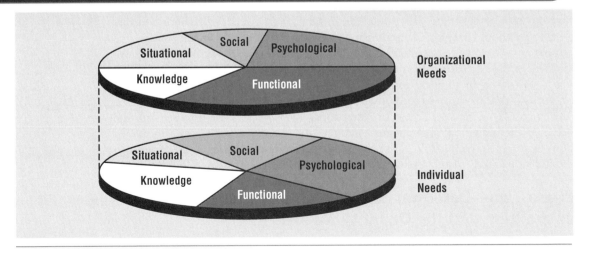

Business buyers' needs are a combination of the buyers' individual needs and the organization's needs.

This particular phase of the buying process involves the consideration and study of the overall situation to understand what is required in the form of a preferred solution. This begins to establish the general characteristics and quantities necessary to resolve the need or problem. Through effective sales conversations, salespeople use their knowledge and expertise at this point to assist the buyer in analyzing and interpreting the problem situation and needs. Salespeople offer valuable knowledge of problem situations and solution options that buyers typically perceive as beneficial.

Phase Three—Description of the Characteristics of the Item and the Quantity Needed

Using the desired characteristics and quantities developed in the previous phase as a starting point, buyers translate that general information into detailed specifications describing exactly what is expected and required. The determination of detailed specifications serves several purposes. First, detailed specifications guide supplier firms in developing their proposals. Second, these specifications provide the buyer a framework for evaluating, comparing, and choosing among the proposed solutions. Postpurchase specifications serve as a standard for evaluation to ensure that the buying firm receives the required product features and quantities. Trust-based buyer–seller relationships allow salespeople to work closely with buyers and collaboratively assist them in establishing the detailed specifications of the preferred solutions.

Phase Four—Search for and Qualification of Potential Sources

Next, buyers must locate and qualify potential suppliers capable of providing the preferred solution. Although buyers certainly utilize information provided by salespeople to identify qualified suppliers, there is an abundance of information available from other sources such as trade associations, product source directories, trade shows, the Internet, advertising, and word of mouth. Once identified, potential suppliers are qualified on their ability to consistently perform and deliver at the level of quality and quantity required. Due to the large number of information sources available to buyers researching potential suppliers, one of the most important tasks in personal selling is to win the position of one of those information sources and keep buyers informed about the salesperson's company, its new products, and solution capabilities.

Phase Five—Acquisition and Analysis of Proposals

Based on the detailed specifications, **requests for proposals** (known in the trade as an **RFP**) are developed and distributed to the qualified potential suppliers. Based on the RFP, qualified suppliers develop and submit proposals to provide the products as specified. Salespeople play a critical and influential role in this stage of the buying process by developing and presenting the proposed solution to the buyers. In this role, the salesperson is responsible for presenting the proposed features and benefits in such a manner that the proposed solution is evaluated as providing higher levels of benefits and value to the buyer than other competing proposals. Consequently, it is imperative that salespeople understand the basic evaluation procedures used by buyers in comparing alternative and competitive proposals so they can be more proficient in demonstrating the superiority of their solution over the competition.

Procedures for Evaluating Suppliers and Products

Purchase decisions are based on the buyers' comparative evaluations of suppliers and the products and services they propose for satisfying the buyers' needs. Some buyers may look for the sales offering that receives the highest rating on the one characteristic

EXHIBIT 3.3 Important Product Information

Characteristics	BondIt #302	AdCo #45	StikFast #217
Ease of application	Excellent	Good	Very good
Bonding time	8 minutes	10 minutes	12 minutes
Durability	10 years	12 years	15 years
Reliability	Very good	Excellent	Good
Nontoxic	Very good	Excellent	Very good
Quoted price	$28 per gal.	$22 per gal.	$26 per gal.
Shelf-life in storage	6 months	4 months	4 months
Service factors	Good	Very good	Excellent

they perceive as being most important. Others may prefer the sales offering that achieves some acceptable assessment score across each and every attribute desired by the buyer. However, research into how purchase decisions are made suggests that most buyers use a compensatory, **multiattribute model** incorporating weighted averages across desired characteristics.[3] These weighted averages incorporate (1) assessments of how well the product or supplier performs in meeting each of the specified characteristics and (2) the relative importance of each specified characteristic.

Assessment of Product or Supplier Performance

The first step in applying the multiattribute model is to objectively rate how well each characteristic of the competing products or suppliers meets the buyers' needs. Let us use the example of General Motors (GM) evaluating adhesives for use in manufacturing. The buyers have narrowed the alternatives to products proposed by three suppliers: BondIt #302, AdCo #45, and StikFast #217. As illustrated in Exhibit 3.3, the GM buying team has assessed the competitive products according to how well they perform on certain important attributes. These assessments are converted to scores as depicted in Exhibit 3.4, with scores ranging from 1 (very poor performance) to 10 (excellent performance).

As illustrated, no single product is consistently outstanding across each of the eight identified characteristics. Although BondIt #302 is easy to apply and uses the buyer's current equipment, it is also more expensive and has the shortest durability time in the field. StikFast #217 also scores well for ease of application, and it has superior durability. However, it has the longest bonding time and could negatively influence production time.

Accounting for Relative Importance of Each Characteristic

To properly compare these performance differences, each score must be weighted by the characteristic's perceived importance. In the adhesive example, importance weights are assigned on a scale of 1 (relatively unimportant) to 10 (very important).

EXHIBIT 3.4 Product Performance Scores

Characteristics	BondIt #302	AdCo #45	StikFast #217
Ease of application	10	5	8
Bonding time	8	6	4
Durability	6	8	9
Reliability	8	10	5
Nontoxic	8	10	8
Quoted price	5	9	7
Shelf-life in storage	9	6	6
Service factors	5	8	10

Weighted Averages for Performance Times Importance and Overall Evaluation Scores									EXHIBIT 3.5
Characteristics	**BondIt #302**			**AdCo #45**			**StikFast #217**		
	P	**I**	**P×I**	**P**	**I**	**P×I**	**P**	**I**	**P×I**
Ease of application	10	8	80	5	8	40	8	8	72
Bonding time	8	6	48	6	6	36	4	6	24
Durability	6	9	54	8	9	72	9	9	81
Reliability	8	7	56	10	7	70	5	7	35
Nontoxic	8	6	48	10	6	60	8	6	48
Quoted price	5	10	50	9	10	90	7	10	70
Shelf-life in storage	9	6	54	6	6	36	6	6	36
Service factors	5	8	40	8	8	64	10	8	80
Overall evaluation score			430			468			446

As illustrated in Exhibit 3.5, multiplying each performance score by the corresponding attribute's importance weight results in a weighted average that can be totaled to calculate an overall rating for each product. The product or supplier having the highest comparative rating is typically the product selected for purchase. In this example, AdCo has the highest overall evaluation totaling 468 points compared with BondIt's 430 points and StikFast's 446 points.

Employing Buyer Evaluation Procedures to Enhance Selling Strategies

Understanding evaluation procedures and gaining insight as to how a specific buyer or team of buyers is evaluating suppliers and proposals is vital for the salesperson to be effective and requires the integration of several bases of knowledge. First, information gathered prior to the sales call must be combined with an effective needs–discovery dialogue with the buyer(s) to delineate the buyers' needs and the nature of the desired solution. This establishes the most likely criteria for evaluation. Further discussion between the buyer and seller can begin to establish the importance the buyers place on each of the different performance criteria and often yields information as to what suppliers and products are being considered. Using this information and the salesperson's knowledge of how their products compare with competitors' offerings allows the salesperson to complete a likely facsimile of the buyers' evaluation. With this enhanced level of preparation and understanding, the salesperson can plan, create, and deliver a more effective presentation using the five fundamental strategies that are inherent within the evaluation procedures used by buyers.

- *Modify the Product Offering Being Proposed.* Oftentimes, in the course of preparing or delivering a presentation, it becomes apparent that the product offering will not maximize the buyer's evaluation score in comparison with a competitor's offering. In this case, the strategy would be to modify or change the product to one that better meets the buyer's overall needs and thus would receive a higher evaluation. For example, by developing a better understanding of the adhesive buyer's perceived importance of certain characteristics, the BondIt salesperson could offer a different adhesive formulation that is not as easy to apply (low perceived importance) but offers improved durability (perceived high importance) and more competitive price (perceived high importance).

- *Alter the Buyer's Beliefs about the Proposed Offering.* Provide information and support to alter the buyer's beliefs as to where the proposed product stands on certain attributes. This is a recommended strategy for cases in which the buyer underestimates the true qualities of the proposed product. However, if the buyer's perceptions are correct, this strategy would encourage exaggerated and overstated claims by the salesperson and should be avoided. In the instance of BondIt #302's low evaluation score, the salesperson could offer the buyer information and evidence that the product's durability and service factors actually perform much better than the buyer initially believed. By working with the buyer to develop a more realistic perception of the product's performance, BondIt #302 could become the buyer's preferred choice.

- *Alter the Buyer's Beliefs about the Competitor's Offering.* For a variety of reasons, buyers often mistakenly believe that a competitor's offering has higher level attributes or qualities than it actually does. In such an instance, the salesperson can provide information to evidence a more accurate picture of the competitor's attributes. This has been referred to as **competitive depositioning** and is carried out by openly comparing (not simply degrading) the competing offering's attributes, advantages, and weaknesses. As an illustration, the BondIt salesperson might demonstrate the *total* cost for each of the three product alternatives, including a quoted price, ease of application, and bonding time. BondIt is much easier to apply and has a faster bonding time. Consequently, less of it needs to be applied for each application, which results in a significantly lower total cost and a much improved evaluation score.

- *Alter the Importance Weights.* In this strategy, the salesperson uses information to emphasize and thus increase the importance of certain attributes on which the product offering is exceptionally strong. In the case of attributes on which the offering might be short, the strategy would be to deemphasize their importance. Continuing the adhesive purchase decision, BondIt's salesperson might offer information to influence the buyer's importance rating for ease of application and storage shelf-life—two characteristics in which BondIt is much stronger than the two competitors.

- *Call Attention to Neglected Attributes.* In the case in which it becomes apparent that significant attributes may have been neglected or overlooked, the salesperson can increase the buyer's evaluation of the proposed offering by pointing out the attribute that was missed. For instance, the BondIt #302 adhesive dries to an invisible, transparent, and semiflexible adhesive compared with the two competitors, which cure to a light gray color that could detract from the final product in cases in which the adhesive flowed out of the joint. The appearance of the final product is a significant concern, and this neglected attribute could substantially influence the comparative evaluations.

Phase Six—Evaluation of Proposals and Selection of Suppliers

The buying decision is the outcome of the buyer's evaluation of the various proposals acquired from potential suppliers. Typically, further negotiations will be conducted with the selected supplier(s) for the purpose of establishing the final terms regarding product characteristics, pricing, and delivery. Salespeople play a central role in gaining the buyer's commitment to the purchase decision and in the subsequent negotiations of the final terms.

Phase Seven—Selection of an Order Routine

Once the supplier(s) has been selected, details associated with the purchase decision must be settled. These details include delivery quantities, locations, and times along with return policies and the routine for reorders associated with the purchase. For cases in which the purchase requires multiple deliveries over a period of time, the routine for placing subsequent orders and making deliveries must be set out and understood. Is the order routine standardized on the basis of a prearranged time schedule, or is the salesperson expected to monitor usage and inventories in order to place orders and schedule shipments? Will orders be placed automatically through the use of electronic data interchange or the Internet? Regardless of the nature of the order routine, the salesperson plays a critical role in facilitating communication, completing ordering procedures, and settling the final details.

Phase Eight—Performance Feedback and Evaluation

The final phase in the buying process is the evaluation of performance and feedback shared among all parties for the purpose of improving future performance and enhancing buyer–seller relationships. Research supports that salespeople's customer interaction activities and communication at this stage of the buying process become the primary determinants of customer satisfaction and buyer loyalty. Consequently, it is critical that salespeople continue working with buyers after the sale. The salesperson's follow-up activities provide the critical points of contact between the buyer and seller in order to assure consistent performance, respond to and take care of problems, maximize customer satisfaction, create new value opportunities, and further enhance buyer–seller relationships.

Understanding Postpurchase Evaluation and the Formation of Satisfaction

Research shows that buyers evaluate their experience with a product purchase on the basis of product characteristics that fall into a **two-factor model of evaluation** as depicted in Figure 3.4.[4] The first category, **functional attributes**, refers to the features and characteristics that are related to *what* the product actually does or is expected to do—its functional characteristics. These functional characteristics have also been referred to as **must-have attributes**, features of the core product that are taken for granted by the customer. These are the attributes that must be present for the supplier or product to even be included among those being considered for purchase. Consequently, they tend to be fairly common across the set of suppliers and products being considered for purchase by a buyer. Characteristics such as reliability, durability, conformance to specifications, competitive pricing, and performance are illustrative of functional attributes.

Psychological attributes make up the second general category. This category refers to *how* things are carried out and done between the buyer and seller. These supplier and market offering characteristics are described as the **delighter attributes**—the augmented features and characteristics included in the total market offering that go beyond buyer expectations and have a significant positive impact on customer satisfaction. The psychological or delighter characteristics are not perceived as being universal features across the evoked set of suppliers and market offerings being considered. Rather, these are the differentiators between the competitors. The competence, attitudes, and behaviors of supplier personnel with whom the buyer has contact, as well as the salesperson's trustworthiness, consideration for the customer, responsiveness, ability to recover when there is a problem, and innovativeness in providing solutions are exemplary psychological attributes.

The Growing Importance of Salespeople in Buyer's Postpurchase Evaluation

Understanding the differential impact of functional (*must-haves*) and psychological (*delighters*) attributes is important for salespeople. Functional attributes possess a close correspondence to the technical and more tangible product attributes whereas the psychological attributes are similar to the interpersonal communication and behaviors of salespeople and other personnel having contact with customers. Numerous research studies across a variety of industries evidences psychological attributes as having up to two times more influence on buyer satisfaction and loyalty than functional attributes. This observation underscores special implications for salespeople, as it is their interpersonal communication and behaviors—what they

FIGURE 3.4   The Two-Factor Model of Buyer Evaluation

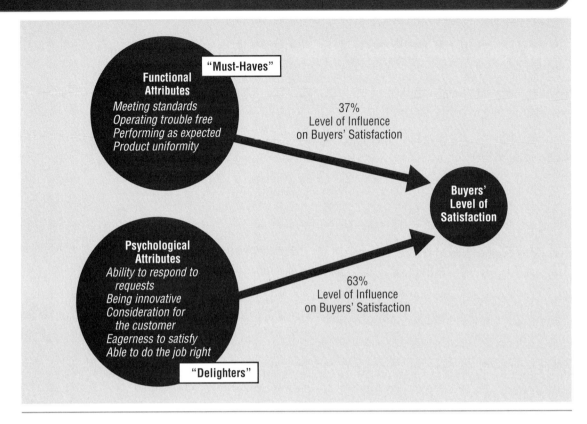

Buyers evaluate functional attributes and psychological attributes of a sales offering to assess overall performance and satisfaction.

do—that make up the psychological attributes. Although both categories of product characteristics are important and have significant influences on buyer satisfaction, the activities and behaviors of the salesperson as she or he interacts with the buyer have more impact on that buyer's evaluation than the features of the product or service itself.

TYPES OF PURCHASING DECISIONS

Buyers are learners in that purchase decisions are not isolated behaviors. Buyer behavior and purchase decisions are based on the relevant knowledge that buyers have accumulated from multiple sources to assist them in making the proper choice. Internally, buyers reflect on past experiences as guides for making purchase decisions. When sufficient knowledge from past experiences is not available, buyers access external sources of information: secondary sources of information (e.g., trade journals, product test reports, advertising) and other individuals the buyer perceives as being trustworthy and knowledgeable in a given area.

The level of experience and knowledge a buyer or buying organization possesses relevant to a given purchasing decision is a primary determinant of the time and resources the buyer will allocate to that purchasing decision. The level of a buyer's existing experience and knowledge has been used to categorize buyer behavior into three types of purchasing decisions: straight rebuys, modified rebuys, and new tasks. As summarized in Exhibit 3.6, selling strategies should reflect the differences in buyer behaviors and decision-making characteristic of each type of buying decision.

	Decision Type		
EXHIBIT 3.6 Three Types of Buying Decisions	**Straight Rebuy**	**Modified Rebuy**	**New Task**
Newness of problem or need	Low	Medium	High
Information requirements	Minimal	Moderate	Maximum
Information search	Minimal	Limited	Extensive
Consideration of new alternatives	None	Limited	Extensive
Multiple buying influences	Very small	Moderate	Large
Financial risks	Low	Moderate	High

Straight Rebuys

If past experiences with a product resulted in high levels of satisfaction, buyers tend to purchase the same product from the same sources. Comparable with a routine repurchase in which nothing has changed, the **straight rebuy decision** is often the result of a long-term purchase agreement. Needs have been predetermined with the corresponding specifications, pricing, and shipping requirements already established by a blanket purchase order or an annual purchase agreement. Ordering is automatic and often computerized by using electronic data interchange (EDI) and e-commerce (Internet, intranet, and extranet). Mitsubishi Motor Manufacturing of America uses a large number of straight rebuy decisions in its acquisition of component parts. Beginning as a primary supplier of automotive glass components, Vuteq has developed a strong relationship with Mitsubishi Motor Manufacturing of America over a period of several years. As a result, Vuteq's business has steadily increased and now includes door trims, fuel tanks, and mirrors in addition to window glass. These components are purchased as straight rebuys by using EDI, allowing Vuteq to deliver these components to Mitsubishi on a minute-to-minute basis, matching ongoing production.

Buyers allocate little, if any, time and resources to this form of purchase decision. The primary emphasis is on receipt of the products and their continued satisfactory performance. With most of the purchasing process automated, straight rebuy decisions are little more than record keeping that is often handled by clerical staff in the purchasing office.

For the in-supplier (a current supplier), straight rebuys offer the advantage of reduced levels of potential competition. Rather than becoming complacent, however, in-salespeople must continually monitor the competitive environment for advances in product capabilities or changes in price structures. They should also follow up on deliveries and interact with users as well as decision makers to make sure that product and performance continue to receive strong and positive evaluations.

Straight rebuy decisions present a major challenge to the out-salesperson. Buyers are satisfied with the products and services from current suppliers and see no need to change. This is a classic case where the buyer perceives no difference or needs gap between their actual and desired state. Consequently, there is no active buying motive to which the out-salesperson can respond. In this case, out-salespeople are typically presented with two strategy choices. First, they can continue to make contact with the buyer so that when there is a change in the buying situation or if the current supplier makes a mistake, they are there to respond. Second, they can provide information and evidence relevant to either the desired or actual states so that the buyer will perceive a needs gap. For example, Vuteq's competitors will find it most difficult to gain this portion of Mitsubishi's business by offering similar or equal products and systems. However, a competitor might adopt future advances in technology that would enable them to offer significant added value over and beyond that being offered by Vuteq. Effectively

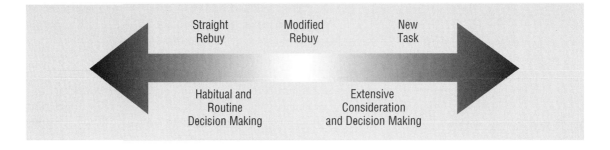

FIGURE 3.5   Continuum of Types of Buying Decisions

communicating and demonstrating their advanced capabilities holds the potential for raising the desired state and thus producing a needs gap favoring their solution over Vuteq's existing sales offering.

New Tasks

The purchase decision characterized as a **new task decision** occurs when the buyer is purchasing a product or service for the first time. As illustrated in Figure 3.5, new task purchase decisions are located at the opposite end of the continuum from the straight rebuy and typify situations in which buyers have no experience or knowledge on which to rely. Consequently, they undertake an extensive purchase decision and search for information designed to identify and compare alternative solutions. Reflecting the extensive nature of this type of purchase decision, multiple members of the buying team are usually involved. As a result, the salesperson will be working with several different individuals rather than a single buyer. Mitsubishi buyers and suppliers were presented with new task decisions when the new Mitsubishi four-wheel-drive sport utility vehicle was moving from design to production. Moving from their historical two-wheel-drive to four-wheel-drive power lines and transmissions presented a variety of new needs and problems.

Relevant to a new task purchasing decision, there is no in- or out-supplier. Further, the buyer is aware of the existing needs gap. With no prior experience in dealing with this particular need, buyers are often eager for information and expertise that will assist them in effectively resolving the perceived needs gap. Selling strategies for new task decisions should include collaborating with the buyer in a number of ways. First, the salesperson can provide expertise in fully developing and understanding the need. The salesperson's extensive experience and base of knowledge is also valuable to the buyer in terms of specifying and evaluating potential solutions. Finally, top salespeople will assist the buyer in making a purchase decision and provide extensive follow-up to ensure long-term satisfaction. By implementing this type of a consultative strategy, the salesperson establishes a relationship with the buyer and gains considerable competitive advantage.

Modified Rebuys

Modified rebuy decisions occupy a middle position on the continuum between straight rebuys and new tasks. In these cases, the buyer has experience in purchasing the product in the past but is interested in acquiring additional information regarding alternative products and/or suppliers. As there is more familiarity with the decision, there is less uncertainty and perceived risk than for new task decisions. The modified rebuy typically occurs as the result of changing conditions or needs. Perhaps the buyer wishes to consider new suppliers for current purchase needs or new products offered by existing suppliers. Continuing the example of buyer—seller experiences at Mitsubishi, the company's recent decision to reexamine their methods and sources for training and education corresponds to the characteristics of a modified rebuy decision. Since its beginning, Mitsubishi Motor Manufacturing of America has used a mix of company trainers, community colleges, and universities to provide education and training to employees. Desiring more coordination across its training programs, the company has requested proposals for the development and continued management of a corporate university from a variety of suppliers, including several current as well as new sources.

Often a buyer enters into a modified rebuy type of purchase decision to simply check the competitiveness of existing suppliers in terms of the product offering and pricing levels. Consequently, in-salespeople will emphasize how well their product has performed in resolving the needs gap. Out-salespeople will use strategies similar to those undertaken in the straight rebuy. These strategies are designed to alter the relative positions of the desired and actual states in a way that creates a perceived gap and influences buyers to rethink and reevaluate their current buying patterns and suppliers.

UNDERSTANDING COMMUNICATION STYLES

Verbal and nonverbal messages can also provide salespeople with important cues regarding buyers' personalities and communication styles. Experienced salespeople emphasize the importance of reading and responding to customer communication styles. Effectively sensing and interpreting customers' communication styles allows salespeople to adapt their own interaction behaviors in a way that facilitates buyer–seller communication and enhances relationship formation. Most sales training programs use a two-by-two matrix as a basis for categorizing **communication styles** into four primary types.[5] As illustrated by Figure 3.6, the four styles are based on two determinant dimensions: assertiveness and responsiveness.

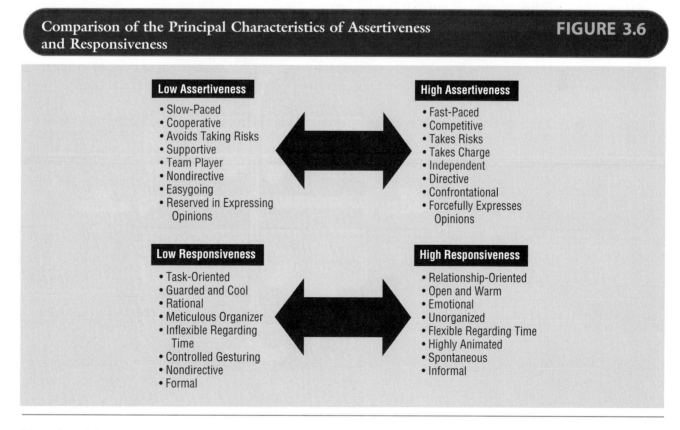

Comparison of the Principal Characteristics of Assertiveness and Responsiveness   **FIGURE 3.6**

Low Assertiveness
- Slow-Paced
- Cooperative
- Avoids Taking Risks
- Supportive
- Team Player
- Nondirective
- Easygoing
- Reserved in Expressing Opinions

High Assertiveness
- Fast-Paced
- Competitive
- Takes Risks
- Takes Charge
- Independent
- Directive
- Confrontational
- Forcefully Expresses Opinions

Low Responsiveness
- Task-Oriented
- Guarded and Cool
- Rational
- Meticulous Organizer
- Inflexible Regarding Time
- Controlled Gesturing
- Nondirective
- Formal

High Responsiveness
- Relationship-Oriented
- Open and Warm
- Emotional
- Unorganized
- Flexible Regarding Time
- Highly Animated
- Spontaneous
- Informal

Most sales training programs use a two-by-two matrix as a basis for categorizing communication styles into four primary types. The four styles are based on two dimensions: assertiveness and responsiveness.

Assertiveness—**Assertiveness** refers to the degree to which a person holds opinions about issues and attempts to dominate or control situations by directing the thoughts and actions of others. Highly-assertive individuals tend to be fast-paced, opinionated, and quick to speak out and take confrontational positions. Low-assertive individuals tend to exhibit a slower pace. They typically hold back, let others take charge, and are slow and deliberate in their communication and actions.

Responsiveness—**Responsiveness** points to the level of feelings and sociability an individual openly displays. Highly-responsive individuals are relationship-oriented and openly emotional. They readily express their feelings and tend to be personable, friendly, and informal. However, low-responsive individuals tend to be task-oriented and very controlled in their display of emotions. They tend to be impersonal in dealing with others, with an emphasis on formality and self-discipline.

The actual levels of assertiveness and responsiveness will vary from one individual to another on a continuum ranging from high to low. An individual may be located anywhere along the particular continuum, and where the individual is located determines the degree to which he or she possesses and demonstrates the particular behaviors associated with that dimension. The following figure illustrates the range of behaviors commonly associated with each dimension.

Overlaying the assertiveness and responsiveness dimensions produces a four-quadrant matrix as illustrated in Figure 3.7. The four quadrants characterize an individual as exhibiting one of four different communication styles on the basis of his or her demonstrated levels of assertiveness and responsiveness. *Amiables* are high on responsiveness but low on assertiveness. *Expressives* are defined as high on both responsiveness and assertiveness. *Drivers* are low on responsiveness but high on

---

FIGURE 3.7　　**Communication Styles Matrix**

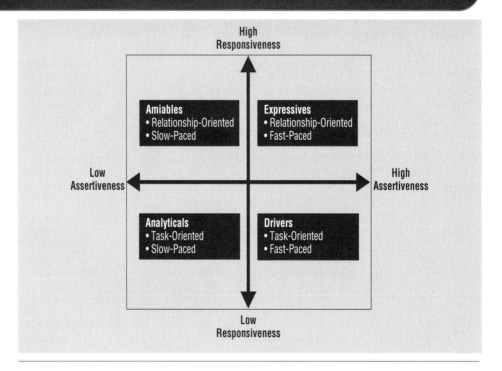

The four quadrants characterize an individual as one of four different communication styles on the basis of his or her demonstrated levels of assertiveness and responsiveness. A salesperson's skill in properly classifying customers can provide valuable cues regarding customer attitudes and behaviors.

assertiveness. *Analyticals* are characterized as being low on assertiveness as well as responsiveness. A salesperson's skill in properly classifying customers can provide valuable cues regarding customer attitudes and behaviors. In turn, these cues allow the salesperson to be more effective by adapting his or her communication and responses to better fit the customer's style.

Amiables—Developing and maintaining close personal relationships is important to **amiables**. Easygoing and cooperative, they are often characterized as friendly backslappers due to their preference for belonging to groups and their sincere interest in other people—their hobbies, interests, families, and mutual friends. With a natural propensity for talking and socializing, they have little or no desire to control others but rather prefer building consensus. Amiables are not risk takers and need to feel safe in making a decision. Somewhat undisciplined with regard to time, amiables appear to be slow and deliberate in their actions. They avoid conflict and tend to be more concerned with opinions—what others think—than with details and facts. When confronted or attacked, amiables tend to submit. In working with an amiable customer, salespeople should remember that their priority "must-have" is to be liked and their fundamental "want" is for attention.

Expressives—**Expressives** are animated and highly communicative. Although very competitive by nature, they also exhibit warm personalities and value building close relationships with others. In fact, they dislike being alone and readily seek out others. Expressives are extroverted and are highly uninhibited in their communication. When confronted or crossed, they will attack. Enthusiastic and stimulating, they seem to talk in terms of people rather than things and have a ready opinion on everything. Yet, they remain open-minded and changeable. Expressives are fast paced in their decision making and behavior and prefer the big picture rather than getting bogged down in details. As a result, they are very spontaneous, unconcerned with time schedules, and not especially organized in their daily lives. They are creative, comfortable operating on intuition, and demonstrate a willingness to take risks. The two keys for expressives that salespeople must keep in mind are the "must-have" of never being hurt emotionally and their underlying "want" is attention.

Drivers—Sometimes referred to as the director or dictator style, **drivers** are hard and detached from their relationships with others. Described as being cool, tough, and competitive in their relationships, drivers are independent and willing to run over others to get their preferred results. As they seek out and openly demonstrate power and control over people and situations, they are difficult to get close to and appear to treat people as things. Drivers are extremely formal, businesslike, and impatient, with a penchant for time and organization. They are highly opinionated, impatient, and quick to share those opinions with those around them. When attacked or confronted, drivers will dictate. Drivers exhibit a low tolerance for taking advice, tend to be risk takers, and favor making their own decisions. Although they are highly task-oriented, drivers prefer to ignore facts and figures and instead rely on their own gut feelings in making decisions—after all, they do know it all. When working with drivers, salespeople should remember that this style's "must-have" is winning and their fundamental "want" is results.

Analyticals—The descriptive name for this style is derived from their penchant for gathering and analyzing facts and details before making a decision. **Analyticals** are meticulous and disciplined in everything they do. Logical and very controlled, they are systematic problem solvers and thus very deliberate and slower in pace. In stressful situations and confrontations, analyticals tend to withdraw. Many times, they appear to be nit-picky about everything around them. They do not readily let their feelings hang out nor are they spontaneous in their behaviors. As a result, they are often seen as being cool and aloof. Analyticals shy away from personal relationships and avoid taking risks. Time and personal schedules are close to being a religious ritual for the analytical. The two fundamentals that salespeople must keep in mind when working with this style are the "must-have" of being right and the underlying "want" for analytical activities.

MASTERING COMMUNICATION STYLE FLEXING

In addition to sensing and interpreting the customer's communication style, sales-people must also be aware of his or her own personal style. Mismatched and possibly clashing styles can be dysfunctional and present significant barriers to communica-tion and relationship building. To minimize possible negative effects stemming from mismatched styles, salespeople can flex their own style to facilitate effective communication. For example, an expressive salesperson calling on an analytical buyer would find considerable differences in both pace and relationship/task-orientation that could hinder the selling process unless adjustments are made. Flex-ing his or her own style to better match that of the buyer enhances communication. In terms of our example, the salesperson would need to make adjustments by slow-ing down his or her natural pace, reining in the level of spontaneity and animation, and increasing task orientation by offering more detailed information and analysis.

Adapting to buyers by flexing his or her own communication style has been found to have a positive impact on salespeople's performance and the quality of buyer–seller relationships. Nevertheless, flexing should not be interpreted as meaning an exact match between a salesperson's style and that of a customer. Not only is it not required, exact matches could even be detrimental. For example, a buyer and seller with matching expressive styles could easily discover that the entire sales call regressed to little more than a personal discussion with nothing of substance being accomplished. However, a buyer and seller matched as drivers could find it difficult, if not impossible, to reach a decision that was mutually ben-eficial. Rather than matching the buyer's style, flexing infers that the salesperson should adjust to the needs and preferences of the buyer to maximize effectiveness. Growmark, an international agricultural product and service organization, teaches their salespeople to flex throughout their interaction with a buyer by studying dif-ferent behaviors a salesperson might demonstrate with each style of buyer (see Exhibit 3.7).[6]

Study and compare the flexing behaviors that Growmark recommends that their salespeople demonstrate while working with each different buyer communication style. Note the differences in recommended salesperson behavior and rationalize them in terms of the specific characteristics of each buyer's style. Overlaying and integrating these two sets of information will enhance the understanding of how to flex to different buyers and why that form of flexing is recommended.

It is not always possible to gain much information about a buyer's communication style, especially if the buyer is new. If this is the case, it may be more appropriate to assume that the buyer is an analytical-driver and prepare for this style. If the buyer proves to be close to an amiable-expressive, then the salesperson can easily adapt. It is much more difficult to prepare for the amiable-expressive and then switch to an analytical-driver style.

MULTIPLE BUYING INFLUENCES

A single individual typically makes routine purchase decisions such as straight rebuys and simpler modified rebuys. However, the more complex modified rebuy and new task purchase decisions often involve the joint decisions of multiple participants within a buying center or team. **Buying teams** (also referred to as **buying centers**) incorporate the expertise and multiple buying influences of people from different departments throughout the organization. As the object of the purchase decision changes, the makeup of the buying team may also change to maximize the relevant expertise of team members. The organization's size, as well as the nature and volume of the products being purchased, will influence the actual number and makeup of buying teams. The different members of a buying team will often have varied goals reflecting their individual needs and those of their different departments.

EXHIBIT 3.7   Recommended Flexing Behaviors for Different Communication Styles

Selling Task or Objective	Selling to the Analytical	Selling to the Driver	Selling to the Amiable	Selling to the Expressive
Setting an Appointment	• Send a business letter specifying details about yourself and the company. • Follow the letter with a phone call to confirm expectations and set an appointment.	• Drivers may not take time to read your letter. • Contact them by phone first and follow up with a letter. • Keep call businesslike and to the point by identifying yourself, explain the business problem addressed by your product, and ask for an appointment. • Letter should simply confirm time and date of appointment and include materials the Driver might review prior to the meeting.	• Send a letter with a personal touch stating who you are and why you are contacting the Amiable. • Letter should include your experience working with clients the prospect knows by reputation or experience, your reliability and follow-through, and the quality of your product/service. • Follow letter with a personal phone call. • Take time to be friendly, open, sincere, and to establish trust in the relationship.	• Generally, a phone call is most appropriate. • Make your call open and friendly, stressing quick benefits, personal service, your experience, and your company's experience with its products and services. • If you send a letter, make it short and personal, stressing who you are, how you know of the Expressive, and what you are interested in talking about.
Opening the Call	• Provide background information about you and the company. • Approach in an advisory capacity acknowledging buyer's expertise. • Show evidence that you have done your homework on buyer's situation. • Offer evidence of providing previous solutions. • Be conscious of how you are using buyer's time.	• Listen and focus on Driver's ideas and objectives. • Provide knowledge and insight relevant to Driver's specific business problems. • Be personable but reserved and relatively formal. • Present factual evidence that establishes the business problem and resulting outcome. • Maintain a quick pace. Drivers value punctuality and efficient use of time.	• Engage in informal conversation before getting down to business. • Demonstrate that you are personally interested in the Amiable's work and personal goals. • You will have to earn the right to learn more personally about the Amiable. • Demonstrate your product/service knowledge by referencing a common acquaintance with whom you've done business.	• Quickly describe the purpose of your call and establish credibility—you must earn the right to develop a business relationship with the Expressive. • Share stories about people you both know. • Share information the Expressive would perceive as exclusive. • Share your feelings and enthusiasm for the Expressive's ideas and goals. • Once the Expressive has confidence in your competence, take time to develop an open and trusting personal relationship.
Gathering Information	• Ask specific, fact-finding questions in a systematic manner. • Establish comprehensive exchange of information. • Encourage buyer to discuss ideas while focusing on factual information. • Be thorough and unhurried—listen. • Explain that you are in alignment with his or her thinking and can support his or her objectives.	• Ask, don't tell. Ask fact-finding questions leading to what the Driver values and rewards. • Make line of questioning consistent with your call objective. • Follow up on requests for information immediately. • Support the buyer's beliefs; indicate how you can positively affect goals. • Clarify the Driver's expectations.	• Create a cooperative atmosphere with an open exchange of information and feelings. • Amiables tend to understate their objectives, so you may need to probe for details and specifics about his or her goals. • Listen responsively. Give ample amounts of verbal and nonverbal feedback. • Verify whether there are unresolved budget or cost justification issues.	• Begin by finding out the Expressive's perception of the situation and vision of the ideal outcome. • Identify other people who should contribute to analysis and planning. • Listen, then respond with plenty of verbal and nonverbal feedback that supports the Expressive's beliefs. • Question carefully the critical data you'll need. • Keep the discussion focused and moving toward a result.

(continued)

EXHIBIT 3.7 Recommended Flexing Behaviors for Different Communication Styles—*Continued*

Selling Task or Objective	Selling to the Analytical	Selling to the Driver	Selling to the Amiable	Selling to the Expressive
Gathering Information (*Continued*)			• Find out who else will contribute to the buying decision. • Summarize what you believe to be the Amiable's key ideas and feelings.	• If the Expressive shows limited interest in specifics, summarize what has been discussed and begin to suggest ways to move the vision toward reality.
Activating the Need to Change	• Use their records to supply information. • Use a logical approach. • Illustrate with dollars and cents.	• Be fast paced and businesslike. Be sure of your figures. Show the Driver the bottom line. Appeal to rational thinking and avoid appeal to emotions.	• Address emotional needs in line with safety and comfort needs. • Use the Amiable's own figures rather than your own. • Do not push!	• Support the Expressive's ideas and goals. • Work toward his/her esteem needs. • Supply data from people seen as leaders to the Expressive.
Engaging in the Sales Conversation	• Provide a detailed written proposal as part of presentation. • Include strongest cost-benefit justifications. • Support with third-party data. • Be reserved and decisive but not aggressive. • Limit emotional or testimonial appeals. • Recommend specific course of action. • Give buyer chance to review all documents related to purchase and delivery.	• Present your recommendation so that the Driver can compare alternative solutions and his or her probable outcomes. • Provide documented options. • Offer the best quality given the cost limitations. • Be specific and factual without overwhelming the Driver with details. • Appeal to esteem and independence needs. • Reinforce the Driver's preference for acting in a forthright manner. • Summarize content quickly, then let Driver choose a course of action.	• Define clearly in writing and make sure the Amiable understands: • What you can do to support the Amiable's personal goals; • What you will contribute and what the Amiable needs to contribute; and • The support resources you intend to commit to the project. • Provide a clear solution to the Amiable's problem with maximum assurances that this is the best solution and that there is no need to consider others. • Ask the Amiable to involve other decision makers. • Satisfy needs by showing how your solution is best now and will be best in the future and support it with references and third-party evidence. • Use testimonials from perceived experts and others close to the Amiable.	• Provide specific solutions to the Expressive's ideas—in writing. • Build confidence that you have the necessary facts, but do not overwhelm the Expressive with details. • Do not rush the discussion. Spend time developing ways to implement ideas. • Appeal to personal esteem needs. • Try to get commitments to action in writing.
Earning Commitment	• Ask for commitment in a low-key but direct manner. • Expect to negotiate changes. • Pay special attention to pricing issues. • Work for commitment now to avoid Analytical's tendency to delay decisions.	• Ask for the order directly. • Put your offer in clear factual terms. • Offer options and alternatives. • Be prepared to negotiate changes and concessions. • Drivers sometimes attach conditions to a sale. • Offer the Driver time to consider the options.	• Ask for the order indirectly—do not push. • Emphasize the guarantees that offer protection to the Amiable. • Do not corner the Amiables, they want a way out if things go wrong. • Guard against "buyer's remorse"—get a commitment even if you have to base it on a contingency.	• When you have enough information to understand the need and have tested the appropriateness of the recommendation, assume the sale and ask for the order in a casual and informal way. • When the opportunity presents itself, offer incentives to encourage the purchase.

Selling Task or Objective	Selling to the Analytical	Selling to the Driver	Selling to the Amiable	Selling to the Expressive

Earning Commitment (*continued*)	• Cite data supporting company's service records.
	• Respond to objections by emphasizing the Analytical's buying principles and objectivity.
		• Anticipate objections in advance and come prepared with facts.
		• Respond to objections based on Driver's values and priorities.
			• Stress your personal involvement after the sale.
			• Encourage the Amiable to involve others in the final purchase decision.
			• Welcome objections and be patient and thorough in responding to them.
			• When responding to objections:
			  • Describe financial justification;
			  • Refer to experts or others the Amiable respects; and
			  • Keep in mind how the Amiable feels about and will be affected by the purchase decision.
				• Do not confuse the issue by presenting too many options or choices.
				• Get a definite commitment. Be sure the Expressive understands the decision to purchase.
				• Save the details until after you have a firm buying decision. The Expressive believes it is the salesperson's job to handle details.
				• In handling objections:
				  • Describe what others have done to get over that hurdle;
				  • Respond to the Expressive's enthusiasm for his/her goals;
				  • Deal with how the recommendation meets with this buyer's options; and
				  • Restate benefits that focus on the satisfaction a buying decision will bring.

Providing Follow-Up	• Provide a detailed implementation plan.
	• Maintain regular contact.
	• Check to confirm satisfactory and on-schedule delivery.
		• Set up communication process with the Driver that encourages quick exchange of information about checkpoints and milestones.
		• Make sure you have a contingency plan to responsively implement corrections and incorporate changes.
		• Make sure there are no surprises.
			• Immediately after the purchase decision is made, make a follow-up appointment.
			• Initiate and maintain frequent contacts providing services such as:
			  • Periodic progress reports on installation;
			  • Arrangements for service and training;
			  • Introduction of new products and services; and
			  • Listening carefully to concerns, even those that seem trivial.
				• As soon as the order is signed, reaffirm the schedule for delivery and your personal relationship with the buyer, and introduce the implementation person or team.
				• A social situation such as a lunch can be a very effective opportunity for following up on business with this buyer.
				• Work toward becoming an ongoing ... ...
				• In c... ...
				  an... ...
				  o...

Buying team members are described in terms of their roles and responsibilities within the team.[7]

- *Initiators*—**Initiators** are individuals within the organization who identify a need or perhaps realize that the acquisition of a product might solve a need or problem.
- *Influencers*—Individuals who guide the decision process by making recommendations and expressing preferences are referred to as **influencers**. These are often technical or engineering personnel.
- *Users*—**Users** are the individuals within the organization who will actually use the product being purchased. They evaluate a product on the basis of how it will affect their own job performance. Users often serve as initiators and influencers.
- *Deciders*—The ultimate responsibility for determining which product or service will be purchased rests with the role of **deciders**. Although buyers may also be deciders, it is not unusual for different people to fill these roles.
- *Purchasers*—**Purchasers** have the responsibility for negotiating final terms of purchase with suppliers and executing the actual purchase or acquisition.
- *Gatekeepers*—Members who are in the position to control the flow of information to and between vendors and other buying center members are referred to as **gatekeepers**.

Although each of these influencer types will not necessarily be present on all buying teams, the use of buying teams incorporating some or all of these multiple influences has increased in recent years. One example of multiple buying influences is offered in the recent experience of an Executive Jet International salesperson selling a Gulfstream V corporate jet to a Chicago-based pharmaceutical company. Stretching over a period of six months, the salesperson worked with a variety of individuals serving different roles within the buying organization:

- *Initiator:* The initiator of the purchase process was the chief operating officer of the corporation who found that the recent corporate expansions had outgrown the effective service range of the organization's existing aircraft. Beyond pointing out the need and thus initiating the search, this individual would also be highly involved in the final choice based on her personal experiences and perceived needs of the company.
- *Influencers:* Two different employee groups acted as the primary influencers. First, were the corporate pilots who contributed a readily available and extensive background of knowledge and experience with a variety of aircraft types. Also playing a key influencer role were members from the capital budgeting group in the finance department. Although concerned with documented performance capabilities, they also provided inputs and assessments of the different alternatives using their capital investment models.
- *Users:* The users provided some of the most dynamic inputs, as they were anxious to make the transition to a higher performance aircraft to enhance their own efficiency and performance in working at marketing/sales offices and plants that now stretched over the continents of North and South America. Primary players in this group included the vice presidents for marketing and for production/operations in addition to the corporate pilots who would be flying the plane.
- *Deciders:* Based on the contribution and inputs of each member of the buying team, the ultimate decision would be made by the chief executive officer. Primarily traveling by commercial carriers, her role as decider was based more on her position within the firm rather than her use of the chosen alternative. As the organization's highest operating officer, she was in a position to move freely among all members of the buying team and make the decision on overall merits rather than personal feelings or desires.
- *Purchaser:* Responsibility for making the actual purchase, negotiating the final terms, and completing all the required paperwork followed the typical lines of authority and was the responsibility of the corporate purchasing department with the director of purchasing actually assuming the immediate contact role.

The purchasing office typically handles purchasing contracts and is staffed to draw up, complete, and file the related registrations and legal documents.

- *Gatekeepers.* This purchase decision actually involved two different gatekeepers within the customer organization: the executive assistant to the chief operating officer and an assistant purchasing officer. The positioning of these gatekeepers facilitated the salesperson's exchange of information and ability to keep in contact with the various members of the buying team. The COO's executive assistant moved easily among the various executives influencing the decision and was able to make appointments with the right people at the right times. However, the assistant purchasing officer was directly involved with the coordination of each member and bringing their various inputs into one summary document for the CEO. The salesperson's positive dealings and good relationships with each of the gatekeepers played a significant role in Executive Jet getting the sale.

A classic and all-too-common mistake among salespeople is to make repetitive calls on a purchasing manager over a period of several months only to discover that a buying team actually exists and that the ultimate decision will be made by someone other than the purchasing manager. Salespeople must gather information to discover who is in the buying team, their individual roles, and which members are the most influential. This information might be collected from account history files, people inside the salesperson's organization who are familiar with the account sources within the client organization, and even other salespeople. A salesperson should work with all members of the buying team and be careful to properly address their varied needs and objectives. Nevertheless, circumstances sometimes prevent a salesperson from working with all members of the team, and it is important that they reach those that are most influential.

CURRENT DEVELOPMENTS IN PURCHASING

Today's business organizations are undergoing profound change in response to ever-increasing competition and rapid changes in the business environment. The world-wide spread of technology has resulted in intense and increasingly global competition that is highly dynamic in nature. Accelerating rates of change have fragmented what were once mass markets into more micro and niche markets composed of more knowledgeable and demanding customers with ever-increasing expectations. In response, traditional purchasing practices are also rapidly changing.

Increasing Use of Information Technology

Buyers and sellers alike are increasingly using technology to enhance the effectiveness and efficiency of the purchasing process. Business-to-business e-commerce is growing at a rate exceeding 33 percent a year. Although EDI over private networks has been in use for some time, nearly all the current growth has been in Internet-based transactions.

Information technology electronically links buyers and sellers for direct and immediate communication and transmission of information and data. Transactional exchanges such as straight rebuy decisions can now be automated with Internet- and World Wide Web-enabled programs tracking sales at the point of purchase and capturing the data for real-time inventory control and order placing. By cutting order and shipping times, overall cycle times are reduced, mistakes minimized, and working capital invested in inventories is made available for more productive applications. Further, the automation of these routine transactions allows buyers and salespeople to devote more time to new tasks, complex sales, and post-sale service and relationship-building activities. In addition to facilitating exchange transactions, applications integrating the Internet are also being used to distribute product and company information along with training courses and materials. Several companies have begun publishing their product catalogs online as a replacement for the

AN ETHICAL DILEMMA

Ashley West is a key account manager for Custom Transportation, a multimodal company specializing in providing inbound and outbound transportation needs of Fortune 1000 companies worldwide. Over the years, West has developed strong relationships with members of the buying teams at each of the 13 companies that comprise her account list. Interlake Heavy Industries, a worldwide producer of large metal castings and forgings, has become west's largest account. In fact, Interlake alone accounts for just over 28 percent of her total annual sales volume. Last week, west took Interlake's director of purchasing—an avid golfer—out for a day of golf at one of Chicago's best private golf clubs. On the tenth tee, West hit her best drive of the day and the Interlake buyer began admiring West's driver. It was a brand new club—

(the technologically advanced TaylorMade Model r7 460) which she had paid $499 for only a few days earlier. At the next tee box, West handed the club to the buyer and insisted that he try it out. He did and drilled a beautiful shot straight down the fairway—and the ball went a good 40 yards longer than any previous drive. The buyer handed the driver back to West with many positive exclamations including the comment that he could not wait to get one for himself. At that point, West tossed the driver back to the buyer saying, ". . . it's in your bag. Just remember to think of me every time you use it."

What do you think about West's latest efforts at building relationships with the Interlake buyer? How would you have handled this situation in you were in West's place?

reams of product brochures salespeople have traditionally had to carry with them. The online catalogs can be easily updated without the expense of obsolete brochures and can be selectively downloaded by salespeople to create customized presentations and proposals.

Relationship Emphasis on Cooperation and Collaboration

More than ever before, the business decisions made by one company directly affect decisions in other companies. Business in today's fast-paced and dynamic marketplace demands continuous and increased levels of interactivity between salespeople and buyers representing the customer organizations. This trend is further underscored by more and more buying organizations emphasizing long-term relationships with fewer suppliers so that they can forge stronger bonds and develop more efficient purchasing processes. As illustrated in "An Ethical Dilemma," this increasing level of buyer–seller interaction and interdependence can create challenging ethical decisions for the salesperson.

Rather than competing to win benefits at the expense of one another, leading organizations are discovering that it is possible for all parties to reduce their risk and increase the level of benefits each receives by sharing information and coordinating activities, resources, and capabilities.[8] These longer-term buyer–seller relationships are based on the mutual benefits received by and the interdependence between all parties in this value network. In addition to being keenly aware of changing customer needs, collaborative relationships require salespeople to work closely with buyers to foster honest and open two-way communication and develop the mutual understanding required to create the desired solutions. Further, salespeople must consistently demonstrate that they are dependable and acting in the buyer's best interests.

Supply Chain Management

Having realized that their success or failure is inextricably linked to other firms in the value network, many organizations are implementing **supply chain management** across an extended network of suppliers and customers. Beyond a buyer–seller

PROFESSIONAL SELLING IN THE 21ST CENTURY

Enhancing Value for the Customer through Mobile Technology

Consistent, effective communication is critical for managing the buyer–seller relationships that deliver successful sales outcomes. Yet, with salespeople increasingly on the road, effective communication becomes a challenge that one needs to address. Harprit Singh, CEO of Intellicomm, a communications services organization, discusses the variety of ways a salesperson can stay productive and work with customers while on the road.

From a communications standpoint, having broadband access is probably number one. Secondly, you want to address the need for a cell phone so that you have a good communication channel. Then, when you have Internet access, you essentially have phone functionality via VoIP (Voice-over-Internet Protocol). You can also use faxes, e-mail, and instant messaging—all powerful tools for keeping in touch. These combinations of communication technologies also enable the use of additional channels such as Web conferencing and teleconferencing, which can help make your communication tasks more efficient. In today's mobile world, with the realities of increased communication requirements, applications that offer unified voice, fax, and data messaging are becoming essential tools for working successfully and staying in touch.

relationship, supply chain management emphasizes the strategic coordination and integration of purchasing with other functions within the buying organization as well as external organizations including customers, customers' customers, suppliers, and suppliers' suppliers. Salespeople must focus on coordinating their efforts with all parties in the network—end users and suppliers alike—and effectively work to add value for all members of the network. As described in "Professional Selling in the 21st Century: Enhancing Value for the Customer through Mobile Technology,"[9] it is clear that advances in mobile communications are making it possible for salespeople to maintain more effective customer communication even while on the road traveling between accounts.

Increased Outsourcing

Broader business involvement and expanded integration between organizations is a natural evolution as buyers and suppliers become increasingly confident of the other's performance capabilities and commitment to the relationship. These expanded agreements often involve **outsourcing** to a supplier certain activities that were previously performed by the buying organization. These activities are necessary for the day-to-day functioning of the buying organization but are not within the organization's core or distinct competencies. Outsourcing these activities allows the organization to focus on what it does best. However, these activities are typically among those in which the supplying organization specializes or even excels. As a result of the outsourcing agreement, the relationship gains strength and is further extended in such a way that all parties benefit over the long term. Outsourcing agreements place increased emphasis on the role of the salesperson to provide continuing follow-up activities to ensure customer satisfaction and nurture the buyer–seller relationship. Changes in customer needs must be continually monitored and factored into the supplier's market offerings and outsourcing activities.

Target Pricing

Using information gathered from researching the marketplace, buyers establish a **target price** for their final products. For example, buyers determine the selling price for a new printing press should be $320,000. Next, they divide the press into its subsystems and parts to estimate what each part is worth in relation to the overall price. Using such a system, buyers might conclude that the maximum price they could pay for a lead roller platen would be $125 and then use this information when working with potential suppliers. In working with targeted pricing requirements, salespeople find they have two fundamental options. They can meet the required cost level, which often entails cutting their prices, or they can work with the buyer to better understand and possibly influence minimum performance specifications. Certain restrictive specifications might be relaxed as a trade-off for lower pricing. For example, a salesperson might negotiate longer lead times, fewer or less complex design features, or less technical support in exchange for lower prices. The latter option requires salespeople to have a high level of knowledge regarding their products, organizational capabilities, and customer applications and needs. Just as important is the ability to create feasible options and effectively communicate them to the buyer.

Increased Importance of Knowledge and Creativity

The increased interdependence between buyer and seller organizations hinges on the salesperson's capabilities to serve as a problem solver in a dynamic and fast-changing business environment. Buyers depend on the salesperson to provide unique and value-added solutions to their changing problems and needs. To shape such innovative solutions, salespeople must have broad-based and comprehensive knowledge readily available and the ability to use that knowledge in creative ways. This includes knowledge of one's own products and capabilities, as well as the products and capabilities of competitors. More important, the salesperson must possess a thorough understanding of product applications and the needs of the customer to work with the buyer in generating innovative solutions.

SUMMARY

1. **Categorize primary types of buyers.** Buyers are classified according to their unique buying situations that influence their needs, motivations, and buying behavior. The most common categorization splits buyers into either consumer markets or business markets. Consumers purchase goods and services for their own use or consumption whereas members of the business market acquire goods and services to use them as inputs into manufacturing, for use in the course of doing business, or for resale. Business markets are further divided into firms, institutions, and governments.

2. **Discuss the distinguishing characteristics of business markets.** Business markets have numerous characteristics that distinguish them from consumer markets. Among the more common characteristics are consolidation, which has resulted in buyers being fewer in number but larger in size; demand that is derived from the sale of consumer goods; more volatile demand levels; professional buyers; multiple buying influences from a team of buyers; and increased interdependence and relationships between buyers and sellers.

3. **List the different steps in the business-to-business buying process.** There are eight sequential and interrelated phases that make up the business buyers' decision process. This process begins with (1) recognition of the problem or need, (2) determination of the characteristics of the item and the quantity needed, (3) description of the characteristics of the item and quantity needed, (4) search for and qualification of potential sources, (5) acquisition and analysis of proposals, (6) evaluation of proposals and selection of suppliers, (7) selection of an order routine, and (8) performance feedback and evaluation.

4. **Discuss the different types of buyer needs**. Organizing what might appear to be an endless and confusing mixture of different needs and problems into their common types helps salespeople better understand the nature of the buyer's needs along with their interrelationships. In turn, salespeople are better able to generate and demonstrate value-added solutions that address the different needs. The five general types of buyer needs are described as follows:

   Situational Needs—Needs that are related to, or possibly the result of, the buyer's specific environment, time, and place.

   Functional Needs—The need for a specific core task or function to be performed—the need for a sales offering to do what it is supposed to do.

   Social Needs—The need for acceptance from and association with others—a desire to belong to some reference group.

   Psychological Needs—The desire for feelings of assurance and risk reduction, as well as positive emotions and feelings such as success, joy, excitement, and stimulation.

   Knowledge Needs—The desire for personal development and need for information and knowledge to increase thought and understanding as to how and why things happen.

5. **Describe how buyers evaluate suppliers and alternative sales offerings by using the multiattribute model of evaluation**. Purchase decisions are based on the buyer's comparative evaluation of how well they perceive a supplier or product compares on the basis of specific characteristics that the buyer judges as being important. Using the multiattribute model, buyers establish the attributes they perceive as important and evaluate the degree to which each of the specified attributes is present (or how well each performs) in a proposed solution. Each evaluation is then multiplied by the attribute's relative level of importance to calculate a weighted average for each attribute. These weighted averages are then totaled to derive an overall score for each supplier or product being compared. The product or supplier having the highest score is favored for purchase.

6. **Explain the two-factor model that buyers use to evaluate the performance of sales offerings and develop satisfaction**. The two-factor model is a special type of multiattribute model in which further analysis of the multiple characteristics results in two primary groupings of factors: functional attributes and psychological attributes. Functional attributes are the more tangible characteristics of a market offering whereas the psychological attributes are primarily composed of the interpersonal behaviors and activities between the buyer and seller. The psychological attributes have been repeatedly found to have higher levels of influence than functional attributes on customer satisfaction and repeat purchase.

7. **Explain the different types of purchasing decisions**. A buyer's level of experience relevant to a given purchasing situation is a primary determinant of the time and resources that the buyer will allocate to a purchasing decision and can be used to categorize buyer behavior into three types of purchasing decisions: straight rebuys, modified rebuys, and new tasks.

   Straight Rebuy. Comparable with a routine repurchase in which nothing has changed, the straight rebuy is often the result of past experience and satisfaction with buyers purchasing the same products from the same sources. Needs have been predetermined with specifications already established. Buyers allocate little, if any, time or resources to this form of purchase decision, and the primary emphasis is on continued satisfactory performance.

   Modified Rebuy. Modified rebuys occupy the middle ground between straight rebuys and new tasks. The buyer has some level of experience with the product but is interested in acquiring additional information regarding alternative products and/or suppliers. The modified rebuy typically occurs as the result of changing conditions or needs. Perhaps the buyer wishes to consider new suppliers for current purchase needs or new products offered by existing suppliers.

New Task. New task decisions occur when a buyer is purchasing a product or service for the first time. With no experience or knowledge on which to rely, buyers undertake an extensive purchase decision and search for information designed to identify and compare alternative solutions. Reflecting the extensive nature of this type of purchase decision, multiple members of the buying center or group are usually involved. As a result, the salesperson often works with several different individuals rather than a single buyer.

8. **Describe the four communication styles and how salespeople must adapt and flex their own styles to maximize communication**. Based on high and low levels of two personal traits, assertiveness and responsiveness, communication styles can be categorized into four primary types:

   - Amiables are high on responsiveness and low on assertiveness.
   - Expressives are defined as high on both responsiveness and assertiveness.
   - Drivers are low on responsiveness but high on assertiveness.
   - Analyticals are characterized as low on assertiveness as well as responsiveness.

   Mismatched styles between a seller and a buyer can be dysfunctional in terms of effective collaboration and present significant barriers for information exchange and relationship building. Differences in styles manifest themselves in the form of differences in preferred priorities (relationships versus task orientation) and favored pace (fast versus slow) of information exchange, socialization, and decision making. To minimize potential communication difficulties stemming from mismatched styles, salespeople should flex their personal styles to better fit the preferred priorities and pace of the buyer.

9. **Explain the concept of buying teams and specify the different member roles**. In the more complex modified rebuy and new task purchasing situations, purchase decisions typically involve the joint decisions of multiple participants working together as a buying team. Team members bring the expertise and knowledge from different functional departments within the buying organization. Team members may also change as the purchase decision changes. Team members are described by their roles within the team: initiators, influencers, users, deciders, purchasers, and gatekeepers.

UNDERSTANDING PROFESSIONAL SELLING TERMS

consumer markets	knowledge needs
business markets	requests for proposals (RFP)
derived demand	multiattribute model
acceleration principle	competitive depositioning
business buyers' purchase process	two-factor model of evaluation
needs	functional attributes
desired states	must-have attributes
actual states	psychological attributes
needs gap	delighter attributes
situational needs	straight rebuy decisions
functional needs	new task decisions
social needs	modified rebuy decisions
psychological needs	communication styles

assertiveness
responsiveness
amiables
expressives
drivers
analyticals
buying teams
buying centers
initiators

influencers
users
deciders
purchasers
gatekeepers
supply chain management
outsourcing
target price

DEVELOPING PROFESSIONAL SELLING KNOWLEDGE

1. How might the following characteristic of business-to-business markets affect the relational selling activities of salespeople:
   - Larger, but fewer, buyers?
   - Derived demand?
   - Higher levels of demand fluctuation?

2. How do the three different types of purchasing decisions (straight rebuy, modified rebuy, new task) influence the time and effort a buyer might allocate to the different steps of the purchase decision process?

3. List and compare the probable functional, situational, psychological, social, and knowledge needs of (a) a large financial investment office and (b) a college student, who are both looking to purchase a new computer printer.

4. How might a salesperson work with and assist a business buyer in each step of the buying process:
   - Recognition of the problem or need
   - Determination of the characteristics of the item and the quantity needed
   - Description of the characteristics of the item and the quantity needed
   - Search for and qualification of potential sources
   - Acquisition and analysis of proposals
   - Evaluation of proposals and selection of suppliers
   - Selection of an order routine
   - Performance feedback and evaluation

5. Explain the role of functional attributes and psychological attributes in the post-purchase determination of customer satisfaction.

6. How might salespeople use their knowledge of the multiattribute evaluation model to plan and deliver their sales presentation to a buyer?

7. What are the implications for a salesperson if, when making a sales call, they discover that there is no needs gap present? Illustrate your answer with an example.

8. Why has knowledge and the capability to creatively apply that knowledge in creating unique solutions become so important for today's salesperson in the business-to-business marketplace?

9. Explain the concept of communication styles and how a salesperson might flex his or her own style to better match the style of a buyer. How would the salesperson's behaviors and activities differ as he/she advances through the different stages of the selling process? Illustrate your answer with examples.

10. What are the implications of buying teams for a salesperson selling complex production equipment to a manufacturer firm? Develop an example to further explain and illustrate your answer.

BUILDING PROFESSIONAL SELLING SKILLS

1. Respond to each of the following buying situations by describing what you would do as (a) an in-salesperson and (b) an out-salesperson.

   - *Straight Rebuy.* This is a buying situation in which the customer is basically reordering an item already in use. Little or nothing has changed in terms of product, price, delivery, the available sources of supply, or any other aspect. This is a low-risk situation involving little cognitive effort and requiring little information. The purchasing department or a clerical person is most often the key decision maker and buyer.
     (a) What do you need to do as an in-salesperson to keep this business? Explain: _____
     _____
     _____
     _____
     _____

     (b) What do you need to do as an out-salesperson to get your foot in the door and persuade this company to buy from you? Explain: _____
     _____
     _____
     _____
     _____

   - *Modified Rebuy.* A buying situation in which the customer is already purchasing the item but some key aspect has changed. For example, there may be a proposed price change, a new competitive source of supply, a problem with delivery, a change in product specifications, or a newly available product or service. These are moderate-risk situations requiring greater effort and necessitating better information and information sources.
     (a) What do you need to do as an in-salesperson to keep this business? Explain: _____
     _____
     _____
     _____
     _____

     (b) What do you need to do as an out-salesperson to get your foot in the door and persuade this company to buy from you? Explain: _____
     _____
     _____
     _____
     _____

2. You are a salesperson for Accu-Press Corporation, a regional manufacturer of metal stamping tools used for the shaping (stamping) of small metal component parts. Accu-Press has just introduced a new line of tools featuring several breakthrough design features. The new equipment is faster and easier to use. Tests indicate that it can increase production by 15 percent over conventional tools while simultaneously reducing the rate of defective parts. You are calling on Federal Metal Stampings, a major supplier to the automotive industry, with the objective of selling them the new line of tools. Federal purchases their tools from two of your competitors, and you have been calling on the buyer at Federal for the past six months. In the past, the buyer has seen no need to switch sources and has ended each call by telling you that they are satisfied with their current suppliers.

Describe how you might use the advanced capabilities of your new tool line to assist the buyer at Federal Metal Stampings to realize a needs gap and thus create an opportunity to sell them the new product.

_____

_____

_____

_____

_____

Situation: Read Item 2.

Characters: Yourself, salesperson for Accu-Press Corporation; the buyer, director of purchasing for Federal Metal Stampings

Scene: _Location_—The office of the director of purchasing at Federal Metal Stampings.

ROLE PLAY

Action—As described, this is the most recent of several sales calls you have made to Federal Metal Stampings. Your objective for this sales call is to utilize the potential increased productivity your new line of tools offers the buyer in order to create a needs gap and thereby create an opportunity to sell them your new products.

Role play how you might create a needs gap for this buyer. Begin with the usual greeting and small talk that might typify a repeat sales call. Proceed to the point where you demonstrate the enhanced production capacity of your new tool line in a manner that will alter the buyer's desired state and create a needs gap that you might address.

Upon completion of the role play, address the following questions:

(a) How do the buyer's perceived actual and desired states of being impact and activate their recognition of a need?

(b) Other than the method role played in the assignment, in what other ways might the salesperson for Accu-Press influence the buyer's recognition of a needs gap?

3. Put yourself in the role of salesperson for National Computer Corporation. You are currently working to sell the College of Business at your university a large number of upgraded personal computers. These computers will be placed in staff and faculty offices for use with a variety of networking, word processing, spreadsheet, and statistical analysis applications. The committee responsible for the purchase decision includes two faculty members and the director of purchasing for the university. Based on your work with these members of the buying team, you have compiled the following list of buyers' expectations of the salesperson and supplier organization:

- Coordinate all aspects of the product/service mix to provide a total package.
- Provide counseling to the customer based on in-depth knowledge of the product, the market, and the customer's needs.
- Engage in problem solving with a high degree of proficiency so as to ensure satisfactory customer service over extended time periods.
- Demonstrate high ethical standards and be honest in all communication.
- Advocate the customer's best interests within the selling organization.
- Be imaginative in meeting the buyers' needs.
- Be well prepared for sales calls.
- Demonstrate a high level of dependability.

From the perspective of this buying scenario:

(a) Explain what each of these buyer expectations mean.

(b) Discuss the implications of each expectation and how it might influence your behavior.

(c) Give an example of how a salesperson might fulfill each buyer expectation using the list below.

1. Coordinate all aspects of the product/service mix to provide a total package.

_____
_____
_____
_____
_____

2. Provide counseling to the customer based on in-depth knowledge of the product, the market, and the customer's needs.

_____
_____
_____
_____
_____

3. Engage in problem solving with a high degree of proficiency so as to ensure satisfactory customer service over extended time periods.

_____
_____
_____
_____
_____

4. Demonstrate high ethical standards and be honest in all communication.

_____
_____
_____
_____
_____

5. Advocate the customer's best interests within the selling organization.

_____
_____
_____
_____
_____

6. Be imaginative in meeting the buyer's needs.

_____
_____
_____
_____
_____

7. Be well prepared for sales calls.

_____
_____
_____
_____
_____

8. Demonstrate a high level of dependability.

_____
_____
_____
_____

4. Use the following Communication Styles Survey[10] to assess your communication style. First, complete the Assertiveness Scale and the Responsiveness Scale by circling the number that best represents your self-evaluation regarding each of the paired characteristics. Give your candid reaction—there is no right or wrong answer. After completing each set, complete the scoring as instructed and plot your scores on the grid chart.

Assertiveness Scale

I perceive myself as being:

Cooperative				Competitive
1	2	3	4	5

Submissive				Authoritarian
1	2	3	4	5

Accommodating				Domineering
1	2	3	4	5

Hesitant				Decisive
1	2	3	4	5

Reserved				Outgoing
1	2	3	4	5

Compromising				Insistent
1	2	3	4	5

Cautious				Risk-Taking
1	2	3	4	5

Patient				Hurried
1	2	3	4	5

Complacent				Influential
1	2	3	4	5

Quiet				Talkative
1	2	3	4	5

Shy				Bold
1	2	3	4	5

Supportive				Demanding
1	2	3	4	5

Relaxed				Tense
1	2	3	4	5

Restrained				Assertive
1	2	3	4	5

Scoring for Assertiveness Scale:

Add the circled numbers on this page and enter the sum here ___

Divide this sum by 14 to compute your Assertiveness Score and enter it here ___

Responsiveness Scale

I perceive myself as being:

Disciplined				Easy-Going
1	2	3	4	5

Controlled				Expressive
1	2	3	4	5

Serious				Light-Hearted
1	2	3	4	5

Methodical				Unstructured
1	2	3	4	5

Calculating				Spontaneous
1	2	3	4	5

Guarded				Open
1	2	3	4	5

Stalwart				Humorous
1	2	3	4	5

Aloof				Friendly
1	2	3	4	5

Formal				Casual
1	2	3	4	5

Reserved				Attention-Seeking
1	2	3	4	5

Cautious				Carefree
1	2	3	4	5

Conforming				Unconventional
1	2	3	4	5

Reticent				Dramatic
1	2	3	4	5

Restrained				Impulsive
1	2	3	4	5

Scoring for Responsiveness Scale:

Add the circled numbers on this page and enter the sum here ___

Divide this sum by 14 to compute your Responsiveness Score and enter it here ___

Use the grid chart on the next page to plot your Assertiveness Score and your Responsiveness Score to determine your individual communication style.

What is your communication style? _____

Do you feel this is an accurate portrayal of your style? Why or why not?

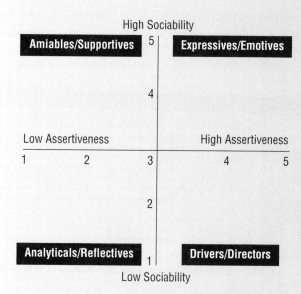

5. Based on your understanding of (a) interpersonal communication styles and (b) your personal communication style, respond to each of the following questions. These questions refer to how and why you would flex your style to better relate to buyers characterized by various communication styles.

   (a) What preparations and style flexing would you make to better relate to and communicate with customers characterized as *Drivers/Directors?*
   (b) What preparations and style flexing would you make to better relate to and communicate with customers characterized as *Analyticals/Reflectives?*
   (c) What preparations and style flexing would you make to better relate to and communicate with customers characterized as *Expressives/Emotives?*
   (d) What preparations and style flexing would you make to better relate to and communicate with customers characterized as *Amiables/Supportives?*

6. **Situation:**   As a key account manager for Hirsch Production Controls, Jerry has developed a strong relationship with St. Louis-based Forrestor Manufacturing and the members of Forrestor's team of buyers. In place for several years now, this relationship has propelled Jerry into Hirsch's top salesperson and transformed Forrestor into Hirsch's best customer—accounting for some 20 percent of the company's business. Jerry has been working with one of Forrestor's competitors, Chicago-based Dorval Products for several months hoping to add them as a customer. As is typical in relationship selling, Jerry has had access to proprietary materials concerning Dorval's manufacturing processes and long-range planning.

   ROLE PLAY

   Characters: Jerry, key account manager for Hirsch Production Controls; Clark Hughley, director of purchasing for Forrestor Manufacturing

   Scene: *Location*—Clark Hughley's office at Forrestor Manufacturing.
   Action—Jerry is on a sales call discussing a new product relevant to Forrestor's production system. While there, Hughley begins asking Jerry about Dorval. It is apparent that Hughley wants to learn anything he can about Dorval's processes and a rumored plant expansion—proprietary or not, he keeps pushing Jerry for information.

Role play the situation that is playing out in Clark Hughley's office. Begin with the usual greeting and approach that might typify a long-standing relationship and proceed to the point where Hughley begins asking questions about Dorval's plans. Demonstrate how you would handle this situation in an ethical and professional manner.

Upon completion of the role play, address the following questions:

(a) Develop a list of five different ways that Jerry might handle this situation. Which one do you believe is the best option? Explain why you feel your choice is better than one of the other four options not selected.

(b) If you were Jerry, what would you do if Hughley continued to ask for information about Dorval? What if he hinted that your business with Forrestor might be in jeopardy if you did not come through with the desired information about Dorval?

7. Personality traits and temperament have been found to be important predictors of individuals' preferences and behaviors. One of the well-researched personality and temperament assessment scales has been made available for individuals to use as an online assessment of their own personality. This same Web site offers a large amount of information explaining the different categories of personality and temperament and how each category can predict certain tendencies in likes and dislikes, communication, and interpersonal behaviors.

Go to the Web site: http://www.keirsey.com. Click on "Take the Keirsey Sorter." After reading the explanatory information, scroll down and click on "Take the Sorter." Complete the self-assessment and get your free individual temperament description. Return to the main "keirsey.com" page. Click on some of the icons found on this page and read about the different temperament styles and how they can predict an individual's behaviors.

(a) What are the different temperament styles identified by the Keirsey Sorter? What are key characteristics of each style?

(b) What was your indicated temperament category? How well do you feel it depicts the image you have of yourself? Why?

(c) Compare and contrast the Keirsey temperament styles with the communication style categories studied in the text.

(d) Having identified your temperament category, what implications might it have for you as a salesperson dealing with other people? What about working with people that are in different categories than you?

MAKING PROFESSIONAL SELLING DECISIONS

Case 3.1: Candoo Computer Corporation

Background

As a salesperson for Candoo Computer Corporation (CCC), you have just received a call from your regional manager regarding a program now underway at one of your key accounts, Farmland Companies. Farmland is a national insurance company with agency offices spread across the United States. The company is in the early stages of designing and specifying a computer system that will place a computer in each agency office. The system will allow each agency to develop, operate, and maintain its own customer database to provide better service to customers. In addition, by linking through the CCC mainframe, agencies, regional offices, and CCC headquarters will be networked for improved internal communications and access to the corporate database.

Current Situation

You have serviced this account for several years, and CCC equipment accounts for the biggest share of computers now in place at Farmland—some 35 to 40 percent of all units. As reflected in your share of this account's business, you and CCC have a good reputation and strong relationship with Farmland. In talking with Aimee Linn, your usual contact in the Farmland purchasing office, you have learned that this agency network system is the brainstorm and pet project of Mike Hughes, a very "hands-on" CEO. Consequently, the probability of the system becoming a reality is high. While faxing a complete set of hardware specs to you, Linn has also let you know that, although Kerris Nicks, director of the Farmland MIS department, is actually heading up this project; the national agency sales director, Tim Long, is also very active in its design and requirement specifications. His interest stems not only from wanting to make sure that the system will do what is needed at the corporate, regional, and agency levels but also from the fact that he brainstormed and spearheaded a similar project two years ago that was never implemented. The previous effort did not have the blessing of Nicks in the MIS department, and it became a political football between the two departments. Each department wanted something different, and both sides accused the other of not knowing what it was doing. Primarily, because the CEO has commanded that it will be done, both sides seem to be playing ball with each other this time.

Linn did hint at one concern, however; although corporate is designing and specifying the system, each agency has to purchase its units out of its own funds. Although the agencies exclusively represent only Farmland Insurance products, each agency is owned by the general agent—not Farmland. Some of the agents are not convinced that the system is worth the projected price tag of $3,500 per system, and Farmland cannot force them to buy the systems.

As with other selling opportunities with Farmland, this has all the makings of a decision that will be made as a result of multiple inputs from an assortment of individuals across the company—a buying team of sorts. As the salesperson having primary responsibility for this account, how would you go about identifying the various members of the buying center? Using the worksheet provided, respond to the following activities.

Questions

1. Identify each member of the buying center and the role each participant plays, and estimate the amount of influence (low, medium, high, very high) each has on the final decision.
2. What are the major problems, needs, and expectations that you will need to address for each of these buying center members?

As you complete this assignment, remember that a single individual can perform multiple roles in the center. Furthermore, it is common to find more than one individual playing the same buying center role.

Situation:	Read Case 3.1.
Characters:	Yourself, salesperson for the Candoo Computer Corporation; Aimee Linn, purchasing manager for Farmland Companies; Kerri Nicks, director of MIS for Farmland Companies; Tim Long, national agency sales director for Farmland Companies; and Mike Hughes, CEO for Farmland Companies.
Scene 1:	*Location*—Linn's office at Farmland Companies. *Action*—You, as the Candoo Computer salesperson, are entering the first meeting with the Farmland buying team. Your goal for this first sales call is to establish a rapport with each of the buying team members and identify the needs and expectations that will determine the purchases

ROLE PLAY

Worksheet for Identifying Buying Team Members and Roles

Buying Team Role	Team Member Playing This Role	Level of Influence	Team Member's Perceived Needs and Expectations
Initiators			
Users			
Influencers			
Purchasers			
Deciders			
Gatekeepers			

for this project. Identifying these needs and expectations is critical so that you can work with your own technology support people and develop a customized system as a solution to Farmland's needs.

Join with a group of fellow students to role play this first sales call and demonstrate how you would (a) build a rapport with the team members, (b) identify the needs and expectations the team members have for this information technology project, and (c) bridge the gap between the sales manager and the MIS director that seemed to kill the project once before.

Scene 2:   *Location*—Aimee Linn's office at Farmland Companies.
Action— Based on the needs and expectations discovered in your first sales call, you have worked with your support team at Candoo Computers to develop a customized

system meeting Farmland's primary needs. You are now making a follow-up sales call for the purpose of presenting your proposed system and making the sale.

Upon completion of the role play, address the following questions:

1. In what way would the different communication styles of the buying team members present complications in the critical stages of building a rapport and discovering the buyers' needs and expectations?

2. How can a salesperson effectively build a rapport with a team of different individuals that have large variations across their communication styles?

3. In a buying team situation, it is typical that certain needs will be championed by specific members while other members will be vocal in support of other needs the solution must address. How might a salesperson best present

the proposed package of features and benefits and recognize the relevant interests of the different buying team members?

4. What suggestions do you have for improving the presentation of the proposed solution and maximizing the positive involvement and buy-in of the different team members?

Case 3.2: American Seating Company Background

You are a salesperson for the American Seating Company (ASC) working with the Seattle Metropolitan Auditorium Authority to replace the seating as part of a major rejuvenation of the auditorium. The remodeling project is being done in response to several private theaters and two universities' entertainment centers that had begun to take major show bookings from the auditorium.

Current Situation

The buyers want the new auditorium seating to be as comfortable as possible and have specified units complete with arms and hinged seats/backs that allow the user to sit upright or slightly recline by leaning back 4 inches. The specifications also specify heavy frames, hardware, and linkage assemblies to yield an expected usable life of 10 years before requiring any form of service or replacement. However, these specifications increase the cost of the chairs by 13 percent. As a result, the buyers are now wanting a lower-grade vinyl fabric in hopes of making up for some of the increased hardware costs.

With your expertise of chairs and fabrics, you have recommended the use of higher-grade nylon velvet rather than vinyl. The velvet will not only be much more comfortable but also more durable than the vinyl. Although both fabrics are equally moisture and stain resistant, the velvet comes with a guaranteed usable life of 10 years compared with the vinyl's 6-year guarantee.

Questions

Use the multiattribute model of evaluation to develop a strategy for reselling the better-grade fabric as the best choice for the new auditorium seating.

ROLE PLAY

Situation: Read Case 3.2.

Characters: Yourself, salesperson for the American Seating Company; the buyer, purchasing manager for Seattle Metropolitan Auditorium Authority.

Scene: *Location*—Buyer's office at the Seattle Metropolitan Auditorium Authority. *Action*—You are presenting the chairs and seating equipment that your company is proposing to sell and install in line with the desired specifications outlined by the design architect and the management for the Seattle Metropolitan Auditorium Authority.

Demonstrate how you might present the advantages and benefits of the higher-grade nylon velvet over the lower-grade vinyl fabric and gain the buyer's commitment to use the better fabric on the seating that is purchased.

Upon completion of the role play, address the following questions:

1. What is the role of the salesperson in explaining and demonstrating that the longer-term added values of a solution with a higher initial cost can make it the lowest lifetime cost alternative?

2. What sales aids could assist the salesperson in demonstrating the longer-term added value and evidencing the greater benefits to the buyer?

CAPTURING THE POWER OF COLLABORATIVE COMMUNICATION IN SALES CONVERSATIONS

Kari Darding, an assistant manager at Wells Fargo Financial, is in charge of putting customers in a better financial situation through a wide array of financial products designed to fit each individual's goals. Wells Fargo Financial prides itself on putting its customers first, as is reflected in their mission statement: "We want to satisfy all our customers' financial needs, help them succeed financially, and be recognized as one of America's great companies."

Many Wells Fargo Financial customers come to the company with "a small financial problem" that is actually a much larger problem than they realize. It is through collaborative communication—including purposeful questioning and active listening—that Darding is able to identify, understand, and solve the customers' larger underlying financial problems. As an example, say a couple takes out a small loan with Wells Fargo when a check arrives in the mail. Wells Fargo Financial often sends such checks in mass mailings designed to generate new business. Once the check is cashed, the customer then has an account with Wells Fargo Financial. In order to prevent identity theft and fraudulent accounts, Darding will call the couple to verify information and to make sure that the name on the account is in fact the person who cashed the check. The manner in which she communicates with her customer is critical in determining how successful she will be in helping better their situation. In that initial discovery conversation, Darding collects information about their dreams, accomplishments, goals, and fears and assesses the customers' financial state. She also asks a variety of questions that will give her a good grasp of what would most benefit the customer. Active listening and purposeful questions are Darding's tools for eliciting pertinent information about the realities of the customers' situation—information that is very important for both parties. For Darding, this collaborative sales conversation enables her to diagnose the customers' situation and develop the depth of understanding required to identify the solution that will best benefit the customer. For the customer, this collaborative sales conversation establishes Darding's credibility and concern for the customer. Just as important, it uncovers real problems, expands the customer's comprehension of the problem and its ramifications, and ignites their desire to resolve the problem.

Based on the customer's expanded knowledge of the problem and desire to solve it, Darding sets an appointment for a follow-up meeting to discuss possible solutions. She usually arranges to meet her customers at their home for their comfort and convenience. In our example, Darding sits at the customers' kitchen table, and within the first few minutes builds a rapport by asking the customers more questions about their lifestyle, their family, and what is most important to them. This conversation is the most important part of the meeting because it is in these few precious minutes that Darding is earning the trust of her customers. If the customers do not trust her, she will not gain their business; however, once they do trust her, she will have loyal customers who will come to her with all their financial needs. Darding was able to determine that this couple most needed a reduction in their monthly obligations to help pay for their children's education. Because of the wide array of products that Wells Fargo Financial offers, she was able to condense their mortgage from a 30-year term to a 15-year term while reducing their monthly

Objectives

After completing this module, you should be able to

1 Explain the importance of collaborative, two-way communication in trust-based selling.

2 Explain the primary types of questions and how they are applied in selling.

3 Illustrate the diverse roles and uses of strategic questioning in trust-based selling.

4 Identify and describe the five steps of the ADAPT questioning sequence.

5 Discuss the four sequential steps for effective active listening.

6 Discuss the superiority of pictures over words for explaining concepts and enhancing comprehension.

7 Describe the different forms of nonverbal communication.

obligation by $300. This couple remains a loyal customer of Darding's and is very thankful for her help.

Darding and others in her position are successful because Wells Fargo Financial practices trust-based selling that emphasizes collaborative sales conversations in which underlying problems are uncovered and customers gain a better understanding of those problems. One motto in Darding's branch is, "We're not order takers; we're order makers." Within the initial 30 seconds of a call, Darding has to determine the customer's communication style, adapt her sales conversation to fit that style, and differentiate herself from every other financial/mortgage company who happens to be calling on the same customer. She must communicate clearly, convey a sense of urgency to set an appointment, and, most important, be able to gain the trust of her customers. Darding believes that, with the proper attitude and the use of clear communication, anyone can be successful at sales.

Darding's experience with the potency of collaborative sales conversations illustrated in the opening vignette is not uncommon. In reality, it is quickly becoming the norm for effective selling. In the past, product-oriented salespeople focused on telling stories about their products' features and benefits. In trust-based selling, salespeople realize that the customer possesses the information relevant to the realities they are experiencing, and the salesperson will not recommend a solution without first diagnosing the customer's situation. The information required to make a diagnosis must come from the customer and can only be obtained through effective questioning and active listening. Trust-based selling is collaborative, two-way communication—a true dialogue. Consequently, the skill and effectiveness of a salesperson's interpersonal communication are fundamental determinants of selling performance. Oddly, communication continues to be one of the least understood and least studied skills for successful selling.

Source: Personal interview with Kari Darding, assistant manager, July 15, 2006.

This module addresses the need to better understand and master the art of collaborative, two-way communication. First, we will examine the basic nature of **trust-based sales communication.** Building on this preliminary understanding, the text breaks down trust-based sales communication into its component and subcomponent parts to facilitate study, application, and mastery. The verbal dimension of communication is examined first with an emphasis on three communication subcomponents: (1) developing effective questioning methods for use in uncovering and diagnosing buyers' needs and expectations, (2) using active listening skills to facilitate the interchange of ideas and information, and (3) maximizing the responsive dissemination of information to buyers to explain and bring alive the benefits of proposed solutions. Finally, the nonverbal dimension of interpersonal communication is examined with an emphasis on its application and meaningful interpretation.

SALES COMMUNICATION AS A COLLABORATIVE PROCESS

Neither people nor organizations buy products. Rather, they seek out the satisfaction and benefits that are provided by certain product features. Although traditional selling has been described as "talking *at* the customer," trust-based selling has been referred to as "talking *with* the customer." Trust-based sales communication is a two-way and naturally collaborative interaction that allows buyers and sellers alike to develop a better understanding of the need situation and work together to generate the best response for solving the customer's needs. Although trust-based selling has become the preeminent model for contemporary personal selling, the situation described in "An Ethical Dilemma" should serve as a reminder that some salespeople and sales organizations continue to practice more traditional and manipulative forms of selling.

AN ETHICAL DILEMMA

Aimee Moore is 23-years-old and recently completed her undergraduate degree in marketing. She accepted a position in the fast-growing financial services field as a financial representative for one of the largest, nationwide organizations in the industry—a company focused on maintaining a growth rate that will assure its continued dominance in the industry and sustain its large customer base. Upon accepting the position, Moore first completed a two-month training program (along with 18 other new recruits) at the company's headquarters in Minneapolis. She describes the training program as being primarily concerned with (a) legal and industry issues in order to get all the necessary licenses and (b) product knowledge so that she would understand the various products and services she was hired to sell. Coverage of basic sales skills was pretty limited and was only addressed on the last two days in Minneapolis.

Upon completion of the two months of training, the newly minted financial representatives returned to their resident offices and were given a list of prospects that they would use for making phone calls. Each new rep was also given a three-ring binder of selling tips to use as needed. The first page of the selling tips contained a motivational message followed by what was titled, "The 5 Keys to Successful Selling." These keys to success were as follows:

Key #1: Everybody needs a financial planner! Make your daily calls, demonstrate the benefits of our products, and ask for the appointment.

Key #2: Prospective buyers do not know what they need in terms of financial products and services! At the appointment, follow the standard selling message showing each of our products, and ask for the order each time until the buyer makes a choice.

Key #3: Always be closing! If you don't ask for the order, nobody will buy!

Key #4: Success in selling is simply a numbers game! Contact enough prospects and you will make your quota. Want to sell more? Make more contacts!

Key #5: Product knowledge is the key! Have a good opening, explain the products, handle objections, and close the sale by leading the buyer where you want them to go.

How does this company's selling philosophy compare with the trust-based, collaborative selling approach we've been discussing? How are these keys to selling success likely to work in today's marketplace? Why?

Trust-based sales communication is the sharing of meaning between buying and selling parties that results from the interactive process of exchanging information and ideas. It is important to note that the purpose of sales communication is not agreement but rather the maximization of common understanding among participants. With this emphasis on establishing understanding, communication is fundamental throughout each stage of the selling process. Effective communication skills are needed to identify buying needs and to demonstrate to buyers how a salesperson's proposed solution can satisfy those needs better than competitors. The critical capabilities for effective selling include questioning, listening, giving information, nonverbal communication, and written communication skills. Although each of these skills is pervasive in everyday life, they are literally the heart and soul of the interpersonal exchange that characterizes trust-based selling.

VERBAL COMMUNICATION: QUESTIONING

There are two ways to dominate or control a selling conversation. A salesperson can talk all the time, or the salesperson can maintain a more subtle level of control by asking well thought out questions that guide the discussion. As highlighted in "Professional Selling in the 21st Century: Importance of Preparation and Well Thought Out Questions,"[1] successful salespeople must be masters at thinking through what they need to know and planning the questions they need to ask. They should know exactly what information they need and which type of question is best suited for eliciting that information from a prospective buyer.

Importance of Preparation and Well Thought Out Questions

Successful salespeople do not rely solely on their instincts during a sales call. They know that in today's environment of sophisticated and knowledgeable buyers they cannot just "wing it"—they must develop a solid precall plan outlining the information they need and the questions they will ask in order to get the information needed from the customer. Mark Shonka and Dan Kosch, copresidents of IMPAX Corporation and sales training consultants to Fortune 500 companies, share their comments regarding the importance of precall planning and knowing what questions you are going to ask before you make the actual sales call.

The information gained in the sales call should build on the research that a salesperson has already gathered from other sources and should provide the salesperson with more detail from the insider's perspective. As there is a limitless amount of knowledge about the target account available, keeping on track and avoiding the social conversation trap requires that the salesperson determines what information he or she needs and what questions he or she might ask prior to making the actual sales call. Typically, the information needed from the insider's perspective can be classified into five distinct categories:

1. *Corporate Profile and Direction*
   - *Get a grasp of the facts and figures that describe the company and make it unique.*

   - *Investigate the issues and activities that influence the company's plans and operations.*
   - *Determine what their plans are for the future.*

2. *Organizational Structure*
   - *Formal Chart—chain of command, how the company is structured.*
   - *Informal Chart—how things actually get done: politics and power don't always follow formal titles.*
   - *Social Chart—the key relationships that affect what happens in the company.*

3. *Key Players & Profiles (Buying Team Roles)*
   - *Personal and professional background information.*
   - *Objectives and priorities.*
   - *Issues and concerns.*

4. *Departmental Profile and Direction*
   - *Profile the internal workings and how it functions.*
   - *Objectives, strategies, and projects.*
   - *Issues and concerns.*

5. *Buying Organization–Selling Organization Business Fit*
   - *Address customer's objectives and issues.*
   - *Focus on decision makers' concerns.*
   - *Aim for a long-term, value-based relationship.*

Purposeful, carefully crafted questions can encourage thoughtful responses from buyers and provide richly detailed information about the buyers' current situation, needs, and expectations. This additional detail and understanding is often as meaningful for the buyer as it is for the salesperson. That is, proper questioning can facilitate both the buyer's and seller's understanding of a problem and its possible solutions.[2] For example, questions can encourage meaningful feedback regarding the buyer's attitude and the logical progression through the purchase decision process. Questioning also shows interest in the buyer and his or her needs and actively involves the buyer in the selling process. Questions can also be used to tactically redirect, regain, or hold the buyer's attention should it begin to wander during the conversation. In a similar fashion, questions can provide a convenient and subtle transition to a different topic of discussion and provide a logical guide promoting sequential thought and decision making.

Questions are typed by the results they are designed to accomplish. Does the salesperson wish to receive a free flow of thoughts and ideas or a simple yes/no confirmation? Is the salesperson seeking a general description of the overall situation or specific details regarding emergent needs or problematic experiences with current suppliers? To be effective, salespeople must understand which type of question will best accomplish his or her desired outcome. In this manner, questions can be typed into two basic categories: (1) amount of information and level of specificity desired and (2) strategic purpose or intent.

Types of Questions Classified by Amount and Specificity of Information Desired

Open-End Questions

Open-end questions, also called nondirective questions, are designed to let the customer respond freely. That is, the customer is not limited to one- or two-word answers but is encouraged to disclose personal and/or business information. Open-end questions encourage buyers' thought processes and deliver richer and more expansive information than closed-end questions. Consequently, these questions are typically used to probe for descriptive information that allows the salesperson to better understand the specific needs and expectations of the customer. The secret to successfully using open-end questions lies in the first word used to form the question. Words often used to begin open-end questions include *what, how, where, when, tell, describe,* and *why.*[3] "What happens when...," "How do you feel...," and "Describe the..." are examples of open-end questions.

Closed-End Questions

Closed-end questions are designed to limit the customers' response to one or two words. This type of question is typically used to confirm or clarify information gleaned from previous responses to open-end questions. Although the most common form is the yes/no question, closed-end questions come in many forms—provided the response is limited to one or two words. For instance, "Do you...," "Are you...," "How many...," and "How often..." are common closed-end questions.

Dichotomous/Multiple-Choice Questions

Dichotomous questions and multiple-choice questions are directive forms of questioning. This type of question asks a customer to choose from two or more options and is used in selling to discover customer preferences and move the purchase decision process forward. An example of this form of question would be, "Which do you prefer, the _____ or the _____?"

Types of Questions Classified by Strategic Purpose

Probing Questions

Probing questions are designed to penetrate below generalized or superficial information to elicit more articulate and precise details for use in needs discovery and solution identification. Rather than interrogating a buyer, probing questions are best used in a conversational style: (1) requesting clarification ("Can you share with me an example of that?" "How long has this been a problem?"), (2) encouraging elaboration ("How are you dealing with that situation now?" "What is your experience with _____?"), and (3) verifying information and responses ("That is interesting, could you tell me more?" "So, if I understand correctly, _____. Is that right?").

Evaluative Questions

Evaluative questions use open- and closed-end question formats to gain confirmation and to uncover attitudes, opinions, and preferences held by the prospect. These questions are designed to go beyond generalized fact finding and uncover prospects' perceptions and feelings regarding existing and desired circumstances as well as potential solutions. Exemplary evaluative questions include "How do you feel about _____?" "Do you see the merits of _____?" and "What do you think _____?"

Tactical Questions

Tactical questions are used to shift or redirect the topic of discussion when the discussion gets off course or when a line of questioning proves to be of little interest or value. For example, the salesperson might be exploring the chances of plant expansion only to find that the prospect cannot provide that type of proprietary information at this early stage of the buyer–seller relationship. To avoid either embarrassing the prospect or him- or herself by proceeding on a forbidden or nonproductive line of questioning, the seller uses a strategic question designed to change topics. An example of such a tactical question might be expressed as "Earlier you mentioned that _____. Could you tell me more about how that might affect _____?"

Reactive Questions

Reactive questions are questions that refer to or directly result from information previously provided by the other party. Reactive questions are used to elicit additional information, explore for further detail, and keep the flow of information going. Illustrative reactive questions are "You mentioned that _____. Can you give me an example of what you mean?" and "That is interesting. Can you tell me how it happened?"

These different groupings of question types are not mutually exclusive. As depicted in the guidelines for combining question types in Exhibit 4.1, effective questions integrate elements from different question types. For example, "How do you feel about the current trend of sales in the industry?" is open end (classified by format) and evaluative (classified by purpose) in nature.

Regardless of the types of questions combined, Robert Jolles, senior sales training consultant for Xerox Corporation, cautions against the natural tendency to use closed-end questions rather than open-end questions. His experience and research indicate that for every open-end question the average salesperson asks, there will be ten closed-end questions.[4] This overuse of closed-end questions is dangerous in selling. The discovery and exploration of customer needs are fundamental to trust-based selling, and discovery and exploration are best done with open-end questions.

EXHIBIT 4.1   Guidelines for Combining Types of Questions for Maximal Effectiveness

		Explore and Dig for Details	Gain Confirmation and Discover Attitudes/Opinions	Change Topics or Direct Attention	Follow Up Previously Elicited Statements
	Discussion and Interpretation	*Open-End* Questions Designed to Be *Probing* in Nature	*Open-End* Questions Designed to Be *Evaluative* in Nature	*Open-End* Questions Designed to Be *Tactical* in Nature	*Open-End* Questions Designed to Be *Reactive* in Nature
Amount and Specificity of Information Desired	Confirmation and Agreement	*Closed-End* Questions Designed to Be *Probing* in Nature	*Closed-End* Questions Designed to Be *Evaluative* in Nature	*Closed-End* Questions Designed to Be *Tactical* in Nature	*Closed-End* Questions Designed to Be *Reactive* in Nature
	Choice from Alternatives	*Dichotomous* or *Multiple-Choice* Questions Designed to Be *Probing* in Nature	*Dichotomous* or *Multiple-Choice* Questions Designed to Be *Evaluative* in Nature	*Dichotomous* or *Multiple-Choice* Questions Designed to Be *Tactical* in Nature	*Dichotomous* or *Multiple-Choice* Questions Designed to Be *Reactive* in Nature

Strategic Objective or Purpose of Questioning

As previously discussed, closed-end questions certainly have their place in selling, but they are best used for clarification and confirmation, not discovery and exploration. An additional issue in overusing closed-end questions is that when they are used in a sequence, the resulting communication takes on the demeanor of interrogation rather than conversation.

Strategic Application of Questioning in Trust-Based Selling

Effective questioning skills are indispensable in selling and are used to address critical issues throughout all stages of the selling process. In practice, salespeople combine the different types of questions discussed earlier to accomplish multiple and closely related sales objectives:

- *Generate Buyer Involvement.* Rather than the salesperson dominating the conversation and interaction, purposeful and planned questions are used to encourage prospective buyers to actively participate in a two-way collaborative discussion.
- *Provoke Thinking.* Innovative and effective solutions require cognitive efforts and contributions from each participant. Strategic questions stimulate buyers and salespeople to thoroughly and pragmatically think about and consider all aspects of a given situation.
- *Gather Information.* Good questions result from advance planning and should be directed toward gathering the information required to fill in the gap between "What do we need to know?" and "What do we already know?"
- *Clarification and Emphasis.* Rather than assuming that the salesperson understands what a buyer has said, questions can be used to further clarify meaning and to further emphasize the important points within a buyer–seller exchange.
- *Show Interest.* In response to statements from buyers, salespeople ask related questions and paraphrase what the buyer has said to demonstrate their interest in and understanding of what the buyer is saying.
- *Gain Confirmation.* The use of simple and direct questions allow salespeople to check back with the prospective buyer to confirm the buyer's understanding or agreement and gain his or her commitment to move forward.
- *Advance the Sale.* Effective questions are applied in a fashion that guides and moves the selling process forward in a logical progression from initiation through needs development and through needs resolution and follow-up.

With the aim of simultaneously targeting and achieving each of these objectives, several systems have been developed to guide salespeople in properly developing and using effective questions. Two of the more prominent questioning systems are SPIN and ADAPT. Both of these systems use a logical sequencing—a sort of funneling effect—that begins with broad-based, nonthreatening, general questions. Questioning progressively proceeds through more narrowly focused questions designed to clarify the buyer's needs and to logically propel the selling process toward the presentation and demonstration of solution features, advantages, and benefits.

SPIN Questioning System

The **SPIN** system sequences four types of questions designed to uncover a buyer's current situation and inherent problems, enhance the buyer's understanding of the consequences and implications of those problems, and lead to the proposed solution.[5] SPIN is actually an acronym for the four types of questions making up the multiple question sequence: situation questions, problem questions, implication questions, and need-payoff questions.

- *Situation Questions.* This type of question solicits data and facts in the form of general background information and descriptions of the buyer's existing situation. **Situation questions** are used early in the sales call and provide salespeople with leads to fully develop the buyer's needs and expectations. Situation questions might include "Who are your current suppliers?" "Do you typically purchase or lease?" and "Who is involved in purchasing decisions?" Situation questions are essential, but they should be used in moderation as too many general fact-finding questions can bore the buyer. Further, their interrogating nature can result in irritated buyers.

- *Problem Questions.* **Problem questions** follow the more general situation questions to further probe for specific difficulties, developing problems, and areas of dissatisfaction that might be positively addressed by the salesperson's proposed sales offering. Some examples of problem questions include "How critical is this component for your production?" "What kinds of problems have you encountered with your current suppliers?" and "What types of reliability problems do you experience with your current system?" Problem questions actively involve the buyer and can assist him or her in better understanding his or her own problems and needs. Nevertheless, inexperienced and unsuccessful salespeople generally do not ask enough problem questions.

- *Implication Questions.* **Implication questions** follow and relate to the information flowing from problem questions. Their purpose is to assist the buyer in thinking about the potential consequences of the problem and understand the urgency of resolving the problem in a way that motivates him or her to seek a solution. Typical implication questions might include "How does this affect profitability?" "What impact does the slow response of your current supplier have on the productivity of your operation?" "How would a faster piece of equipment improve productivity and profits?" and "What happens when the supplier is late with a shipment?" Although implication questions are closely linked to success in selling, even experienced salespeople rarely use them effectively.

- *Need-Payoff Questions.* Based on the implications of a problem, salespeople use **need-payoff questions** to propose a solution and develop commitment from the buyer. These questions refocus the buyer's attention to solutions rather than problems and get the buyer to think about the positive benefits derived from solving the problems. Examples of need-payoff questions are "Would more frequent deliveries allow you to increase productivity?" "If we could provide you with increased reliability, would you be interested?" "If we could improve the quality of your purchased components, how would that help you?" and "Would you be interested in increasing productivity by 15 percent?" Top salespeople effectively incorporate a higher number of need-payoff questions into sales calls than do less successful salespeople.

ADAPT Questioning System

As illustrated by Figure 4.1, the **ADAPT** questioning system uses a logic-based funneling sequence of questions, beginning with broad and generalized inquiries designed to identify and assess the buyer's situation. Based on information gained in this first phase, further questions are generated to probe and discover more details regarding the needs and expectations of the buyer. In turn, the resulting information is incorporated in further collaborative discussion in a way that activates the buyer's motivation to implement a solution and further establishes the buyer's perceived value of a possible solution. The last phase of ADAPT questioning transitions to the buyer's commitment to learn about the proposed solution and grants the salesperson permission to move forward into the presentation and demonstration of the sales offering. ADAPT is an acronym for the five stages of strategic questioning and represents what the salesperson should be doing at each stage: assessment questions, discovery questions, activation questions, projection questions, and transition questions.[6]

- *Assessment Questions.* This initial phase of questioning is designed to be nonthreatening and to spark conversation that elicits factual information about the customer's current situation that can provide a basis for further exploration and probing. As illustrated in Exhibit 4.2, **assessment questions** do not seek conclusions—rather, at a macro or 40,000-foot level of focus, these questions

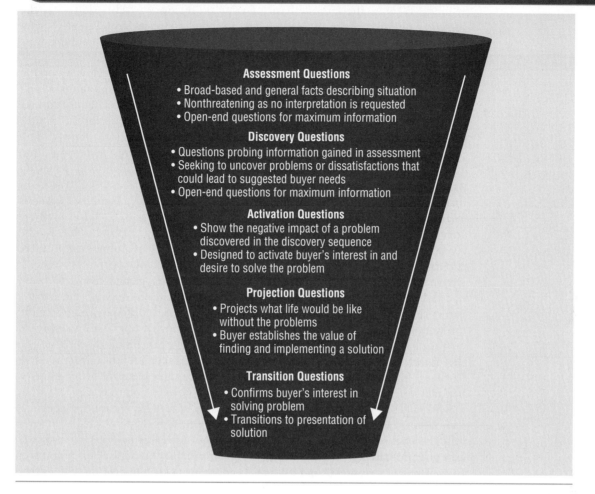

Funneling Sequence of ADAPT Technique for Needs Discovery   FIGURE 4.1

Assessment Questions
- Broad-based and general facts describing situation
- Nonthreatening as no interpretation is requested
- Open-end questions for maximum information

Discovery Questions
- Questions probing information gained in assessment
- Seeking to uncover problems or dissatisfactions that could lead to suggested buyer needs
- Open-end questions for maximum information

Activation Questions
- Show the negative impact of a problem discovered in the discovery sequence
- Designed to activate buyer's interest in and desire to solve the problem

Projection Questions
- Projects what life would be like without the problems
- Buyer establishes the value of finding and implementing a solution

Transition Questions
- Confirms buyer's interest in solving problem
- Transitions to presentation of solution

The ADAPT questioning technique logically sequences questions from broad and general inquiries through increasingly detailed questions for effective needs discovery.

Assessment Questions   EXHIBIT 4.2

These questions are designed to elicit factual information about the customer's current situation. These questions do not seek conclusions; rather they seek information that describes the customer and his or her business environment. The information sought should augment or confirm precall research.

Examples:

1. **Question—"What types of operating arrangements do you have with your suppliers?"**
    Answer—We use a Just-in-Time (JIT) system with our main suppliers .
2. **Question—"Who is involved in the purchase decision-making process?"**
    Answer—I make the decisions regarding supplies . . .

Assessment questions are generally open end; however, closed-end questions are used when seeking confirmation or basic descriptive information. For example, "So, you currently work with 10 different suppliers?" or "How many years have you been in business?" Assessment questions are necessary for drawing out information early in the sales cycle.

should address the buyer's company and operation, goals and objectives, market trends and customers, current suppliers, and even the buyer as an individual. The information sought should augment or confirm precall research. Examples would include "What is the current level of your production?" "How long has the current equipment been in place?" "How many suppliers are currently being used?" "What are the growth objectives of the company?" and "What individuals have input into purchase decisions?"

- *Discovery Questions.* As portrayed in Exhibit 4.3, these questions follow up on the responses gained from the preceding assessment questions. At a more micro and ground-level focus, **discovery questions** should drill down and probe for further details needed to fully develop, clarify, and understand the nature of the buyer's problems. Facts as well as the buyer's interpretations, perceptions, feelings, and opinions are sought in regard to the buyer's needs, wants, dissatisfactions, and expectations relevant to product, delivery requirements, budget and financing issues, and desired service levels. The goal is to discover needs and dissatisfactions that the salesperson's sales offering can resolve. Examples of discovery questions might include "How often do these equipment failures occur?" "How well are your current suppliers performing?" "What disadvantages do you see in the current process?" "How satisfied are you with the quality of components you are currently purchasing?" and "How difficult are these for your operators to use?"

- *Activation Questions.* The implied or suggested needs gained from discovery questions are not usually sufficient to gain the sale. Often, a buyer will believe that a particular problem does not cause any significant negative consequences, hence the motivation to solve the problem will carry a low priority. Successful salespeople help the customer realistically evaluate the full impact of the implied need through the use of **activation questions**. As detailed in Exhibit 4.4, the objective is to "activate" the customer's interest in solving discovered problems by helping him or her gain insight into the true ramifications of the problem and to realize that what may initially seem to be of little consequence is, in fact, of significant consequence. Examples include "What effects do these equipment breakdowns have on your business operations?" "To what extent are these increases in overtime expenses affecting profitability?" "How will the supplier's inability to deliver on time affect your planned expansion?" and "When components fail in the field, how does that influence customer satisfaction and repurchase?"

- *Projection Questions.* As a natural extension of the activation questions, **projection questions** encourage and facilitate the buyer in "projecting" what it would be like without the problems that have been previously "discovered" and

---

EXHIBIT 4.3   Discovery Questions

Discovery questions are used to uncover problems or dissatisfactions the customer is experiencing that the salesperson's product or company may be able to solve. Basically, these questions are used to "distill" or "boil down" the information gained from the preceding assessment questions and from precall research into suggested needs.

Examples:

1. **Question—"I understand you prefer a JIT relationship with your suppliers—how have they been performing?"**
   Answer—Pretty well . . . an occasional late delivery . . . but pretty well.
2. **Question—"How do you feel about your current supplier occasionally being late with deliveries?"**
   Answer—It's real problem . . . for . . . instance . . .

The *suggested* needs gained from discovery questions are used as a foundation for the rest of the sales call. Yet, a *suggested* need is usually not sufficient to close the sale. Often, a customer will believe that a particular problem does not cause any significant negative consequences. If this is the case, finding a solution to the problem will be a very low priority. The professional salesperson must then help the customer to reevaluate the impact of the *suggested* need by asking activation questions.

Activation Questions   EXHIBIT 4.4

Activation questions are used to show the impact of a problem, uncovered through discovery questions, on the customer's entire operation. The objective is to "activate" the customer's interest in solving the problem by helping him or her to gain insight into the true ramifications of the problem and realize that what may seem to be of little consequence is, in fact, of significant consequence.

Examples:

1. **Question—"What effect does your supplier's late delivery have on your operation?"**
   Answer—It slows production . . . Operating costs go up . . .
2. **Question—"If production drops off, how are your operating costs affected, and how does that affect your customers?"**
   Answer—Customer orders are delayed . . . Potential to lose customers . . .

Activation questions show the negative impact of a problem so that finding a solution to that problem is desirable. Now, the salesperson can help the customer to discover the positive impact of solving the problems by using projection questions.

"activated." The use of good projection questions accomplishes several positive outcomes. First, the focus is switched from problems and their associated consequences to the upside—the benefits to be derived from solving the problems. What were initially perceived as costs and expenses are now logically structured as benefits to the buyer and his or her organization—the payoff for taking action and investing in a solution. Second—and equally important—the benefit payoff allows the buyer to establish the realistic value of implementing a solution. In this manner, the benefit payoff is perceived as a positive value received and serves as the foundation for demonstrating what the solution is worth—what the buyer would be willing to pay. As illustrated in Exhibit 4.5, projection questions encourage the buyer to think about how and why he or she should go about resolving a problem. In essence, projection questions assist the buyer in selling himself or herself by establishing the worth of the proposed solution. The customer, rather than the salesperson, establishes the benefits of solving the problem. This reinforces the importance of solving the problem and reduces the number of objections that might be raised. Examples of projection questions include "If a supplier was never late with a delivery, what effects would that have on your overall operation?" "What would be the impact on profitability if you did not have problems with limited plant capacity and the resulting overtime expenses?" "How would a system that your operators found easier to

Projection Questions   EXHIBIT 4.5

Projection questions help the customer to "project" what life would be like without the problems or dissatisfactions uncovered through activation questions. This helps the customer to see value in finding solutions to the problems developed earlier in the sales call.

Examples:

1. **Question—"If a supplier was never late with a delivery, what effects would that have on your JIT operating structure?"**
   Answer—It would run smoother and at a lower cost . . .
2. **Question—"If a supplier helped you meet the expectations of your customers, what impact would that have on your business?"**
   Answer—Increased customer satisfaction would mean more business . . .

These questions are used to let the customer tell the salesperson the benefits of solving the problem. By doing so, the customer is reinforcing in his or her mind the importance of solving the problem and reducing the number of objections that might be raised.

EXHIBIT 4.6   **Transition Questions**

Transition questions are simple closed-end questions that confirm the customer's desire to solve the problem(s) uncovered through the previous questions.

Examples:

1. Question—"So, having a supplier who is never late with deliveries is important to you?"
   Answer—Yes, it is.
2. Question—"If I can show you how our company ensures on-time delivery, would you be interested in pursuing a formal business arrangement with our company?"
   Answer—Yes, if I'm convinced your company can guarantee on-time delivery . . .

The primary function of these questions is to make the transition from need confirmation into the sales presentation. In addition, these questions can lead to a customer commitment, provided the salesperson adequately presents how his or her company can solve the customer's problems.

---

use affect your business operations?" and "If component failures were minimized, what impact would the resulting improvement in customer satisfaction have on financial performance?"

- *Transition Questions.* **Transition questions** are used to smooth the transition from needs discovery into the presentation and demonstration of the proposed solution's features, advantages, and benefits. As exemplified in Exhibit 4.6, transition questions are typically closed end and evaluative in format. These questions confirm the buyer's desire to seek a solution and give their consent to the salesperson to move forward with the selling process. Examples include "So, having suppliers that are consistently on time is important to you—if I could show you how our company ensures on-time delivery, would you be interested?" "It seems that increasing capacity is a key to reducing overtime and increasing profitability—would you be interested in a way to increase capacity by 20 percent through a simple addition to your production process?" and "Would you be interested in a system that is easier for your operators to use?"

VERBAL COMMUNICATION: LISTENING

Listening is the other half of effective questioning. After all, asking the customer for information is of little value if the salesperson does not listen. Effective listening is rated among the most critical skills for successful selling. Yet, as illustrated by "Professional Selling in the 21st Century: Effective Listening Is the Foundation for Trust-Based Selling," most of us share the common problem of being a lot better at sending messages than receiving them. Considerable research identifies effective listening as the number one weakness of salespeople.[7]

Poor listening skills have been identified as one of the primary causes of salesperson failure.[8] In order to get the information needed to best serve, identify, and respond to needs, and nurture a collaborative buyer–seller relationship, salespeople must be able to listen and understand what was said *and* what was meant. Nevertheless, situations similar to the one depicted in "An Ethical Dilemma" are all too common. As illustrated by Figure 4.2, effective listening can be broken down into six primary facets:

1. *Pay attention*—Listen to understand, not to reply. Resist the urge to interrupt and receive the full message the buyer is communicating.
2. *Monitor nonverbals*—Make effective eye contact and check to see if the buyer's body language and speech patterns match what is being said.
3. *Paraphrase and repeat*—Confirm your correct understanding of what the buyer is saying by paraphrasing and repeating what you have heard.
4. *Make no assumptions*—Ask questions to clarify the meaning of what the buyer is communicating.

Effective Listening Is the Foundation for Trust-Based Selling

Jerry Acuff is president of Delta Point—The Sales Agency, a Scottsdale Arizona based consultancy, that assists leading companies in finding new and innovative ways to increase the effectiveness of their selling and marketing programs. Acuff emphasizes that meetings with customers should be a conversation, not merely a sales call and that this means the salesperson should be intently listening to the customer at least half of the time spent in the meeting. He also discusses that, as necessary as it is for trust-based selling, listening is hard work and something that most of us are just not very good at doing.

Listening is hard work, and many of us do not listen as well as we should. Jiddu Krishnamurti, the Indian philosopher offers insight as to why it's so difficult:

"To be able really to listen one should abandon or put aside all prejudices, preformulations, and daily activities. When you are in a receptive state of mind, things can be easily understood; you are listening when your real attention is given to something. But unfortunately, most of us listen through a screen of resistance. We are screened with prejudices, whether religious or spiritual, psychological, or scientific; or with our daily worries, desires, and fears. . . . It is extremely difficult to put aside our training, our prejudices, our inclination, our resistance, and, reaching beyond the verbal expression, to listen so that we understand instantaneously."

I suspect the only way to overcome the noisy buzz of our opinions, ideas, prejudices, background, and impulses is through practice. We must learn to consciously turn down the volume of our own prejudiced thoughts in order to focus on what the other person is saying. Salespeople must understand that only after you have heard and absorbed what the other person has said should you respond with your opinions, ideas, and all the rest.

5. *Encourage the buyer to talk*—Encourage the flow of information by giving positive feedback and help the buyer stay on track by asking purposeful, related questions.
6. *Visualize*—Maximize your attention and comprehension by thinking about and visualizing what the buyer is saying.

The practiced listening skills of high performance salespeople enable them to pick up, sort out, and interpret a higher number of buyers' verbal and nonverbal messages more than lower-performing salespeople. In addition to gaining information and understanding critical to the relational selling process, a salesperson's good listening behaviors provide the added benefits of positively influencing the formation and

AN ETHICAL DILEMMA

People describe Brian Reed as an enthusiastic and very outgoing person. He graduated with a double major in Applied Computer Systems and Marketing and is very knowledgeable in the areas of computer technology, software applications, and networking systems. Bringing together his personality traits and educational background, Reed works as a salesperson for Business Systems & Solutions, a major technology consultancy and business systems design organization. Even though Reed finished his training at the top of his class, his sales success in the field has been consistently below average, and a number of his existing accounts have been lost to the competition. Hoping to assist Reed in realizing his true potential, his sales manager recently spent several days with him out in the field calling on new prospects as well as existing customers. During these ride-a-longs, the sales manager has observed that Reed has a tendency to interrupt when the buyer is discussing problems and desired outcomes. Rather than allowing buyers to describe the nature of a given situation or need fully, Reed interjects his own opinions based on his own knowledge and experience. While he continues to successfully close sales, Reed's hit ratio is considerably below average and needs to improve if he is to remain in his current position with Business Systems & Solutions.

What is going on in terms of Reed's sales conversations with his customers that might explain his below average performance? If you were Reed's sales manager, what changes would you suggest to him? Why?

> **FIGURE 4.2** Six Facets of Effective Listening

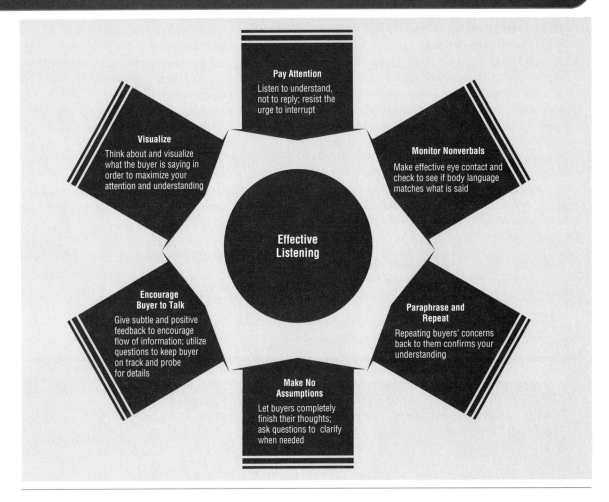

The six facets of effective listening enable salespeople to better pick up, sort out, and interpret buyers' verbal and nonverbal messages.

continuation of buyer–seller relationships. The effective use and demonstration of good listening skills by a salesperson are positively associated with the customer's trust in the salesperson and the anticipation of having future interactions with the salesperson.[9] Clearly, effective listening is a critical component in trust-based, relational selling, and success requires continuous practice and improvement of our listening skills.

Using Different Types of Listening

Communications research identifies two primary categories of listening: *social* and *serious*.[10] **Social listening** is an informal mode of listening that can be associated with day-to-day conversation and entertainment. Social listening is characterized by low levels of cognitive activity and concentration and is typically used in conversation with a friend or a store clerk or listening to music, a concert, a television program, or even a play. The received messages are taken at face value and do not require a high degree of concentration or thinking to sort through, interpret, and understand. However, **serious listening** is associated with events or topics in which it is important to sort through, interpret, understand, and respond to received messages. The serious form of listening is often referred to as *active listening*, as it requires high levels of concentration and cognition about the messages being received. *Concentration* is required to break through the distractions and other interference to facilitate receiving and remembering

SIER Hierarchy of Active Listening   FIGURE 4.3

Active listening is a cognitive process of actively sensing, interpreting, evaluating, and responding to verbal and nonverbal messages from buyers and prospects.

specific messages. *Cognition* is used to sort through and select the meaningful relevant messages and interpret them for meaning, information, and response.

Active Listening

Active listening in a selling context is defined as "the cognitive process of actively sensing, interpreting, evaluating, and responding to the verbal and nonverbal messages of present or potential customers."[11] This definition is very useful to those wishing to master active listening skills. First, it underscores the importance of receiving and interpreting both verbal and nonverbal cues and messages to better determine the full and correct meaning of the message. Second, it incorporates a well-accepted model of listening. As illustrated in Figure 4.3,[12] the **SIER** model depicts active listening as a hierarchical, four-step sequence of sensing, interpreting, evaluating, and responding.[13] Effective active listening requires each of these four hierarchical process activities to be carried out successfully and in proper succession.

- *Sensing.* Listening is much more than simply hearing. Nevertheless, the first activities in active listening are **sensing** (i.e., hearing and seeing) and receiving (i.e., paying attention to) the verbal and nonverbal components of the message being sent. Sensing does not occur without practice and should not be taken for granted. In fact, research indicates that most of us listen at only 25 percent of our capacity. Think about yourself. How often have you had to ask someone to repeat what he or she said or perhaps assumed you knew what the sender was going to say before he or she could say it? Increased concentration and attention can improve sensing effectiveness. Taking notes, making eye contact with the sender, and not interrupting can improve sensing skills. Let the sender finish and provide the full content of the message. This not only improves the concentration of the receiver but also encourages the sender to provide more information and detail.
- *Interpreting.* After the message is received, it must be correctly interpreted. **Interpreting** addresses the question of "What meaning does the sender intend?" Both content and context are important. That is, in addition to the semantic meaning of the words and symbols, we must consider the experiences, knowledge, and attitudes of the sender to fully understand what was meant. Hold back the temptation to evaluate the message until the sender is through. Note the nonverbal and verbal cues along with possible consistencies and inconsistencies

between them. Incorporate knowledge of the sender's background and previous relevant statements and positions into the message interpretation.

- *Evaluating.* Active listening requires the receiver to decide whether he or she agrees with the sender's message. The results from the interpretation stage are evaluated to sort fact from opinion and emotion. Too often, receivers complete this activity prior to receiving the full message, and on hearing something with which they disagree, the sender is effectively tuned out. As a result, communication is stifled. **Evaluating** can be improved through improved concentration and thoughtful consideration of the full message. Summarizing the key points as if they were going to be reported to others can further enhance evaluation skills. Searching for areas of interest rather than prejudging the message can also facilitate the evaluation process.
- *Responding.* **Responding** is both an expectation and requirement for active listening to be effective. Collaborative, two-way communication requires that the listener respond to the sender. Responses provide feedback to the other party, emphasize understanding, encourage further elaboration, and can serve as a beginning point for the receiver to transition into the role of sender for the next message sent. Responses can take many forms. Nonverbal cues such as nodding and smiling can indicate that the sender's message was received. Responses in the form of restating and paraphrasing the sender's message can provide strong signals of interest and understanding. Asking questions can elicit additional details and clarification.

The SIER model provides a useful framework for evaluating communication accuracy and pinpointing the sources of problems. Similarly, it can be effectively used for planning activities and behaviors designed to improve communication effectiveness. As depicted by the SIER model, active listening is a hierarchical and sequential process. One must sense the message before it can be interpreted. In turn, the message must be interpreted before it can be evaluated. Finally, it must be effectively evaluated prior to generating a proper response. When diagnosing a listening breakdown, one should look for the lowest level in the hierarchy where the breakdown could have originated and take proper action to remedy the problem. Exhibit 4.7[14] describes ten specific keys to effective listening that can be used in conjunction with the SIER model to pinpoint and improve listening problems.

VERBAL COMMUNICATION: GIVING INFORMATION

Verbal information refers to statements of fact, opinion, and attitude that are encoded in the form of words, pictures, and numbers in such a way that they convey meaning to a receiver. However, many words and symbols mean different things to different people. Different industries, different cultures, and different types of training or work experience can result in the same word or phrase having multiple interpretations. For instance, to a design or production engineer, the word *quality* might mean "manufactured within design tolerance." However, to a customer it might be translated as "meeting or exceeding expectations." To maximize clarity and minimize misunderstandings, understand and use the vocabulary and terminology that corresponds with the perspective of the customer.

Understanding the Superiority of Pictures over Words

Studies in cognitive psychology have found that pictures tend to be more memorable than their verbal counterparts.[15] The fact that pictures enhance understanding and are more easily recalled than abstract words and symbols has several implications for effective selling.

- The verbal message should be constructed in a manner that generates a mental picture in the receiver's mind. For example, the phrase "Tropicana juices are bursting with flavor" is more visual than the more abstract version "Tropicana

	Ten Keys to Effective Listening **EXHIBIT 4.7**	
The Key Practice	**The Weak Listener**	**The Strong Listener**
1. Find areas of interest	Tunes out dry subjects	Actively looks for opportunities of common interest
2. Judge content, not delivery	Tunes out if the delivery is poor	Skips over delivery errors and focuses on content
3. Hold your fire until full consideration	Evaluates and enters argument prior to completion of message	Does not judge or evaluate until message is complete
4. Listen for ideas	Listens for facts	Listens for central themes
5. Be flexible	Takes intensive and detailed notes	Takes fewer notes and limits theme to central theme and key ideas presented
6. Work at listening	Shows no energy output; attention is faked	Works hard at attending the message and exhibits active body state
7. Resist distractions	Distracted easily	Resists distractions and knows how to concentrate
8. Exercise your mind	Resists difficult expository material in favor of light recreational materials	Uses complex and heavy material as exercise for the mind
9. Keep an open mind	Reacts to emotional words	Interprets color words but does not get hung up on them
10. Capitalize on fact that thought is faster than speech	Tends to daydream with slow speakers	Challenges, anticipates, mentally summarizes, weighs evidence, and listens between the lines

juices have more flavor." This can also be accomplished by providing a short and illustrative analogy or illustrative story to emphasize a key point and bring it alive in the buyer's mind.

- Rather than abstract words that convey only a broad general understanding, use words and phrases that convey concrete and detailed meaning. Concrete expressions provide the receiver with greater information and are less likely to be misunderstood than their abstract counterparts. For example, "This Web transfer system will increase weekly production by 2,100 units" provides more detail than "This Web transfer system will increase production by 10 percent." Similarly, "This conveyor is faster than your existing system" does not deliver the same impact as "This conveyor system will move your product from production to shipping at 50 feet per second as compared with your current system's 20 feet per second."

- Integrate relevant visual sales aids into verbal communication. Sales support materials that explain and reinforce the verbal message will aid the receiver's understanding and enhance recall of the message. As an additional benefit, sales aids such as samples, brochures, graphs, and comparative charts can be left with the buyer to continue selling until the salesperson's next call on the buyer.

Impact of Grammar and Logical Sequencing

Grammar and logical sequencing are also important in the process of giving information to others. The use of proper grammar is a given in business and social communication. In its absence, the receiver of the message tends to exhibit three closely related behaviors.

First, the meaning and credibility of the message are significantly downgraded. Second, the receiver begins to focus on the sender rather than the message, which materially reduces the probability of effective communication. Last, the receiver dismisses the sender and the sender's organization as being unqualified to perform the role of an effective supplier and partner. The importance of proper grammar should not be overlooked.

Similarly, whether one is engaged in simply explaining details or making a formal proposal, logical sequencing of the material is critical. The facts and details must be organized and connected in a logical order. This is essential to clarity and assists the receiver in following the facts. A discussion or presentation that jumps around risks being inefficient and ineffective. At best, the receiver will have to ask a high number of clarification questions. At worst, the receiver will dismiss the salesperson as incompetent and close off the sales negotiation. Advance planning and preparation can improve organization. Outline what needs to be covered and organize it into a logical flow. The outline becomes the agenda to be covered and can serve as an aid for staying on track.

NONVERBAL COMMUNICATION

Nonverbal behaviors have been recognized as an important dimension of communication since medieval times. As early as 1605, Francis Bacon focused on the messages conveyed by *manual language*. Verbal communication deals with the semantic meaning of the message itself while the nonverbal dimension consists of the more abstract message conveyed by how the message is delivered. **Nonverbal communication** is the conscious and unconscious reactions, movements, and utterances that people use in addition to the words and symbols associated with language. This dimension of communication includes eye movements and facial expressions; placement and movements of hands, arms, head, and legs as well as body orientation; the amount of space maintained between individuals; and variations in voice characteristics. Collectively, the various forms of nonverbal communication carry subtle as well as explicit meanings and feelings along with the language message and are frequently more informative than the verbal content of a message.[16]

Research indicates that highly successful salespeople are capable of picking out and comprehending a higher number of behavioral cues from buyers than less successful salespeople are able to sense and interpret. In addition, evidence shows that 50 percent or more of the meaning conveyed within the communication process stems from nonverbal behavior.[17] As the nonverbal components of a message carry as much or more meaning than the language portions, it is critical for salespeople to effectively sense, accurately interpret, and fully evaluate the nonverbal elements of a message in addition to the verbal components. In addition to sensing verbal messages, learn to sense between the words for the thoughts and feelings not being conveyed verbally.

Facial Expressions

Possibly reflecting its central point of focus in interpersonal communication, the various elements of the face play a key role in giving off nonverbal messages. Frowning, pursed lips, and squinted eyes are common in moments of uncertainty, disagreement, and even outright skepticism. Suspicion and anger are typically accompanied by tightness along the jaw line. Smiles are indicative of agreement and interest while biting of one's lip can signal uncertainty. Raised eyebrows can signify surprise and are often found in moments of consideration and evaluation.

Eye Movements

In North America and western Europe, avoidance of eye contact results in a negative message and is often associated with deceit and dishonesty. However, increased eye contact by the sender infers honesty and self-confidence. Increased eye contact by the receiver of the message signals increasing levels of interest and concentration. However, when eye contact becomes a stare and continues unbroken by glances away or blinking, it is typically interpreted as a threat or inference of power. A blank stare or eye contact directed away from the conversation can show disinterest and boredom. Repeated glances made toward one's watch or possibly an exit door often indicate that the conversation is about to end.

Placement and Movements of Hands, Arms, Head, and Legs

Smooth and gradual movements denote calm and confidence, whereas jerky and hurried movements are associated with nervousness and stress. Uncrossed arms and legs signal openness, confidence, and cooperation. However, crossed arms and legs psychologically close out the other party and express disagreement and defensiveness. Increased movement of the head and limbs hints at increasing tension, as does the tight clasping of hands or fists. The placement of a hand on the chin or a tilted head suggests increased levels of evaluation, whereas nodding of the head expresses agreement. Growing impatience is associated with drumming of the fingers or patting of a foot. The fingering of one's hair and rubbing the back of the neck signifies increasing nervousness and apprehension.

Body Posture and Orientation

Fidgeting and shifting from side to side is generally considered to be a negative message associated with nervousness and apprehension. Leaning forward or sitting forward on the edge of a chair is a general sign of increasing interest and a positive disposition in regard to what is being discussed. Similarly, leaning away can indicate disinterest, boredom, or even distrust. Leaning back with both hands placed behind one's head signifies a perceived sense of smugness and superiority. A rigid erect posture can convey inflexibility or even defensiveness whereas sloppy posture suggests disinterest in the topic. Similar to sitting backward in a chair, sitting on the edge of the table or the arm of a chair is an expression of power and superiority.

Proxemics

Proxemics refers to the personal distance that individuals prefer to keep between themselves and other individuals and is an important element of nonverbal communication. The distance that one places between oneself and others implies a meaningful message and affects the outcome of the selling process. If a salesperson pushes too close to a prospect who requires more distance, the prospect may perceive the salesperson to be manipulative, intimidating, and possibly threatening. However, salespeople who put too much distance between themselves and the customer risk being perceived as rigidly formal, aloof, or even apprehensive.

Proxemics differ across cultures and regions of the world. For example, in North Africa and Latin America business is conducted at a much closer distance than in North America. As depicted in Figure 4.4, North Americans generally recognize four distinct proxemic zones. The *intimate zone* is reserved for intimate relationships with immediate family and loved ones. The *personal zone* is for personal relationships with close friends and associates. The *social zone* is for business client relationships and is the zone in which most business is conducted. The *public zone* is for the general public and group settings such as classrooms and presentations.

It is critical that salespeople understand proxemics and monitor the progression of their buyer–seller relationships so as to properly position themselves with different customers. Typically, salespeople begin working with a prospect at the far end of the *social zone*. As the salesperson–buyer relationship develops, the salesperson is in a position to move closer without violating the customer's space and causing him or her to become defensive.

Variations in Voice Characteristics

Nonverbal voice characteristics such as speaking rates, pause duration, pitch or frequency, and intensity have been linked to communication effectiveness and selling performance.

FIGURE 4.4   Personal Space and Interpersonal Communication

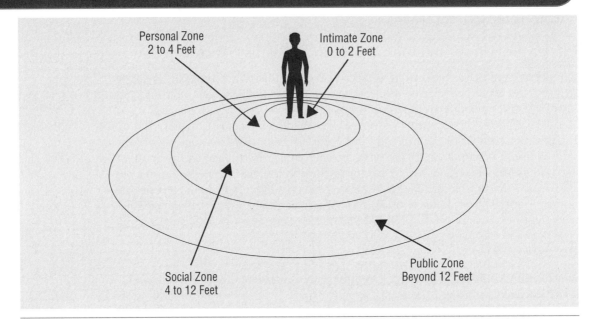

Individuals utilize four preferred spatial zones for interaction in different social and business situations.

These voice characteristics convey direct as well as subtle and implied meanings and feelings that can complement or accent the corresponding verbal message.[18]

Speaking Rates and Pause Duration

Within normal speaking rates, faster speakers are generally evaluated more favorably than slower speakers. Contrary to the often-cited fast-talking salesperson being perceived as high pressure, faster rates of speech and shorter pause duration are actually associated with higher levels of intelligence, credibility, and knowledge.[19] Slower speakers are perceived as being less competent as well as less benevolent. However, speech rates that are jerky and beyond normal rates of speech can present problems in sensing and interpreting the complete message. Varying the rate of speech has also been found to be conducive to maintaining interest.

Pitch or Frequency

Voice pitch carries a great deal of information to the receiver. Varying pitch and frequency during the course of a message is used to encourage attentiveness of the listener and to accent certain forms of statements. A rising pitch during the message is associated with questions and can often be perceived as reflecting uncertainty. Just the opposite, a falling pitch is associated with declarative statements and completion of the message. Overall, high-pitched voices are judged as less truthful, less emphatic, less potent, and more nervous. Lower-pitched voices have been found to be more persuasive and truthful and have a positive impact on selling performance.

Intensity and Loudness

Dominance, superiority, intensity, and aggression are commonly associated with loud voices, whereas soft voices characterize submission and uncertainty. However, it is the variability of intensity that has been found to be most effective in communication. Varying levels of loudness allow the sender to adapt to different situations and environments. Variation also increases the receiver's attention and can provide additional information inputs by accenting key points of a message.

Using Nonverbal Clusters

Nonverbal clusters are groups of related expressions, gestures, and movements. Similar to a one-word expression, a single isolated gesture or movement should not be taken as a reliable indication of the true intent or meaning of a message. Sensing and interpreting groups or clusters of nonverbal cues provide a more reliable indicator of the message and intent. When the individual behaviors and gestures begin to fit together, they form a common and unified message that should be considered by the salesperson. Common nonverbal clusters applicable to selling communication are described in Exhibit 4.8.[20]

Just as nonverbal messages can be interpreted by salespeople to better interpret and understand communication with prospects and buyers, those same prospects and buyers can also sense and interpret the nonverbal messages being sent by the salesperson. Consequently, it is important that salespersons monitor the nonverbal cues they are sending to ensure consistency with and reinforcement of the intended message.

Common Nonverbal Clusters   **EXHIBIT 4.8**

Cluster Name	Cluster Meaning	Body Posture and Orientation	Movement of Hands, Arms, and Legs	Eyes and Facial Expressions
Openness	Openness, flexibility, and sincerity	• Moving closer • Leaning forward	• Open hands • Removing coat • Unbutton collar • Uncrossed arms and legs	• Slight smile • Good eye contact
Defensiveness	Defensiveness, skepticism, and apprehension	• Rigid body	• Crossed arms and legs • Clenched fists	• Minimal eye contact • Glancing sideways • Pursed lips
Evaluation	Evaluation and consideration of message	• Leaning forward	• Hand on cheek • Stroking chin • Chin in palm of hand	• Tilted head • Dropping glasses to tip of nose
Deception	Dishonesty and secretiveness	• Patterns of rocking	• Fidgeting with objects • Increased leg movements	• Increased eye movement • Frequent gazes elsewhere • Forced smile
Readiness	Dedication or commitment	• Sitting forward	• Hands on hips • Legs uncrossed • Feet flat on floor	• Increased eye contact
Boredom	Lack of interest and impatience	• Head in palm of hands • Slouching	• Drumming fingers • Swinging a foot • Brushing and picking at items • Tapping feet	• Poor eye contact • Glancing at watch • Blank stares

SUMMARY

1. **Explain the importance of collaborative, two-way communication in trust-based selling.** The two-way exchange process inherent in collaborative communication facilitates accurate and mutual understanding of the objectives, problems, needs, and capabilities of each of the parties. As a result of this heightened level of understanding, solutions and responses can be generated that provide mutual benefits to all participants. Without mutual sharing, this would not be possible, and one party or the other would benefit at the expense of the other. Although this might be good for the "winning" party, the disadvantaged party would be less inclined to continue doing business and would seek out other business partners.

2. **Explain the primary types of questions and how they are applied in selling.** Questions can be typed into two basic categories according to (1) the amount of information and level of specificity desired and (2) the strategic purpose of the question.

   - **Typed by the Amount of Information and Level of Specificity Desired.** This category includes open-end questions, closed-end questions, and dichotomous questions. *Open-end questions* are designed to let the customer respond freely and deliver richer and more expansive information than more directed forms of questioning. They are typically used to probe for descriptive information that allows the salesperson to better understand the specific needs and expectations of the customer. *Closed-end questions* are designed to limit the customer's response to one or two words. This type of question is typically used to confirm or clarify information gleaned from previous responses to open-end questions. *Dichotomous questions* are directive forms of questioning in which the buyer is requested to make a choice between two or more alternatives. These questions are used to discover buyer preferences and move the selling process forward.

   - **Types of Questions Classified by Strategic Purpose.** This category of questions includes questions designed for (1) probing, (2) evaluative, (3) tactical, and (4) reactive purposes. *Probing questions* are designed to penetrate beneath surface information to provide more useful details. *Evaluative questions* use an open-end format to uncover how the buyer feels about things (e.g., attitudes, opinions, and preferences held by the prospect). *Tactical questions* are used to shift the topic of discussion when a line of questioning proves to be of little interest or value. *Reactive questions* respond to previous information provided by the other party and ask for additional details about the previous information. Salespeople *use reactive questions to elicit additional details regarding facts, attitudes, or feelings the customer has mentioned.*

3. **Illustrate the diverse roles and uses of strategic questioning in trust-based selling.** The most obvious use of questioning is to elicit detailed information about the buyer's current situation, needs, and expectations. Properly applied, questioning facilitates both the buyer's and seller's understanding of a problem and proposed solutions. Questioning can also test the buyer's interest in a problem or solution and increase their cognitive involvement and participation in the selling process. Questions can also be used to subtly and strategically redirect, regain, or hold the buyer's attention should it begin to wander during the conversation. Similarly, questions can provide a convenient and subtle transition to a different topic of discussion and provide a logical guide promoting sequential thought and decision making while advancing the selling process in moving forward.

4. **Identify and describe the five steps of the ADAPT questioning sequence.** Corresponding to the ADAPT acronym, the five steps making up this sequence

of effective questioning are assessment questions, discovery questions, activation questions, projection questions, and transition questions.

- *Assessment Questions.* These are broad and general questions designed to be nonthreatening and to spark conversation. Rather than asking for feelings or conclusions, assessment questions elicit factual information about the customer's current situation that can provide a basis for further exploration and probing. These questions should address the buyer's company and operation, goals and objectives, market trends and customers, current suppliers, and even the buyer as an individual.

- *Discovery Questions.* Following up responses from assessment questions, discovery questions drill down and probe for further details needed to further clarify and understand the buyer's problems. In addition to facts, the buyer's interpretations, perceptions, feelings, and opinions are sought in regard to their needs, wants, dissatisfactions, and expectations relevant to product, delivery requirements, budget and financing issues, and desired service levels. The goal is to discover needs and dissatisfactions that the salesperson's sales offering can resolve.

- *Activation Questions.* The implied or suggested needs that might be gained from discovery questions are not usually sufficient to gain the sale. Often a buyer will believe that a particular problem does not cause any significant negative consequences, hence the motivation to solve the problem will carry a low priority. Activation questions help the customer realistically evaluate the full impact of the implied need. The objective is to "activate" the customer's interest in solving discovered problems by helping him or her to gain insight into the true ramifications of the problem and realize that what may initially seem to be of little consequence may, in fact, carry significant consequence to the buyer's organization.

- *Projection Questions.* A natural extension of the activation questions, projection questions encourage and facilitate the buyer in "projecting" what it would be like if the problems or needs did not exist. Projection questions switch the focus from problems to the benefits to be derived from solving the problems—the payoff for taking action and investing in a solution. Focusing on the benefit payoff allows the buyer to establish his or her perceived value of implementing a solution. In this manner, the benefit payoff is perceived as what the solution is worth—what the buyer would be willing to pay. Projection questions assist the salesperson in selling himself or herself by establishing the worth of the solution. More important, the customer, rather than the salesperson, establishes the value of solving the problem.

- *Transition Questions.* Transition questions smooth the transition from needs discovery and activation into the presentation and demonstration of the proposed solution's features, advantages, and benefits. Typically, closed end and evaluative in format, these questions confirm the buyer's desire to seek a solution and give his or her consent to the salesperson to move forward with the selling process.

5. **Discuss the four sequential steps for effective active listening.** Active listening consists of the sequential communication behaviors of (1) sensing, (2) interpreting, (3) evaluating, and (4) responding.

- *Sensing.* The first activity in active listening is to sense and receive the verbal and nonverbal components of the message. Sensing is much more than just hearing the message and requires practice and concentration. Poor or weak sensing can create significant problems in the latter stages of interpreting and evaluating.

- *Interpreting.* After sensing and receiving the message, it must be correctly interpreted in terms of what the sender actually meant. In addition to the meaning of the words and symbols, the experiences, knowledge, and attitudes of the sender should be considered to fully understand what was meant.

- *Evaluating.* Effective communication requires the receiver to decide whether or not he or she agrees with the sender's message. This requires evaluating the results from the interpretation stage to sort fact from opinion and emotion.

- *Responding.* Collaborative communication requires listeners to provide feedback to the other party. Responses can take the form of restating and paraphrasing the sender's message, answering questions, or asking questions to gain additional details and clarification.

6. **Discuss the superiority of pictures over words for explaining concepts and enhancing comprehension.** Evidence is provided by studies in cognitive psychology supporting pictures as being more memorable than words. Using descriptive words to "draw" mental pictures in the buyer's mind can enhance understanding and are more easily recalled than abstract words and symbols. This carries several implications for successful selling:

- Understanding and recall can be aided by providing a short and illustrative analogy or illustrative story to emphasize a key point and bring it alive in the buyer's mind.

- Rather than abstract words that convey only a broad general understanding, utilize words and phrases that convey concrete and detailed meaning. Concrete expressions provide the receiver with greater information and are less likely to be misunderstood than their abstract counterparts.

- Integrate relevant visual sales aids into verbal communication. Sales support materials that explain and reinforce the verbal message will aid the buyer's understanding and enhance recall of the message.

7. **Describe the different forms of nonverbal communication.** Nonverbal behaviors are made up from the various movements and utterances that people use in addition to the words and symbols associated with language. These can be conscious or unconscious and include eye movement and facial expressions; placement and movements of hands, arms, head, and legs as well as body orientation; the amount of space maintained between individuals; and variations in voice characteristics. Sensing and interpreting groups or clusters of nonverbal cues can provide a reliable indicator of the underlying message and intent. When the individual behaviors and gestures begin to fit together, they form a common and unified message that should be considered by the salesperson. Evidence shows that 50 percent or more of the meaning conveyed in the process of interpersonal communication is carried by nonverbal behaviors. Consequently, it is critical that salespeople learn to effectively sense, accurately interpret, and fully evaluate the nonverbal elements of a message.

UNDERSTANDING PROFESSIONAL SELLING TERMS

trust-based sales communication	implication questions
open-end questions	need-payoff questions
closed-end questions	ADAPT
dichotomous questions	assessment questions
probing questions	discovery questions
evaluative questions	activation questions
tactical questions	projection questions
reactive questions	transition questions
SPIN	social listening
situation questions	serious listening
problem questions	active listening

SIER	responding
sensing	nonverbal communication
interpreting	proxemics
evaluating	nonverbal clusters

DEVELOPING PROFESSIONAL SELLING KNOWLEDGE

1. Explain why talking *with* buyers rather than talking *at* buyers is critical to success in selling.

2. Discuss how salespeople use effective questioning to maintain subtle control over the buyer–seller communication dialogue.

3. Distinguish between open-end and closed-end questions, and describe how each of these question formats might best be used in the trust-based selling process.

4. Explain the difference in the uses of probing, evaluative, tactical, and reactive questions in trust-based selling.

5. Discuss how effective questioning skills help accomplish the seven closely related sales objectives identified in this module.

6. Identify and explain each of the individual steps involved in the SPIN sequence of questioning. Develop two example questions for each step.

7. Identify and explain each of the individual steps involved in the ADAPT sequence of questioning. Develop two example questions for each step.

8. Discuss how the four sequential elements of sensing, interpreting, evaluating, and responding (SIER) combine to create what is referred to as active listening.

9. Explain what is meant by nonverbal clusters and why they are important to salespeople.

10. What is meant by proxemics? Why is it important for salespeople to understand the concept of proxemics?

BUILDING PROFESSIONAL SELLING SKILLS

1. Listening skill development is an ongoing process. Good listening is a key to success in any business environment. Discovering your attitude about listening and assessing your listening behaviors are important for self-development and improvement. Complete the following exercise and score your listening habits. If the statement describes your listening habits, check "Yes," if not, check "No." After completing the assessment, score your listening habits according to the scale following the checklist.[21]

	YES	NO
a. I am interested in many subjects and do not knowingly tune out dry-sounding information.	☐	☐
b. I listen carefully for a speaker's main ideas and supporting points.	☐	☐
c. I take notes during meetings to record key points.	☐	☐
d. I am not easily distracted.	☐	☐
e. I keep my emotions under control.	☐	☐
f. I concentrate carefully and do not fake attention.	☐	☐
g. I wait for the speaker to finish before finally evaluating the message.	☐	☐

	YES	NO
h. I respond appropriately with a smile, a nod, or a word of acknowledgment as a speaker is talking.	☐	☐
i. I am aware of mannerisms that may distract a speaker and keep mine under control.	☐	☐
j. I understand my biases and control them when I am listening.	☐	☐
k. I refrain from constantly interrupting.	☐	☐
l. I value eye contact and maintain it most of the time.	☐	☐
m. I often restate or paraphrase what the speaker said to make sure I have the correct meaning.	☐	☐
n. I listen for the speaker's emotional meaning as well as subject matter content.	☐	☐
o. I ask questions for clarification.	☐	☐
p. I do not finish other people's sentences unless asked to do so.	☐	☐
q. When listening on the phone, one hand is kept free to take notes.	☐	☐
r. I attempt to set aside my ego and focus on the speaker rather than myself.	☐	☐
s. I am careful to judge the message rather than the speaker.	☐	☐
t. I am a patient listener most of the time.	☐	☐

The following scale will help you interpret your present listening skill level based on your current attitudes and habits.

1–5 "NO" answers	You are an excellent listener. Keep it up!
6–10 "NO" answers	You are a good listener but can improve.
11–15 "NO" answers	Through practice you can become a much more effective listener in your business and personal relationships.
16–20 "NO" answers	Listen up!!

How do your listening skills compare to those of your class peers? What steps might you take to strengthen your listening skills?

2. Developing ADAPT question sequences takes thought and practice. Using the ADAPT questioning process discussed in this module as a guide, develop a scripted series of salesperson questions and possible buyer responses that might be typical in the following selling situation. For your convenience, a sample ADAPT questioning script template is included following the description of the selling scenario.

THE SELLING SCENARIO

This scenario involves a salesperson representing the Direct Sales Department of American Seating Company (ASC) and Rodney Moore, a buyer representing the Seattle Music Arts Association (SMAA). Although there are some 12 major manufacturers of auditorium seating, ASC's market share of 21 percent makes the company a leader in this industry. ASC's selling efforts are organized on a basis of market types: one department sells direct to end-users and a second department sells to distributors who in turn sell to retailers of business furniture. Direct sales to end-users are restricted to minimum orders of $200,000.

As an integral part of a major remodeling project, SMAA wants to replace the seats in the Seattle Metropolitan Auditorium. ASC estimates a potential sale of between

$350,000 and $500,000. This range represents differences in both quantity and types of seating desired. According to the Request for Proposals, funding for this project is being provided through a bond issue. From this very basic level of knowledge of the buyer's situation, the salesperson is working through the ADAPT questioning sequence with the buyer to better identify and confirm the actual needs and expectations regarding seating.

Use the following ADAPT script template to develop a series of salesperson questions and anticipated buyer responses that might apply to this selling situation.

Assessment Questions:

Seller: _____
Buyer: _____

Seller: _____
Buyer: _____

Seller: _____
Buyer: _____

Seller: _____
Buyer: _____

Discovery Questions:

Seller: _____
Buyer: _____

Seller: _____
Buyer: _____

Seller: _____
Buyer: _____

Seller: _____
Buyer: _____

Activation Questions:

Seller: _____
Buyer: _____

Seller: _____
Buyer: _____

Seller: _____
Buyer: _____

Seller: _____
Buyer: _____

Projection Questions:

Seller: _____
Buyer: _____

Seller: _____
Buyer: _____

Seller: _____

Buyer: _____

Seller: _____

Buyer: _____

Transition Questions:

Seller: _____

Buyer: _____

Seller: _____

Buyer: _____

Seller: _____

Buyer: _____

Seller: _____

Buyer: _____

ROLE PLAY

Situation:	Read the selling scenario in item 2.
Characters:	Yourself, salesperson for American Seating Company (ASC); Rodney Moore, director of purchasing for the Seattle Music Arts Association (SMAA)
Scene:	*Location*—Rodney Moore's office at the Seattle Music Arts Association (SMAA).
	Action—As an integral part of the remodeling of the Seattle Metropolitan Auditorium, SMAA will be replacing all the seating. As a salesperson for ASC, you are making an initial sales call to Moore for the purpose of identifying and detailing the specific needs and expectations SMAA has for seating in the new auditorium.

Role play this needs discovery sales call and demonstrate how you might utilize SPIN or ADAPT questioning sequences to identify the needs for seating.

Upon completion of the role play, address the following questions:

(a) What additional information does the salesperson need in order to fully understand the seating needs of SMAA? Develop assessment and discovery questions designed to elicit the needed information.

(b) What additional activation and projection questions might be effective for motivating the buyer to take action and advance the sale forward?

3. Used in combination, open- and closed-end questions help salespeople uncover and confirm customer needs, dissatisfactions, and opportunities. Observe a salesperson calling on a new prospect and notice the different types of questions used and the information that is received in exchange.

- What open-end questions did the salesperson use?
- What types of information were gathered by using these open-end questions?
- What closed-end questions did the salesperson use?
- What types of information were gathered by using these closed-end questions?

ROLE PLAY

4. **Situation:** MidComm specializes in providing cell phones and wireless services for small businesses with 10 to 100 employees having needs that call for mobile, wireless communication. As an account development specialist for MidComm, you are making an initial sales call to Dan Goebel, the director of your university's maintenance division to assess their current use and needs for wireless mobile communication. According to the initial information you

gained from a short phone conversation with Goebel, they are currently using Sprint cellular service for a number of their maintenance supervisors. Having staff members wirelessly linked and able to communicate from anywhere on campus has proven beneficial in terms of efficiency and productivity. In fact the university is considering rolling cell phones out to all building maintenance workers. They have been pleased with the positive aspects of wireless communication, but during your phone conversation Goebel made a couple of comments that there might be some problems with the present vendor and concerns about potential employee misuse of the phone services.

Characters: Yourself, salesperson for MidComm; Dan Goebel, director of facilities maintenance for your university

Scene: *Location*—Dan Goebel's office at the university.
Action—Role play this needs discovery sales call and demonstrate how you might utilize SPIN or ADAPT questioning sequences to identify the needs and concerns of the prospect.

Upon completion of the role play, address the following questions:

(a) What additional information does the salesperson need in order to fully understand the communication needs and concerns? Develop assessment and discovery questions designed to elicit the needed information.

(b) What additional activation and projection questions might be effective for motivating the prospect to take action and advance the sale forward?

5. Strong and effective interpersonal communication skills play a critical role in trust-based selling. The Northwest Regional Educational Laboratory (NWREL) focuses on the study of communication with the goal of developing tools and programs that enable interested individuals to improve their communication effectiveness. Their *E.A.R. Indicators for Effective, Appropriate, and Responsive Customer Service Communication* provides clear and specific guidelines for effective communication in any type of seller–buyer exchange. As such, this set of guidelines can serve as an instrument for assessing one's own interpersonal communication behaviors and identifying strong areas for continued emphasis and weak areas for improvement.

Go to the Web site http://www.nwrel.org/assessment/pdfRubrics/csr.PDF and read through the rubrics that NWREL has developed for effective customer service communication. The first page of the PDF file, *E.A.R. Indicators for Effective, Appropriate, and Responsive Customer Service Communication*, summarizes the communication competencies that comprise the three dimensions of customer service communication: effectiveness, appropriateness, and responsiveness. The subsequent three pages focus on each of these three dimensions, one at a time, in order to further detail the communication activities and behaviors associated with three different levels of performance: Exceptional, Developing, and Emerging.

Read and study this web-based set of guidelines for effective customer communication and address each of the following questions:

(a) Compare the activities and competencies described in the NWREL *E.A.R. Indicators for Effective, Appropriate, and Responsive Customer Service Communication* with the activities and behaviors you have learned as comprising trust-based selling. How are they similar? How are they different? Why?

(b) Identify the five competencies in the *E.A.R. Indicators for Effective, Appropriate, and Responsive Customer Service Communication* that you would rate yourself as *Exceptional* in performing. For each, explain why.

(c) Identify the five competencies in the *E.A.R. Indicators for Effective, Appropriate, and Responsive Customer Service Communication* that you would rate yourself as *Emerging* in terms of performance. For each of these emergent competencies, explain what you will do to improve your skill and performance in that area.

MAKING PROFESSIONAL SELLING DECISIONS

Case 4.1: Pre-Select, Inc.

Background

You are a salesperson for Pre-Select, Inc. (PSI), the Chicago-based industry leader in preinterview assessment and testing for the insurance industry. Focusing primarily on sales-related recruiting and selection, PSI's Interactive Employee Assessment System (IEAS) has been successful in lowering overall payroll costs by reducing sales agent turnover rates. Because of its highly recognized rate of success, PSI's customers include 13 of the top 20 insurance companies in the United States.

Although the system is continuously revised and updated, the basic program has been operating for six years. Using a personal computer in the field—usually at the branch office or general agency location—the IEAS consists of three computer-based components:

1. Preinterview attitude and aptitude testing.
2. Interactive simulations of critical work situations for use as part of the interview process.
3. Periodic posthiring assessment for input into future training needs.

Current Situation

Ron Lovell, national agency director for Secure Future Insurance Company (SFIC), is interested in improving his company's recruiting and selection process for sales agents. SFIC is a national company with 150 agents across the United States. Although not ranked among the top 20 insurers, SFIC is a large and successful firm listed in the *Fortune 1000.* You have met with Lovell on four previous occasions exploring problems, opportunities, and needs. During these meetings, you discovered that SFIC's turnover rate among its sales agents approaches 42 percent. Compared with industry averages, that is not all that bad, but it does require hiring 375 new salespeople every year. SFIC's own estimate of hiring, training, and licensing costs is $7,500 per new salesperson hired, for a total annual cost exceeding $2.8 million. Well-documented field experience indicates that, using PSI's computer-based system, turnover would drop to an average turnover rate ranging from 15 to 20 percent, which offers considerable savings to SFIC.

You have been working up the figures for implementing the system at SFIC's headquarters and in each of the company's 150 general agency offices. One-time hardware costs total $610,000. Although minimal training is required, installation and training would be priced out at $75,000 plus another $5,500 for chargeable travel expenses. Software licensing fees would total $135,000 per year.

Sales tax on the hardware and software would be computed at 6.5 percent. Finally, software maintenance fees run 15 percent of the annual licensing cost. According to the technical support department, this installation could be completed, with the full system operating and all staff training completed, in just four months from the date of the order.

The Learning Assignment

Review your text materials discussing "Verbal Communication: Giving Information." This section details three fundamentals for maximizing information exchange: (1) generating mental pictures in your buyer's mind, (2) using phrases that convey concrete and detailed meaning, and (3) integrating effective visual aids to enhance your buyer's understanding. Demonstrate your understanding of these three concepts by responding to the following discussion items:

Questions

1. Think through and create a seller–buyer script that explains the advantageous capabilities and beneficial outcomes of your assessment system.
2. Develop a set of visual aids that could be used to illustrate the capabilities and beneficial outcomes identified.

Situation:	Read Case 4.1.
Characters:	Yourself, salesperson for Pre-Select, Inc.; Ron Lovell, national agency director for Secure Future Insurance Company.
Scene:	*Location*—Ron Lovell's office at Secure Future Insurance Company. *Action*—This is your fifth sales call to Secure Future. On the previous sales calls, you have worked with Lovell to discover and detail a great deal of information about the prospect's problems and needs to do a better job in selecting and hiring sales agents. Lovell has requested this meeting so that you might illustrate how your Interactive Employee Assessment System (IEAS) program can help them address and resolve these problems.

ROLE PLAY

Role play this meeting with Lovell and demonstrate how you might explain the capabilities of and beneficial outcomes offered by IEAS as they are described in Case 4.1.

Upon completion of the role play, address the following questions:

1. What might the salesperson do to generate vivid mental pictures of the advantages offered by the IEAS program?

2. What other ways might the salesperson maximize the detailed meaning and understanding through the use of concrete expressions?

3. What other visual sales aids could be used to further support and illustrate the capabilities and benefits of this system?

Case 4.2: STAGA Financial Services

Background

Bart Waits, account manager for Data Intelligence, LLC, arrived just a few minutes early for his 9:00 A.M. meeting with Kerri Williams, director of purchasing for STAGA Financial Services. This was his first in-person call at STAGA, and he had flown in explicitly for this meeting to present his proposal for a data-mining software package that would be used by the client's IT department. Upon arrival, Waits did the obligatory check-in with the receptionist in the main lobby. After contacting the purchasing office, the receptionist informed him that they would be right down to escort him to Williams' office. About 12 minutes later, Williams' executive assistant entered the lobby and advised Waits that she would escort him to the office where they would be meeting. The executive assistant was friendly and open and provided Waits with a fresh cup of coffee just before taking him into Williams' office.

Current Situation

Upon entering the large and well-furnished office, Waits noticed that the layout was a bit different than he had expected. Williams was sitting behind a large walnut executive desk that was located at an angle in one corner and faced toward the opposite wall of windows. No guest chairs were located adjacent to the desk. Rather, the chairs were set some 10 to 12 feet from the desk, adjacent to a small table, and facing the desk. In another area of the room, there was a worktable with several chairs pulled up to it.

Williams was on the phone as Waits entered and signaled for him to go ahead and be seated. It was obvious that the conversation was drawing to a close, and she made eye contact and smiled at him once or twice to acknowledge his presence. When the phone call was over, she popped up from the desk and walked over to meet him. While shaking hands, each of them introduced themselves, and she mentioned that he should address her as Kerri. She apologized for being on the phone and inquired about his flight. After some small talk, Waits transitioned into his presentation by first outlining the

needs as specified in STAGA's original Request for Proposals (RFP). As Waits provided many additional details beyond those in the RFP, Williams smiled and looked him in the eye as she shifted her chair closer to the table and commented that it was apparent that he had done his homework on the company.

Several times during his presentation, she placed her hand on her cheek and shifted forward to ask numerous questions. Although sparingly, she also took notes at several points of his presentation. Waits' appointment was for one and one-half hours, and he figured that he would need every minute of it. However, about 50 minutes into the meeting he noticed that Williams would glance at her watch occasionally. After making a major point and demonstrating several significant benefits to STAGA, he noticed that Williams uncrossed her legs and leaned forward with her glasses on the tip of her nose as she began asking him a series of questions about his software package.

Questions

1. Identify the different nonverbal cues that the buyer was providing to Waits.

2. If you were in Waits' place, how would you have interpreted and responded to these different nonverbal cues?

Situation:	Read Case 4.2.
Characters:	Bart Waits, account manager for Data Intelligence, LLC; Kerri Williams, director of purchasing for STAGA Financial Services
Scene:	*Location*—Kerri Williams' office at STAGA Financial Services. *Action*—Waits has arrived for his first meeting with Williams. As he is escorted to Williams' office to begin his sales call, he begins to pick up a variety of verbal and nonverbal cues that might prove very useful as he advances through the agenda of this initial sales call.

ROLE PLAY

Role play this meeting between Waits and Williams as described in Case 4.2.

Upon completion of the role play, address the following questions:

1. Based on the patterns of verbal and nonverbal clusters, what interpretations might the salesperson make as to the meaning of these various communication signals?

2. How should Waits respond to these nonverbal cues in order to further advance his sales call objectives?

Initiating Customer Relationships

The two modules in Part Two concentrate on initiating relationships with customers. Module 5 discusses prospecting, the process of locating and screening potential customers. Strategic prospecting and various prospecting methods are presented as means of overcoming unique challenges in this early stage of the sales process. Preparing for sales dialogue is also discussed in Module 5. In this process, salespeople gather and study information to be used in subsequent sales calls.

In Module 6, we offer insights into how to plan sales dialogues and presentations as well as how to approach the customer. A comprehensive checklist provides a framework for sales dialogue and presentation planning. The checklist reminds salespeople to define the buying situation, buyer needs and motives, the competitive situation, presentation objectives, and additional information needed to plan a successful sales interaction. Module 6 also gives valuable advice on how to engage the customer, which involves securing an appointment and getting the sales dialogue and presentation off to a good start.

STRATEGIC PROSPECTING AND PREPARING
FOR SALES DIALOGUE

IDENTIFYING SALES OPPORTUNITIES: THREE EXAMPLES

The Polling Company provides research services to clients involved in political campaigns. The company was growing, but a large percentage of sales revenue was being generated by a few large clients. Concerned about this situation, the company expanded its line of research services and made a concerted effort to bring in new clients. Salespeople used targeted mailing and cold calls to attract new clients, but their efforts were not very successful. Eventually, the morale of the sales force began to be affected. In addition, salespeople were spending so much time trying to get new clients that they did not have time to develop additional business with existing clients. The company changed course, and salespeople began to look for opportunities to sell additional services to existing customers. This approach was very successful—sales increased by 20 percent.

When Paul Brancaleone purchased Foster's Promotional Goods, company sales had been stagnant for several years. Prospecting for new customers was largely through cold calls by salespeople. Brancaleone decided to expand prospecting efforts by placing ads in the Yellow Pages and on a local radio station. These efforts were expensive, but they did not generate much new business. Looking for a better approach to identify good sales opportunities, Brancaleone started using an e-mail blasting method. He identified more than 3,000 existing customers and prospects he had met at trade shows in the company database. Each contact in the database now receives a quarterly e-mail with product photos and special offers. This approach does not cost very much and typically produces an immediate response from existing customers or new prospects. For example, a recent e-mail produced a $12,000 order within days. Those who respond represent good sales opportunities because they are interested in exploring making a purchase. In addition to the increase in sales, Brancaleone's salespeople are happier—they do not have to make cold calls anymore.

Anu Shukla founded RubiconSoft three years ago. As is typical for business start-ups, the online marketing service company's team was busy taking care of its initial customers, but the time had come to start adding new clients. However, the company had limited time and financial resources to search for new clients. Shukla turned to free online services. She used an online social networking service to identify the appropriate contacts at two large prospective customer organizations. Another online service identified an executive she knew that had moved to another company. This company represented an excellent sales opportunity for RubiconSoft. These and other online services helped Shukla land several new clients without spending any money.

Sources: Charles Butler, "Get'Em in Gear," *Business Week SmallBiz* (Winter 2005): 47; Jeanette Borzo, "End of the Cold Call?" *The Wall Street Journal* (May 8, 2006): R10.

Prospecting is extremely important to most salespeople. Salespeople who do not regularly prospect are operating under the assumption that the current customer base will be sufficient to generate the desired level of future revenue. This is a shaky assumption in that market conditions may change, causing existing customers

Objectives

After completing this module, you should be able to

1 Discuss why prospecting can be a challenging task for a salesperson.

2 Explain strategic prospecting.

3 Explain where salespeople find prospects.

4 Understand the importance of gathering and studying precall information to prepare for sales dialogue.

to buy less. Another possibility is that customers may go out of business or be bought by another firm, with the buying decisions now being made outside the salesperson's territory. The salesperson may simply lose customers due to competitive activity or dissatisfaction with the product, the salesperson, or the selling firm. Because there is typically a considerable time lag between the commencement of prospecting and the conversion of prospects to customer status, salespeople should spend some time prospecting on a regular basis. Otherwise, lost sales volume cannot be regained quickly enough to satisfy the large majority of sales organizations—those that are growth oriented.

The examples in the opening vignette illustrate the importance and complexity of identifying sales opportunities. Most salespeople have to cultivate future business if they are to sustain the sales growth objectives established by their company. Salespeople typically achieve sales growth objectives by finding the right balance between getting new customers and generating additional business from existing customers. A variety of approaches are available with each having advantages and disadvantages. New technological advances are increasing the tools salespeople can use to determine the best sales opportunities. The purpose of this module is to examine the importance and challenges of prospecting, introduce the strategic prospecting process, present different strategic prospecting methods, and discuss preparing for sales dialogue.

PROSPECTING: IMPORTANCE AND CHALLENGES

Despite its importance, salespeople will often say that they find it difficult to allocate enough time to prospecting. Truthfully, the biggest reason most salespeople find prospecting challenging is their fear of rejection. Today's buyers are busy, and many are reluctant to see salespeople. There are several reasons that buyers may not take the time to see a salesperson:

1. They may have never heard of the salesperson's firm.
2. They may have just bought the salesperson's product category, and there is presently no need.
3. Buyers may have their own deadlines on other issues, and they are not in a receptive mood to see any salespeople.
4. Buyers are constantly getting calls from salespeople and do not have time to see them all.
5. Gatekeepers in any organization screen their bosses' calls and sometimes are curt and even rude.

Salespeople can overcome the challenges of prospecting and become more effective in determining the best sales opportunities by following a strategic sales prospecting process, utilizing a variety of prospecting methods, developing a strategic prospecting plan, and preparing for sales dialogue with prospects.

Strategic Prospecting

The first step in the trust-based sales process presented in Module 1 is strategic prospecting. **Strategic prospecting** is a process designed to identify, qualify, and prioritize sales opportunities, and whether they represent potential new customers or opportunities to generate additional business from existing customers. The basic purpose of strategic prospecting is to help salespeople determine the best sales opportunities in the most efficient way. Effective strategic prospecting helps salespeople spend their valuable selling time in the most productive manner.

The strategic prospecting process (illustrated in Figure 5.1) is called a **sales funnel** or **sales pipeline**, because it visualizes the trust-based sales process vertically in the form of a funnel, rather than horizontally as depicted in Module 1. The funnel is very wide at the top as salespeople typically have a large number of potential sales

Sales Funnel   FIGURE 5.1

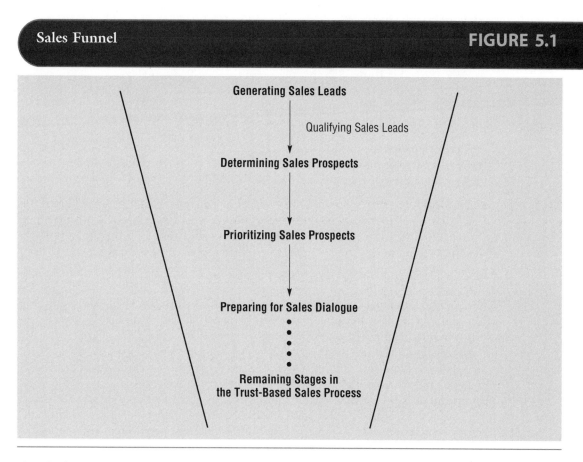

Generating Sales Leads

Qualifying Sales Leads

Determining Sales Prospects

Prioritizing Sales Prospects

Preparing for Sales Dialogue

**Remaining Stages in
the Trust-Based Sales Process**

The sales funnel presents the trust-based sales process and highlights the major steps of the strategic prospecting process.

opportunities. As salespeople move through the strategic prospecting process and the other stages in the trust-based sales process, the funnel narrows because only the best sales opportunities are pursued and not all sale opportunities result in a sale or new customer relationship. For the most productive salespeople, the sales funnel is normally much wider at the bottom than the bottom of the funnel for less productive salespeople. The most productive salespeople pursue the best sales opportunities and translate a larger percentage of these opportunities into actual sales than less productive salespeople. We will now discuss each step in the strategic prospecting process.

Generating Sales Leads

The first step in the strategic prospecting process is to identify sales leads. **Sales leads** or **suspects** are organizations or individuals who might possibly purchase the product or service offered by a salesperson. This represents the realm of sales opportunities for a salesperson. So, if a salesperson is selling copiers in business markets, any organization that might need a copier would be a sales lead. Although more sales leads are usually better than less leads, the identified organizations represent different types of sales opportunities. For example, large organizations might represent better sales opportunities, because they probably need more copiers than smaller organizations. Other organizations may have just purchased copiers or are very satisfied with their current copiers, which would mean they do not represent good sales opportunities. If salespeople merely generate leads and pursue most of them, they are likely to be spending a great deal of their time with organizations that are unlikely to purchase from them.

Determining Sales Prospects

The most productive salespeople evaluate sales leads to determine which ones are true prospects for their product or service. This evaluation process is usually called **qualifying sales leads**. Salespeople search for, collect, analyze, and use various types of screening procedures to determine if the sales lead is really a good sales prospect. Although specific companies define sales prospects in different ways, a **sales prospect** is typically an individual or organization that:

- Has a need for the product or service.
- Has the budget or financial resources to purchase the product or service.
- Has the authority to make the purchase decision.

Those that meet these criteria move down the sales funnel (see Figure 5.1) into the sales prospect category, while those that do not are set aside. Salespeople who spend the time and effort qualifying their leads limit the time wasted on making calls with a low probability of success and focus their efforts on the more fruitful opportunities.

Prioritizing Sales Prospects

Even though the qualifying process has culled out the least promising sales leads, the remaining prospects do not all represent the same sales opportunity. The most productive salespeople create an **ideal customer profile** and they analyze their sales prospects by comparing them to this ideal customer profile. Those that fit the profile the best are deemed to be the best sales prospects. Another approach is to identify one or more criteria, evaluate sales prospects against these criteria, and either rank all of the sales prospects based on this evaluation or place the sales prospects into A, B, and C categories with A sales prospects representing the best sales opportunities. The sales funnel becomes even narrower as the most promising sales opportunities, which are pursued and the least promising are put aside.

Preparing for Sales Dialogue

The final step in the strategic prospecting process is to prepare for the initial contact with a sales prospect by planning the sales dialogue. The information accumulated to this point in the process is helpful, but additional information is usually required to increase the chances of success in the initial sales dialogue. The types of additional information required are discussed later in this module.

LOCATING PROSPECTS

Many different sources and methods for effective strategic prospecting have been developed for use in different selling situations. A good selling organization and successful salespeople will have a number of ongoing prospecting methods in place at any given time. The salesperson must continually evaluate prospecting methods to determine which methods are bringing in the best results. New methods must also be evaluated and tested for their effectiveness. Many popular prospecting methods are presented in Exhibit 5.1.

Cold Canvassing

Cold canvassing occurs when salespeople contact a sales lead unannounced with little if any information about the lead. **Cold calling** is the most extreme form of cold canvassing, because salespeople merely "knock on doors" or make telephone calls to organizations or individuals. This is a very inefficient prospecting method. Typically, a very small percentage of cold calls produce qualified prospects or lead to future sales dialogue with qualified prospects. Since there is so much rejection, many salespeople do not like to cold call sales leads. The examples of the Polling Company and Foster's Promotional Goods in this module's opening vignette illustrate the difficulties in cold calling.

Prospecting Methods **EXHIBIT 5.1**			
Cold Canvassing	**Networking**	**Company Sources**	**Published Sources**
• Cold Calling • Referrals • Introductions	• Centers of Influence • Noncompeting Salespeople	• Company Records • Advertising Inquiries • Telephone Inquiries • Trade Shows • Sales Seminars	• Lists and Directories • Commercial Lead Lists • Web Sites

The success of cold calling can be improved by using referrals or introductions. A **referral** is a sales lead provided by a customer or some other influential person. Salespeople are often trained to ask customers and others for the names and contact information of potential prospects. Sometimes salespeople can also obtain sufficient information to qualify the lead as a good sales prospect. Salespeople also can get permission to use the person's name when contacting the prospect. In some cases, the person might agree to provide an **introduction** by writing a letter or making a phone call to introduce the salesperson to the prospect. An example of cold calling with referrals is presented in "Professional Selling in the 21st Century: Getting Appointments over the Phone."

Networking

Salespeople can use various types of networking as effective methods for prospecting. Many salespeople join civic and professional organizations, country clubs, or fraternal organizations, and these memberships provide the opportunity for them to build relationships with other members. Sometimes these relationships yield prospects. Some members might be influential people in the community or other organizations, making them **centers of influence** for the salesperson and potentially providing help in locating prospects. Accountants, bankers, attorneys, teachers, business owners, politicians, and government workers are often good centers of influence.

PROFESSIONAL SELLING IN THE 21ST CENTURY

Getting Appointments over the Phone

John Klich, college unit director and agent for Northwestern Mutual Financial Network in Skokie, Illinois, understands the importance of prospecting to gain new business. Here are a few of his thoughts on how he uses the telephone in his prospecting process:

I need to make two appointments per day to be successful and meet my personal selling targets. Many times it takes 25 to 40 phone calls to make those two good appointments. I understand that the phone is my lifeline. If I don't get a commitment in a matter of seconds, I have lost the prospect. This means that my *primary points have to be direct, compelling, and brief—very brief. I have to be well organized. I don't use a script, but I do have my key points outlined on paper and in front of me when I make my prospecting calls.*

My philosophy is to keep my opening short and sweet. I briefly introduce myself. I mention referrals right away when I can, and I resist the temptation to make a full-blown sales presentation over the phone. I try to sell the appointment. It may sound obvious, but always be polite. One last thought, if someone already has a good relationship with an agent, I thank him or her for their time and let them know that I'm available if anything changes.

Networking with salespeople from noncompeting firms can also be a good source of prospects. Business Networking International (BNI) is a formal organization with each local group consisting of **noncompeting salespeople**. The basic purpose of this organization is for the members to generate prospects for each other. There are other sales and marketing organizations that salespeople can join to create the opportunity to identify prospects by networking with members.

An example of how noncompeting salespeople can help each other was demonstrated when a Hershey Chocolate, U.S.A., salesperson went out of his way to tell a Hormel sales representative about a new food mart going into their territory. The Hormel representative was the first of his competitors to meet with the new food mart management team and was given valuable shelf space that his competitors could not get. A few months later, the Hormel sales representative returned the favor when he found out that an independent grocer was changing hands. The Hershey salesperson was able to get into the new owner's store early and added valuable shelf space for his products. The operating principle of "you scratch my back, and I scratch yours" works when information flows in both directions.[1]

It is important for salespeople to strike up conversations with other sales representatives while waiting to see buyers. Noncompeting salespeople can be found everywhere and can help in getting valuable information about prospects.

Company Sources

Many companies have resources or are engaged in activities that can help their own salespeople with strategic prospecting. **Company records** can be a useful source of prospects, as illustrated in this module's opening vignette. The use of a company database by Foster's Promotional Goods shows how salespeople can use company records to generate qualified sales prospects. Salespeople can also review company records to identify previous customers who have not placed an order recently. Contacting previous customers to determine why they have stopped ordering could provide opportunities to win back business. Examining the purchasing behavior of existing customers can also help in identifying opportunities to sell additional products to specific customers.

Advertising inquiries are potentially a good source of prospects. For example, one manufacturer's rep in the natural gas industry speaks highly of his company's advertising plan. They only advertise in trade magazines that they believe their buyers read. The salesperson's territory includes Idaho, Utah, Montana, and Wyoming. Their advertising message is simply, "If we can help you with any of your natural gas needs (e.g., flow meters, odorizers), please give us a call." These leads are then turned over to the salesperson who calls on that territory. Territories of this size cannot be covered extensively by one salesperson. The advertising program qualifies the prospect (with the help of the telephone) before the salesperson is sent out on the call.[2]

Many organizations today use both inbound (prospect calls the company) and outbound (salesperson contacts the prospect) telemarketing. **Inbound telemarketing** involves a telephone number (usually a toll-free number) that prospects or customers can call for information. Companies distribute toll-free numbers by direct mail pieces (brochures), advertising campaigns, and their **outbound telemarketing** program. United Insurance Agency in Muncie, Indiana, uses both inbound and outbound telemarketing to serve their market niche of hotels across America.[3] They use outbound telemarketing to generate and then qualify leads for their sales force. Qualified leads are turned over to experienced salespeople. Usually, interns do all the outbound telemarketing. Inbound telemarketing is used to resolve problems, answer questions of prospects, as well as take orders from existing customers.

Attending conventions and **trade shows** presents salespeople with excellent opportunities to collect leads. Generally, the company purchases booth space and sets up a stand that clearly identifies the company and its offerings. Salespeople are available at the booth to demonstrate their products or answer questions. Potential customers walk by and are asked to fill out information cards indicating an interest in

Tom Linker has sold office furniture for the past ten years. The second year he was with the company he won a district contest and placed eighth in the national contest during his third year. The past seven years have been very disappointing. Tom has had some success at getting his current clients to upgrade and make repeat purchases. His downfall has been his inability to locate new business. Linker's boss, Larry Davis, started a new prospecting program in which each salesperson had to contact five new leads per month and discuss them at their monthly sales meetings. After several months, Linker still seems to be having problems generating new business from the leads that he has been turning in to his boss. After six months of no new business, Davis decided to investigate to find out what Linker's problem might be. Davis had to make only three phone calls to determine that Linker had been turning in names that he had never called on! What should Davis do?

the company or one of its products. The completed information card provides leads for the salesperson. Trade shows can stimulate interest in products and provide leads. For example, bank loan officers attend home improvement trade shows and can offer the homeowner immediate credit to begin a project. Those who sign immediately may be offered a reduction in interest rate.

Firms can use **seminars** to generate leads and provide information to prospective customers. For example, a financial planner will set up a seminar at a local hotel, inviting prospects by direct mail, word of mouth, or advertising on local television and radio, to give a presentation on retirement planning. The financial consultant discusses a technique or investing opportunities that will prepare the audience for retirement. Those present will be asked to fill out a card expressing their interest for follow-up discussions. The financial consultant hopes this free seminar will reward him or her with a few qualified prospects.

"An Ethical Dilemma" illustrates the difficulty in getting sales reps to locate potential new business.

Published Sources

A variety of sources published in print and electronic form can be very useful in prospecting. Published **lists and directories** (also often available in electronic form) offer an inexpensive, convenient means of identifying leads. Telephone books today contain a business section that lists all the community's businesses. This list is usually broken down further by business type. Manufacturers, medical facilities, pharmacies, and grocery stores, to name a few, can be easily identified by using the business pages of the phone book. Many lists and directories exist, such as chamber of commerce directories, trade association lists, *Moody's Industrial Directory, Standard & Poor's Register of Corporations, Directors, and Executives.*

Directories are a gold mine of information if they are used correctly. A salesperson must remember that the day these lists are published they start to become obsolete. Sending a letter to a buyer who is no longer with the company makes the salesperson look bad. Companies change their names, merge with others, and even change their addresses. Salespeople must verify information before using it. Exhibit 5.2 refers to many of the directories that salespeople have at their disposal.

A large variety of list providers offer **commercial lead lists** designed to focus on virtually any type of business and/or individual. Available on paper or in convenient computer formats such as Excel and Word, commercial lead lists range from simple listings of names, addresses, and phone numbers to more detailed listings with a full profile of the different entities included in the list. Salespeople should keep in mind that even while list services guarantee a range of accuracy, commercial lists typically contain a number of errors. Also, response rates with commercial lists are usually lower than for more customized lists compiled by the individual salesperson. Typically, only a few prospects will be generated for every 100 names on the lead list.

EXHIBIT 5.2   List of Secondary Lead Sources

1. *Harris Directory,* Harris InfoSource, Indiana, Illinois, Kentucky, Michigan, Ohio, Pennsylvania, Virginia, West Virginia; features company profiles, key contacts with titles, street and mailing addresses, extended zip codes, phone, fax, and toll-free numbers, headquarters location and phone, employment figures, import/export, product description, annual sales, facility size, and more. Find information at www.harrisinfo.com.

2. *Sales & Marketing Management* magazine discusses strategies and tactics of marketing and evaluates the market for various products and services. Of more interest to salespeople in the field is its *Annual Survey of Buying Power,* which helps salespeople determine how many individuals in a particular territory can afford their particular product or service. It also provides information about the most promising sales targets and tips on applying statistical data to your particular marketing plans. See www.salesandmarketing.com.

3. *Moody's Industrial Directory* is an annual publication with a wide range of statistical information about particular firms that might be prospects for a specific product or service. Names of executives, description of the company business, and a brief financial statement for more than 10,000 publicly held firms are on the Web at www.moodys.com.

4. *Standard & Poor's Register of Corporations, Directors, and Executives* is an excellent source of personal information about individuals in companies. Such information can be used for qualifying prospects and for learning enough about them to plan an effective approach and presentation. This annual publication lists names, titles, and addresses for 50,000 firms. See www.standardandpoors.com.

5. *Thomas Register of American Manufacturers,* published annually, provides information about who makes what and where almost anything may be purchased. Information is also provided about the corporate structure of the manufacturer and about its executives. If a company sells supplies, raw materials, or components used by a certain type of manufacturer, a salesperson can find an exhaustive list of all companies that might need that product. If a company markets a service, a salesperson can find companies in his or her area whose business fits the description of the ideal client. An index allows recovery of information by geographic location, by product or service, by company name, and by product trade name. Find more information at www.thomasregister.com.

6. *Polk City Directory* supplies detailed information on individuals living in specific communities. Polk publishes more than 1,100 directories covering 6,500 communities throughout the United States and Canada. The local chamber of commerce should have access to this directory. See www.citydirectory.com.

7. *Trade Shows & Professional Exhibits* lists more than 3,500 trade shows including their location, when they are held, and attendance expected.

8. *The International Corporate 1000* provides information and profiles of the 1,000 largest companies in the world: 350 are from the United States and Canada; the remaining 650 are from Europe, South America, the Pacific Basin, and the Middle East.

9. *Database America* has 14 million businesses and 104 million households in their databases. They provide prospect lists (perfect for sales lead generation and telemarketing), tape and PC diskettes (enables printing of sales leads and labels), and mailing labels (useful for direct mail campaigns). Visit the Web site: http://www.databaseamerica.com.

10. *Million Dollar Directory* (Dun & Bradstreet) lists names, addresses, and business lines of firms worth more than $1 million. See www.dnbibl.com/mddi.

11. *Encyclopedia of Associations* (Thomson Gale) lists 22,200 national associations, more than 22,300 international organizations, and more than 115,000 regional, state, and local organizations.

12. *Directory of Corporate Affiliations.* The Web site www.corporateaffiliations.com provides information on 170,000 parent companies, affiliates, subsidiaries, and divisions worldwide.

13. *World Scope: Industrial Company Profiles* (Wright Investor's Service) provides extensive coverage of 5,000 companies from 25 countries, within 27 major industry groupings. See www.wisi.com.

14. *National Trade and Professional Associations* (Columbia Books) lists more than 7,500 trade and professional associations, along with pertinent information about each. See www.columbiabooks.com.

Many firms today have turned to **Web sites** to attract potential customers. A Web site is a collection of information about the company that usually includes company history, products, prices, and how to order or reach a salesperson if there is an interest in the products. Companies today are creatively using text, pictures, sound, and video to attract prospects. Advertising and promotion campaigns focus on Web site addresses and encourage prospects to browse their site.

The disadvantage of using a Web site occurs if companies do not update them periodically. One farm implement dealer learned this the hard way when posting used farm equipment on its Web site. Seventy-five percent of the equipment was sold the first month the Web site was available. Before the site was updated later that year, sales reps had to tell prospective buyers that the equipment had been sold. In fact, almost everything on the site was sold. Some companies find they have to update their sites weekly and even daily.

STRATEGIC PROSPECTING PLAN

The most productive salespeople use a variety of prospecting methods and follow the strategic prospecting process by generating leads, qualifying them to identify true prospects, and then prioritizing these prospects so that they pursue the best sales opportunities. An example of one effective approach is presented in "Professional Selling in the 21st Century: What Is Your Prospecting Advantage?" The use of a strategic prospecting plan can help salespeople continuously improve their prospecting effectiveness.

A **strategic prospecting plan** should fit the individual needs of the salesperson. As illustrated in Figure 5.2, the focal point of a prospecting plan should be the goal stating the number of qualified prospects to be generated. Formalized goals serve as guides to what is to be accomplished and help to keep a salesperson on track. The plan should also allocate an adequate and specific daily or weekly time period for prospecting. Having specific time periods set aside exclusively for prospecting helps to prevent other activities from creeping in and displacing prospecting activities. A good **tracking system** should also be a part of the prospecting plan. A tracking system can be as low-tech as a set of 3- by 5-inch note cards or employ one of the many computerized and online contact management or customer relationship management software applications. An example of a simple, but effective, paper and pencil tracking form can be found in Exhibit 5.3. The tracking system should record comprehensive information about the prospect, trace the prospecting methods used, and chronologically archive outcomes from any contacts with the prospect. A fourth element of the prospecting plan is a system for analyzing and

---

PROFESSIONAL SELLING IN THE 21ST CENTURY

What Is Your Prospecting Advantage?

Greg Burchett, district sales manager from Moore Wallace, spends quite a bit of time with each of his sales reps going over Moore Wallace's prospecting advantage.

I know every Moore Wallace product or service has some advantage over the others on the market. By defining our advantages and then fitting them to the market, we make prospecting a more rewarding activity. I have my salespeople list their present customers and how they use Moore Wallace's products, what they like about it, *and what benefits it has brought to them. Next, we have them make a list of prospects they think could use our products. Next, we have them cross-match the lists to show which benefits would fit each prospect. Those who cross-match in many ways will be priority prospects. Those who do not cross-match at all are very low-priority prospects. By assigning a numerical value to each prospect, we automatically eliminate wasted prospecting time and develop a prospecting advantage image of our ideal prospect. When it's time to prospect again, we already know exactly what prospects will be the best for Moore Wallace to call.*

FIGURE 5.2   Prospecting Plans Are the Foundation for Effective Prospecting

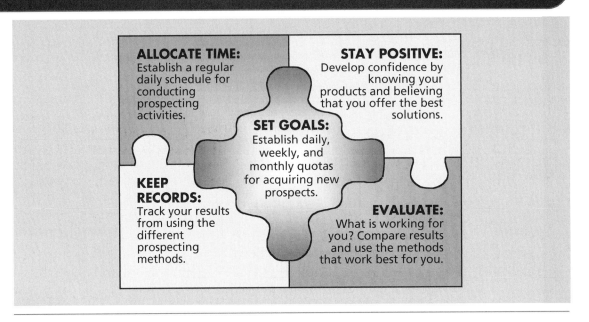

The strategic prospecting plan sets goals, allocates specific times to be used for prospecting, and continuously evaluates results in order to maximize the effectiveness of prospecting time and effort.

evaluating the results of prospecting activities. Continuous evaluation should be employed to assure the salesperson is meeting prospecting goals and using the most effective prospecting methods. The fifth and final element of a prospecting plan should be a program to review and stay up-to-date on product knowledge and competitor information to emphasize and underscore that the salesperson's products and services offer the best solutions to customer needs and problems. Self-confidence is critical to success in selling and a base of comprehensive knowledge and understanding is the key to believing in one's self.

As with all phases of the sales process, salespeople must exercise judgment and set priorities in prospecting. There is a limited amount of time for prospecting, and a better understanding of the concepts and practices illustrated in this module can help a salesperson be more productive. An added bonus is that the sales process is more enjoyable for salespeople calling on bona fide prospects who can benefit from the salesperson's offering.

PREPARING FOR SALES DIALOGUE: GATHERING AND STUDYING PROSPECT INFORMATION

Once potential customers are identified, the salesperson must begin the process of collecting information. During this stage, the salesperson gathers information about the prospect that will be used to formulate future sales interactions. Buyer's needs, buyer's motives, and details of the buyer's situation should be determined. Some organizations spend a great amount of time determining the salesperson's and buyer's communication style. Effectively sensing and interpreting customers' communications styles allow salespeople to adapt their own interaction behaviors in a way that facilitates buyer–seller communication and enhances relationship formation.

The more the salesperson knows about his or her buyer, the better chance he or she has to sell. Over time, the salesperson should be able to accumulate knowledge about the prospect. The information that the salesperson needs varies with the kind

Personal Prospecting Log

Name   _Tom Jenkins_

Team   _Indianapolis Commercial_   Date   _4/16_

1st Contact	Organization	Contact Person	Source of Lead	Phone	Date of Appointment	Outcome of Call	Follow-Up Activity
6/02/05	Cummins Engine	Tyler Huston	Personal contact	765-444-1234	4/11 8:30 A.M.	Need info on printer	Send in mail
9/01/04	Cosco	Fred Banks	Referral Tom Oats John Deere	219-888-4111	Will call with dates/times	Liked our numbers decision next week	Send info on satisfied customers
9/02/04	Ball-Foster	MaryLou Hinkle	Called in on 800#	765-365-4242	4/13 Lunch	Great lunch need proposal	Will work up proposal, set date and present
4/19/05	Ontario Systems	Darrell Beaty	Referral	765-223-4117	4/19 4 P.M.		
4/17/05	Cincinnati Reds	Sharon Bristow	Referral Stacey Jones Indianapolis, Indiana	513-452-REDS	4/17 8 A.M.		
2/02/05	BANK ONE	Alice Arnold	Direct mail sent back 6/02	317-663-2214	4/16 Lunch	Didn't seem impressed need more work	Need more contact with Alice PACER GAME?
2/03/05	Davis & Davis	Frank Chapman	800# call in	317-211-8811	Bob Evans 4/15 Breakfast 7 A.M.	Will include their DP department at next call	Schedule DP
3/03/05	ABB	Jerome Parker	Personal contact	317-927-4321	4/14 2 P.M.	Liked our proposal	Call Monday for answer
3/03/05	Thomson Consumer Electronics	Doug Lyon	Phone	317-212-4111	4/15 3 P.M.	Had bad experience with us several year ago	This one will take time

of product that he or she is selling. As a rule, a salesperson should definitely know a few basic things about his or her customers (e.g., the prospect's name, correct spelling, and correct pronunciation). A salesperson can learn a great deal about a customer over time by collecting bits and pieces of information, sorting them out, and developing a personalized presentation for the customer.

Obtaining Information on the Buyer

A salesperson must do some preliminary homework once a company has been identified as a potential client. The first stage of information gathering is to concentrate on the individual prospect. Several questions need to be answered that will identify how the buyer will behave toward the salesperson. Exhibit 5.4 details some of the questions that a salesperson needs to ask.

EXHIBIT 5.4 Information to Gather on a Prospect and Who to Contact

Information Needed	How to Collect Information
The prospect's name.	Correct spelling and pronunciation can be gathered by asking the receptionist or secretary to verify information.
The prospect's correct title.	This can be determined by asking the gatekeepers to verify.
Is this prospect willing to take risks? Are they confident with decision making?	The salesperson may have to ask the prospect about willingness to take risks.
Is the prospect involved in the community? Does the prospect belong to any clubs or professional organizations?	The salesperson may be able to observe club or organizational honors displayed in the office.
Does the prospect have hobbies or interests he or she is proud of? (coin collector, sports enthusiast)	Observation of the office might give away this information.
What is the prospect's personality type? Easygoing? All business?	Observation and experience with the buyer will give the answer to the salesperson.
Where was the prospect educated? Where did this prospect grow up?	Look for diploma on the wall. The salesperson may have to ask for this information.

It is not unusual for gatekeepers to prohibit the salesperson access to the buyer over the phone if the salesperson mispronounces the buyer's name. Mail is thrown away without being opened if the name is misspelled or the title is incorrect.

Precall information should be used to develop a rapport with the prospect and to eventually tailor the presentation to fit the buyer's needs. A salesperson can establish a relationship with a prospect by discussing such mutual points of interest as an alumni association with the same college or support for the same athletic team. As illustrated in "An Ethical Dilemma," information gathering must be done thoughtfully. It can take many sales calls and months to gather all the useful information needed by a salesperson.

Gathering Information on the Prospect's Organization

Gathering information about the prospect's company helps salespeople better understand the environment in which they will be working. Exhibit 5.5 details some of the questions that provide useful information about the prospect's organization. Is the prospect presently buying from a single supplier? How long has the prospect been buying from this supplier? If the answer is 20 years and he or she is extremely satisfied with the current salesperson, products, and services, then the prospect should be thanked for his or her time, and the salesperson should move on to other accounts.

Sources of Information

A good salesperson uses all available information sources to gather valuable information. Lists and directories will have names, addresses, phone numbers, and other key information. The Web can be a valuable tool as companies provide more than enough vital information for a salesperson. Walker Group in Indianapolis has one person dedicated to daily seeking critical Web information about their clients and competitors.[4] Salespeople have access to a large quantity of current information and should use it to gain a competitive edge over their competitors.

Secretaries and receptionists can be a friendly source of information. They can certainly be used to verify name, title, pronunciation, and correct spelling. Also, noncompeting salespeople can help a salesperson fill in information on accounts.

Teresa Wolf had just completed her sales training with Foster Supply (a distributor of component parts for small engines), and she really took to heart the importance of precall information gathering. Her company kept a customer profile and planning sheet that gathered information such as

Name _____

Address _____

Type of Business _____

Name of Buyer _____

Buyer's Hobbies _____

Decision Maker _____

Key Influences in the Company _____

Buyer Profile _____

Buyer Personality Type _____

Name of Owner _____

Age of Company _____

Primary Products Produced, etc. _____

She had only been in her territory two weeks when her sales manager, Ted Hart, started receiving complaints from Wolf's prospects and customers. The callers complained that she had been aggressively collecting information on their company and buyers by interviewing everyone in their respective companies that would agree to see her. One caller, Jane VanWay (the lead buyer for Wisconsin Power Corporation and a key account for Foster Supply) even termed one of her sales calls an "interrogation." Upon reviewing her profile sheets, Hart was amazed at how complete they were. Nevertheless, there was still the problem in how Wolf was going about getting the information. If you were Wolf, how might you go about researching and collecting the needed company and individual buyer information in a fashion that would not be perceived as so intrusive and aggressive?

Finally, a salesperson should be gathering information about each of its companies and buyers. Some companies provide the sales force with contact management software like ACT or Goldmine. Salespeople may develop their own system for gathering pertinent information. Exhibit 5.6 illustrates the types of information that can be gathered in a customer profile.

Determining Other Buyers' Influences

As products become more complex, we often see an increase in the number of buying influencers and decision makers involved in the purchase. The salesperson should attempt to determine the various buying influencers. For example, if a salesperson concentrates on the purchasing agent in an organization and ignores other key players (e.g., department head, data processing) in the decision-making process, the salesperson takes the risk that he or she is potentially selling to the wrong person.

Gathering Information about the Organization   EXHIBIT 5.5

Information Needed	How to Collect Information
What type of business are we dealing with: manufacturer, wholesaler, retailer, government, educational, medical, financial institution?	This can be gathered from a directory.
To what market does the company sell? Who are the organization's primary competitors? What does the company make and sell?	Annual reports may be helpful in answering these questions.
Who does the prospect presently buy from? Do they buy from a single vendor? Multiple vendors? How long have they purchased from their suppliers? What problems does the company face? In what volume does the company buy? What is the organization's financial position?	The salesperson may have to ask for this information.

EXHIBIT 5.6   Customer Profile

1. Name of Business _____
2. Address _____
3. Phone _____
4. Name of Buyer(s) _____ Title _____
   Personality, Hobbies, Interests _____
   _____ Title _____
   _____ Title _____
   _____ Title _____
5. Source of prospect (i.e., referral, cold call) _____
6. Other Key People
   Receptionists _____
   Personality, Hobbies, Interests _____
   Secretaries _____
   Personality, Hobbies, Interests _____
   Department Heads _____
   Personality, Hobbies, Interests _____
   Other Influencers—Who? _____
   Personality, Hobbies, Interests _____
7. What products does the company produce? _____
8. History and current standing in the industry _____
9. How many employees? _____
10. Extent of operations—local, regional, national, international _____
11. Is buying done by individuals or committee? _____
12. Does the company buy from single or multiple sources? _____

The salesperson must use **observation** and questioning to determine the role of each member of the buying team and the amount of influence each exerts; each member's needs should be determined before or during the presentation. Department heads may be interested in how the product will benefit their department, whereas the CFO may only care about the price. During group presentations, all the members of the buying party must feel involved. The salesperson must be sure to direct questions and comments to all potential decision makers in the group.

If a salesperson has only one contact (e.g., purchasing agent) in an organization, he or she runs the risk that the key contact could die, get fired, change jobs, get transferred, or retire. By having contact with many influencers in an organization, the salesperson will always have a number of people who have had previous experiences to pass on to the new purchasing agent or team member. In the first instance, the salesperson must start the entire relationship process again; in the second, the salesperson will have help keeping the relationship in place.

SUMMARY

1. **Discuss why prospecting can be a challenging task for a salesperson.** Prospective buyers may be difficult to contact because they have never heard of a salesperson's firm and do not want to take the time with a potential new supplier. Buyers are constantly getting calls from salespeople and do not have time to see them all. Gatekeepers have been trained to screen their bosses' calls and often are not pleasant to the salesperson.

2. **Explain strategic prospecting.** Strategic prospecting involves the identification of qualified potential customers, usually called prospects. When we say a prospect is qualified, it means that the prospect meets or exceeds screening criteria that have been established by the salesperson or the sales organization. Prospects

must meet criteria such as being financially capable of making the purchase, able to truly benefit from what is being sold, accessible to the salesperson, and in a position to make or support a purchase decision.

3. **Explain where salespeople find prospects.** A good sales organization and salesperson will have a number of ongoing prospecting methods in place at any given time. Asking present customers for leads (referrals), working with noncompeting sales people, buying directories or lists, advertising for interested companies to call or mail in their interest, telemarketing, the Web, direct mail, and observation are a few of the techniques that salespeople can use to generate leads.

4. **Understand the importance of gathering and studying prospect information to prepare for sales dialogue.** Salespeople must gather information about the prospect that will be used to help formulate the sales presentation. Buyer's needs, buyer's motives, and details about the buyer's situation should be determined. The more a salesperson knows about the buyer, the better chance he or she will have to meet the buyer's needs and eventually earn the commitment.

UNDERSTANDING PROFESSIONAL SELLING TERMS

strategic prospecting	company records
sales funnel	advertising inquiries
sales pipeline	inbound telemarketing
sales leads	outbound telemarketing
qualifying sales leads	trade shows
sales prospect	seminars
ideal customer profile	lists and directories
cold calling	commercial lead lists
referral	Web sites
introduction	strategic prospecting plan
centers of influence	tracking system
noncompeting salespeople	observation

DEVELOPING PROFESSIONAL SELLING KNOWLEDGE

1. Why should a salesperson be concerned with prospecting—isn't it enough to concentrate on your present customers and grow your new business from them?

2. What should be the objectives of strategic prospecting?

3. Why is prospecting difficult for some salespeople?

4. Why should a salesperson wait until they have a track record with a buyer before they ask for a referral?

5. Why is there the potential for cold calls to be an ineffective prospecting method?

6. At a minimum, what criteria should be used to qualify prospects?

7. Why is it important to collect information on the buyer and the company to prepare for sales dialogue?

8. What sources of information can a salesperson use to gather information on their prospects?

9. Why is it important to determine other buying influences?

10. What are some typical objectives a salesperson might hope to accomplish when calling on a prospect?

BUILDING PROFESSIONAL SELLING SKILLS

1. You have recently graduated from college and are selling a new line with X-tra Clear Copiers. You have been assigned to a new territory in a city of 100,000 near your campus. You do not have any clients who currently own X-tra Clear Copiers. Your boss asks you to develop a prospect list in ten days. How might you go about generating this list of prospects?

   Provide a list of sources that you might use to generate leads.

   1. _____
   2. _____
   3. _____
   4. _____
   5. _____
   6. _____
   7. _____
   8. _____
   9. _____
   10. _____

   Provide a list of establishments that would be prospects for X-tra Clear Copiers. Can you identify a person to call on? What information should you try to collect?

   1. Company _____
      Whom to call on _____
      Info to collect _____

   2. Company _____
      Whom to call on _____
      Info to collect _____

   3. Company _____
      Whom to call on _____
      Info to collect _____

   4. Company _____
      Whom to call on _____
      Info to collect _____

   5. Company _____
      Whom to call on _____
      Info to collect _____

   6. Company _____
      Whom to call on _____
      Info to collect _____

   7. Company _____
      Whom to call on _____
      Info to collect _____

   8. Company _____
      Whom to call on _____
      Info to collect _____

   9. Company _____
      Whom to call on _____
      Info to collect _____

   10. Company _____
       Whom to call on _____
       Info to collect _____

2. **Situation:**   Read the Ethical Dilemma on page 151.

   Characters: Teresa Wolf, salesperson for Foster Supply; Jane VanWay, lead buyer for Wisconsin Power Corporation

   Scene: *Location*—Jane VanWay's office at Wisconsin Power Corporation. *Action*—Teresa Wolf has been doing a commendable job in getting complete company and buyer profile information to complete the account profile sheets that her company requires her to complete and keep updated. However, Wolf's sales manager has received a number of complaints about her aggressiveness in getting the information. VanWay, lead buyer for Wisconsin Power Corporation and long-time key account for Foster Supply, has even complained that Wolf seems to interrogate everyone who is willing to see her.

ROLE PLAY

Role play a sales call interaction with Jane VanWay and demonstrate how information about the buyer and the buyer's company might be collected without it being an interrogation.

Upon completion of the role play, answer the following questions:

2a. What other methods might Wolf use to gain the information she needs?

2b. How might Wolf handle the fact that many of her prospects and buyers have developed a negative impression of her information-gathering techniques?

3. **Situation:**   Read "Professional Selling in the 21st Century" on page 143.

   Characters: John Klich, salesperson for Northwestern Mutual Financial Network; Tracy Hanna, high school math teacher

   Scene: *Location*—John Klich's office at Northwestern Mutual Financial Network.
   Action—Klich is making his daily phone calls to qualify prospects and set up appointments to present a variety of financial services and products as solutions for individual life insurance and retirement needs. He has obtained Hanna's name and phone number from a lead list of community teachers.

ROLE PLAY

Role play the phone conversation between Klich and Hanna as Klich gathers the information needed to screen Hanna as a qualified prospect and gain an appointment for an initial sales call to explore Hanna's needs for financial services and products and begin developing the relationship as a satisfied client.

Upon completion of the role play, answer the following questions:

3a. What other ways might Klich introduce himself, generate Hanna's positive involvement, and gain the appointment?

3b. Why is it important for Klich to avoid making a full-blown sales presentation to Hanna over the phone?

4. As an account manager for Chemical Coating Corporation (CCC) you have the national responsibility for selling Syntex, a new paint additive that significantly extends the shelf life and improves the application of all forms of latex-based paints. This is a breakthrough product just coming onto the market and you are in the process of identifying, qualifying, and prioritizing latex paint manufacturers across the United States that offer high potential for buying the new additive.

Prior information gathered from CCC's customer account records indicates that the best prospects would be larger manufacturers of latex paint. The larger manufacturers tend to be characterized by having an asset base of $10 million or higher and 25 or more employees.

Having become a regular user of the Internet and World Wide Web in digging out business-related information on prospects and accounts, you are aware that the *Thomas Net* site has the capability to search specific product categories by name, identify manufacturers, and provide a summary profile of each company identified.

Access the *Thomas Net* site at the URL http://www.thomasnet.com/indexhtml and generate a list of firms manufacturing the product described as latex paint. Print the list in a format suitable to hand in to your instructor. You may have to complete a free registration process to use the site.

- On the *ThomasNet* home page, select the "Product/Service" tab, enter the product name "latex paint" into the "search box," and select your "state or territory."
- Click on the hot link heading "paints: latex" to pull up a more detailed page listing the companies by name and location.
- Click on the "Company Profile" hot link to access a more detailed profile of the company including asset size, number of employees, and a full description of what the organization does.

(a) How many total leads did you find?

(b) Use CCC's description of the characteristics that denote major manufacturers to provide an initial qualification screen. How many of the leads pass this initial screening test?

(c) Prioritize the remaining accounts according to CCC's screening criteria and list the companies in the order of priority for contact.

(d) What problems do you see with using a commercial database such as the *Thomas Net* as a lead generating tool? Explain.

5. A large number of computer-based and online tools are available to facilitate tracking prospects and customers. Some of these tools are known simply as contact management applications while others have evolved into full customer relationship management tools. ACT! is one of the consistent leaders in this category of products and is used by a large number of companies of all sizes.

Access the ACT! Web site at the URL http://www.act.com. Click on the link to see the ACT! demo after identifying the subject of interest. This tour will walk you through the features of the newest release and allow you to experience firsthand how versatile these contact management tools have become.

(a) As a salesperson, how might you use ACT! to increase your selling effectiveness?

(b) What five features of ACT! would be most beneficial to you? Why?

MAKING PROFESSIONAL SELLING DECISIONS

Case 5.1: How to Prospect for New Customers
Background

Pete Tsuleff has been interested in the food and beverage industry since he was a little boy. His father owned a restaurant/tavern. Tsuleff spent his evenings, weekends, and summers working in the restaurant. At age 21, he began to work as a bartender. He had firsthand experience ordering food, hiring, firing, and running the entire operation by the time he was 25. At age 30, he bought his father out.

During the next ten years, he opened another restaurant/bar and two package liquor stores. Tsuleff's first love was experimenting with new recipes. He had a chili that won competitions in his hometown. He made a spaghetti sauce that was world class. His garlic bread and garlic cheese bread were legendary. Tsuleff decided to get out of the tavern and liquor business, and he opened a line of spaghetti shops. Sales over the first five years were outstanding, and he opened a new store every six months.

Tsuleff continued to experiment with recipes and developed a line of barbecue sauces. He believes that he is the first to dual franchise spaghetti and barbecue in the same building.

Current Situation

Tsuleff is convinced that a good market exists (e.g., groceries, restaurants, gas stations) for his garlic bread and spaghetti and barbecue sauces. He has seen his sales grow by 18 percent per year over the past five years, and the trend is expected to continue for at least the next three years.

One of his first problems is to obtain a list of prospects.

Questions

1. What prospecting methods should Tsuleff use?
2. How can Tsuleff qualify the leads he receives? What qualifying factors will be most important?
3. How can Tsuleff organize his prospecting activities?
4. How should he keep records of his prospects?
5. What precall information is needed by Tsuleff? How will he collect this information?

ROLE PLAY

Situation: Read Case 5.1.

Characters: Pete Tsuleff, owner and salesperson for Specialty Foods & Sauces; Sue Almont, specialty products buyer for Cub Food Stores.

Scene: *Location*—Pete Tsuleff's office at Specialty Foods & Sauces.
Action—In the course of Tsuleff's prospecting activities, Sue Almont and Cub Food stores have scored a high priority as a qualified prospect for his new line of garlic breads and sauces. Cub Food stores is a major supermarket chain with significant market penetration in Iowa, Missouri, Illinois, and Indiana.

Role play the phone conversation between Tsuleff and Almont as Tsuleff introduces himself and his company to Almont, gathers needed information about the prospect, and asks for an appointment for an initial sales call.

Upon completion of the role play, answer the following questions:

1. In what other ways might Tsuleff introduce himself and his company?
2. How might Tsuleff elicit sufficient interest from Almont to gain an appointment for a sales call?
3. Why is it important for Tsuleff to avoid making a full-blown sales presentation to Almont over the phone?

Case 5.2: Prospecting and Gaining Prospect Information
Background

Preston Adams has just completed the sales training program for the Office Equipment Division of Xerox. Adams has been assigned a territory in Illinois that includes the metro areas of Bloomington, Decatur, and Peoria. The company once commanded a significant market share in these markets. However, due to a problem with a previous salesperson in these markets three years ago, Xerox has not been directly working this particular region of central Illinois. Although there are a large number of Xerox machines still in use across this territory, it has been a while since a salesperson has called on any accounts. As with any geographic area, there have likely been a lot of changes with existing companies moving or even going out of business and new companies opening up.

Current Situation

Adams' sales manager, Eric Waits is coming in two weeks to spend three days in the field with Adams calling on prospective accounts. Adams is working to develop a list of leads that he can qualify and then contact in order to set up the sales calls he will be making with his manager.

Questions

1. What prospecting methods and sources might Adams use to develop his list of leads?
2. How might Adams go about qualifying the leads he develops? What qualifying factors will be most important?
3. What prospect information would be needed by Adams?
4. How might Adams go about obtaining that information?

Situation:	Read Case 5.2.
Characters:	Preston Adams, salesperson for Xerox Business Machines Division; Jerri Spencer, office manager with purchasing responsibilities for Peoria-based McKelvey and Walters, Attorneys-at-Law.
Scene:	*Location*—Preston Adam's office at Xerox Business Machines Division.

ROLE PLAY

Action—In the course of Adams' prospecting activities, Spencer and the McKelvey and Walters law firm have come up as a strong prospect for Xerox's new line of professional copiers. McKelvey and Walters operate a large office in Peoria that occupies most of two floors in the Planter's Bank Building and a branch office in Bloomington. They were previously a customer of Xerox, but the information that Adams has obtained indicates that they are using an unspecified variety of different brands of copiers.

Role play the phone conversation between Adams and Spencer as Adams introduces himself and his company to Spencer, gathers needed information to better qualify the prospect, and asks for an appointment for an initial sales call.

Upon completion of the role play, answer the following questions:

1. In what other ways might Adams introduce himself and his company?
2. How might he handle the likely questions as to why it has been so long since they have heard from a Xerox salesperson?
3. What information does Adams need in order to qualify McKelvey and Walters as a good prospect?

SUCCESSFUL SALES PRESENTATIONS REQUIRE PLANNING, CUSTOMER FOCUS

In large corporations, small entrepreneurial firms, and professional services firms, a major change is occurring in how sellers communicate with buyers. Top-performing salespeople are focusing increasingly on the customer when planning their sales calls. Having a clear understanding of the buyer's situation, needs, and priorities is essential to success.

Major companies such as Google, Abbot Laboratories, and Altera Corp. are working hard to better understand their customers. Altera, a computer chipmaker with 1,100 salespeople, devotes four weeks of training to getting their salespeople to understand how their customers think. After technology markets slumped in 2000, the company had to adapt to a more cautious market, which meant that Altera's salespeople had to become better listeners and become more adept at working with risk averse customers. Since 2002, the company has spent more than $11 million training its sales force on how to identify with customers' situations, motives, and feelings. Altera's most recent sales results strongly suggest that the new sales model is more than paying for its investment in training.

Entrepreneur Shelly McMahan is president of Smart Design, Inc., a fabrication firm that creates trade show designs, museum exhibits, and commercial interiors. When she visits prospective customers, she brings along a checklist of important questions to ensure that she gets an accurate picture of the prospect's needs. She says, "It is more than giving a sales presentation and writing up an order; it's correctly identifying customers' needs and matching them to a product that we offer. I can show them what *they* want and need and how they can have it."

Professional service providers such as John Graziano (CPA) and Patrick Flanagan (certified financial planner), advocate a customer-based selling approach: "It doesn't focus on the product. Instead, its goal is to clearly define a client's needs and objectives and secure the client's agreement that these needs should be addressed. Techniques that keep the clients involved in the process, actively translate their feelings into actions, and maintain their ongoing interest in continuing to work toward their goals are all critical to consultative selling."

When planning sales dialogues and presentations, top salespeople think like the customer, present information the way customers want to receive it, and measure their success by the customer action taken.

Sources: Cliff Edwards, "Death of a Pushy Salesman," *Business Week* (July 3, 2006): 108–109; John E. Graziano and Patrick J. Flanagan, "Explore the Art of Consultative Selling," *Journal of Accountancy* (January 2005): 34–37; Renee Houston Zemanski, "Self Starter," *Selling Power* (June 2006): 27–28.

PLANNING SALES DIALOGUE AND PRESENTATION

In Module 1, we illustrated the trust-based sales process (see Figure 1.4) in which, salespeople must have a basic understanding of the value they and their companies can deliver to customers. Further, they must recognize that what constitutes value

Objectives

After completing this module, you should be able to

1 Understand alternative ways of communicating with prospects and customers through canned sales presentations, written sales proposals, and organized sales dialogues or presentations.

2 Explain why organized sales dialogues and presentations are more frequently used than canned presentations or written sales proposals.

3 Discuss the nine components in the planning template for an organized sales dialogue or presentation.

4 Explain how to write a customer value proposition statement.

5 Link buying motives to benefits of the seller's offering, support claims made for benefits, and reinforce verbal claims made.

6 Engage the customer by setting appointments.

will typically vary from one customer to the next. Finally, as the process continues and relationships are established with customers, salespeople must work continually to increase the value received by their customers. Throughout the process, selling strategy must focus on customer needs and how the customer defines value.

In this module we discuss the necessary elements in planning productive sales dialogues and presentations. A **sales call** takes place when the salesperson and buyer or buyers meet in person to discuss business. This typically takes place in the customer's place of business, but may take place elsewhere, such as in the seller's place of business or at a trade show.

Most sales calls involve **sales dialogue,** defined in Module 1 as business conversations between buyers and sellers that take place over time as salespeople attempt to initiate, develop, and enhance customer relationships. The term **sales conversation** is used interchangeably with sales dialogue. Some sales calls involve **sales presentations** as part of the dialogue. Sales presentations are comprehensive communications that convey multiple points designed to persuade the prospect or customer to make a purchase. The best sales presentations focus on customer value and only take place after the salesperson has completed the **ADAPT** process (introduced in Module 4). As a reminder, the ADAPT process means the salesperson has: **A**ssessed the customer's situation; **D**iscovered their needs, buying processes, and strategic priorities; **A**ctivated the buyer's interest in solving a problem or realizing an opportunity; helps the buyer **P**roject how value can be derived from a purchase; and then made a **T**ransition to the full sales presentation. Salespeople who attempt to make a sales presentation before building a foundation through sales dialogue, risk being viewed as not-customer oriented and overly aggressive.

To better understand the process of planning sales dialogues and presentations, we will now discuss the three most common approaches: the canned sales presentation, the written sales proposal, and the sales dialogue. Each of these alternatives varies greatly in terms of how much customization and customer interaction is involved. Of the three, the sales dialogue is the most focused on individual customer characteristics, so a planning template that serves as a guide for sales dialogues and comprehensive presentations will be presented, concluding with a discussion of how to foster better sales dialogues when attempting to initiate relationships with customers.

SALES COMMUNICATIONS FORMATS

In planning customer encounters, salespeople must decide on a basic format, such as a canned sales presentation, a written sales proposal, or an organized sales dialogue. Exhibit 6.1 summarizes the types of communications used by sales professionals. A salesperson might use one or more of these formats with a particular customer. Each format has unique advantages and disadvantages. To be successful, these communications must be credible and clear. In addition, the salesperson must communicate in the right environment at an appropriate time to maximize the probability of a successful outcome.

For any of the three communications types, salespeople must plan to be as specific as possible in developing their sales message. For example, it is better to tell a prospect "This electric motor will produce 4800 RPM and requires only one hour of maintenance per week" than to say "This motor will really put out the work with only minimum maintenance."

Canned Sales Presentations

Canned sales presentations include scripted sales calls, memorized presentations, and automated presentations. Automated presentations rely heavily on computer images, movies, tapes, or slides to present the information to the prospect.

Most canned sales presentations have been tested for effectiveness with real customers before dissemination to the sales force. Canned presentations are usually complete and logically structured. Objections and questions can be anticipated in

Types of Sales Communications   EXHIBIT 6.1

Canned Presentations
- Include
  - scripted sales calls
  - memorized presentations
  - automated presentations
- Should be tested for effectiveness
- Must assume buyer needs are the same

Written Sales Proposals
- The proposal is a complete self-contained sales presentation
- Customer may receive a proposal and a follow-up call to explain and clarify the proposal
- Thorough assessment should take place before a customized proposal is written

Organized Sales Dialogues and Presentations
- Address individual customer and different selling situations
- Allow flexibility to adapt to buyer feedback
- Most frequently used format for sales professionals

advance, and appropriate responses can be formulated as part of the presentation. The highly structured and inflexible canned sales presentation does not vary from customer to customer. When properly formulated, it is logical and complete and minimizes sales resistance by anticipating the prospect's objections. It can be used by relatively inexperienced salespeople and perhaps is a confidence builder for some salespeople.

Canned sales presentations make an implicit assumption that customer needs and buying motives are homogeneous. Therefore, canned presentations fail to capitalize on a key advantage of personal selling—the ability to adapt to different types of customers and various selling situations. Most consumer-based telemarketing sales calls are canned and follow this formula. The canned presentation can be effective but is not appropriate for many situations—simply because customer opportunity to interact is minimized. During a memorized presentation, the salesperson talks 80 to 90 percent of the time, only occasionally allowing the prospect to express his or her feelings, concerns, or opinions. Unfortunately, the salesperson does not attempt to determine the prospect's needs during the sales interview but gives the same memorized sales talk to all prospects. The salesperson can only assume the buyer's need and must hope that a lively presentation of product benefits will cause the prospect to buy. The major limitation of the canned sales presentation is that it fails to capitalize on the strength of personal selling—the ability to tailor the message to the prospect. Further, it does not handle interruptions well, may be awkward to use with a broad product line, and may alienate buyers who want to participate in the interaction.

Despite its limitations, the canned sales presentation can be effective in some situations. If the product line is narrow and the sales force is relatively inexperienced, the canned presentation may be suitable. Also, many salespeople find it effective to use a sales dialogue to introduce their company, to demonstrate the product, or for some other limited purpose.

Written Sales Proposals

The second basic type of sales communication is the **written sales proposal**. The proposal is a complete self-contained sales presentation, but it is often accompanied by other verbal sales presentations before or after the proposal is delivered. In some cases, the customer may receive a proposal and then request that the salesperson make a sales call to further explain the proposal and provide answers to questions. Alternatively, preliminary sales presentations may lead to a sales proposal. In any event, the sales proposal should be prepared after the salesperson has made a thorough assessment of the buyer's situation as it relates to the seller's offering.

The sales proposal has long been associated with important, high-dollar-volume sales transactions. It is frequently used in competitive bidding situations and in situations involving the selection of a new supplier by the prospect. One advantage of the proposal is that the written word is usually viewed as being more credible than the spoken word. Written proposals are subject to careful scrutiny with few time constraints, and specialists in the buying firm often analyze various sections of the proposal.

Sales proposal content is similar to other sales presentations, focusing on customer needs and related benefits offered by the seller. In addition, technical information, pricing data, and perhaps a timetable are included. Most proposals provide a triggering mechanism such as a proposed contract to confirm the sale, and some specify follow-up action to be taken if the proposal is satisfactory.

With multimedia sales presentations becoming more routine, it is natural to think that written sales proposals would be declining in importance. Actually, the opposite is true. With the widespread use of multimedia, the standards for all sales communication continue to rise. Buyers expect clear informative sales messages, and they are less tolerant of sloppy communication. Because everyone knows that word processing programs have subroutines to check spelling and grammar, for example, mistakes are less acceptable than ever.

Because written communication provides a permanent record of claims and intentions, salespeople should be careful not to over promise, while still maintaining a positive and supportive tone. No buyer wants to read a proposal full of legal disclaimers and warnings, yet such information may be a necessary ingredient in certain written communication. As with all communication, salespeople should try to give buyers the information they need to make informed decisions.

Writing Effective Proposals

Whether the proposal is in response to a buyer's request for proposals (RFP) or generated to complement and strengthen a sales presentation, it is essential that the proposal be correctly written and convey the required information in an attractive manner. Tom Sant, an author and consultant who works with many Fortune 100 companies, gives these reasons why proposals may fail[1]:

1. Customer does not know the seller.
2. Proposal does not follow the specified format.
3. Executive summary does not address customer needs.
4. Proposal uses the seller's (not the customer's) company jargon.
5. Writing is flat and technical and without passion.
6. Generic material contains another customer's name.
7. Proposal is not convincing.
8. Proposal contains glaring grammatical errors.
9. Proposal does not address key decision criteria.
10. Proposal does not build a persuasive value proposition.

Clearly, developing a quality proposal takes time and effort. However, the process of writing an effective proposal can be simplified by breaking the proposal down into its primary and distinct parts. The five parts common to most proposals are an executive summary, a needs and benefits analysis, a company description, the pricing and sales agreement, and the suggested action and timetable.[2]

Executive Summary

This summary precedes the full proposal and serves two critical functions. First, it should succinctly and clearly demonstrate the salesperson's understanding of the customer's needs and the relevance of the proposed solution. An effective summary will spell out the customer's problems, the nature of the proposed solution, and the resulting benefits to the customer. A second function of the summary is to build a desire to read the full proposal. This is important as many key members of the organization often read little more than the information provided in the summary. A question commonly asked by new salespeople refers to the length of the executive summary. A good rule of thumb is that an executive summary should be limited to two typewritten pages—especially if the main body of the report is fewer than 50 pages in length.

Needs and Benefits Analysis

This section is typically composed of two primary parts. First, the situation analysis should concisely explain the salesperson's understanding of the customer's situation, problems, and needs. Second, the recommended solution is presented and supported with illustrations and evidence on how the proposed solution uniquely addresses the buyer's problems and needs. The emphasis in this section should be on the benefits resulting from the solution and not on the product or service being sold. It is important that these benefits be described from the perspective of the customer. Proprietary information required in the proposal can be protected in a number of ways. The most common method is to place a notice on the cover (i.e., "Confidential" or "For Review Purposes Only"). Many technology companies ask the prospect to sign a nondisclosure agreement that is part of the overall document, and in some instances, the selling organization will even copyright the proposal.

Company Description

Information about the supplier company offering the proposal is included to demonstrate why the company is the best vendor for this solution. This section offers a succinct overview and background of the firm, but the emphasis should be on the company's capabilities. Case histories of customers for whom the company solved similar problems with similar solutions have proved to be an effective method to document and illustrate organizational capabilities and past successes.

Pricing and Sales Agreement

The previous sections are designed to build the customer-value of the proposed solution. Once this value has been established, the proposal should "ask for the order" by presenting pricing information and delivery options. This information is often presented in the form of a sales agreement for the buyer to sign off on and complete.

Suggested Action and Timetable

The purpose of this section is to make it as easy as possible for the buyer to make a positive purchase decision. In effect, this section should say "...if you like the proposal and want to act on it, this is what you do." There may be a contract to sign, an order form to fill out, or instructions regarding who to call to place an order or request further information. A timetable that details a schedule of key implementation events should also be included.

The specific content of a written proposal will vary from situation to situation. Nevertheless, there are certain content expectations and contextual issues that are universal. Salespeople desiring to enhance their proposal writing skills should evaluate the completeness and accuracy of each proposal they write. Exhibit 6.2[3] presents a "Proposal Writing Scorecard" that can provide an effective checklist for evaluating and improving writing skills.

The expectation for *perfect* spelling and grammar is universal. Misspelling a customer's name or misstating the title of the recipient or the exact name of the organization risks turning off a prospect. After all, the quality of a salesperson's written documents is a surrogate for that salesperson's competence and ability as well as the capabilities and overall quality of the organization. For this reason, salespeople are well advised to follow the "Twelve Simple Rules for Writing"

EXHIBIT 6.2   The Proposal Writing Scorecard

The following scorecard evaluates five dimensions that should be contained in effective written proposals: reliability, assurance, tangibles, empathy, and responsiveness. Scoring each of the items in the five sections can assist you in detecting strengths as well as weaknesses. Score each item using this scale: 5 = *Excellent*; 4 = *Good*; 3 = *Average*; 2 = *Poor*; and 1 = *Inadequate*.

Reliability: reflects your (the seller's) ability to identify creative, dependable, and realistic solutions and strategies and match them to the buyer's needs and wants.

Does the Proposal:
_____ 1. Clearly articulate proposed solutions and strategies?
_____ 2. Provide creative and innovative solutions and strategies for the buyer?
_____ 3. Present solutions and strategies appropriate for the buyer's business operation and organization?
_____ 4. Provide financial justifications that support the proposed solutions and strategies?
_____ 5. Provide references that support and reflect dependability?
_____   TOTAL FOR RELIABILITY

Assurance: builds the buyer's trust and confidence in your ability to deliver, implement, produce, and/or provide the benefits.

Does the Proposal:
_____ 1. Assure the buyer that the proposing organization has qualified, experienced, and competent leadership and staff?
_____ 2. Provide adequate specifications and/or benefits that substantiate ability and capability statements?
_____ 3. Present techniques, methodologies, or processes for assuring quality performance?
_____ 4. Concisely and adequately define project or implementation roles and responsibilities?
_____ 5. Clearly identify and define all fees, prices, and expenses for completing the project?
_____   TOTAL FOR ASSURANCE

Tangibles: enhance and support the communication of your message and invite readership by its overall appearance, content, and organization.

Does the Proposal:
_____ 1. Provide a logical flow of information, ideas and sense of continuity for solving the buyer's business problems?
_____ 2. Convert the intangible elements of the solutions or strategies into tangibles?
_____ 3. Demonstrate high standards for excellence in format, structure, grammar, spelling, and appearance?
_____ 4. Provide positive indicators to differentiate the proposing organization from their competition?
_____ 5. Contain a letter of transmittal, executive summary, needs and benefits analysis, company description, and the pricing and sales agreement?
_____   TOTAL FOR TANGIBLES

Empathy: confirms your thorough understanding of the buyer's business and their specific needs and wants.

Does the Proposal:
_____ 1. Clearly identify the buyer's specific needs and wants?
_____ 2. Demonstrate a thorough understanding of the buyer's business operation and organization?
_____ 3. Provide solutions and strategies that fit within the buyer's business goals?
_____ 4. Fulfill the buyer's original expectations?
_____ 5. Identify and discuss financial and nonfinancial benefits in terms of their impact on the buyer's unique operation and organization?
_____   TOTAL FOR EMPATHY

(continued)

The Proposal Writing Scorecard—*Continued*   EXHIBIT 6.2

Responsiveness: developed in a timely manner and demonstrates a willingness to provide solutions for the buyer's needs and wants and to help measure results.

Does the Proposal:

_____ 1. Meet or beat the completion deadline?

_____ 2. Reflect a genuine willingness to understand the buyer's business operation and organization and provide viable and flexible solutions and strategies?

_____ 3. Reflect the proposing organization's willingness to work closely with the buyer by enthusiastically asking questions, gathering information, presenting options, and reviewing draft proposals?

_____ 4. Did the proposing organization thoroughly review the final proposal with the buyer and respond to their questions or clarify any outstanding issues and concerns?

_____ 5. Are the proposed solutions or strategies within the buyer's budget and implementation time frames?

_____ TOTAL FOR RESPONSIVENESS

set out in Exhibit 6.3.[4] Although a well-written proposal is no guarantee of making the sale, a poorly written proposal will certainly reduce the probability of success.

Next, the sales presentation checklist is presented as a tool that salespeople can use to make the task of customizing the sales presentation easier.

Sales Dialogues and Presentations

Sales dialogues may precede or follow other sales communications such as a written sales proposal. Sales dialogues are much more than mere conversation—they are a chance for the salesperson to seek information and/or action from the prospect and to explore the business reasons the prospect has for continuing the dialogue with the salesperson (e.g., solving a problem or realizing an opportunity). Feedback from the prospect is encouraged, and therefore this format is less likely to offend a

Twelve Simple Rules for Writing   EXHIBIT 6.3

- Double check company names, titles, and individuals' names.
- The spelling of words you are not sure of should always be looked up. Do not rely on your word processor's spelling checker.
- Write the proposal and get away from it before proofreading. Give your mind some time away from the document so that it will be fresh when it is time to begin the editing process.
- Proofread and edit for improvements rather than to simply catch mistakes. How can the message be improved in clarity and crispness?
- Repeat the proofreading process and, when possible, have a third party read for meaning, clarity, grammar, and spelling. Another set of eyes can find problems that the writer often overlooks. Don't submit your first draft, as it won't be your best.
- Use hyphens to avoid confusion, but do not place a hyphen after an adverb that ends with *ly*.
- Separate things in a series with a comma, and set off nonessential clauses with a comma.
- Use *that* in restrictive clauses; use *which* in nonrestrictive clauses. (e.g., The sales quota that he announced is too low. He announced the new sales quota, which is too low.)
- Avoid starting sentences with the words *and* or *but*.
- Use *like* for direct comparisons; use *such as* for examples.
- Use a dash to set off and end a thought in a sentence that differs from the preceding concept or thought.
- Periods, commas, and question marks go within quotation marks; semicolons go outside quotation marks.

Tom Lawrence was not one who liked to do a lot of precall planning or ask questions of his prospects. Lawrence had a good idea about which of his products' features were hot buttons for most prospects. During each of his sales calls, he hammered home those features that he thought were important to most of his prospects. His sales manager made calls with him for a few days and made the observation that Lawrence should do more questioning and listening and only sell those features and benefits that were relevant to each prospect. Lawrence stated: "I feel that is a waste of time. Most of my buyers are busy. They don't have time to answer questions all day. I'm the expert, I should know what they need." What are the dangers in the way Lawrence thinks? What can his sales manager do to help Lawrence change?

participation-prone buyer. "An Ethical Dilemma" demonstrates the problem for a salesperson who is not willing to ask questions and gain feedback.

Sales dialogues are not scripted in advance as is the case with canned sales presentations; however, salespeople should think ahead about what questions and statements to include in the conversation and be prepared to hold up their end of the conversation with an appropriate amount of detail.

In most situations, the process of converting a prospect into a customer will take several sales conversations over multiple encounters. For example, salespeople often speak by telephone with a qualified prospect to get an appointment for a later meeting. The second conversation with the customer typically focuses on fact finding and parallels the ADAPT process. The next step would come after the salesperson has developed a tailored solution for the customer. The salesperson may make a comprehensive sales presentation, but it should be designed for dialogue with the customer throughout. This type of sales presentation is referred to as an **organized sales presentation**. To reiterate, this is not a one-way presentation or monologue—it is a sales dialogue with a high level of customer involvement. Accordingly, the organized presentation is also referred to as an **organized sales dialogue**.

When the situation calls for a full sales presentation, the organized sales presentation is usually favored over both the canned presentation and the written proposal. Such an approach allows much-needed flexibility to adapt to buyer feedback and changing circumstances during the presentation. Organized presentations may also include some canned portions. For example, a salesperson for Caterpillar may show a videotape to illustrate the earth-moving capabilities of a bulldozer as one segment of an organized presentation. Due to its flexibility during the sales call and its ability to address various sales situations, the organized presentation is the most frequently used format for professional sales presentations.

One reality of this presentation format is that it requires a knowledgeable salesperson who can react to questions and objections from the prospect. Steve Kehoe, president of Kehoe Financial Services, confirms this in "Professional Selling in the 21st Century: Being Prepared for My Sales Calls." Further, this format may extend the time horizon before a purchase decision is reached, and it is vulnerable to diversionary delay tactics by the prospect. Presumably, those who make these arguments think that a canned presentation forces a purchase decision in a more expedient fashion.

The trust-based relational selling presentation often referred to as the need-satisfaction/consultative model, is a popular form of an organized presentation. The first stage of the process, the need development stage, is devoted to a discussion of the buyer's needs. As seen in Figure 6.1, during this phase the buyer should be talking 60 to 70 percent of the time. The salesperson accomplishes this by using the first four questioning techniques of the ADAPT process. The second stage of the process (need awareness) is to verify what the buyer thinks his or her needs are and to make the buyer aware of potential needs that may exist. For instance, fast-food restaurants were generally slow to recognize the need to offer more low-fat and low-carbohydrate menu items until their sales volume suffered. Others, such as Subway, gained a

Being Prepared for My Sales Calls

Steve Kehoe, president of Kehoe Financial Services in Cincinnati, Ohio, knows the importance of planning and organizing each of his sales calls.

My clients are very knowledgeable, they want answers to questions and I must be prepared to answer them. It may sound simple but my clients want to know what I am selling and why do they need it. If they have high schoolers, it's my job to explain the college savings plan and how it works. I represent many different companies so my clients want to know what company

I am recommending and why. It is not unusual to be asked if I have other satisfied clients using the product. I have to be prepared to talk about my satisfied clients and how I helped them. Yes, price always comes up and my clients want to know if my prices are truly competitive. We're not always the lowest, but we better be close. Many of my clients are not confident in their decision making. I must be prepared to explain why they need to act now and not wait. I cannot go into my sales calls having not thought about these questions. As a professional salesperson, I must plan for them before the fact and be ready to answer them.

competitive advantage by working with their suppliers to formulate a significant number of menu alternatives for the health-conscious consumer. The need-awareness stage is a good time to restate the prospect's needs and to clarify exactly what the prospect's needs are. During the last stage of the presentations, (the need-fulfillment stage), the salesperson must show how his or her product and its benefits will meet the needs of the buyer. As seen in Figure 6.1, the salesperson during the need-fulfillment stage will do more of the talking by indicating what specific product will meet the buyer's needs. The salesperson, by being a good listener early in the process, will now have a better chance to gain the buyer's interest and trust by talking about specific benefits the buyer has confirmed as being important.

Overall, however, most agree that the organized presentation is ideal for most sales situations. Its flexibility allows a full exploration of customer needs and appropriate

The Trust-Based Selling Process: A Need-Satisfaction Consultative Model   FIGURE 6.1

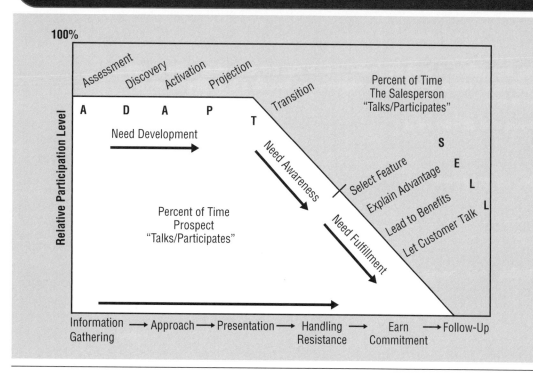

adaptive behavior by the salesperson. By fully participating in the dialogue, both buyer and seller have an opportunity to establish a mutually beneficial relationship.

Sales Dialogue and Presentation Template

A **sales dialogue and presentation template** (see Exhibit 6.4) is a useful tool to ensure that all pertinent content areas are covered with each prospect. The template is flexible and can be used either to plan a comprehensive organized sales presentation or to guide sales dialogues of a more narrow scope. The template is not meant to be a script for a sales encounter, but rather an aid in planning and assembling the information required of the salesperson.

By addressing the issues noted in the template, salespeople can facilitate trust-building by demonstrating their competence and expertise, customer orientation, candor, dependability, and compatibility. It is true that trust is built through behavior not just by planning and having good intentions; however, salespeople who are aware of what it takes to earn the customer's trust in the planning stages have a better chance of earning that trust in subsequent encounters with the customer. The sales dialogue and presentation template is organized into nine sections, each of which is discussed individually.

EXHIBIT 6.4   **Sales Dialogue and Presentation Planning Template**

1. Prospect Information

  A. Company Name:_____   Type of Business: _____

  Key-Person Information

  B. Prospect's Name (Key Decision Maker)_____   Job Title: _____

  C. Other people involved in the purchase decision:

Name(s)/Job Title	Departments	Role in Purchase Decision

2. Customer Value Proposition: A brief statement of how you will add value to the prospect's business by meeting a need or providing an opportunity. Include a brief description of the product or service:

  A. Product/Service that delivers value:

  B. Value Proposition Statement:

3. Sales Call Objective (must require customer action):

(continued)

Sales Dialogue and Presentation Planning Template—*Continued* EXHIBIT 6.4

4. Linking Buying Motives, Benefits, Support Information, and other Reinforcement Methods.
(Repeat for each influencer who will be involved in the upcoming sales call.)

A. *Buying Motives:* What is most important to the prospect(s) in making a purchase decision? **Rational** motives include economic issues such as quality, cost, service capabilities, and the strategic priorities of the prospect's company. **Emotional** motives include fear, status, and ego-related feelings. List all relevant buying motives in order of importance.	B. *Specific Benefits Matched to Buying Motives:* Benefits to be stressed are arranged in priority order (sequence to be followed unless prospect feedback during the presentation indicates an alternative sequence). Each benefit should correspond to one or more buying motives.	C. *Information needed to support claims for each benefit.*	D. *Where appropriate, methods for reinforcing verbal content* (Audio/Visual, collateral material, illustrations, testimonials, etc.).
1.			
2.			
3.			
4.			

5. Current Suppliers (if applicable) and Other Key Competitors:

Competitors	Strengths	Weaknesses

6. Beginning the Sales Dialogue:

Plans for the first few minutes of the sales presentation:
Introduction, thanks, agreement, then: begin ADAPT as appropriate or transition into other sales dialogue or presentation:
Assessment _____
Discovery _____
Activation _____
Project _____
Transition to Presentation _____
Note: The ADAPT process may take place over several sales conversations during multiple sales calls. In other cases, it may be concluded in a single sales call, then immediately followed by a sales presentation during the same sales call.

(continued)

EXHIBIT 6.4   Sales Dialogue and Presentation Planning Template—*Continued*

7. Anticipated Prospect Questions and Objections, with Plan Responses:

Questions/Objections	Responses

8. Earn Prospect Commitment

A preliminary plan for how the prospect will be asked for a commitment related to the sales call objective:

9. Build Value through Follow-Up Action

Statement of follow-up action needed to ensure that the buyer–seller relationship moves in a positive direction:

Section 1: Prospect Information

This section is used to record specific information on the prospect such as the company name, key decision maker's name and job title, and the type of business. In most business-to-business situations, it is critical to know who else is involved in the buying decision and what role he or she plays, such as gatekeeper, user, or influencer. (Refer to Module 4 if you need to review the buying center concept.) It is also important that the salesperson make sure that all of the key players are receiving the appropriate information and getting the proper attention they deserve. A mistake often made by salespeople is not identifying all the buying influencers.

Section 2: Customer Value Proposition

In this section, the salesperson develops a preliminary **customer value proposition**, which is a statement of how the sales offering will add value to the prospect's business by meeting a need or providing an opportunity. Essentially, the customer value proposition summarizes the legitimate business reason for making the sales call by answering the prospect's question, "Why should I spend my time with you?" A good customer value proposition clearly states why the customer will be better off by doing business with the salesperson and his or her firm, but at this point does not try to list all of the reasons.[5]

At the planning stage, the customer value proposition is preliminary. The salesperson has good reason to believe that customer value can be enhanced by delivering on the contents of the proposition, but, the true value of the proposition will be accepted or rejected by the customer as the sales process moves along. It is during this sales dialogue process that the actual customer value to be delivered will be refined and modified. This section of the template provides a point of departure for planning purposes and assumes that the value proposition is likely to be modified prior to the purchase decision. In writing the preliminary customer value proposition, salespeople should attempt to:

1. Keep the statement fairly simple so that the direction for upcoming sales dialogues is clear.
2. Choose the key benefit(s) likely to be most important to the specific customer who is the audience for this particular dialogue or presentation. (At this point, it is not necessary to list all of the benefits of their offerings.)
3. Make the value proposition as specific as possible on tangible outcomes (e.g., improvements to revenues, cost containment or reduction, market share, process speed and efficiency) and/or the enhancement of the customer's strategic priority.
4. Reflect any product or service dimensions that add value, whether or not they are paid for by the customer. For example, some companies offer delivery, installation, and training along with the purchase of their products. Added value may also accrue from what the seller's sales team provides (e.g., work in the field with a distributor's salespeople or certification training for the buyer's technicians).
5. Promise only what can be consistently delivered. Strictly speaking, a customer value proposition in the planning stage is not a guarantee, it is a belief based on the salesperson's knowledge and best judgment. As the sales process moves along, appropriate guarantees can be made.

Using these points as a guide, this is an example of a customer value proposition that could provide clear direction for planning an upcoming sales presentation or a series of sales dialogues.

> "ABC Company can improve its market share by a minimum of four percentage points in a one-year period in its San Francisco and Dallas markets by implementing our customer satisfaction and retention training for its customer service personnel."

By contrast, here is an example of a poorly constructed customer value proposition.

> "By adopting our customer satisfaction and retention programs, ABC Company will see a dramatic increase in its market share."

This second proposition opens the salesperson to a potential barrage of questions:

> Dramatic increase in market share? What's dramatic?
>
> "We operate in 22 markets. Are you saying that we will increase market shares in all 22 markets?"
>
> What do you mean by programs? Are you referring to training programs?

In the planning stages, salespeople may or may not be fully aware of the prospect's needs and priorities—and, until they are aware of these needs and priorities, the sales dialogue should focus on the first two stages of the ADAPT process: assessing the prospect's situation and discovering their needs. Unless these stages are completed, the customer value proposition will not contain enough detail to be useful.

Section 3: Sales Call Objective

Section 3 asks the salesperson to determine the objective for his or her sales call. Salespeople must have an objective for each sales call. Many salespeople think that there is only one objective and that is to get an order. Other sales objectives do exist. For instance, during an introductory call the objective may be simply to introduce the salesperson and his or her company and to gather information on the buyer's needs. Eventually, the major sales presentation objective will be to earn a commitment from the customer by making a sale. After the sale is made, the objective may be to follow up and determine whether or not the customer is satisfied with the salesperson's efforts. The salesperson can also look for openings to cover additional objectives. Gwen Tranguillo of Hershey's always looks for ways to introduce other products in her presentation if the buyer expresses interest. Tranguillo made a major sales presentation on a Halloween display of king-size candies and found that the buyer was very interested in adding more king sizes immediately. She shifted gears and gained a commitment on the new king-size display and later in the presentation went back to her Halloween proposal. At the very least, the heart of any presentation should be to advance the process toward an order.

Section 4: Linking Buying Motives, Benefits, Support Information, and other Reinforcement Methods

In Section 4 of the planning template, the prospect's buying motives are linked to specific benefits offered. For each benefit identified, the salesperson will also assemble the information needed to support the claims to be made in the upcoming dialogue or presentation. In some cases, verbal claims must be reinforced with audio-visual portrayal, illustrations, printed collateral material, or testimonials from satisfied customers, as appropriate to the situation.

Buying motives refers to the most important factors from the customer's perspective in making a purchase decision. In other words, What will motivate the buyer to make a purchase? Buying motives may be rational or emotional, or a combination of both rational and emotional. **Rational buying motives** typically relate to the economics of the situation, including cost, profitability, quality, services offered, and the total value of the seller's offering perceived by the customer. **Emotional motives** such as fear, the need for security, the need for status, or the need to be liked, are sometimes difficult for salespeople to uncover as prospects are generally less likely to share such motives with salespeople. In business-to-business selling, rational motives are typically the most important buying motives, but salespeople should not ignore emotional motives if they are known to exist.

In linking benefits to buying motives, benefits should be distinguished from features. **Features** are factual statements about the characteristics of a product or service, such as "This is the lightest electrical motor in its performance category." **Benefits** describe the added value for the customer—the favorable outcome derived from a feature. For example, is "The lightweight motor supports your mobile repair service strategy in that it is very portable. The ease of use allows your technicians to complete more service calls per day, thus increasing impact on your profitability." To make such a claim about increasing profitability, the salesperson would need to gather specific information to support it. For example, in this case the claim that technicians can complete more service calls per day because the motor is easy to use might call for competitive comparisons and actual usage data, and/or a demonstration.

Some situations may lead the salesperson to decide that a product demonstration and testimonials from satisfied customers will reinforce the spoken word. In other cases, third-party research studies or articles in trade publications might be used to reinforce oral claims. Another powerful option is material developed by the salesperson, such as a break-even chart showing how quickly the customer can recoup the investment in the new product or service. A note of caution: It is always a good idea to use these types sales support materials sparingly—some prospects do not react positively to information overload. Module 7 discusses in greater detail sales tools and how they can enhance the sales effort.

Section 5: Competitive Situation

Understanding the competitive situation is essential in planning sales dialogues and presentations. Because buyers make competitive comparisons in their decision processes, salespeople should be prepared for it. This section of the planning template asks the salesperson to identify key competitors and to specify their strengths and weaknesses. By knowing their own product's strengths and weaknesses as well as those of their competitors, salespeople are better equipped to articulate customer value relative to their competitors. This competitive positioning is important, as most major purchase decisions are made in a highly competitive business environment. If the prospect is already buying a similar product, knowledge about the current supplier can give the salesperson critical insight into which buying motives and product attributes are likely to be affecting the buyer's decisions.

Section 6: Beginning the Sales Dialogue

Section 6 addresses the critical first few minutes of the sales call. During this period, salespeople will greet the prospect and introduce themselves, if necessary. There is typically some brief polite conversation between the salesperson and buyer as the salesperson is welcomed to the buyer's office, then both parties are usually eager to get down to business as quickly as possible. It is recommended that the salesperson propose an agenda, which may or may not have been previously agreed to. Then, depending on the situation, the salesperson will proceed with questions designed to assess the prospect's situation, discover their needs, or make a transition into a sales dialogue or presentation. A typical first few minutes might sound like this:

> **Buyer:** Come on in, Pat. I am John Jones. Nice to meet you. (*Introduction/greeting.*)
>
> **Seller:** Mr. Jones, I am Pat Devlin with XYZ Company. Nice to meet you, too. I appreciate the time that you are spending with me today. (*Thanks, acknowledges importance of the buyer's time.*)
>
> **Buyer:** Glad you could make it. We've had a lot of cancellations lately due to the bad weather. Did you have any problems driving over from Orlando? (*Polite conversation, may last for several minutes depending on the buyer–seller relationship and on how much the buyer wants to engage in this sort of conversation.*)
>
> **Seller:** Not really, it was pretty smooth today. Say, I know you are busy, so I thought we could talk about a couple of key ways I think we can really help you build market share with your end-user market. How does that sound? (*A simple illustration of getting the buyer to agree to the agenda.*)
>
> **Buyer:** Sure, let's get right to it. What do you have in mind?
>
> **Seller:** Well, based on our phone call last week, I believe that our training programs for your customer service representatives can improve your customer satisfaction ratings and customer retention. I can share the details with you over the next 20 minutes or so.... (*Transition to a sales dialogue or presentation based on customer needs and customer value.*)

In planning the first few minutes of the sales call, salespeople should remind themselves to be friendly and positive. They should also remain flexible in terms of their proposed agenda—customers like to have an agenda but sometimes want to modify it. The salesperson should be prepared to make an adjustment on the spot. For example, in the previous dialogue, the prospect might have said, "Yes, I want to hear about your training programs for our customer service reps, but I am also interested in your thoughts on how we can build a service-based culture across our entire marketing organization." The salesperson might respond accordingly, "I would be happy to do that. In fact, let me start with an overview that shows you the big picture from a strategy and company culture perspective, then later I will show you how the customer service training piece fits into the overall strategy. How does that sound?"

These first few minutes are critical in the trust-building process. By showing sensitivity to customer needs and opinions, and by asking questions to clarify the customer's perspective, salespeople demonstrate a customer orientation. Salespeople can demonstrate their expertise and competence by being sharp and well prepared. First impressions are crucial in all human interactions, so time spent on planning the first few minutes is a good investment on the salesperson's part. But remember that the planning

Making a Good First Impression

Kim Davenport, district manager for Shering-Plough, has seen his industry change since 1977, in regard to what is accepted as professional dress. Salespeople are allowed to wear beards and mustaches as long as they are groomed properly (i.e., short, neatly trimmed, not shaggy). What salespeople are allowed to wear has changed dramatically over the years. Today (particularly in the south during the summer season) men and women sales representatives routinely wear short-sleeve golf shirts that have Shering-Plough's name on the front for identification. Davenport says it is almost a necessity in towns like Scottsdale, Arizona, where temperatures reach 120 degrees in the summer. First impressions are still important according to Davenport and looking professional is the key. Dressing attractively and giving special attention to grooming will always pay off.

template is not intended as a script. It is imperative that salespeople think logically—and from the buyer's point of view—in planning what to say after greeting the customer.

Initiating Contact

Kim Davenport, district manger for Shering-Plough, discusses the importance of making a good first impression in "Professional Selling in the 21st Century: Making a Good First Impression."

In planning the first few minutes of the sales dialogue or presentation, there are a few ironclad rules—the appropriate sequence will be dictated by the situation and the prospect's preferences—but a few general rules do apply:

- Following an adequate introduction of the salesperson and the salesperson's company, questions, careful listening, and confirmation statements should be used to clarify and define explicit customer needs and motives as related to the salesperson's offering.
- Benefits should be presented in order of importance according to the prospect's needs and motives, and these benefits may be repeated during the presentation and at the conclusion of the presentation.
- If the sales presentation is a continuation of one or more previous sales calls, a quick summary should be made of what has been agreed on in the past, moving quickly into the prospect's primary area of interest.
- As a general rule, pricing issues should not be focused on until the prospect's needs have been defined and the salesperson has shown how those needs can be addressed with the product or service being sold. After prospects fully understand how the product or service meets their needs, they can make informed judgments on price/value issues.

Obviously, the first few minutes of the sales call will be greatly influenced by previous interaction (if any) between the buyer and the salesperson. For example, if previous sales calls have established buyer needs and the buyer has agreed to a sales presentation, the first few minutes will be quite different than if this is the first sales call on this prospect. The ADAPT questioning process (refer to Module 4) can be used in part or whole to acquire needed information and make a transition to the sales dialogue or presentation. As a guide, the salesperson should respect the buyer's time and get to the presentation as soon as circumstances allow. The salesperson should not rush to get to the presentation, and certainly should not launch into a presentation without establishing buyer needs and interest in it.

Section 7: Anticipate Questions and Objections

For reasons to be explained fully in Module 8, prospects will almost always have questions and objections that salespeople must be prepared to answer. In the planning stages, salespeople can prepare by asking themselves, "If I were the buyer, what would I want to be certain about before I make a purchase?" By anticipating these issues and preparing responses, salespeople can increase their chances of ultimate success.

Section 8: Earn Prospect Commitment

As sales dialogues and presentations progress, there eventually comes a critical time to ask for a customer's purchase decision. In many cases, this is an obvious point in the sales conversation, but at other times the salesperson may feel the need to probe to see if the timing is right. Earning a commitment from a customer as discussed in Module 8 should be a natural step in the conversation, not a forced or high-pressure attempt by the salesperson. Although circumstances will dictate exactly when and how commitment will be sought, a preliminary action plan for seeking customer commitment should be part of the overall planning process. Most buyers expect the salesperson to seek a commitment—and, if the commitment is sought at the right time, buyers appreciate that effort from the salesperson.

Section 9: Build Value through Follow-Up Action

Finally, the salesperson must always be looking for ways to enhance the relationship and move it in a positive direction. The salesperson should always make a note of any promises that he or she has made during the sales calls and especially during the proposal presentation. The buyer may ask for information that the salesperson is not prepared to give during the presentation. By taking notes, the salesperson ensures that the appropriate follow-up activities will happen.

This planning template for sales dialogues and presentations is an extremely useful tool for all salespeople and especially to inexperienced salespeople. It guarantees that all the appropriate steps are covered and that all of the pertinent information needed is collected. Using this template will make the task of customizing sales dialogues and presentations easier.

ENGAGING THE CUSTOMER

Most initial sales calls on new prospects require an appointment. Requesting an appointment accomplishes several desirable outcomes. First, the salesperson is letting the prospect know that the salesperson thinks the prospect's time is important. Second, there is a better chance that the salesperson will receive the undivided attention of the prospect during the sales call. Third, setting appointments is a good tool to assist the salesperson in effective time and territory management. The importance of setting appointments is clearly proclaimed in a survey of secretaries, administrative assistants, and other "gatekeepers" responsible for scheduling appointments. A majority of respondents thought that arriving unannounced to make a sales call is a violation of business etiquette.[6] Given this rather strong feeling of those who represent buyers, it is a good idea to request an appointment if there is any doubt about whether one is required.

Appointments may be requested by phone, mail (including e-mail), or personal contact. By far, setting appointments by telephone is the most popular method. Combining mail and telephone communications to seek appointments is also commonplace. Regardless of the communication vehicle used, salespeople can improve their chances of getting an appointment by following three simple directives: give the prospect a reason why an appointment should be granted; request a specific amount of time; and suggest a specific time for the appointment. These tactics recognize that prospects are busy individuals who do not spend time idly.

In giving a reason why the appointment should be granted, a well-informed salesperson can appeal to the prospect's primary buying motive as related to one of the benefits of the salesperson's offering. Being specific is recommended. For example, it is better to say that "you can realize gross margins averaging 35 percent on our product line" than "our margins are really quite attractive."

Mary Clark has been selling computer systems for more than 10 years. She has not had the success she once had in telephoning prospects and setting appointments. She stumbled onto a technique one day to get past the gatekeeper by suggesting to the secretary that she was conducting research and their company had been selected to participate. All she needed was a few minutes of the data processing manager's time. Clark was surprised to find how easy it was now to get past the gatekeeper. She was having a great deal of success with this method. What do you think of Clark's tactics? Is there any potential for future problems?

The above "An Ethical Dilemma" demonstrates the importance of trust and why doing an end run around a gatekeeper is unacceptable.

Specifying the amount of time needed to make the sales presentation alleviates some of the anxiety felt by a busy prospect at the idea of spending some of his or her already scarce time. It also helps the prospect if the salesperson suggests a time and date for the sales call. It is very difficult for busy individuals to respond to a question such as, "What would be a good time for you next week?" In effect, the prospect is being asked to scan his or her entire calendar for an opening. If a suggested time and date are not convenient, the interested prospect will typically suggest another. Once a salesperson has an appointment with the prospect and all the objectives have been established, the salesperson should send a fax or e-mail that outlines the agenda for the meeting and reminds the buyer of the appointment.

SUMMARY

1. **Understand alternative ways of communicating with prospects and customers through canned sales presentations, written sales proposals, and organized sales dialogues or presentations.** Canned sales presentations include scripted sales calls, memorized presentations, and automated presentations. Most canned presentations have been tested with real customers before they are used by an entire salesforce. Canned sales presentations are usually complete and logically structured. Objections are anticipated in advance, and appropriate responses can be formulated as part of the presentation. A written sales proposal is a complete, self-contained sales presentation. A sales proposal should be prepared after the salesperson has made a thorough assessment of the buyer's situation as it relates to the seller's offering. An organized sales dialogue or organized sales presentation is tailored to the prospect's particular situation and needs. It is a flexible format that allows for maximum input and feedback from the prospect. Sales dialogues and organized sales presentations (sometimes referred to as sales conversations) can take place over multiple sales calls before a purchase decision is made.

2. **Explain why organized sales dialogues and presentations are more frequently used than canned presentations or written sales proposals.** Although canned presentations and written sales proposals are effective in some situations, most business-to-business sales calls involve sales dialogue. An organized sales presentation is a form of sales dialogue in which the buyer is an active participant. Most business buyers want to be actively involved in the dialogue, which allows a full exploration of the buyer's needs, requirements, and preferences. Because the organized dialogue is tailored to each customer, it is more effective in more situations than a generic approach such as a canned presentation.

3. **Discuss the nine components in the planning template for an organized sales dialogue or presentation.** The Sales Dialogue and Presentation Template consists of nine sections: (1) prospect information; (2) customer value proposition; (3) sales call objective; (4) situation and needs analysis—linking buying motives, benefits, support information, and other reinforcement methods; (5) competitive situation; (6) beginning the sales dialogue; (7) anticipate questions and objections; (8) earn prospect commitment; and (9) building value through follow-up action.

4. **Explain how to write a customer value proposition statement.** A customer value statement should be simple, so that it provides a clear direction for upcoming sales dialogues. Salespeople should not attempt to include all of their benefits in a value proposition statement—rather, they should choose the key benefit(s) that are likely to be most important to the specific customer. The value proposition should be as specific as possible, on listing tangible outcomes such as revenue improvement, cost containment or reduction gain in market share, process speed and efficiency, or the enhancement of a customer's strategic priority. Value proposition statements should promise only what can be consistently delivered. Strictly speaking, a customer value proposition in the planning stage is not a guarantee, it is a belief based on the salesperson's knowledge and best judgment. As the sales process moves along, appropriate guarantees can be made.

5. **Link buying motives to benefits of the seller's offering, support claims made for benefits, and reinforce verbal claims made.** Organized sales dialogues and presentations should focus on the most important motives for a given buyer. Benefits must be linked to both rational and emotional motives, and supporting information must be given for each claim made of a benefit. In some cases, the claim needs support beyond the spoken word (for example, through audio-visual content, printed collateral material, third-party research studies, or testimonials from satisfied customers).

6. **Engage the customer by setting appointments.** Salespeople customarily set an appointment, at least for their initial sales calls on new prospects. Appointments may be arranged by telephone, e-mail, or a combination of phone and mail and should include a request for a specific time and date as well as the amount of time being requested for the sales call. Salespeople have a better chance of securing an appointment if they are prepared to give the customer a good reason for spending time with them.

UNDERSTANDING PROFESSIONAL SELLING TERMS

sales call	sales dialogue and presentation
sales dialogue	template
sales conversations	customer value proposition
sales presentations	buying motives
ADAPT	rational buying motives
canned sales presentations	emotional motives
written sales proposal	features
organized sales presentation	benefits
organized sales dialogue	

DEVELOPING PROFESSIONAL SELLING KNOWLEDGE

1. Why is sales dialogue and presentation preplanning important?
2. Do you see the need for a salesperson to ever use a canned sales presentation?

3. Most salespeople use organized sales dialogues and presentations today. Why?

4. Explain why both verbal and written communication are a necessity for a successful salesperson.

5. Explain the key elements of written proposals.

6. Why is the planning template for sales dialogue and presentation an important tool for today's salesperson?

7. Why is it important for a salesperson to establish objectives for each sales call?

8. What are the characteristics of a well-written customer value proposition?

9. What is the difference between buying motives and benefits?

10. How can salespeople enhance their chances of securing an appointment with a prospect?

BUILDING PROFESSIONAL SELLING SKILLS

1. Sales skills can be developed by understanding how buyers think. In this exercise, assume that you are the director of food-service operations for a large hospital. Among your priorities for the year is to help contain the cost of food service provided by your hospital without sacrificing the quality of patient care. You are meeting with a sales representative from a firm that manufactures disposable plastic tableware such as plates, bowls, and flatware. The sales representative has just recommended that you replace your glass tableware and stainless steel flatware with plastic disposables, claiming that your annual savings will be more than $30,000. To achieve this savings, a large institutional dishwasher will be sold to a used-equipment dealer and two employees will be eliminated from the payroll. As director of the food-service operation, what information would the salesperson have to supply to convince you that the claim of saving $30,000 per year is valid?

ROLE PLAY

2. **Situation:**   Read the Ethical Dilemma on page 166.

   Characters: Tom Lawrence, sales representative; sales manager; customer

   Scene 1:   *Location*—Lawrence in his sales manager's office.
   Action—Sales manager addresses his concern that Lawrence does not do enough precall planning and talks about features that are not relevant to the buyer.

   Role play Lawrence and his boss' conversation.

   Scene 2:   *Location*—Lawrence in one of the offices his customers.
   Action—Lawrence begins his sales conversation without asking any questions and determining needs. He goes right into features.

   Role play Lawrence and his customer's conversation.

   Upon completion of the role plays, address the following questions:

   2a. What are the potential problems for Lawrence?

   2b. Can you think of any reason why Lawrence may be afraid to precall plan and ask questions?

ROLE PLAY

3. **Situation:**   Read the Ethical Dilemma on page 176.

   Characters: Mary Clark, salesperson; secretary

   Scene 1:   *Location*—Client's office.
   Action—Clark calls in-person on company on which she has used this technique.

   Role play the secretary asking Clark why she was selling under the guise of research when she was really calling for an appointment. The secretary and data processing manager had compared notes and knew Clark was less than truthful.

Scene 2:   *Location*—Clark's office.
                   Action—Clark calls on the phone to the secretary.

Role play the secretary asking Clark a few questions about what kind of research she is doing. Who does Clark work for? For what will she use the data she is collecting?

Upon completion of the role plays, address the following questions:

3a. What happens when the secretary starts asking questions?
3b. What are the potential long-term ramifications of Clark's actions? Short term?

4. Go to a search engine like Yahoo.com. Type in "sales, planning the call" or "sales, precall planning." What did you find? Browse through some of these Web sites. What do the so-called experts have to say about precall planning? Write a memo to your boss suggesting some actions that your office can take to improve their precall planning based on the Web site information that you found. Make sure you reference the Web sites you browsed.

MAKING PROFESSIONAL SELLING DECISIONS

Case 6.1: The New Salesperson

Lon Taylor has been working for three months for a large chemical company that sells fertilizers to farm co-ops and distributors. He has just completed his training and is ready to go into the field. He has been taught how to gather precall information and prepare for his presentation. He has targeted his biggest distributor for his first call. The appointment has been set; he is ready to go in for a fact-finding call and hopefully some preliminary talk about one of his new products that has been launched in the past two weeks. Taylor is calling on Perry Martin, general manager of the distributorship. Taylor was in for a big surprise. Martin greeted Taylor with, "I've been waiting for you, follow me." Taylor followed Martin out to the warehouse where he directed Taylor attention to three large pallets of Taylor products. The top pallet was leaking chemicals all over the pallets below and onto the floor. Martin went on to complain that he'd called the 800 number service hotline three times trying to get someone out to take care of the mess. This totally caught Taylor off guard.

Questions

1. What should Taylor do now?
2. Taylor has a well-prepared presentation on his new product that he wants to give. What should he do about this information gathering call?

Situation:	Read Case 6.1.
Characters:	Lon Taylor, sales representative; Perry Martin, general manger; Todd Cravens, Taylor's boss
Scene 1:	*Location*—Distributor's warehouse. *Action*—A rather agitated Martin points out the leaking chemicals.

ROLE PLAY

Role play Taylor's response to Martin.

Scene 2:	*Location*—Taylor on the phone to his boss, Todd. *Action*—Taylor tries to get to the bottom of why customer service has not let anyone know about his customer's problem.

Role play Taylor's call to his boss, Craven.

Upon completion of the role plays, address the following questions:

1. How should Taylor handle an agitated Martin?
2. How should sales and customer service work together in the future to make sure that this does not happen again?

Case 6.2: The Overhead Door Company

Mary Tyler sells for The Overhead Door Company. She has sold garage doors to contractors and individual home owners for two years. When Tyler first began selling, she used to introduce herself as the name of her company. Next, she made a brief opening remark and then moved quickly into her presentation. Although this resulted in selling many garage doors, Tyler thought that there must be a better method.

Questions

1. What can you recommend to Tyler to strengthen the introduction of her sales calls?
2. If Tyler is successful using her present method, why should she change?

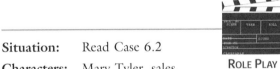

Situation:	Read Case 6.2
Characters:	Mary Tyler, sales representative; customer

ROLE PLAY

Scene 1:	*Location*—Tyler is on the phone calling a new prospect. *Action*—Tyler introduces herself.

Role play Tyler's introduction and try different approach techniques.

Upon completion of the role play, address the following questions:

1. Do you think some openings are more effective than others?
2. Which ones do you find effective?
3. Which approach techniques do you find difficult to use? Why?

Developing Customer Relationships

Part Three is comprised of two modules that focus on the interpersonal interaction which results in an established relationship between the buyer and seller. In Module 7, we concentrate on establishing a productive buyer–seller dialogue. To accomplish a productive dialogue, the salesperson must understand how to communicate benefits to the buyer in an effective manner. The use of sales aids such as audiovisual support material is discussed. Module 7 concludes with a section on special strategies and tactics for selling to groups.

Module 8 discusses why buyers may raise objections or resist the sales proposition and how salespeople can deal with resistance in a professional, ethical manner. We present specific methods for handling objections and earning a commitment from the buyer without employing high-pressure tactics.

MAKING THE SALES CALL: CREATING AND COMMUNICATING VALUES

FACE-TO-FACE WITH THE CUSTOMER: SALESPERSON BEHAVIOR IS KEY TO SUCCESS

Marshall McLuhan's statement, "the media is the message" became a classic largely because it contains so much truth. In professional selling, salespeople are not the entire message, but they are a big part of it. According to consulting firm The HR Chally Group, more customers make buying decisions based on the salesperson than on any other factor, including price and quality. Thus, when interacting with customers, it is of paramount importance that salespeople reinforce the overall sales message through their behaviors.

In addition to planning appropriate sales dialogues or presentations, salespeople should focus on three key behaviors when they are face-to-face with customers: (1) They should show enthusiasm and be energetic about what they are selling; (2) they should be superb listeners; and (3) they should avoid negative selling. Sales trainer and author Brian Tracy advocates writing out an objective before each sales call to clarify the purpose and generate enthusiasm for the product or service. Tracy says that the very act of writing the objective increases the chance that it will be achieved.

The importance of listening cannot be overemphasized. It is easy to *say* that you will be a good listener, but it can be hard to *do*—that is because we can process information approximately five to six times faster than most people talk. As a result, we tend to do other things while listening, which leads to poor listening. When face-to-face with a customer, good salespeople focus on the buyer, ask questions to keep the conversation on track, limit how much they talk, take limited notes, and do not finish the buyer's sentences.

To support a productive sales dialogue, salespeople should concentrate on the positive aspects of how they can provide customer value and refrain from taking cheap shots at the competition. Although salespeople must know their competitors' offerings and be able to illustrate how their own offerings match up, buyers are usually turned off by a sales presentation that focuses on the shortcomings of competitors—especially if those shortcomings are a matter of opinion, not absolute fact.

Smart salespeople know that their time with customers is precious. To maximize the opportunity, they plan carefully and are guided by a written sales call objective. They show enthusiasm and energy, listen well, and keep the dialogue focused on positive ways that they can deliver customer value.

When the objective of a sales call is to make a sale, the salesperson expands on the rapport, knowledge, and understanding established in the preceding portions of the sales process and during previous sales calls. It is in this phase of the selling process that the salesperson presents a solution to the buyer's needs, nurtures the buyer's perceived value of the sales offering as a unique solution for the individual buyer, and confirms the buyer's understanding of and interest in obtaining the benefits offered by the salesperson's solution.

Objectives

After completing this module, you should be able to

1 Describe the difference between features, potential benefits, confirmed benefits, and the role they play in benefits selling.

2 Construct complete selling points using feature and benefit statements.

3 Discuss the advantages of using response-checks in the selling presentation.

4 List and explain the different forms of presentation tools and sales aids that can increase the impact of a presentation.

5 Delineate the four steps of the SPES process for effectively utilizing sales aids in presentations.

6 Explain some of the special considerations in making sales presentations to groups.

Sources: Theodore B. Kinni, "You Are the Message!" *Selling Power* (July/August 2006): 18–19; William Kendy, "Learning to Listen," *Selling Power* (July/August 2006): 25; Renee Houston Zemanski, "When the Competition Gets Tough," *Selling Power* (April 2006): 17–19.

EXHIBIT 7.1   Keys to Effective Sales Dialogue and Presentations

1. Sales dialogue and presentations should be guided by at least one major objective that requires customer action as a result of the presentation.
2. Sales dialogue and presentations should have a clear, easy to follow structure. The use of the Sales Dialogue and Presentation Planning Template (see Module 6) provides such a structure.
3. Understand customer needs before making a complete sales presentation.
4. Focus on needs and buying motives that the customer confirms as being important.
5. Present the solution, or value proposition, in terms of benefits that the customer will experience as a result of making a purchase.
6. Seek confirmation from the customer that the benefits offered are important to the customer, and that your proposition can deliver them.
7. Plan for, and encourage, customer interaction. Strive for a productive two-way dialogue, which can be achieved through active listening and questioning.
8. Use audiovisuals and other sales tools to reinforce key points, but do not let technology and sales tools overwhelm the message.
9. Guard against using annoying mannerisms and statements. Be positive and specific.
10. Be prepared for success. Make it easy for the customer to make a purchase.

Preparing and completing this phase of the sales process successfully has been compared to doing surgery in that it is complex and requires preparation, knowledge, and skill.[1] Prior to conducting surgery, the doctor has acquired a great deal of relevant information from a variety of sources and developed a comprehensive understanding of the patient's problems and needs. Based on this understanding of the patient's needs, the surgeon utilizes his or her training and skills in combination with an assortment of tools to conduct a surgical procedure unique to the individual patient's needs. Continuing the analogy, up to the point of the presentation in the selling process the salesperson has been developing his or her knowledge and understanding of the buyer's situation and needs. Now, in the form of an effective presentation, the salesperson presents a solution that is specific and customized to the needs of the buyer, illustrates and demonstrates the benefits of the solution, and confirms the buyer's belief in and desire to obtain the benefits.

Good salespeople are very much like good surgeons in that they are serious in what they do and leave nothing to chance. They work with the prospective buyer to identify, diagnose, and clarify unsatisfied needs or problems and then show the buyer how much better the situation would be by purchasing the proposed product or service. For some keys to effective sales dialogue and presentations see Exhibit 7.1.

NEEDS-GAP ANALYSIS: SELECTING APPROPRIATE CUSTOMER OFFERINGS BY ASSESSING NEEDS

The simple fact that a qualified prospect can buy does not translate that he or she will buy. Need alone is not sufficient. A prospect will buy after concluding that by purchasing your product, he or she will be substantially better off. Given the high level of competition in most industries, salespeople must have a clear understanding of their customers' needs to be considered seriously. Using a questioning sequence such as **SPIN** or **ADAPT** (for a full discussion of SPIN and ADAPT see Module 4, "Communication Skills") the salesperson explores the buyer's situation to identify missed opportunities, dissatisfactions, needs, and problems. The salesperson must ask questions, probe for details, and listen carefully to what the prospective buyer is saying. This may take more than one sales call depending on the amount of probing and clarifying that must take place to understand the prospect's needs. The salesperson's primary goal is to uncover the prospect's specific needs or problems and then focus on what products or services will solve the problem or meet the specific needs.

Tracey Wise has been selling computer systems for just over nine years and earned the position of senior account manager for one of the leading companies in the industry. For several months, Wise has been working with a major insurance company that is looking for an automated information system that will solve the company's growing backlog of worker compensation claims. After reviewing the information from previous sales calls with the buyer, Wise and her tech-support team decided that the R740 system offered the greatest benefits to this particular customer. However, a special sales promotion provided company salespeople additional commissions and double points toward the annual sales incentive trip to Hawaii for each R800 system sold. The higher priced R800 had all the same features and capabilities of the R740 along with many more. However, few of these additional capabilities would ever be of value to the insurance company. During her last sales call, Wise explained and demonstrated the R740 and the R800 and persuaded the buyer that they would quickly "grow into the additional features" making the R800 the best deal. Based on Wise's presentation and stated benefits, the company purchased the R800 and Wise received the bonus commission and qualified for the Hawaii sales incentive trip.

What happened here? What are the dangers in overselling a customer?

Based on the prospective buyer's identified and confirmed needs, the salesperson reviews the possible product and service options in order to select or create a solution that satisfies the buyer's needs and problems. The salesperson describes and builds desire for the recommended solution by detailing features of the solution as they relate to specific needs of the prospective buyer and demonstrating the benefits provided by each of the relevant features. Solution features and benefits are linked to the buyer's specific needs in a way that generates the buyer's desire to purchase and acquire the recommended solution. As illustrated in "An Ethical Dilemma," basing a presentation on anything other than a customer's true needs is a questionable tactic.

CREATING VALUE: LINKING SOLUTIONS TO NEEDS

It is unlikely that the customer will be interested in every detail of the salesperson's product or service offering, and certainly some aspects of the offering will be more important to a particular prospect than will others. Essentially, salespeople should strive to communicate three crucial factors: (1) How buyer needs will be met or how an opportunity can be realized as a result of a purchase; (2) how the product features translate, in a functional sense, into benefits for the buyer; and (3) why the buyer should purchase from you as opposed to a competitive salesperson. To assist salespeople in effectively communicating these three factors, most sales training programs emphasize a form of benefit selling, sometimes referred to as **FAB** (for features, advantages, and benefits).

BENEFIT SELLING: FEATURES, POTENTIAL BENEFITS, AND CONFIRMED BENEFITS

Any given product or service is comprised of multiple **features** that have the capability to produce different **potential benefits** and **confirmed benefits**. Features are traditionally defined as a quality or characteristic of a product or service that is designed to provide value to a buyer. Features answer the question, "What is it?" A benefit is the value provided by a feature to the buyer and addresses the always present buyer's question, "What's in it for me?" However, not all benefits will be valued at the same level by all buyers, thus the categorization of potential benefits versus confirmed benefits. A potential benefit describes a general form of value that is assumed to be of importance by the salesperson but not yet acknowledged as such by the buyer. Once the prospective buyer acknowledges the importance of a benefit to his or her buying situation, it is a confirmed benefit. Because confirmed benefits represent customer value that is provided by the proposed solution, some sales programs refer to one or more confirmed benefits as the value proposition.

Research tells us that buyers do not purchase products and features. Rather, buyers purchase the value and satisfaction provided to them in the form of relevant benefits. Consequently, features have very little persuasive power. Salespeople can be more effective by selling benefits rather than features. However, to be most effective and gain the buyer's confirmation, stated benefits must be relevant to the prospective buyer's needs and phrased in a format that clearly translates the benefit from a generic "one-size-fits-all" description to a unique and customized benefit that has immediate meaning for the prospective buyer. While the one-size-fits-all benefit statements do not require much cognitive effort on the part of the salesperson, they typically do not pass from potential benefits to confirmed benefits. As illustrated in Exhibit 7.2, benefit statements that build on the salesperson's understanding and appreciation of the buyer's situation and are tailored to the individual buyer's needs and expectations are more likely to be confirmed by the buyer as being important.

By themselves, features and potential benefits risk the buyer thinking or asking, "So what?" Confirmed benefits are persuasive and advance the sale forward on the basis of creating added value for the buyer. This is the foundation of benefit selling. In benefit selling, the salesperson describes the benefits as they relate to specific needs of the prospective buyer and limits the role of features to simply supporting and

---

EXHIBIT 7.2   Features/Potential Benefits/Confirmed Benefits

Salesperson in golf shop selling Titleist golf balls to a weekend golfer.		Confirmed Benefit?	Explanation
Feature:	Solid 1.58" diameter core		
Potential Benefit:	Higher initial velocity and launch angle.	No	The typical weekend golf customer would not immediately see how the benefit of higher velocity and launch angle will benefit him or her.
Feature:	Solid 1.58" diameter core		
Potential Benefit:	Provides more distance on shots for the typical golfer and lowers your score.	Yes	Longer shots and lower scores are a primary interest of the typical weekend golfer. Customers can immediately understand the benefit to themselves.

Selling a new Frito-Lay snack to a regional supermarket chain.		Confirmed Benefit?	Explanation
Feature:	Daily delivery		
Potential Benefit:	Retailer can reduce inventory costs.	No	This prospective buyer considers inventory costs a regular cost of doing business. The potential benefit is not perceived as being important.
Feature:	Daily delivery		
Potential Benefit:	Assures product freshness, which will lead to high customer satisfaction.	Yes	Prospective customer places tremendous emphasis on customer satisfaction. Consequently, this potential benefit is confirmed as being valuable.

evidencing the presence of confirmed benefits. This combination of a specific feature and its meaningful benefit statement are referred to as a **selling point**. As the following illustrates, selling points should be phrased in a conversational tone and clearly describe the benefit in a manner that emphasizes its applicability and importance to the individual buyer.

- "This particular copier automatically selects the paper size that best matches your original document. Based on the experience of other customers using this model, it will speed up reproduction of your longer reports and reduce waste. Not only will this save you money in terms of reduced waste, but it will also increase the efficiency of your office staff, which you expressed as one of your major concerns."
- "The design of this particular golf club provides you with an expanded sweet-spot for maximum ball contact. This will not only increase the distance of your shots, but will also provide the improved accuracy that you are looking for."
- "Our unique use of overnight express for merchandise delivery reduces your need for back-up inventory while eliminating the possibility for out-of-stock and disappointed customers that you mentioned were costing you business."

Most sales trainers and successful salespeople would agree that showing the buyer potential benefits of relevant features will sometimes lead to successful sales calls. A sale may be made—but, if not, at least the dialogue has been advanced in a positive manner, which sets the stage for subsequent sales calls. However, there is no question that the chances of a successful sales call are greatly improved by getting the buyer to agree that one or more benefits are indeed important to him or her.

The use of confirmed benefits is further explained in "Professional Selling in the 21st Century: Using Confirmed Benefits."[2] In selecting specific features and benefits to be stressed, salespeople should focus on any unique benefits not offered by the competition, as long as the benefits are of interest to the prospective buyer. These might include product benefits along with nonproduct benefits such as delivery, financing, extraordinary customer service, or additional sales support available to the buyer.

PROFESSIONAL SELLING IN THE 21ST CENTURY

Using Confirmed Benefits

Jamie Howard, vice president of Chicago-based Active Solutions, emphasizes selling benefits rather than features to advance the sale.

In today's competitive business environment it has become more difficult for sales professionals to separate their solutions from the competition. It is important to realize that what advances the sale to the next step is not always directly related to the features of the product, but instead to the value the benefits of the product creates.

The contract furniture industry is as competitive as any other industry. When a large corporation is in the market for new furniture, as many as five competitors will be asked to bid. In one high profile project last year, creating value through showing our solution's benefits was the only chance to win. The products being proposed had very similar features and our price was slightly

higher. My team had to develop a strategic plan to create value for what we were offering. When everything is perceived to be similar, features will not be the deciding factor in the client's decision. The majority of the time the client will make his or her decision based on other variables. In this case, our price was higher and the features were similar. We had to create value for our product by focusing on the benefits rather than the features. The benefits had to be tied to the buyer's needs, which we developed during the questioning phase of the sales cycle. By identifying the client's needs, we were able to present the benefits that created added value over the competition. The customer's perceived value of our solution separated us from the competition. Following months of strategic meetings, we won the high profile project—the largest in our company's history. The client acknowledged that understanding how our solution benefited them was the key in their decision-making process because we had solved a problem for them instead of just offering a product.

ENCOURAGING BUYER FEEDBACK

In productive sales dialogues and presentations, salespeople continually assess and evaluate the reactions and responses of prospective buyers. In contrast, less successful salespeople often rush through the entire presentation from beginning to end and never stop to invite feedback from the buyer. Feedback from the prospective buyer provides the salesperson with important information measuring the climate between the salesperson and the buyer, the buyer's level of interest in the product's features and benefits, whether the salesperson has successfully responded to the buyer's concerns, and how well the presentation is progressing toward the buyer making a purchase decision.

As detailed and discussed in Module 4, the observant salesperson can receive a great deal of continual feedback in the form of the buyer's nonverbal cues. In addition to observing nonverbal cues, high performing salespeople incorporate verbal probes at key points in order to evaluate the buyer's interest and assess the progress of the sales dialogue. These verbal probes are typically confirmatory forms of questions in search of simple "yes" or "no" responses from the buyer.

The phrases **check-backs** and **response-checks** have become common names for this form of questioning seeking feedback from the buyer. While feedback can be sought at any point in the conversation, response checks are commonly employed in two key points: (1) After a specific feature-benefit sequence in order to confirm the benefit and better assess the prospective buyer's level of interest and (2) following the response to an objection in order to evaluate the level to which the salesperson has handled the problem. Exhibit 7.3 provides an illustrative selection of response-check examples that salespeople indicate are typical of those they commonly use.

The effective use of response-checks offers a number of advantages. Probably the most evident is increased buyer involvement. Asking for buyer feedback helps to ensure that the dialogue remains a two-way, collaborative exchange. The effective use of response-checks also helps the salesperson evaluate the level of the buyer's understanding and keeps the salesperson on the right track. If feedback indicates a lack of understanding—or even worse a lack of interest—on the part of a prospective buyer, the salesperson must make changes to improve alignment with the needs and expectations of the buyer. On the other hand, positive feedback indicating a high level of understanding and interest on the part of the buyer would signal the salesperson to stay the course and advance the presentation toward gaining the buyer's purchase commitment. A series of positive response-checks indicates that the buyer is nearing a purchase decision. The more positive affirmations a salesperson receives in relation to his or her response-checks, the easier the final purchase decision becomes and the more confident the prospective buyer is in having made the appropriate decision.

EXHIBIT 7.3   Illustrative Examples of Response-Checks

- "How does this sound to you?"
- "Does this make sense to you so far?"
- "Would this particular feature be useful to you in your current operations?"
- "What do you think?"
- "So this is something that would be valuable to you?"
- "Isn't that great?"
- "Do you like this color?"
- "From your comment, it sounds like you would want the upgraded memory. Is that correct?"
- "Does that answer your concern?"
- "Would this be an improvement over what you are doing right now?"
- "Is this what you had in mind?"

SALES TOOLS FOR MAXIMIZING PRESENTATION EFFECTIVENESS

The benefit selling approach is designed to create a prospective buyer's awareness of the value provided by a proposed solution in line with his or her needs and problems, generate interest in learning more about the solution and its benefits, and stimulate the buyer's desire to obtain the benefits confirmed as being important. However, simply informing the prospect about the benefits and their value to the buyer is seldom sufficient to generate the level of interest and desire required to result in a purchase decision. To maximize the effectiveness of the sales dialogue, salespeople utilize sales tools that capture and hold the buyer's attention, boost the buyer's involvement and understanding, increase the believability of the claims, and build the buyer's retention of information (see Exhibit 7.4).

As illustrated in Figure 7.1, salespeople have a variety of sales tools available for use in presentations. These various sales tools can be categorized in five ways: verbal support, sales call setting, proof providers, visual aids, and electronic media.

Many times, these sales tools are provided by the selling organization. However, experienced salespeople are quick to comment that some of their most effective sales tools are those that they developed themselves for specific prospects and selling situations. A rapidly growing trend is the development and use of online libraries of sales aids and tools. These are typically developed by selling organizations for the exclusive use of their salespeople and access is restricted through the use of password authentication. Hewlett-Packard maintains an extensive online database and library of sales tools that include product brochures and specification sheets, graphics, proposal templates, competitive comparisons, and an archive of PowerPoint presentations. Content can be downloaded and printed as is or customized to better fit a specific need. Equipped with a hand-held or laptop computer and portable color printer, a salesperson can produce professional quality sales aids or a full-color proposal in a matter of minutes.

Not all sales tools are suitable for all products, selling situations, or buyers. Nor should a salesperson feel the need to use each and every tool in any given sales call. A salesperson should think through and visualize the presentation that he or she is developing. Based on what the salesperson envisions, he or she should consider several questions to arrive at a decision on what tools to incorporate:

- "How might the presentation be made stronger?"
- "What tools would help to capture and hold the buyer's attention?"
- "What sales aids could aid the buyer's understanding and retention?"
- "Which sales aids would better evidence and build the buyer's believability of the benefits and value offered by this solution?"

Verbal Support

Among the five categories of sales tools and aids, the elements comprising the **verbal support** group are immediately available to the salesperson. More importantly, they

Reasons for Using Sales Tools and Aids	**EXHIBIT 7.4**

- Capture prospective buyer's attention.
- Generate interest in the recommended solution.
- Make presentations more persuasive.
- Increase the buyer's participation and involvement.
- Provide the opportunity for collaboration and two-way communication.
- Add clarity and enhance the prospect's understanding.
- Provide supportive evidence and proof to enhance believability.
- Augment the prospect's retention of information.
- Enhance the professional image of the salesperson and selling organization.

> ## FIGURE 7.1 — Key Sales Tools and Aids
>
> **VISUAL AIDS**
> - Product demonstrations and models
> - Printed materials
> - Photographs and illustrations
> - Graphs and charts
>
> **SALES CALL SETTING**
> - Location
> - Positioning and seating arrangements
> - Disruptions
>
> **PROOF PROVIDERS**
> - Statistics
> - Testimonials
> - Case histories
>
> **Sales Tools and Aids**
>
> **VERBAL SUPPORT**
> - Voice characteristics
> - Examples and anecdotes
> - Comparisons and analogies
>
> **ELECTRONIC MEDIA**
> - Computer-based presentations
> - Video
> - Slides
> - Overhead transparencies

To make sales dialogues and presentations more effective, salespeople should utilize the right combination of sales tools and aids. The five key categories of sales tools and aids are visual aids, the sales call setting, proof providers, verbal support, and electronic media.

are very effective in holding the prospective buyer's attention, building interest, and increasing both understanding and retention of information. Primary components of the verbal support group are **voice characteristics**, **examples and anecdotes**, and **comparisons and analogies**.

Voice Characteristics

As emphasized in "Professional Selling in the 21st Century: Energizing Sales Dialogues,"[3] a salesperson can know his or her product inside and out, but if there is

---

PROFESSIONAL SELLING IN THE 21ST CENTURY

Energizing Sales Dialogues

David Jacoby, sales instructor for CDW Corporation emphasizes the importance of energizing your sales presentation through the effective use of voice characteristics, nonverbal communication, and mentally painting pictures of solutions and benefits in the buyer's mind.

When presenting, your voice says it all—literally. This is especially true in telesales, where the entire sales cycle takes place over the phone. Our research underscores that in a face-to-face conversation, vocalization accounts for 38 percent of a customer's comprehension, while in a phone conversation it accounts for 86 percent. Assuming one has successfully identified all of the confirmed needs through the ADAPT questioning process, it is up to the salesperson to present the solution in a way that prompts the customer to take action. Vocalization can keep the customer's attention and create impact through speaking rates and pause duration, pitch and frequency, and intensity and volume. While presenting, maintain control of your vocalization through self-monitoring. At various intervals ask yourself, "If I were on the other end of the phone, would I be intently listening or daydreaming about my next meeting?" It will be hard at first, but try to see your presentation from your customer's perspective to make it more effective. By developing vocal skills and adding them to your sales arsenal, you will be able to create and maintain customer interest. Remember, your voice says it all.

no energy and passion in his or her voice, the potential for making the sale will be seriously impaired. Voice coach Jeffrey Jacobi emphasizes that, "Your voice and how you use it determines how people respond to you. The sound of your voice relays to people whether you are confident, likable, boring, unpleasant, honest, or even dishonest."[4] Voice quality can be used to bring excitement and drama to the presentation by doing three things: varying the pitch, fluctuating the speed, and altering the volume.

Varying and changing pitch on key words adds emphasis and increases impact. It is analogous to putting different colors and hues into your voice. The increased intensity and vividness grabs attention, holds interest, and helps the buyer remember what is said. Fluctuating the speed of speech can add emphasis and guide the buyer's attention to selected points of the presentation. Important details—especially quantitative information—should be provided at a slower, more careful pace. Less critical information can be presented at a faster pace in order to grab the buyer's attention and redirect his or her interest. Changes in volume can be used to add emphasis to an important phrase or topic while a softer volume—almost a whisper—can build intrigue and pull the prospect into the conversation. Altering of volume from loud to soft can better grab and hold the buyer's interest while simultaneously adding clarity and emphasis to increase understanding.

Examples and Anecdotes

An example is a brief description of a specific instance used to illustrate features and benefits. Examples may be either real or hypothetical and are used to further explain and emphasize a topic of interest. Anecdotes are a type of example that is provided in the form of a story describing a specific incident or occurrence. While a salesperson's use of examples and anecdotes bring clarity into the presentation in order to improve the buyer's understanding and retention, they also contribute proof and believability of benefit claims.

A production equipment salesperson might further explain the purpose of an infrared guidance control by using the following example:

> . . . for example, if the feedstock coming off the main paper roll gets out of line by as little as $1/16$ of an inch, the infrared guidance control will sense it and automatically make the correct adjustments. This prevents a paper jam from shutting down your package printing line and costing lost time and wasted product.

Similarly, a Snap On tool salesperson might use the following anecdote as an explanation of the Snap On lifetime guarantee:

> . . . for instance, one of your mechanics uses this ratchet handle as a substitute hammer to drive a retaining pin into an axle and damages the ratchet mechanism. Snap On will replace the broken tool at no charge, even though the damage was caused by misuse.

Comparisons and Analogies

A comparison is a statement that points out and illustrates the similarities between two points. An analogy is a special and useful form of comparison that explains one thing in terms of another. Analogies are useful for explaining something complex by allowing the buyer to better visualize it in terms of something familiar that is easier to understand. Comparisons add interest and clarity while improving the retention of information. The substantiation of claims that is provided through comparisons and analogies is also effective in providing proof to the claims of benefit and value.

A salesperson wishing to add emphasis and meaning to his or her verbal description of the Honda S2000's performance capabilities might use a direct comparison to the performance capabilities of a competitive model that the prospective buyer might also be considering:

> You have the performance specifications on both cars, and as you can see …the 6 second 0 to 60 performance of the S2000 outperforms the Audi TT by a good 10 percent. Isn't that the kind of performance that you are looking for?

A salesperson for Newell-Rubbermaid might illustrate the benefits of setting up an end-of-aisle display of special occasion containers by using the following comparison to the store manager's sales goals for the product category:

> …sales data from stores similar to yours indicate that adding an end-of-aisle display for these seasonal containers will increase their sales by 35 to 40 percent during the fourth quarter holiday season. This would certainly help you achieve—and possibly exceed—the store's goal of a 20 percent increase for this general product category.

A BMW salesperson presenting to an Air Force pilot the option of an in-car global positioning system map and tracking system might use the following analogy:

> …having the onboard map and tracking system is like having a friendly flight controller with you on every trip. You will always know exactly where you are and what route you should travel to reach your destination. You will never get lost or be delayed because you took the wrong turn.

Sales Call Setting

Many times the salesperson has little or no control over the setting in which the sales call will take place. Nevertheless the setting can influence results, and salespeople should consider the two primary elements of sales settings—**location, positioning and seating arrangements, and disruptions**—as they address the following questions:

- Will the atmosphere be supportive and nonthreatening?
- Where would the prospect feel more open to ideas and willing to listen?
- What location will minimize potential distractions?

Location

Where the sales presentation takes place can have a strong positive or negative influence on its success. Most sales presentations take place in the prospect's office. If the prospective buyer has a private office and interruptions can be controlled, it will usually be the best location. The familiar surroundings put the buyer at ease. As the guest, the salesperson is duly treated with respect. In those instances where interruptions cannot be controlled or the prospect has a reputation for being highly domineering, meeting off-site at a neutral location is often more productive. The off-site meeting could be at a related third-party's facility or perhaps a lunch meeting where the salesperson assumes the psychological role of host.

Positioning and Seating Arrangements

Although most sales calls are made while seated with the prospective buyer at a desk or table, many sales calls are actually made standing up. For instance, a detail representative for pharmaceutical companies such as Pfizer or Merck often makes sales calls while walking down the hall with the doctor as he or she moves from one patient's examining room to another. An agriculture chemical salesperson for Dow or Growmark might find himself or herself making a presentation to a farmer out in the demonstration field next to the application equipment.

Whether sitting or standing, the salesperson should be aware of interpersonal communication and behavior concepts such as proxemics that were discussed in

Module 4. If standing, collaborative communication can be facilitated by the salesperson positioning himself or herself two to four feet from the buyer and at an angle rather than straight across from the buyer. Standing too close and straight across from the buyer can be unconsciously as well as consciously perceived as threatening. If the presentation is going to be made from a seated position, read the prospective buyer's nonverbal cues as to what seat to take and when to be seated. As with standing, seating yourself directly across from the buyer can be seen as threatening or intimidating. If the office is arranged so that the only seat available is in front of the desk and directly across from the buyer, make the most of it by sitting at a bit of an angle. Not only will this take the edge off any unconscious intimidation, but it is also less formal and will make it easier to show and demonstrate visual aids. The ideal seating arrangement is around a small table or at the side of the prospective buyer's desk where the salesperson can direct the buyer's attention and effectively share visual aids and other presentation tools while being able to observe the buyer's nonverbal cues and feedback.

Disruptions

Interruptions and disruptions are any occurrences that distract the buyer's attention away from the sales dialogue. Some, such as something related to the buyer's job or home life are not directly controllable by the salesperson. However, many distractions and interruptions can be directly controlled or at least influenced by the salesperson. For instance, asking prior to beginning the presentation whether others will be joining the meeting can prevent having to start over when a late comer unexpectedly strolls into the room. Is there activity going on outside the office window that might momentarily distract the buyer's concentration? If so, it might be possible to position yourself so that the buyer's line of sight is redirected away from the window. These are but a few examples of how the salesperson can minimize distractions. However, to be successful in doing so the salesperson must be observant of the surroundings and proactively influence sources of potential disruptions. Even the best-prepared salespeople will occasionally encounter a disruption that must be handled effectively. As detailed in Exhibit 7.5, when that happens, the salesperson must quickly read the

How to Handle Disruptions   EXHIBIT 7.5

- Be patient and observe the situation. Look and listen for verbal and nonverbal cues. Some disruptions are momentary distractions while others demand the prospect's attention and may take some time.

If Disruption Is Momentary in Nature and Controllable	If Disruption Requires More of Buyer's Attention and Is Not Controllable
• Redirect the customer's attention pointing out an interesting detail or asking a question. • Restate the selling points of interest that were being discussed just prior to the disruption. • Make sure you are covering details that the customer perceives as being important; if not, change to a different selling point that would be of more importance to the buyer. • Incorporate the use of sales aids to increase the buyer's involvement and participation in the dialogue.	• Suggest that it might be better to continue at a time more convenient for the buyer. • Set and confirm a specific day and time to return. • Be slightly early for the next appointment. • Briefly summarize where you were in the previous appointment. • Restate and gain the buyer's reconfirmation of the features and benefits that had already been covered prior to the disruption. • Continue the dialogue, making sure to cover details the customer perceives as being important; if not, change to a different selling point that would be of more importance to the buyer.

verbal and nonverbal cues and decide whether to tactfully regain the prospect's attention or make an appointment to return at a better time.

Proof Providers

As discussed earlier in this module, confirmed benefits answer the buyer's question, "What's in it for me?" In a similar fashion, proof providers such as **statistics**, **testimonials**, and **case histories** can be utilized to preempt the buyer from asking, "Can you prove it?" or "Who says so?" Claims of benefits and value produced and provided to the buyer need to be backed up with evidence to highlight their believability.

Statistics

Facts and statistics lend believability to claims of value and benefit. When available, statistics from authoritative, third-party sources carry the highest credibility. Among others, third-party sources include independent testing organizations and labs (e.g., *Consumer Reports*, Underwriters Laboratory), professional organizations (e.g., American Dental Association, Risk and Insurance Management Society), research companies (e.g., Booz Allen Hamilton, The Industry Standard, PricewaterhouseCoopers), institutions (e.g., Sandia, MIT), and various governmental entities (e.g., Census Bureau, state licensing bureaus, Department of Commerce). Statistics prepared by the selling organization as well as the salesperson can also be useful in providing evidence for claims. Facts and statistics are most powerful when they fairly represent all sides to the story and are presented in printed form rather than simply stated orally. Not only does the printed word carry more credibility, but it is also convenient and can be left as a reminder to aid the prospect's retention of information.

Testimonials

Testimonials are similar to facts and statistics, but in the form of statements from satisfied users of the selling organization's products and services. Supportive statements from current users are excellent methods to build trust and confidence. They predispose the prospective buyer to accept what the salesperson says about the benefits and value offered by a recommended solution and reduce the prospect's perceived risk in making a purchase decision. As shown in "An Ethical Dilemma," the power of testimonials sometimes tempts salespeople to misuse them.

Written testimonials are especially effective when they are on the recommending user's letterhead and signed. However, testimonials that list customers, trade

AN ETHICAL DILEMMA

Jane Rafael is an account manager for International Supply and Uniform (ISU), a major provider of work wear and uniforms to companies, institutions, and individuals throughout North America. During her recent sales presentation to the Dallas-based Waits Manufacturing Corp., Rafael was well into the presentation of her proposed weekly uniform supply program when the buyer asked about the quality of the uniforms. Rafael responded that J. D. Powers (a well-known organization rating product and service quality) had recently rated them as one of the highest quality providers of work uniforms. This appeared to satisfy the buyer and the sale was closed. Upon leaving the buyer's office, the sales assistant working with Rafael that day asked about the J. D. Powers rating, commenting "I can't believe I missed something that important. Where can I get a copy of it?" Rafael replied, "Actually, J. D. Powers has never rated uniform suppliers that I know of. The buyer was ready to make the commitment and just needed some kind of quality reference to help him make the decision. "Don't worry about it. Nobody ever checks things like that. Besides, our quality is excellent. There will be no problems." What are the dangers in how Rafael uses references and testimonials? How might the sales assistant help Rafael change this habit?

publications, trade associations, and independent rating organizations along with one-sentence comments in a presentation can also be effective. For instance:

- "The American Dental Association has endorsed the new Laserlite drilling system as being safe and painless for the patient."
- "In January, *Fortune* magazine recognized CDW as the top-rated technology vendor on the basis of services provided to the buying customer."
- "The *RIMS Quality Scorecard* rated Arthur J. Gallagher & Co. as the highest rated insurance broker in North America in terms of value and service provided to its clients."

Testimonials are used extensively across industry and product/service types. To maximize their effectiveness, testimonials should be matched according to relevance and recognition to the prospective buyer. It is critical that the organization or person providing the supporting testimony be known or recognized by the prospect, above reproach, and in a position of respect.

Case Histories

Case histories are basically a testimonial in story or anecdotal form. Their added length allows more detail to be presented in order to further clarify an issue or better itemize the proof for a given statement. Case histories can also break the monotony of a long presentation. Like their counterpart testimonials, case histories should only be used when they clearly illustrate a particular point and are appropriate for the prospective buyer. Unrelated or tangential stories not only distract the customer but can be a source of irritation that works against credibility building. Case histories should be short and to the point lasting no more than a minute. They should support the presentation rather than becoming the center of attention.

Visual Aids

Visual aids allow the salesperson to involve one or more of the buyer's senses in the presentation and help to illustrate features and benefits. Visual aids add clarity and dramatization to impact the effectiveness of a sales presentation and advance the sale toward a purchase commitment. Among the variety of visual aids available to a salesperson, **product demonstrations and models**, **printed materials, photographs and illustrations**, along with **charts and graphs** have proven to be very effective in adding impact to and reinforcing the sales presentation.

Product Demonstrations and Models

The product itself is often the most effective sales aid because it provides the prospective buyer with an opportunity for hands-on experience. When the actual product does not lend itself to being demonstrated, models can be used to represent and illustrate key features and benefits of the larger product. The value of an actual product demonstration is applicable to all types of products and services. For example, Boeing salespeople use scale models to give the buyer a detailed and realistic feel for the aircraft, which cannot be tucked into the salesperson's briefcase. As the sale progresses, the prospective buyer's team will be given actual hands-on experience with the real product. Simmons and Sealy, leading manufacturers of quality sleep products require that their registered dealers have demonstration models of mattress sets on display and available for customers to try out. Major vendors of office furniture will set up an actual model office so that the prospective client can experience its actual use. Pharmaceutical companies provide doctors with actual samples of the product for trial use with selected patients.

As detailed in Exhibit 7.6, the salesperson should make sure the product being demonstrated is typical of what is being recommended. Furthermore, it should be checked to assure that it is in good working order prior to the demonstration and that setup and removal do not detract from the presentation. The last thing the salesperson wants is to have to apologize for poor appearance or inadequate performance.

EXHIBIT 7.6   Guidelines for Product Demonstrations

- Assure the appearance of the product is neat and clean.
- Check for problem-free operation.
- Be confident and able to skillfully demonstrate the product.
- Practice using the product prior to the demonstration.
- Anticipate problems and have back-up or replacement parts on hand.
- Setup and knockdown should be easy and quick.

Printed Materials

Printed materials include such items as brochures, pamphlets, catalogs, articles, reprints, reports, testimonial letters, and guarantees. Well-designed printed materials can help the salesperson communicate, explain, and emphasize key points of the selling organization and products. They are designed to summarize important features and benefits and can be effectively used not only during the presentation but left behind as reminder pieces for the buyer after the salesperson has left. During subsequent phone calls with the buyer, the salesperson can review important topics and point out information to the buyer that is included in the printed material. When printed materials are left with a buyer, the salesperson's name and contact information should be clearly printed on the material or an attached business card. Exhibit 7.7 provides salespeople with a number of tips for preparing printed materials and visuals.

As with all sales aids, when using printed materials with a prospective buyer, they should be placed directly in front of the buyer. If anyone must read upside down, it should be the salesperson and not the buyer. To draw the buyer's attention to a certain section of the printed material, the salesperson can highlight the selected areas with a marker prior to the presentation. Then, during the presentation the salesperson can use a pen or pointer to direct the buyer's attention to the specific section that is relevant to the feature or benefit under discussion.

Photographs and Illustrations

Photographs and illustrations are easy to produce and relatively inexpensive. Using images allows the salesperson to present a realistic portrayal of the product or service. Many products cannot be taken into a prospective buyer's office because of their size. A well-detailed image can give the prospect an idea of the product's appearance and size. Line drawings and diagrams can show the most important details of a product. Images are most effective when they illustrate and simplify a more complex product or feature and make it easy to communicate information about size, shape, construction, and use.

EXHIBIT 7.7   Tips for Preparing Printed Materials and Visuals

- Printed materials and visuals should be kept simple.
- When possible, use phrases and let the buyer's mind complete the sentences.
- Use the same layout and format throughout to tie the presentation together.
- Check for typographical and spelling errors.
- Use colors sparingly and for functional rather than decorative purposes.
- Leave plenty of white space; don't crowd the page too full.
- Each visual should present only one idea.
- Target using a maximum of seven words per line and seven lines per visual.
- Where possible use graphics (charts and graphs) rather than tables.
- Use bullet points to emphasize key points.
- Never read the presentation directly from the visual.
- Clearly label each visual with titles and headings to guide the prospective buyer.

Charts and Graphs

Charts and graphs are useful in showing trends and illustrating relationships. As such they can show the prospect what the problem is costing them or how a solution might work. Charts and graphs often illustrate relationships in terms of bars, lines, circles, or squares. For example, a salesperson for an office equipment vendor might get the cost figures associated with their use of an outside copy center for the previous two years. This information could then be used in a comparative bar graph to better illustrate the savings possible if they had their own copier. Salespeople for a leading medical technology company use a chart format to compare the features and benefits of their product versus the competitors' equipment the buyer is considering. The chart format succinctly and effectively supports statements of superiority made during the presentation.

Electronic Media

Salespeople today can customize graphic presentations using their laptops and hand-held computers, DVDs, and slide and overhead projectors. Customizing and enriching presentations by using electronic multimedia can be done inexpensively and in a fairly short period of time. Microsoft PowerPoint, for example, allows the salesperson to quickly build a complete, high-impact graphic presentation customized for an individual prospect. The availability of technologies such as **computer-based presentations**, **video, slides**, and **overhead transparencies** leaves the salesperson with no reason to deliver a "canned presentation."

Computer-Based Presentations

The computing power of today's laptops and even hand-held computers combined with presentation software such as PowerPoint allows the salesperson to create powerful multimedia presentations. Pictures of products, video testimonials of satisfied customers, as well as product demonstrations and competitive comparisons can all be included in a PowerPoint presentation. Editing with computer-based artwork and different fonts further enhances the presentation. Exhibit 7.8 provides some tips for preparing PowerPoint slides.[5] Once completed, the PowerPoint software produces notes that can be used as convenient handouts during the presentation.

Video

The rapidly shrinking size of video players and monitors combined with the ability to replay digitized video from a compact disk or DVD direct to a laptop or hand-held computer screen have further advanced the popularity and effectiveness of video in presentations. Unlike slides, pictures, and printed materials, video has the advantage of both sound and action. The product can be shown in action, for example, the prospect can be taken on a virtual tour of the selling organization and see the product being produced or he or she can simultaneously see and hear a personal message

---

PowerPoint Tips   EXHIBIT 7.8

- **Avoid Needless Animation.** Occasional animation can be used for emphasis, but don't overdo it as it gets annoying.
- **Get a Fresh Background.** Acquire a background that is not a stock template in PowerPoint and incorporate your company's logo and visual branding into the design.
- **Cut Down on the Number of Slides.** Ten slides should be the limit for a 30-minute presentation. Too much slide flipping detracts from the message.
- **Run Spell Check.** Grammatical errors and typos suggest that your company pays little attention to detail.

from the president of the selling organization as well as testimonials from satisfied customers.

Slides

Many companies produce relatively inexpensive slides for their salespeople to use in presentations. GlaxoSmithKline uses before-and-after slides to depict the effectiveness of a topical cream it sells. The first slide shows an affected area of the skin, and the next slide shows the cleared skin after three days of treatment. The slides also indicate that 93 percent of the patients on this cream clear up after just three days. Slide shows can be easily changed depending on the audience and have become more sophisticated through the use of multiple projectors and the addition of soundtracks.

Overhead Transparencies

The proliferation of computers and the availability of small, lightweight, and powerful projectors have practically eliminated the use of transparencies and overhead projectors. However, transparencies and overhead projectors are still widely used when more sophisticated methods are not available. Transparencies are easy to make and inexpensive to produce. Last minute changes can be made on a copying machine and color printers can produce full-color transparencies for greater impact. Because of their ease of production and low cost, many salespeople carry transparencies and a portable projector as a back-up to their more sophisticated computer presentations.

Using Tools and Sales Aids in the Presentation

Practice! Practice! Practice! Rehearsal of the presentation is the final key to making effective sales presentations. Understand what features are relevant and what benefits are meaningful to the prospective buyer in terms of value to be realized. Be confident in developing and using multiple sales aids to add impact to the presentation itself. As the following further details, using the **SPES Sequence** can facilitate the effectiveness of presentation tools and sales aids: **S** = *State selling point and introduce the sales aid;* **P** = *Present the sales aid;* **E** = *Explain the sales aid;* **S** = *Summarize.*[6]

State the Selling Point and Introduce the Sales Aid

This means stating the full selling point including the feature and potential benefit and then introducing the sales aid. For instance, "To demonstrate this benefit, I'd like you to take a look at this video" or "This graph summarizes the increased performance you will experience with the Honda S2000." This prepares the buyer for the visual aid and informs him or her that attention is required.

Present the Sales Aid

This involves presenting the sales aid to the customer and allowing a few moments for examination and familiarization before saying anything. For example, when using printed materials, place the material directly in front of the customer and allow it to be reviewed momentarily in silence. Allow the customer to review the sales aid and satisfy their natural curiosity before using it.

Explain the Sales Aid

No matter how carefully a sales aid is prepared, it will not be completely obvious. The customer will not necessarily understand the significance unless the salesperson provides a brief explanation. Do not rely on a chart or graph to fully illustrate the points being supported. Similarly, a product demonstration might be enjoyed by the prospect while they totally miss the information or experience supporting the presentation. The salesperson should point out the material information and explain how it supports his or her points.

Summarize

When finished explaining the significance of the sales aid, summarize its contribution and support and remove the sales aid. If not removed, its presence can distract the prospective buyer's attention from subsequent feature and benefit points.

GROUP SALES PRESENTATIONS

Sales presentations to groups are fairly commonplace in business-to-business selling. For example, retail chains often employ buying committees when considering the addition of new products for their stores. Hospitals use cross-functional teams comprising medical and administrative personnel to choose vendors such as food service providers. The decision of which advertising agency will be chosen is usually made by a group of marketing and upper-management people. Corporations often depend on representatives from several departments to make purchase decisions that affect all employees, such as the choice of insurance providers.

Delivering sales presentations to groups presents special challenges and opportunities. In addition to the basic fundamentals of planning and delivering sales presentations to individual buyers, there are additional strategies and tactics that can enhance sales presentations to groups.

When selling to groups, salespeople can expect tough questions and should prepare accordingly. While buyer questions are part of most sales presentations whether to individuals or groups, they are particularly crucial when there are multiple buyers. Most buying groups are assembled to tap the individual expertise and interests of the group members. For example, a buying committee for a company's computer information system could include technical specialists; finance and accounting personnel; and representatives from production operations, logistics, management, and marketing. All of these individuals are experts and demand in-depth information in order to make a decision. In some situations, this calls for a sales team to adequately address all questions, while in some cases, an individual salesperson has the cross-functional expertise required to make the sale.

When selling to a group, salespeople should take every opportunity to **presell** individual group members prior to the group presentation. Preselling to individual buyers or subgroups of buyers takes place before a major sales presentation to the entire group. Buying procedures in a given company may or may not allow preselling. If it is an option, the salesperson should definitely work with the individuals comprising the buying group prior to presenting to the group as a whole. By doing so, the salesperson can better determine individual and group interests and motives and possibly build a positive foundation for the group presentation. Preselling can also reveal the roles of the individuals in the buying center as discussed in Module 3. Knowing who the decision maker is, along with the other roles such as users and influencers, is crucial for success in group sales presentations. In the following discussion, we will focus on two key areas: tactical suggestions for group presentations, and handling questions in group settings.

Sales Tactics for Selling to Groups

Assuming that the salesperson or sales team has planned a comprehensive presentation and done as much preselling as possible, there are some specific sales tactics that can enhance presentations to groups. Sales tactics for group presentations fall into three general categories: arrival tactics, eye contact, and communications tips during presentation delivery.

Arrival Tactics

Try to arrive at the location for the presentation before the buying group arrives. This provides an opportunity to set up and check audio-visual equipment, prepare collateral material for distribution to the group, and become familiar and comfortable with the surroundings. It also sets the stage for the salesperson to personally greet individuals from the buying team as they enter the room. In a symbolic way, it also signals territorial command, or that the salesperson is in charge of the meeting. Though the control of the presentation meeting is typically shared with the buying group, arriving first sends a message that the salesperson is prepared to start promptly at the appointed time, thus showing respect for the buyer's time.

From the very beginning, the salesperson is hoping to connect with each individual in the group, rather than connecting only at the group level. By arriving first, the salesperson may have the opportunity to talk briefly with each individual. If nothing more, a friendly greeting, handshake, and introduction can help establish a rapport with individuals in the group. When not allowed to arrive first, salespeople should attempt individual introductions when joining the group. If that is not practical, salespeople must try and engage each individual through eye contact and, if appropriate, introductory remarks early in the presentation that recognizes the individual interests of those present. For example, a salesperson for a food service company might begin a presentation to a hospital with the following:

> Thank you for the opportunity to discuss our food service programs with you today. In planning for our meeting, I recognize that the dietary group is most concerned about the impact of any proposed change on the quality of patient care. Linda (the head dietitian), I believe we have a program that will actually enhance the quality of care that your patients receive. John (the head of finance), we will also propose an efficient, cost-effective alternative...

Opening remarks such as these, when kept brief, can be most effective in building involvement with all individuals in a small group.

Eye Contact

For both small and large groups, establishing periodic eye contact with individuals is important. With small groups, this is easily accomplished. With larger groups, especially formal presentations where the salesperson is standing and the group is sitting, there may be a tendency to use the so-called overhead approach. This method calls for looking just over the heads of the group, with the idea that those seated furthest from the presenter will feel included as part of the group. This method should be avoided. It might be fine for a formal speech to a large audience in a convention hall, but is far too impersonal for groups of 10 to 25 individuals. Also avoid a rapid scanning from side-to-side. This gives the appearance of nervousness and is ineffective in connecting with individual group members. The most effective eye contact is to try and connect with each individual or small subgroups for only a few seconds, moving through the entire group over the course of the presentation. Professional entertainers often use this method to connect with audience members, and salespeople can do the same.

Communications Tips

When selling to groups, it is essential to make all members of the group feel that their opinions are valuable. It is also important to avoid being caught in the middle of disagreements between members of the buying group. For example, if one member likes the salesperson's proposal and another thinks it is too expensive, any resolution of this disagreement must be handled carefully. While the salesperson may present information that resolves the issue, in some cases, disagreements among group buying members may be resolved outside the meetings. It is to the salesperson's advantage if disagreements can be handled during the presentation, as it keeps the sales process moving while unresolved issues can stall the sales process. As an example of how salespeople can play a peacemaker role, consider this exchange:

Buyer A: "I really like this system and think we should install it as soon as possible."

Buyer B: "I like it too, but it's way too expensive. Is there a less expensive alternative?"

Buyer A: "Sure, but they won't do the job."

Salesperson: (Directed to Buyer B) "Could I add something here? I believe we have a cost-effective system, and that our lease-to-purchase plan reduces the capital expenditure and allows a favorable payback period. Could we take another look at the numbers?"

The point is that salespeople must be diplomatic as a participant in discussions that might develop between members of the buying group. This sometimes means remaining silent while the discussion comes to a resolution, and sometimes it means playing an active role. There are no hard and fast rules in this area, and salespeople must simply use their best judgment to guide their actions.

In delivering group presentations, it is important to maintain contact with group members. Thus, reading or overrelying on densely worded slides should be avoided. Think of slides and other audio-visual aids as support tools, not as a "roll-and-scroll" presentation to be read to the group. Contact with the group can also be enhanced by natural movement. Too much pacing about can be detrimental to holding the group's attention, just as remaining tethered to a laptop can detract from group communication. When possible, salespeople should stand to the left of visual aids, as people read right-to-left. When standing to the left, it is easier to direct attention to the visual aids while momentarily deflecting attention away from the speaker. In this way, the salesperson becomes an unobtrusive narrator and the visual aid has maximum impact.

Body language can add or detract to sales effectiveness in the group setting. In general, posture should reflect an energetic, relaxed person. Conventional wisdom dictates that presenters should avoid contact with their own bodies while presenting. Salespeople who stuff their hands in their pockets, scratch their heads, or cross their arms are creating distractions to their own messages.

Handling Questions in Group Presentations

Just as is the case with sales presentations to individuals, questions from buyers in a group are an important part of the buyer–seller interaction that leads to a purchase decision. Salespeople should recognize that questions fill information gaps, thus allowing buyers to make better decisions. In a group setting, questions can also add a dramatic element, making the presentation more interesting for those in attendance. To the extent that it is possible, salespeople should anticipate group questions, then decide whether to address the question before it arises, or wait and address the question should it arise during the presentation.

To effectively handle questions that arise during the presentation, salespeople should listen carefully and maintain eye contact with the person asking the question. Generally, it is a good idea to repeat or restate the question. Questions should be answered as succinctly and convincingly as possible.

By listening carefully to the question, salespeople should show proper respect to the person asking the question. At the same time, they are helping direct the attention of the group to the question. As the question is posed, it is important for the salesperson to maintain eye contact with the person asking the question. Again, this demonstrates respect for the person and for his or her right to ask questions. This may require some practice, as salespeople may be tempted to glance at sales materials or perhaps their watch when the attention is shifted to the person asking the question. To do so could insult the questioner who may feel slighted by the lack of attention.

In many cases, it is a good idea to repeat or, in some cases, restate the question. This will ensure that everyone understands the question. It also signals a shift from the individual back to the group. Additionally, it allows the salesperson to state the key issue in the question succinctly. This is often important because not all questions are well-formulated and are sometimes accompanied by superfluous information. Consider this dialogue:

> Buyer: "You know, I have been thinking about the feasibility of matching our Brand X computers with Brand Y printers. Not too long ago, matching multiple brands would have been a disaster. Are you telling me now that Brand X computers are totally compatible with Brand Y printers?"

> Seller: "The question is: Are your computers compatible with our printers? Yes they are—with no special installation requirements."

When restating questions, salespeople must be careful to accurately capture the essence of the buyer's concern. Otherwise, they could be perceived as avoiding the question or trying to manipulate the buyer by putting words in his or her mouth. Therefore, when in doubt, it is a good practice when restating a question to seek buyer confirmation that the restated question is an accurate representation of the original question. For example, salespeople might say, "Ms. Jackson, as I understand the question, you are concerned about the effectiveness of our seasonal sales promotion programs. Is that correct?"

When answering questions, there are three guidelines. First, salespeople should not attempt to answer a question until he or she and the group members clearly understand the question. Second, salespeople should not attempt to answer questions that they are not prepared to answer. It is far better to make a note and tell the group you will get back to them with the answer than to speculate or give a weak answer. Third, try to answer questions as directly as possible. Politicians are often accused of not answering the questions posed during press conferences, but rather steering the answer toward what they wish to talk about. Salespeople will quickly lose credibility if they take a long time to get to the point in their answer. To answer convincingly, start with a "yes" or "no," then explain the exceptions to the general case. For example, say, "Yes, that is generally the case. There are some exceptions, including…" This is preferred to answering, "Well that depends…" then explaining all of the special circumstances only to conclude with "but, generally, yes, that is the case."

When answering questions, it is important to address the entire group rather than the individual who asked the question. Otherwise, salespeople may lose the attention of other group members. When salespeople conclude their answers, they have the option of going back to the person who asked the question, continuing their presentation, or taking a question from another group member. Salespeople can rely on their common sense and experience to decide what is appropriate in a given situation.

In larger groups, it is particularly important to avoid getting locked into a question-and-answer dialogue with one person if other people are showing an interest in asking questions. Indeed, it is important to take all questions, but it is also important to spread the opportunity to ask questions around the room, coming back to those who have multiple questions until all questions are answered. If one person is a dominant force within the buying group, other group members will typically defer their questions until that person has asked all of their questions at different points in the presentation.

When selling to a group, salespeople should have a clear objective for their presentation. To get the group to take the desired action, salespeople must make a convincing case, motivate the group to take action, and make it easy for the group to take the desired action. Some of the methods for handling buyer objections and earning a commitment as discussed in Module 8 will prove useful for accomplishing these tasks.

In some cases, the group will wish to deliberate and let the salesperson know of their decision at a later time. This is not uncommon, because the group may need a frank discussion without outsiders to reach a final decision. Should this occur, salespeople should be certain that the group has all the information they need or offer to provide the needed information promptly and offer to follow-up within a specified time period.

The process for planning and delivering a group presentation is much the same as it is for sales presentations to individuals. By paying attention to the special considerations in this section, salespeople can build on their experience with sales presentations to individuals and deliver effective sales presentations to groups.

SUMMARY

1. **Describe the difference between features, potential benefits, and confirmed benefits and the role that they play in benefits selling.** Any given product or service is comprised of multiple features that produce different benefits. Features are defined as a characteristic of a product or service that provides value. Features answer the question, "What is it?" A benefit is the value provided by a feature and addresses the buyer's question, "What's in it for me?" Not all benefits will be valued at the same level by all buyers, thus the categorization of potential benefits versus confirmed benefits. A potential benefit describes a general form of value that is assumed to be of importance but not yet acknowledged as such by the buyer. Once the prospective buyer acknowledges the importance of a benefit to his or her buying situation, it is a confirmed benefit. Because confirmed benefits represent customer value that is provided by the proposed solution, some sales programs refer to the confirmed benefit as the value proposition. Confirmed benefits are important because buyers do not purchase features. Rather, they purchase value that is provided in the form of confirmed benefits.

2. **Construct complete selling points using feature and benefit statements.** Selling points are the foundation of benefit selling. In benefit selling, the salesperson describes the benefits as they relate to the specific needs of the prospective buyer and uses a description of the feature to support and evidence the presence of confirmed benefits. This combination of a specific feature and its meaningful benefit statement are referred to as a selling point. Selling points are most effective when they are phrased in a conversational tone and clearly describe the benefit in a manner that emphasizes its applicability and importance to the individual buyer.

3. **Discuss the advantages of using response-checks in the selling presentation.** Response-checks are confirmatory probes used by the salesperson to gather feedback from the buyer. Effective use of response-checks offers a number of advantages including increasing buyer involvement and ensuring that the presentation remains a two-way, collaborative exchange. Response-checks also help the salesperson evaluate the level of the buyer's understanding and keep the salesperson on the right track. If feedback indicates a lack of understanding or lack of interest on the part of a prospective buyer, the salesperson must make changes to the presentation and its features and benefits so that they are better aligned with the needs and expectations of the buyer. On the other hand, positive feedback indicating a high level of understanding and interest on the part of the buyer would signal to the salesperson to stay the course and advance the presentation toward gaining the buyer's purchase commitment. A series of positive response-checks indicates that the buyer is nearing the readiness stage for wrapping up the details and closing the sale.

4. **List and explain the different forms of presentation tools and sales aids that can increase the impact of a presentation.** To maximize the effectiveness of the sales presentation, salespeople utilize sales aids and tools that capture and hold the buyer's attention, boost the buyer's involvement and understanding, increase the believability of the claims, and build the buyer's retention of information. Salespeople have a variety of different types of sales aids available for use in

presentations. These various sales aids can be categorized into five categories of sales presentation tools: Verbal Support (*voice characteristics, examples and anecdotes, comparisons and analogies*), Sales Call Setting (*location, positioning and seating arrangements, disruptions*), Visual Aids (*product demonstrations and models, printed materials, photographs and illustrations, graphs and charts*), Proof Providers (*statistics, testimonials, case histories*), and Electronic Media (*computer-based presentations, video, slides, overhead transparencies*).

5. **Delineate the four steps of the SPES process for effectively utilizing sales aids in presentations.** The SPES Sequence provides the salesperson with guidelines for effectively incorporating sales aids into a selling presentation. Each letter stands for a specific set of actions to be undertaken by the salesperson: S = *State selling point and introduce the sales aid;* P = *Present the sales aid;* E = *Explain the sales aid;* S = *Summarize.*

   - *State the Selling Point and Introduce the Sales Aid.* State the full selling point and then introduce the sales aid. For instance, "This graph summarizes the increased performance that you will experience with the Honda S2000." This prepares the buyer for the visual aid and informs him or her that attention is required.

   - *Present the Sales Aid.* Present the sales aid to the customer and allow a few moments for examination and familiarization before saying anything. For example, when using printed materials, place the material directly in front of the customer and allow it to be reviewed momentarily. This allows the customer to review the sales aid and satisfy his or her natural curiosity before using it.

   - *Explain the Sales Aid.* No matter how carefully a sales aid is prepared, it will not be completely obvious. The customer will not necessarily understand the significance unless the salesperson provides a brief explanation. The salesperson should point out the material information and explain how it supports his or her points.

   - *Summarize.* When finished explaining the significance of the sales aid, summarize its contribution and support and remove the sales aid. If not removed, its presence can distract the prospective buyer's attention from subsequent feature and benefit points.

6. **Explain some of the special considerations in making sales presentations to groups.** Making a sales presentation to a group requires all of the preparation and selling skills necessary in selling to individuals. In addition, salespeople should expect especially tough questions when selling to a group of buyers because individuals in a group are typically experts in their specialty area, and the individual interests of buyers in a group can be quite varied. When possible, salespeople should presell individuals or subgroups prior to making a group presentation. It is important for salespeople to try to establish an individual connection with group members and to pay particular attention to handling questions from the group.

UNDERSTANDING PROFESSIONAL SELLING TERMS

SPIN	confirmed benefits
ADAPT	selling point
benefit selling	check-backs
FAB	response-checks
features	verbal support
potential benefits	voice characteristics

examples and anecdotes

comparisons and analogies

sales call setting

location

positioning and seating arrangements

disruptions

proof providers

statistics

testimonials

case histories

visual aids

product demonstrations and models

printed materials

photographs and illustrations

charts and graphs

electronic media

computer-based presentations

video

slides

overhead transparencies

SPES Sequence

presell

DEVELOPING PROFESSIONAL SELLING KNOWLEDGE

1. How do the questioning sequences SPIN and ADAPT relate to benefits selling?

2. What are the relationships and differences between features, potential benefits, and confirmed benefits? How should they be used in effective sales dialogues and presentations?

3. What are response-checks and how do they advance the selling process forward toward the commitment stage?

4. What are some reasons for using sales tools and aids to enhance sales dialogues and presentations?

5. What are the different sales presentation tools and how can they be used to enhance the persuasive power of the presentation?

6. Explain the SPES Sequence as it applies to the use of sales tools and aids.

7. Why and how is selling to a group different from selling to an individual? What impact do these differences have on a salesperson's presentation?

8. What is the purpose of preselling buyers or subgroups of buyers prior to the major presentation to the group?

9. What advantages might a salesperson gain by arriving early for a group presentation?

10. What is the best way for a salesperson to handle questions from the audience in a group presentation?

BUILDING PROFESSIONAL SELLING SKILLS

1. Visit one retail store in each of the following categories: bedding, sporting goods, and computers. Take notes on the different presentation tools and sales aids, if any, that you observed or experienced being used in selling a product. What presentation tools and sales aids would you have used in making each of the three presentations? Why?

2. Develop a list of presentation tools and sales aids that you might use in a job interview to enhance the presentation of your skills and capabilities. Describe how you would go about using each of your listed items.

3. Assume the role of a computer salesperson for the CanDo Computer Company selling to a small company wanting to equip their field sales force of five salespeople with laptop computers.

    a. Assume the laptops you are selling have the following four features: (1) lightweight; (2) preloaded e-mail, contact management, and account profile software; (3) durable; and (4) full video and graphics capabilities. For each of these features, develop a list of potential benefits. How would you determine which features and benefits would be most important to this particular customer? How would you determine if a benefit could be classified as a confirmed benefit?

b. Describe what sales tools and aids you might use to enhance your presentation.

ROLE PLAY

Situation:	Read item 3.
Characters:	Yourself—salesperson for the CanDo Computer Company; the buyer/director of purchasing for MidWest Supply
Scene:	*Location*—The office of the Director of Purchasing for MidWest Supply. *Action*—As described, MidWest Supply is considering equipping their five-person sales force with laptop computers. You are there to present your line of laptops, gain a sale, and begin a long-term relationship with MidWest Supply.

Role play the three uses of the four different feature–benefit combinations, and demonstrate how you might use the sales tools and aids that you feel would be effective in adding power to your presentation.

Upon completion of the role play, address the following questions:

a. Were you effective at moving the sale forward?

b. What other ways could these features/benefits be presented that might be more effective?

c. How well/positively did the sales tools and aids affect the selling presentation (e.g., attention, clarification, retention, proof, etc.)?

d. What other sales aids might have been used effectively?

4. Jane Gilmore is a salesperson for Nike athletic shoes. She is meeting with Sarah Franklin, head buyer for The Athlete's Foot—a regional chain of athletic shoe stores headquartered in St. Louis—with the objective of selling several new styles to the 12-store chain. Gilmore has put a great deal of preparation into her sales call including a bound set of printed materials consisting of product brochures, competitive charts, and forecasts of financial performance. The sales aids must have been very effective. Gilmore opened the binder and placed it in front of the buyer so that Gilmore could point out several of the supporting materials during her presentation. However, shortly after beginning her presentation, the buyer picked the binder up and began browsing through it before Gilmore ever had an opportunity to use any of the material in her presentation.

a. What should Gilmore do now?

b. What could Gilmore have done differently that might have prevented this interruption from happening?

ROLE PLAY

Situation:	Read item 4.
Characters:	Jane Gilmore—salesperson for Nike athletic shoes; Sarah Franklin—head buyer for The Athlete's Foot
Scene:	*Location*—The office of Sarah Franklin at the headquarters of The Athlete's Foot. *Action*—As described, Gilmore is presenting a new line of athletic shoes for consideration by The Athlete's Foot as stocking items in each of their stores. Gilmore had intended to use a binder of printed sales materials to reinforce several points in her presentation. However, shortly after getting started with her presentation, the buyer has picked up the binder and begun to browse through it.

Role play how you might regain control over the presentation and refocus the buyer's attention on the presentation instead of the binder of materials.

Role play how you could have used the binder in a different way so as to minimize or even prevent the buyer from taking control of the materials.

Upon completion of the role plays, address the following questions:

   a. How well do you think the demonstrated method for regaining control over the presentation would work in reality?
   b. What other actions might Gilmore employ that could also be effective?
   c. In what other ways could Gilmore have better prevented Franklin from taking control of the sales aids and losing her focus and participation in the presentation?

5. Epson, a leading manufacturer of presentation equipment and materials, sponsors a Web site exclusively dedicated to the improvement of individual presentations. Among the more interesting links at the site are What's New, Basics, Tutorials, Resources, and The Presenters Club.

   - **What's New** is an ever-changing series of articles and graphics explaining the latest developments in research, equipment, and software. It is a great source for keeping up to date on major product introductions from all companies, not just Epson.
   - **Basics** offers free online tips for planning and delivering presentations, including the use of visual aids.
   - **Tutorials** guide the user through the use of PowerPoint and projectors, including running a projector from a laptop computer.
   - **Resources** presents the user with a large and ever-growing stock of innovative PowerPoint templates, clip art, and sound clips. The entire library of interesting elements is available for downloading into presentations at no charge.
   - **The Presenters Club** is a "members only" part of the Web site that contains additional clip art, templates, and digital images. Possibly the greatest feature of The Presenters Club is that membership is also free of charge. All you need to do is complete and submit the short registration form and you are in.

   Go the Presenters Online Web site at **http://www.presentersonline.com**.

   - Take time to look around and familiarize yourself with this site. It has a great deal of content that can give you a competitive advantage in classes as well as in your work after graduation.
   - Click on "Basics."
   - Scroll down and take in the different categories of online training, such as Delivery, Content, and Visuals. These are offered at no charge and each of the topic areas is short and can be completed in a few minutes. Note that the displayed items are a selection of the larger library archive that is also available to you.
   - Browse through the training topics available and locate three subjects that are of some interest to you—something you might enjoy and benefit from knowing.
   - One at a time, click on each of your selected three topics.
   - Read through and study the materials offered. Take notes and build your understanding and skills.

   Write a summary reaction paper that identifies each of the three subjects you selected to study. Under each subject, briefly explain what you learned and how you might use the knowledge and abilities gained.

MAKING PROFESSIONAL SELLING DECISIONS

Case 7.1: Texas Paint & Coatings (TPC)

Background

Texas Paint & Coatings (TPC) is a producer of specialty paints and coatings for industrial and agricultural equipment manufacturers. In business for more than 25 years, TPC has established a strong reputation as a competitive supplier of high-quality acrylic and resin-based coatings. Working with the NASA Space Research Center in Houston, TPC is rolling out a breakthrough, self-priming paint product that offers several significant benefits to equipment manufacturers. By totally eliminating the need for any form of a primer coat, the new product can cut application time in half and eliminates about one-third of the material cost involved in the typical paint process. The self-priming paint can be directly applied to any clean metal surface using either a low-pressure spray or roller. An additional benefit is its flash-drying characteristic, which means it dries and cures after only 3 to 5 minutes of exposure to room temperature air. In just 5 minutes after application it is fully cured, rock hard, and highly scratch, chemical, and fade resistant.

Current Situation

Richard Henry is an account manager for TPC and has been working to establish John Deere's Fort Worth, Texas facility as an account. With the previous line of traditional paint products, he had been successful in gaining about 10 percent of the plant's annual paint requirements. However, that seemed to be the limit. Even with the great relationship he has established with Tim Dickerson, head paint and coating buyer for Deere's Fort Worth construction equipment plant, Henry has not been able to gain additional share of the plant's paint requirements.

Henry sees the self-priming product as his path to capturing a majority share of the plant's paint needs. The cost and time savings will certainly be a major item of interest. But first, he must convince Dickerson that the new paint meets and even exceeds the performance specifications. As he is looking through the information he has in his database, he sees that there is a wealth of NASA test data and competitive information that will document the performance of the new coating, but he is pondering how he might organize and present it in a way that will be most effective. He is also trying to think of an effective demonstration he might provide that will give Dickerson a hands-on experience with the paint's superior performance.

Questions

1. What are the benefits of self-priming paint?
2. What different sales tools and aids might Richard use to enhance his presentation of the new self-priming paint?
3. Once he has established the superior performance of the new paint, what should Henry do?

ROLE PLAY

Situation:	Read Case 7.1.
Characters:	Richard Henry—salesperson for Texas Paint & Coatings; Tim Dickerson—head paint and coating buyer for John Deere–Fort Worth
Scene:	*Location*—The office of Tim Dickerson at John Deere–Fort Worth. *Action*—As described, Henry is presenting a revolutionary new self-priming paint. While cost savings will be important, his first concern is to establish that the new paint exceeds all performance requirements.

Role play how Henry might incorporate different presentation tools and sales aids to make his presentation to Dickerson more effective.

Role play how Henry might collaborate with Dickerson to illustrate the possible cost savings provided by the new paint.

Upon completion of the role plays, address the following questions:

1. What other tools and sales aids might prove useful in demonstrating the performance of the new paint?
2. What information will Henry need in order to substantiate the possible cost savings to Dickerson? Where and how might he get that information?

Case 7.2: All Risk Insurance and National Networks

Background

The All Risk Insurance Company has 3,200 sales agents spread across five regions that cover the United States. They are moving toward the development of a national network that would tie each of the agent offices together with the regional offices and corporate headquarters. The improved communication capability will allow all company personnel to have full access to customer records and form the core of a comprehensive customer relationship management system that is to be rolled out in 18 months.

Current Situation

Jim Roberts is a network account specialist for National Networks, a specialist in large corporate network solutions, and has been working with the technology-buying group at All Risk Insurance for several months now. Roberts has worked through several meetings with the buying group members and has a meeting scheduled for next Wednesday to present his recommendations and demonstrate why they should select National Networks as the supplier for this sizable project. The final decision will be made by Joyce Fields (director of information systems), John Harris (comptroller and CFO), Mike Davis (director of agent services), and Dianne Sheffield (director for customer services). Roberts also knows that there is one other competitor who will be making a presentation in hopes of landing the project. The equipment being proposed by both vendors is virtually identical due to the detailed specifications that All Risk Insurance had included in the RFP. Prices are also likely to be pretty similar. The decision will most likely come down to the services each competitor includes in their proposals. Based on the information that Roberts has collected from different sources, he has come up with a comparison of customer services offered by National Networks and the competitor (see the table at the bottom of page).

Questions

1. For each of the features and benefits, describe several presentation tools and sales aids that Roberts might use to enhance his presentation.

2. What recommendations might you have for Roberts as he prepares to present to the group of buyers at All Risk Insurance?

ROLE PLAY

Situation:	Read Case 7.2.
Characters:	Jim Roberts—salesperson for National Networks; Joyce Fields—director of information systems for All Risk Insurance; John Harris—comptroller and CFO for All Risk Insurance; Mike Davis—director of agent services for All Risk Insurance; Dianne Sheffield—director for customer services for All Risk Insurance
Scene:	*Location*—A conference room at All Risk Insurance. *Action*—As described, Jim Roberts is presenting the National Networks proposal for a corporate computer network linking All Risk Insurance's corporate offices with each of its five regional offices and 3,200 sales agents out in the field.

Role play Roberts' presentation of each of the feature–benefit sets incorporating sales tools and aids suitable for use in the group presentation.

Upon completion of the role play, address the following questions:

1. What other sales tools and aids might prove useful to Roberts in presenting his proposed solution to the All Risk Insurance buying team?
2. How might Roberts employ other tactics for selling to a group that could increase the effectiveness of his presentation and advance the sale to the point of gaining an order?

Features	Capability of National Networks	Capability of Competitor	Benefits
Service and repair centers	175 affiliated service and repair centers across the United States	21 affiliated service and repair centers across the United States	Ensures fast and reliable repairs for hardware and software
Installation and testing	Installation and testing done by National Networks employees	Installation and testing outsourced to several different companies	Knowledge that all installations will be done the right way
Customer call center	24 hour, 7 days per week, and staffed by National Networks employees	24 hour, 7 days per week, and staffed by an outsource commercial provider	Knowledgeable staff always available to assist All Risk Insurance employees with problems

FEWER EARNING COMMITMENT TECHNIQUES WORK!

Steve Roe of King Systems (a medical manufacturer) has changed his selling style over the past 30 years. He states, "I remember coming out of college and going to my sales training seminar. The focus back then was to learn a lot of closing techniques and use them *all*, if you had enough time. A previous employer of mine would focus on hiring good closers. At a national sales meeting it was stated by one of our speakers that the best closers are the best salespeople. I've learned from experience that this is not true. The best salespeople are the best information gatherers. Buyers do not like to be hammered on with lots of closing techniques. I noticed when I was team selling with some of my colleagues that too much pressure on closing make the prospect uncomfortable. I also noticed these reps had trouble getting back in to see the buyer after one of these high-pressure sales calls. I studied these experiences carefully and pared down the list of earning commitment techniques I use on my sales calls. I've concluded: when it comes to earning commitment, less is better."

ADDRESSING CONCERNS

An objection or sales resistance is anything the buyer says or does that slows down or stops the buying process. The salesperson's job is to uncover these objections and answer them to the prospect's or client's satisfaction. It is very difficult for a salesperson to earn commitment if there is doubt or concern on the buyer's part. Thus, the salesperson must uncover and overcome any and all objections. In doing so, the salesperson strengthens the long-term relationship and moves the sales process closer to commitment. At the very least, concerns open dialogue between the salesperson and the prospect.

A brief discussion follows on why it is important for salespeople to anticipate and negotiate buyer concern. Following a discussion of why prospects raise objections, this module covers the five major types of objections. Next, different approaches to handling sales resistance are explained. Finally, techniques to earn commitment are reviewed.

Source: Interview with Steve Roe, July 10, 2006.

ANTICIPATE AND NEGOTIATE CONCERNS AND RESISTANCE

Over the years, many sales forces were taught that **sales resistance** was bad and would likely slow down or stop the selling process. Salespeople were also told that if they received resistance, then they had not done a good job explaining their product or service.

Objectives

After completing this module, you should be able to

1   Explain why it is important to anticipate and overcome buyer concerns and resistance.

2   Understand why prospects raise objections.

3   Describe the five major types of sales resistance.

4   Explain how the LAARC method can be used to overcome buyer objections.

5   Describe the traditional methods for responding to buyer objections.

6   List and explain the earning commitment techniques that enhance relationship building.

These notions have changed over the years to where objections are now viewed as opportunities to sell. Salespeople should be grateful for objections and always treat them as questions. The buyer is just asking for more information. It is the salesperson's job to produce the correct information to help buyers understand their concern. Inexperienced salespeople need to learn that sales resistance is a normal, natural part of any sales conversation. The prospect that does not question price, service, warranty, and delivery concerns is probably not interested.

Although many salespeople fear sales resistance from their prospects or customers, it should be viewed as a normal part of the sales process. At a minimum, the salesperson now has the prospect involved. The salesperson can now start to determine customer interest and measure the buyer's understanding of the problem. In some situations, a salesperson cannot overcome resistance (for example, delivery dates do not match; technology does not fit). Under these circumstances, the successful salesperson gracefully ends the sales call while leaving open the option for further business.[1] Finally, if the sales resistance is handled correctly, the outcome can lead to customer acceptance.

Reasons Why Prospects Raise Objections

There are many reasons why prospects will raise objections.

1. The prospect wants to avoid the sales interview. Some prospects do not want to create any more work for themselves than they already have. Granting a sales interview takes time, and buyers already have a busy schedule handling normal day-to-day tasks. Buyers may want to avoid the salesperson because they view his or her call as an interruption in their day. Most buyers do not have the time to see every salesperson that knocks on their door.

2. The salesperson has failed to prospect and qualify properly. Sometimes, poor prospects slip through the screening process. The prospect may have misunderstood the salesperson's intentions when asked for the interview. The salesperson should attempt to qualify the prospect during the sales call. For example, a computer software company used telemarketing to qualify prospects. Leads were turned over to the sales force for in-person visits. The major product line was an inventory control package that cost $20,000. The salesperson asked the owner of the company if she had a budget for this project. The owner answered $5,000. The salesperson gave the owner the names of a couple of inexpensive software companies, thanked the owner for her time, and moved on. The owner was not about to spend $20,000 and said so early in the sales conversation. This resistance actually helped the salesperson. What if this condition had stayed hidden for four to six weeks while the salesperson continued to call on the owner? Both the salesperson's and owner's time would have been wasted.

3. Objecting is a matter of custom. Many purchasing agents have a motto never to buy on the first call with a salesperson. Trust has not yet been developed, and a thorough understanding of the salesperson, his or her company, and the products have not been accomplished. The buyer will need most of this information to make a decision. Many buyers may say no during the first few calls to test the salesperson's persistence.

4. The prospect resists change. Many buyers like the way that they are presently doing business. Thus, buyers will tell the salesperson that they are satisfied with what they have now. Many prospects simply resist change because they dislike making decisions. Prospects may fear the consequences of deciding and dread disturbing the status quo. A purchase usually involves dismissing the present supplier and handling all the arrangements (price, terms, delivery, and product specifications) to smoothly move the new supplier in. Once a buyer is comfortable with his or her suppliers, he or she will generally avoid new salespeople until a major need arises.

5. The prospect fails to recognize a need. The prospect may be unaware of a need, uninformed about the product or service, or content with the present situation.

Why Prospects Raise Objections and Strategies for Dealing with Them   **EXHIBIT 8.1**

- Buyer wants to avoid the sales interview.
  Strategy: Set appointments to become part of the buyer's daily routine.
- Salesperson has failed to prospect and qualify properly.
  Strategy: Ask questions to verify prospect's interest.
- Buyer won't buy on the first sales call.
  Strategy: Regular calls on the prospect lets the prospect know the salesperson is serious about the relationship.
- Prospect does not want to change the present way of doing business.
  Strategy: Salesperson must help the prospect understand there is a better solution than the one the prospect is presently using.
- Prospect has failed to recognize a need.
  Strategy: Salesperson must show evidence that sparks the prospect's interest.
- Prospect lacks information on a new product or on the salesperson's company.
  Strategy: Salesperson must continually work to add value by providing useful information.

In any case, the lack of need creates no motivation to change suppliers. Many purchasing agents were content with their overnight mail service and were slow to recognize the fax machine as a viable solution to getting information to their customers quickly. The poor quality of the reproduced document turned away many buyers. Only when the need for the information outweighed the aesthetics of the document did the buyers readily embrace the fax machine.

6. The prospect lacks information. Ultimately, all sales resistance comes back to the fact that the prospect simply lacks the information he or she needs to comfortably make a decision. The salesperson must view this as an opportunity to put the right information in front of the buyer. If the salesperson diagnoses correctly and presents the right information, then the resistance problem can be more easily overcome. Exhibit 8.1 summarizes why prospects raise objections and lists strategies for dealing with them.

Types of Objections

Although there appears to be an infinite number of objections, most fall into five or six categories. Buyers use delay techniques to avoid taking immediate action. Comments such as "Give me a couple of weeks to think it over" can save the buyer the discomfort of saying no at the end of a presentation. "Your price is too high" or "I have no money" are easy ways for purchasing agents not to buy a salesperson's offering. Price is probably the most often cited objection but usually is not the most important issue. It is obvious that buyers do not buy merely on price; if this were true, then the lowest price supplier would get all the business and eventually be the only supplier left selling the product. "No need at this time" is another typical objection. The buyer may not be in the market to purchase at this point in time.

It is not unusual for salespeople to encounter product objections. Most buyers have fears associated with buying a product. The buyer may be afraid that the product's reliability will not perform up to the standards the salesperson said it would. Not only do the salespeople have to demonstrate that their product will perform at the level they say it will, they must also show how it stacks up to the competition. A competitor introducing a new technology (e.g., e-commerce) may change the way a salesperson competes on a particular product line (e.g., office products).

Many buyers are constantly assessing their supplier on service (e.g., delivery, follow-up, warranties, guarantees, repairs, installation, and training). If the service is good and department heads are not complaining, the buyer is likely to stay with the status quo. Service is one variable that companies and salespeople can use to differentiate

EXHIBIT 8.2   Types of Objections

No Need	Buyer has recently purchased or does not see a need for the product category "I'm not interested at this time."
Product or Service Objection	Buyer may be afraid of product reliability "I'm not sure the quality of your product meets our needs." Buyer may be afraid of late deliveries, slow repairs, etc. "I'm happy with my present supplier's service."
Company Objection	Buyer is intensely loyal to the present supplier "I am happy with my present supplier."
Price Is Too High	Buyer has a limited budget "We have been buying from another supplier who meets our budget constraints."
Time/Delaying	Buyer needs time to think it over "Get back with me in a couple of weeks."

their product. Enterprise Rent-a-Car will deliver cars to the home of the renter and has made this an issue in its advertising. A salesperson for a wholesale distributor may make the point to a prospect that their fresh fruit, fish, and meat can be delivered daily when their competitors only deliver three times per week.

Many buyers will feel intense loyalty to their present suppliers and use this as a reason not to change. Buyers may be equally committed to the salesperson from whom they are presently buying. As a nonsupplier to the company, the salesperson must continue to call on the buyer and look for opportunities to build trust with the prospect. The salesperson may want to investigate whether the buyer has had any previous bad experience with his or her company that is causing the buyer not to do business with that company. Some salespeople and their buyers will not hit it off. The salesperson has to recognize these feelings and move on if several calls do not result in an eventual sale.

At first glance, an inexperienced salesperson may be overwhelmed with the thought of how they will handle all the different types of objections buyers will raise. Salespeople need to develop skills in evaluating objections.[2] It does not take long, however, for a salesperson to learn that most objections fall into just a few categories. When preparing to buy a product or service, a prospect generally obtains information in five areas: need, product or service features, company or source, price, and timing of the buy. Objections could come from any of these areas, as shown in Exhibit 8.2. A more detailed look at each of these areas follows.

Need Objections

Without a need, prospects have little or no reason to talk to a salesperson. If the prospect has been qualified properly, the salesperson believes the prospect has a need for the product. Many buyers have been conditioned to say automatically, "I don't need your product" (i.e., **need objection**). This may be the result of the buyer being out of budget or not having the time to look at your product or proposal. Other buyers may respond, "We are getting along just fine without your product. No one in my company is asking for your product. Call back in a few months and maybe something will change."

The salesperson has a tough challenge ahead if the buyer sincerely believes they have no need. It is the salesperson's job to establish a need in the buyer's mind; if the salesperson cannot do this, then logically, an objection can be expected.

Many prospects do not know they have a specific need for a product until a situation occurs that makes them aware of it (i.e., engineering calls and needs a special software package). Therefore, objections to the need require the salesperson to stimulate the need awareness of the prospect with relevant information—features and

> **Possible Need Objections   EXHIBIT 8.3**
>
> "I have all I can use (all stocked up)."
> "I don't need any."
> "The equipment I have is still good."
> "I'm satisfied with the company we use now."
> "We have no room for your line."

benefits that peak the prospect's interest. Exhibit 8.3 summarizes a number of the no-need objections.

Product or Service Objections

Often the product or service lacks something that the buyer wants and the salesperson can't deliver. A competitive advantage for Ontario Systems, a large software firm, is that they have 24-hour/800 service available to all of their customers. Their number one competitor offers only 8:00 A.M. to 8:00 P.M. call-in phone service. For those clients that run three shifts and need 24-hour service, their choice is easy: they buy from Ontario.

Other prospect objections could be simply emotional—the prospect does not like the way the product looks or feels (i.e., **product or service objection**). Still others have a problem with the products' performance characteristics (i.e., "I need a copier that has color and staples in the bin"). The salesperson also must do an adequate job of fact-finding and qualifying. Many of these issues can be resolved by knowing what the prospect is looking for.

Objections toward the product center around understanding the fit between the product and the customer's needs. The salesperson's job is to learn what product features are important to the buyer and sell those features. Products are bundles of benefits that customers seek to fit their needs. Tying the benefits to the customer's needs helps the prospect bridge the gap from no-need to need. Exhibit 8.4 summarizes a number of product or service objections.

Company or Source Objections

Marty Reist is a manufacturer's representative for a small company in the sporting goods industry. He has to go against the big boys daily. Sales representatives from Nike, Titleist, and Reebok probably do not have to work really hard to get past the gatekeepers. Reist, on the other hand, must justify his existence everyday. "I've never heard of your company" (i.e., **company or source objection**) is something Reist must overcome.

Other buyers may be happy with their present supplier. It is not unusual for buyer/seller relationships to last 10 to 15 years and even longer. Robert Carroll, a former sales representative from Monsanto Agricultural Division heard the following quote from many of his farmers and farm co-ops, "I'm perfectly happy with

> **Possible Product or Service Objections   EXHIBIT 8.4**
>
> "I don't like the design, color, or style."
> "A maintenance agreement should be included."
> "Performance of the product is unsatisfactory (i.e., the copier is too slow)."
> "Packaging is too bulky".
> "The product is incompatible with the present system (i.e., we prefer Apple over IBM)."
> "The specifications don't match what we have now."
> "How do I know if you'll meet our delivery requirements?"
> "The product is poor quality"

EXHIBIT 8.5   Company or Source Objections

"Your company is too small to meet my needs."
"I've never heard of your company."
"Your company is too big; I'll get lost in the shuffle."
"Your company is pretty new; how do I know you'll be around to take care of me in the future?"
"Your company was recently in the newspaper. Are you having problems?"

Monsanto, my crops look good. I've been buying from them for years, and they have always treated me right." This is one of the hardest objections to overcome, especially if the prospect feels genuine loyalty to his or her present supplier.

Professional salespeople never criticize their competitors. The salesperson can point out any superior features they might have. They can also ask for a single order and ask for an evaluation against their present supplier.

Another form of source objection is a negative attitude a buyer might have about the salesperson's company or the poor presentation of a previous salesperson. A buyer might remember a late or damaged order the company did not properly handle. A former salesperson may have made promises to the buyer and did not follow through on them. The salesperson must investigate any and all source objections. The salesperson may uncover source problems that can be overcome with time. Exhibit 8.5 outlines typical company or source objections.

Price Objections

Most sales experts agree that price is the most common form of buyer resistance.[3] This objection has the prospect saying they can't afford the product, the price is too high, or the product is not in their budget at this time (i.e., **price objection**). This objection may be a request for the salesperson to justify to the prospect how they can afford the product or how they can work it into their budget. Most salespeople feel the price objection is an attempt by the buyer to get the salesperson to lower their price. The salesperson must address the price objection by citing how the benefits (value) outweigh the cost. To do this, the product's value must be established before the salesperson spends time discussing price.[4] Many companies never sell as the low-cost option. Stryker Medical sells hospital beds and stretchers to hospitals and emergency rooms. They are never the lowest cost. Stryker's salespeople almost always hear the price objection. First, they have to educate their prospects and customers that their products last 25 to 50 percent longer than their competitors. They can demonstrate with evidence their product will still be around 5 to 10 years after their competitor's has been discarded. If one of their stretchers is $1,500 more than their competitors, they must break down the price over the entire life of the stretcher. They can actually show a savings over time. By providing the right information, Stryker can show value over their competitor's offering.

Price objections probably occur more frequently than any other type. Price objections may be used to cover the real reason for a reluctance to buy. Probing and asking questions are the salesperson's tools to get to the real reasons for a buyer's objection. Exhibit 8.6 summarizes a number of price objections.

EXHIBIT 8.6   Price Objections

"We can't afford it."
"I can't afford to spend that much right now."
"That's 30 percent higher than your competitor's comparable model."
"We have a better offer from your competitor."
"I need something a lot cheaper."
"Your price is not different enough to change suppliers."

Time Objections   **EXHIBIT 8.7**

"I need time to think it over."
"Ask me again next month when you stop by."
"I'm not ready to buy yet."
"I haven't made up my mind."
"I don't want to commit myself until I've had a chance to talk to engineering (i.e., any other department)."

Time Objections

The **time objection**, or as some salespeople call it, the stalling objection, is used by buyers to put off the decision to buy until a later date. Many inexperienced salespeople hear this technique and believe the prospect is going to buy in the future, but just not today. Some buyers use this technique to get rid of salespeople so that the buyer does not have to formally reject the salesperson and his or her sales proposal. Sometimes proposals are very complex and the buyer does need time to think them over. The salesperson must be sensitive to this and not push too hard to get an answer until the buyer has had adequate time to make a decision. It is acceptable for the salesperson to review the reasons to act now or soon. Waiting can have consequences (i.e., prices rise, new tax begins the first of the year, etc.) and the buyer should be made aware of these. Exhibit 8.7 illustrates possible time objections.

Using LAARC: A Process for Negotiating Buyer Resistance

The term **LAARC** is an acronym for listen, acknowledge, assess, respond, and confirm and describes an effective process for salespeople to follow to overcome sales resistance. The LAARC method is a customer-oriented way to keep the sales dialogue positive. In the early days of sales, buyers and sellers were not always truthful with each other, and manipulation was the norm. Salespeople who said whatever it took to get an order—who overpromised and underdelivered and misrepresented their offering—were sometimes looked on favorably by their selling organization. Professional sellers today want to keep the dialogue open and build goodwill by adding value to their proposition. By listening to buyers' concerns and negotiating through open dialogue, the seller increases the likelihood of purchase decisions being made on a favorable basis, and this leads to long-term relationships. Thus, it is the salesperson's job to communicate and demonstrate value when sales resistance arises.

Here is a description of LAARC:

- *Listen:* Salespeople should listen to what their buyers are saying. The ever-present temptation to anticipate what buyers are going to say and cut them off with a premature response should be avoided. Learning to listen is important—it is more than just being polite or professional. Buyers are trying to tell the salesperson something that they consider important.
- *Acknowledge:* As buyers complete their statements, salespeople should acknowledge that they received the message and that they appreciate and can understand the concern. Salespeople should not jump in with an instantaneous defensive response. Before responding, salespeople need a better understanding about what their buyers are saying. By politely pausing and then simply acknowledging their statement, salespeople set themselves up to be a reasonable person—a professional who appreciates other people's opinions. It also buys salespeople precious moments for composing themselves and thinking of questions for the next step.
- *Assess:* This step is similar to assessment in the ADAPT process of questioning. This step in dealing with buyer resistance calls for salespeople to ask assessment

Todd Mackey had been in sales for several years and had run into a number of sales objections recently. He was having trouble handling sales resistance and saw quite a few orders go to his competitor. Mackey remembered a tactic he learned many years ago, when he received an objection he could not immediately answer, he should tell the prospect "I am going to cover your concern later in my presentation." Mackey knew he didn't have an answer and he hoped the prospect would not bring it up again. What do you think about Mackey's tactics? What would you do in this situation?

questions to gain a better understanding of exactly what their buyers are saying and why they are saying it. Equipped with this information and understanding, salespeople are better able to make a meaningful response to the buyer's resistance.

- *Respond:* Based on his or her understanding of what and why the buyer is resisting, the salesperson can respond to the buyer's resistance. Structuring a response typically follows the method that is most appropriate for the situation. The more traditional methods of response (see Exhibit 8.8) include forestalling, direct denial, indirect denial, translation (or boomerang), compensation, question, third-party reinforcement (or feel-felt-found), and "coming to that." In "An Ethical Dilemma" Todd Mackey uses one technique that should never be used by a professional salesperson.

  These techniques have been used both positively and negatively. Professional salespeople use these techniques to add value to their proposal. For instance, the translation or boomerang technique can be used quite effectively if the salesperson has gathered the appropriate information to support his or her response. The buyer might state, "Your company is too big, and we might slip through the cracks as a small customer." The salesperson might respond, "That is exactly why you want to do business with us. We are larger, and we are going to be able to offer you all of the levels of expertise you said you needed. Smaller companies won't be able to do this, and you will eventually have to search for another supplier. We're one-stop shopping, and we'll make sure you won't fall through the cracks." Here, the salesperson took a reason not to buy and translated it into a reason to buy. Much dialogue had to go on before this for the salesperson to be able to provide the proper information to overcome the concern. Exhibit 8.8 includes examples of how a salesperson might respond to buyer concerns in a professional manner.

- *Confirm:* After responding, the salesperson should ask confirmatory questions—response-checks to make sure that the buyer's concerns have been adequately met. Once this is confirmed, the presentation can proceed. In fact, experience indicates that this form of buyer confirmation is often a sufficient buying signal to warrant the salesperson's attempt to gain a commitment.

Recommended Approaches for Responding to Objections

A brief summary of traditional methods for responding to objections follows. Exhibit 8.8 summarizes how each technique works.

Forestalling

When salespeople hear an objection arising repeatedly, they may decide to include an answer to the objection within their sales presentation before it is voiced by the prospect (i.e., **forestalling**). Marty Reist of MPRS Sales, Inc., often tells his prospects he realizes he's not Nike, Titleist, or Reebok, but his size has not kept him from providing outstanding service to his customers. Reist can add a third-party testimonial to back up

Techniques to Answer Concerns EXHIBIT 8.8

Technique	How It Works	Example
Forestalling	Take care of the objection before the prospect brings it up.	Many of my customers have had a concern going into my presentation that we don't have a warranty program. Let me put this to rest that we have one, three and five year warranty programs that match our competitors. I hope this answers your concern.
Direct Denial	A rather harsh response that the prospect is wrong.	You have heard incorrectly. We are not raising prices.
Indirect Denial	Softening the blow when correcting a prospect's information.	We've heard that rumor, too—even some of our best customers asked us about it. Our senior management team has guaranteed us our prices will hold firm through the rest of the year.
Translation or Boomerang	Turn a reason *not* to buy into a reason *to* buy.	Buyer: Your company is too small to meet our needs. Salesperson: That is just the reason you want to do business with us. Because we're smaller, you'll get the individual attention you said you wanted....
Compensation	Counterbalance the objection with an offsetting benefit.	Yes, our price is higher, but you are going to get the quality you said that you needed to keep your customers happy.
Questioning or Assessing	Ask the buyer assessment questions to gain a better understanding of what they are objecting to.	Your concern is price. Can you please tell me who you are comparing us to and does their quote include any service agreement?
Third-Party Reinforcement	Use the opinion or data from a third-party source to help overcome the objection.	Marty Middleton from Dial Electronics had the same concern going in. Let me tell you why she is comfortable with our proposal....
(Or Feel-Felt-Found)	Salesperson relates that others actually found their initial opinions to be unfounded.	Buyer: I don't think my customers will want to buy a product with all those features. We generally sell scaled down models. Salesperson: I can certainly see how you *feel*. Tammy Richardson down the road in Louisville *felt* the same way when I first proposed that she go with these models. However, after she agreed to display them in the front of her store, she *found* that her customers started buying the models with more features—and that, in turn, provided her with larger margins. In fact, she called me less than a week later to order more!
Coming-to-That	The salesperson tells the buyer that he or she will be covering the objection later in his or her presentation.	Buyer: I have some concerns about your delivery dates. Salesperson: I'm glad you brought that up. Before fully discussing our delivery, I want to go over the features that you said were important to you that will help you better understand our product. Is this ok?

his statements and put his prospect's mind at ease. This technique should only be used when there is a high probability that the prospect will indeed raise the objection.[5]

Direct Denial

When using the **direct denial** technique to handle sales resistance, the salesperson is directly telling the customer that he or she is mistaken. Prospects may have incorrect facts or may not understand the information they have.

The prospect might say the following:

Prospect: I hear you don't offer service agreements on any of your products.

The salesperson knowing this is not true cannot soft pedal his or her answer. In this situation the prospect is clearly incorrect and the direct denial is the best solution.

Salesperson: I'm sorry, that is not correct. We offer three- and five-year service contracts, and our warranty is also five years.

The important part of using the direct denial is to not humiliate or anger the prospect. The direct denial should be used sparingly, but it may be easier to use when the salesperson has a good feel for the relationship that he or she has with the buyer.

Indirect Denial

Sometimes it is best not to take an objection head on. The indirect approach takes on the objection, but with a softer more tactful approach. With the **indirect denial**, the salesperson never tells the prospect directly that he or she is wrong. The best way to utilize this method is to think of it as offering sympathy with the prospect's view and still managing to correct the invalid objection of the buyer. An example follows:

Prospect: I heard that your emergency room beds are $4,000 higher than your competitor's.

Salesperson: Many of our customers had a similar notion that our beds are much more expensive. The actual cost is only $1,200 higher. I have testimonials from other hospitals stating that our beds last up to five years longer. You actually save money.

The salesperson here tries to soften the blow with the opening sentence. Then the salesperson must correct the misconception. Techniques can be combined as the salesperson adds information from a third party to add credibility to his or her statement.

Translation or Boomerang

The **translation** or **boomerang** method converts the objection into a reason that the prospect should buy. What the salesperson is trying to do is to take a reason not to buy and turn it into a reason to buy. Our friend, Marty Reist of MPRS Sales, Inc., offers the following advice. Reist states:

Whenever I hear the objection "I don't think your company is large enough to meet our service needs," I immediately come back with "That is exactly the reason you should do business with us. We are big enough to meet your service needs. In fact, you will be calling an 800 number with a larger company and you won't know who you'll get to help you. With our company, anytime you have a problem, question, or concern, you'll call me and talk to a familiar voice."

Another example using the price objection might go like this:

Buyer: "Your price appears to be high."

Salesperson: "Our high price is an advantage for you; the premium sector of the market not only gives you the highest margin, but it is the most stable sector of the market."

The goal of the translation or boomerang method is to turn an apparent deficiency into an asset or reason to buy.

Compensation

There may be a time when a salesperson has to admit that his or her product does have the disadvantage that the prospect has noticed. The **compensation** technique is an attempt to show the prospect that a benefit or advantage compensates for an objection. For example, a higher product price is justified by benefits such as better service, faster delivery, or higher performance.

A buyer may use the objection that your company's lead time is 14 days compared to 10 days for your leading competitor. The salesperson's response could be: "Yes, our required lead time is 14 days, but we ship our orders completely assembled. This practically eliminates extra handling in your warehouse. My competitor's product will require assembly by your warehouse workers." With the compensation method the objection is not denied at all—it is acknowledged, then balanced by compensating features, advantages, and benefits.

Questioning or Assessing

Another potentially effective way to handle buyer resistance is to convert the objection into a question. This technique calls for the salesperson to ask **questions** or **assess** to gain a better understanding of the exact nature of the buyer's objections. Sometimes it is difficult for the salesperson to know the exact problem. This technique is good for clarifying the real objection. This technique can also be effective in resolving the objection if the prospect is shooting from the hip and does not have a strong reason for the objection. Dave Wheat, in "Professional Selling in the 21st Century: Sales Resistance Means Your Buyer Is Thinking," describes how he views sales resistance today versus how he viewed it when he first started in sales. Exhibit 8.9 illustrates the question method as a tool to overcome sales resistance.

Third-Party Reinforcement (or Feel-Felt-Found)

The **third-party reinforcement** technique uses the opinion or research of a third person or company to help overcome and reinforce the salesperson's sales points. A wide range of proof statements can be used by salespeople today. Consumer reports, government reports, and independent testing agencies can all be used to back up a salesperson's statement. Secondary data such as this or experience data from a reliable third party could be all that is needed to turn around a skeptical prospect. A salesperson must remember this technique will only work if the buyer believes in the third-party source that the salesperson is using.

PROFESSIONAL SELLING IN THE 21ST CENTURY

Sales Resistance Means Your Buyer Is Thinking

Dave Wheat of TransWestern Publishing states:

I remember early in my career I dreaded objections. I took objections personally. Generally, I probably was not prepared enough to handle all the different types of objections that came my way. One of our senior reps at the time took me aside and told me to think of objections as, "Your buyer is thinking about your proposal. Doesn't it make sense that you want your buyer thinking about and questioning you on price, delivery, service and warranty?"

That really opened my eyes. I didn't take sales resistance so personally anymore. I listened to their concerns and worked on getting them the information they needed to make a sound decision. It is better that your prospect or client is still thinking about your proposal rather than already having his or her mind made up and the answer is NO! If any buyer is thinking, then I still have an opportunity to earn their business.

EXHIBIT 8.9 Questioning (Assessing) to Overcome Sales Resistance

Example 1
Buyer: I'm not sure I am ready to act at this time.
Salesperson: Can you tell me what is causing your hesitation?

Example 2
Buyer: Your price seems to be a little high.
Salesperson: Can you tell me what price you had in mind? Have other suppliers quoted you a lower price?

Example 3
Buyer: Your delivery schedule does not work for us.
Salesperson: Who are you comparing me to? Can you please tell me what delivery schedule will work for your company?

A version of using third-party reinforcement is the feel-felt-found method. Here, the salesperson goes on to relate that others found their initial thoughts to be unfounded after they tried the product. Salespeople need to practice this method—when used in the correct sequence, it can be very effective. Again, the strength of the person and company being used as an example is critical to how much influence the reference will have on the prospect.

Coming-to-that or Postpone

Salespeople need to understand that objections may and will be made to almost everything concerning them, their products, and their company. Good salespeople anticipate these objections and develop effective answers, but sometimes it may make sense to cover an objection later in the presentation, after additional questioning and information is provided. The salesperson should evaluate how important the concern is to the prospect—and, if the objection seems to be critical to the sale, the salesperson should address it immediately.

Once the salesperson has answered all the buyer's questions and has resolved resistance issues that have come up during the presentation, the salesperson should summarize all the pertinent buying signals.

SUMMARIZING SOLUTIONS TO CONFIRM BENEFITS

The mark of a good salesperson is the ability to listen and determine exactly the customer's needs. It is not unusual for salespeople to incorporate the outstanding benefits of their product into the sales presentation. A salesperson can identify many potential benefits for each product and feature. However, it does not make sense for a salesperson to talk about potential benefits that the buyer may not need. The salesperson must determine the confirmed benefits and make these the focal point of the sales summary before asking for the business. A salesperson must be alert to the one, two, or three benefits that generate the most excitement to the buyer. The confirmed benefits that are of greatest interest to the buyer deserve the greatest emphasis. These benefits should be summarized in such a way that the buyer sees a direct connection in what he or she has been telling the salesperson over the course of the selling cycle and the proposal being offered to meet his or her needs. Once this is done, it is time to ask for the business.

SECURING COMMITMENT AND CLOSING

Ultimately, a large part of most salespeople's performance evaluation is based on their ability to gain customer commitment, often called closing sales. Because of this close relationship between compensation and getting orders, traditional selling has tended to overemphasize the importance of gaining a commitment.[6] In fact, there are those who think that just about any salesperson can find a new prospect, open a sale, or take an order. These same people infer it takes a trained, motivated, and skilled professional to close a sale. They go on to say that the close is the keystone to a salesperson's success, and a good salesperson will have mastered many new ways to close the sale. This outmoded emphasis on closing skills is typical of transaction selling techniques that stress making the sales call at all costs.

Another popular but outdated suggestion to salespeople is to "close early and often." This is particularly bad advice if the prospect is not prepared to make a decision, responds negatively to a premature attempt to consummate the sale, and then (following the principles of cognitive consistency) proceeds to reinforce the prior negative position as the salesperson plugs away, firing one closing salvo after another at the beleaguered prospect. Research tells us that it will take several sales calls to make an initial sale, so it is somewhat bewildering to still encounter such tired old battle cries as "the ABCs of selling, which stand for Always Be Closing." Research based on more than 35,000 sales calls over a 12-year period suggests that an overreliance on closing techniques actually reduces the chance of making a sale.[7]

Manipulative closing gimmicks are less likely to be effective as professional buyers grow weary with the cat-and-mouse approach to selling that is still practiced by a surprising number of salespeople. It is also surprising to find many salespeople who view their customers as combatants over whom victory is sought. Once the sale is made by salespeople who have adversarial, me-against-you attitudes, the customer is likely to be neglected as the salesperson rides off into the sunset in search of yet another battle with yet another lowly customer.

One time-honored thought that does retain contemporary relevance is that "nobody likes to be sold, but everybody likes to buy." In other words, salespeople should facilitate decision making by pointing out a suggested course of action but should allow the prospect plenty of mental space within which a rational decision can be reached.[8] Taken to its logical conclusion, this means that it may be acceptable to make a sales call without asking for the order. Salespeople must be cognizant, however, of their responsibility to advance the relationship toward a profitable sale, lest they become the most dreaded of all types of salespeople—the paid conversationalist.

It has already been mentioned that the salesperson has taken on the expanded roles of business consultant and relationship manager, which is not consistent with pressuring customers until they give in and say yes. Fortunately, things have changed to the point that today's professional salesperson attempts to gain commitment when the buyer is ready to buy. The salesperson should evaluate each presentation and attempt to determine the causes of its success or failure with the customer. The difference between closing and earning commitment is that commitment is more than just securing an order. Commitment insinuates the beginning of a long-term relationship.

Guidelines for Earning Commitment

Earning commitment or gaining commitment is the culmination of the selling process. However, it should not be viewed as a formal stage that only comes at the end of the presentation. Many salespeople fail to recognize early buyer commitment by focusing on their presentation and not the comments being made by the buyer. **Commitment signals** are favorable statements that may be made by the buyer, such as:

- I like that size.
- That will get the job done.
- The price is lower than I thought it would be.
- I didn't realize you delivered everyday.

These statements should be considered green lights that allow the salesperson to move the process forward. They also may come in the form of trial commitments.

Throughout the presentation it is appropriate to determine a prospect's reaction to a particular feature or product. At this time, a trial commitment is a question designed to determine a prospect's reaction without forcing the prospect to make a final yes or

Close When It Is Appropriate

Kelly Osterling, a sales representative for R.R. Donnelly, states:

I close when it's appropriate. Now that begs the question, When is it appropriate? This is really a two part answer. First, I close when the buyer is ready to close. I had a friend in the copier industry who walked into a prospect's office the day after their copier broke. The office had a lot of deadlines to meet, so the office manager was ready to buy at that moment. Not much selling went on during that sales call. The buyer wanted a loaner immediately, and the rest of the details (i.e., price, warranty, and service agreement) could be worked out later. Those kinds of customers don't come along often—but when they do you have to be ready to read the buyer, understand the situation, and provide an immediate solution.

The second part of earning commitment centers on when the buyer has enough information to make an intelligent decision. It is my job to make sure during my presentations and demonstrations that I am providing the right information that will reduce the risk in their decision-making process. If I ask the right questions, I'll know what information my buyer needs to make a decision.

So, I close when the buyer is ready to buy. That comes about by providing the right information for my buyers to make a sound decision. Once the information has been thoroughly digested by my buyers, then I attempt to earn their commitment.

no buying decision. The trial commitment is an effort to elicit how far along the prospect is in his or her decision making. Confirmation on the prospect's part on key features helps the salesperson determine how ready the prospect is to buy.

Open-ended questions are a good way to test prospect readiness. A salesperson might ask during his or her presentation, "What do you think of our computer's larger memory capacity?" The answer to this will help direct the salesperson to his or her next sales points. However, many statements made by buyers should be considered red lights, a formal objection. The salesperson must consider each of these objections and work to overcome them. Red light statements might include:

- I'm not sure that will work.
- The price is higher than I thought it would be.
- Your delivery schedule does not work for us.
- I don't see the advantage of going with your proposal.

Red light statements are commitment caution signals and must be resolved to the buyer's satisfaction before asking for a commitment. Closing early and often and having a closing quota for each sales call are traditional methods that are not liked by buyers. The salesperson should put himself or herself in the buyer's shoes and think about how he or she would like to be hammered with many closes throughout a sales presentation, particularly if a few red lights are introduced. Many times, the best method for earning commitment is to simply ask for the business. If the prospect has been qualified properly and a number of confirmed benefits have been uncovered, then the natural next step is to ask for the business. When does the salesperson ask for the business? When the buyer is ready to buy. Kelly Osterling, in "Professional Selling in the 21st Century: Close When It Is Appropriate," states that she makes sure that her buyer has the appropriate information needed to make an intelligent decision. Then she asks for the business.

Techniques to Earn Commitment

Some sales trainers will try to teach their sales forces literally hundreds of commitment techniques. One trainer recommended to his sales force that the salespeople learn two new commitment techniques per week. Then at the end of the year, they would have more than 100 commitment techniques ready to use. Relationship managers today do not need many commitment techniques. A few good ones will suffice. Five techniques that are conducive to relationship building follow:

1. **Ask for the Order/Direct Commitment.**

   It is not unusual for inexperienced salespeople to lose an order simply by not asking the customer to buy. Professional buyers report that an amazing number of salespeople fear rejection. When the buyer is ready to buy, the salesperson must be prepared to ask for the buyer's commitment. The **direct commitment** is a straightforward request for an order. A salesperson ought to be confident if he or she has covered all the necessary features and benefits of the product and matched these with the buyer's needs. At this time, the salesperson cannot be afraid to ask "Tom, can we set up an office visit for next week?" or "Mary, I'd like to have your business, if we can get the order signed today, delivery can take place early next week." Many buyers appreciate the direct approach. There is no confusion as to what the salesperson wants the buyer to do.

2. **Legitimate Choice/Alternative Choice.**

   The **legitimate choice** asks the prospect to select from two or more choices. For example, will the HP 400 or the HP 600 be the one you want? An investment broker might ask his or her prospect, "Do you feel your budget would allow you to invest $1,000 a month or would $500 a month be better?" The theory behind this technique suggests buyers do not like to be told what to do but do like making a decision over limited choices.

3. **Summary Commitment.**

   A very effective way to gain agreement is to summarize all the major benefits the buyer has confirmed over the course of the sales calls. Salespeople should keep track of all of the important points covered in previous calls so they can emphasize them again in summary form.

   In using the **summary commitment** technique, a computer salesperson might say:

   > Of course, Tom, this is an important decision, so to make the best possible choice, let's go over the major concepts we've discussed. We have agreed that Thompson Computers will provide some definite advantages. First, our system will lower your computing costs; second, our system will last longer and has a better warranty, thus saving you money; and finally, your data processing people will be happier because our faster system will reduce their workload. They'll get to go home earlier each evening.

   The summary commitment is a valuable technique in that it reminds prospects of all the major benefits that have been mentioned in previous sales calls.

4. **The T-Account or the Balance Sheet Commitment.**

   The **T-account commitment** or **balance sheet commitment** is essentially a summary commitment on paper. With the T-account commitment, the sales representative takes out a sheet of paper and draws a large "T" across it. On the left-hand side, the salesperson and buyer brainstorm the reasons to buy. Here, the salesperson will list with the buyer all the positive selling points (benefits) they discussed throughout the selling process. Once this is completed, the salesperson asks the buyer for any reasons that he or she would not want to purchase. Visually, the left-hand side should help the buyer make his or her decision as seen in Exhibit 8.10. This will not work if the weight of the reasons not to buy outweighs the reasons to buy. In the example in Exhibit 8.10, the buyer wants to act, but does not have the money at this time.

5. **Success Story Commitment.**

   Every company has many satisfied customers. These customers started out having problems, and the sales representative helped solve these problems by recommending the product or products that matched the customer's needs. Buyers are thankful and grateful when the salesperson helps solve problems. When the salesperson relates a story about how one of his or her customers had a similar problem and solved it by using the salesperson's product, a reluctant buyer can be reassured that the salesperson has done this before successfully. If the salesperson

EXHIBIT 8.10 T-Account Close

Reasons to Buy	Reasons Not to Buy
• Daily delivery schedule meets our needs • Warranty agreement is longer than the one I have now (5 years versus 3 years) • You provide a training program • Your service department is located in our city	• Because of extra services • Your price *is too high*

decides to use the customer's name and company, then the salesperson must be sure to get permission to do so. A **success story commitment** may go something like this:

> Tom, thanks for sharing your copier problems with me. I had another customer you might know, Betty Brown, who had the same problem over at Thompson Electronics. We installed the CP 2000 and eliminated the problem completely. Please feel free to give Betty a call. She is very happy with our solution.

Some companies will use the success story commitment by actually taking the prospect to a satisfied customer. The salesperson may leave the prospect alone with the satisfied customer so the two can talk confidentially. A satisfied customer can help a salesperson earn commitment by answering questions a reluctant prospect needs answered before they can purchase. A summary of relationship-building earning commitment techniques can be found in Exhibit 8.11.

Probe to Earn Commitment

Every attempt to earn commitment will not be successful. Successful salespeople cannot be afraid to ask a prospect why he or she is hesitating to make a decision. It is the salesperson's job to uncover the reason why the prospect is hesitating by asking a series of questions that get at the key issues. For instance, a buyer may state that he or she is not ready to sign an order. The salesperson must ask, "Mary, there must be a reason why you are reluctant to do business with me and my company. Do you mind if I ask what it is?" The salesperson must then listen and respond accordingly. A salesperson cannot be afraid to ask why a prospect is reluctant to purchase.

Traditional Methods

Sales trainers across the nation teach hundreds of techniques to earn commitment. Exhibit 8.12 is a summary of the traditional commitment techniques. The vast majority of these are not conducive to building a strong buyer–seller relationship. As prospects become more sophisticated, most will be turned off by these techniques and they will be ineffective. "An Ethical Dilemma" asks the question, "How many times should a salesperson ask for the order during each sales call?"

Research has clearly shown that buyers are open to consultative techniques of handling objections (for example, questioning and assessing, direct denial with facts, and

EXHIBIT 8.11 Techniques to Earn Commitment

1. Direct Commitment—Simply ask for the order.
2. Legitimate Choice/Alternative Choice—Give the prospect a limited number of choices.
3. Summary Commitment—Summarize all the confirmed benefits that have been agreed to.
4. T-Account/Balance Sheet Commitment—Summary close on paper.
5. Success Story Commitment—Salesperson tells a story of a business that successfully solved a problem by buying his or her product.

	Traditional Commitment Method **EXHIBIT 8.12**
Method	**How to Use It**
Standing-Room-Only Close	This close puts a time limit on the client in an attempt to hurry the decision to close. "These prices are only good until tomorrow."
Assumptive Close	The salesperson assumes that an agreement has been reached. The salesperson places the order form in front of the buyer and hands him or her a pen.
Fear or Emotional Close	The salesperson tells a story of something bad happening if the purchase is not made. "If you don't purchase this insurance and you die, your wife will have to sell the house and live on the street."
Continuous Yes Close	This close uses the principle that saying yes gets to be a habit. The salesperson asks a number of questions, each formulated so that the prospect answers yes.
Minor-Points Close	Seeks agreement on relatively minor (trivial) issues associated with the full order. "Do you prefer cash or charge?"

AN ETHICAL DILEMMA

Katie Short has just returned from a training session where the sales trainer told all the associates they had to close at least three times during each sales call. Her boss was eager to see if she would be more aggressive in earning commitment. After several calls, her boss confronted her because she was not closing at least two or three times on each sales call. Short's previous company had not been nearly this aggressive. She felt uncomfortable—and felt her buyers were uncomfortable—when she was closing all the time. How should Short handle this situation with her boss?

so on) and earning commitment (for example, asking for the order in a straightforward manner, summarizing key benefits). On the other hand, buyers have stated that standard persuasive (traditional) tactics that have been used for years are unacceptable. They now view traditional techniques of handling objections (for example, forestalling, postponing) and earning commitment (for example, standing room only, fear) as overly aggressive and unprofessional.[9]

SUMMARY

1. **Explain why it is important to anticipate and overcome buyer concerns and resistance.** During the early years of selling, salespeople looked at sales resistance as a negative that was a likely indication that their buyer was not going to buy. This notion has changed over the years and now objections are viewed as opportunities to sell. Salespeople should be grateful for objections and always treat them as indications that the prospect needs more information, and if the salesperson provides the correct information, they are moving closer to gaining the sale.

2. **Understand why prospects raise objections.** Some prospects are happy with their present suppliers and want to avoid the sales interview. In other instances, the salesperson has failed to properly qualify the prospect. A prospect who has

recently purchased a product is probably not in the market for another. Sometimes, prospects simply lack information on the salesperson's product category and they are uncomfortable making a decision.

3. **Describe the five major types of sales resistance.** Typically, objections include: "I don't need your product," "Your product is not a good fit," "I don't know your company," "Your price is too high," and "This is a bad time to buy."

4. **Explain how the LAARC method can be used to overcome buyer objections.** LAARC allows the salesperson to carefully listen to what the buyer is saying. It allows the salesperson to better understand the buyer's objections. After this careful analysis, the salesperson can then respond. The buyer feels the salesperson is responding to his or her specific concern rather than giving a prepared answer.

5. **Describe the traditional methods for responding to buyer objections.** Salespeople have a number of traditional techniques at their disposal to handle resistance. Some of the more popular techniques include: forestalling, answering the objection before the prospect brings it up; direct denial; indirect denial, softens the answer; translation or boomerang, turn a reason not to buy into a reason to buy; compensation, offset the objection with superior benefits; question, use questions to uncover the buyer's concerns; and third-party reinforcements, use the opinion or research of others to substantiate claims.

6. **List and explain the earning commitment techniques that enhance relationship building.** Many techniques can be used to earn commitment. Most are gimmicky in nature and reinforce the notion of traditional selling. Successful relationship-building techniques include the summary commitment, the success story commitment, and the direct commitment or ask for the order.

UNDERSTANDING PROFESSIONAL SELLING TERMS

sales resistance
need objection
product or service objection
company or source objection
price objection
time objection
LAARC
forestalling
direct denial
indirect denial
translation or boomerang
compensation
questions or assess
third-party reinforcement

commitment signals
direct commitment
alternative choice
legitimate choice
summary commitment
T-account or balance sheet
    commitment
success story commitment
standing-room-only close
assumptive close
fear or emotional close
continuous yes close
minor-points close

DEVELOPING PROFESSIONAL SELLING KNOWLEDGE

1. Why is it important for a salesperson to anticipate a buyer's concerns and objections?

2. Is one type of sales resistance (i.e., need, price) more difficult to handle than another (i.e., source, product, time)?

3. Should the direct denial method ever be used?

4. Some trainers have been heard to say, "If a salesperson gets sales resistance, then he or she has not done a very good job during the sales presentation." Do you agree with this?

5. Under what circumstances does a salesperson want sales resistance?

6. Are there ever going to be situations where the salesperson can't overcome sales resistance?

7. Some trainers and sales experts think that closing is the most important stage of the sales process. Do you feel this way?

8. Why should salespeople have many closing techniques ready to use during a sales call? Explain.

9. Can the LAARC method be used for all types of sales resistance? Explain.

10. What is the best method to handle sales resistance?

BUILDING PROFESSIONAL SELLING SKILLS

1. Explain why each of the following statements would be considered a signal of commitment.
   a) The prospect makes a positive statement.
   b) A worried look is replaced by a happy look.
   c) The prospect starts playing with a pen or the order form.
   d) The prospect looks at the product with a favorable expression.
   e) The prospect touches the product.
   f) The prospect is using or trying out the product.
   g) The prospect's tone of voice changes or his or her body relaxes.
   h) The prospect questions price, usage, or delivery.

2. Using the following list, address each of the indicated buyer objections by using the LAARC process. The Listen step is implicit and omitted from the written responses. Take time to write out your answers. Responses will be used in class discussion.
   a) Your price is too high.
      Acknowledge
      Assess
      Respond
      Confirm
   b) I like what I see, but I need to talk with my boss before I do anything.
      Acknowledge
      Assess
      Respond
      Confirm
   c) I just don't think we need it; we already use your competitor's products and they work alright.
      Acknowledge
      Assess
      Respond
      Confirm
   d) I'm just not sure our employees can adapt to the new technology.
      Acknowledge
      Assess
      Respond
      Confirm

e) The last time we bought from your company we had problems with product reliability.
Acknowledge
Assess
Respond
Confirm

ROLE PLAY

3. **Situation:** Read the Ethical Dilemma on page 218.

Characters: Todd Mackey, sales representative; Emma Jones, sales trainer; Mary Sutton, purchasing agent

Scene 1: *Location*—Sales training room.
Action—The sales trainer, Jones, tells the class one technique they might use with a tough objection is to forestall the objection.

Role play answering a difficult objection. Use the response that it will be covered later. How did your buyer respond?

Scene 2: *Location*—Mary Sutton's office.
Action—Mackey tells Sutton he is going to cover a concern later in his presentation.

Role play Sutton asking Mackey to cover the concern, now she does not want to wait until later!

Upon completion of the role plays, address the following questions:

3a. What are the potential problems with telling the buyer you will cover the concern later knowing you don't plan to cover the concern later?

3b. Is it ever alright to tell a prospect or customer you don't know the answer?

ROLE PLAY

4. **Situation:** Read the Ethical Dilemma on page 227.

Characters: Katie Short, salesperson; buyer

Scene: *Location*—Buyer's office.
Action—Short has begun her sales presentation.

Role play Short trying three to five closes during her presentation.

Upon completion of the role play, address the following questions;

4a. Were you comfortable using three to five closes during the presentation?

4b. What risks does the salesperson run by closing several times during his or her presentation?

5. The ability to handle sales resistance and earn commitment are two crucial areas that have much to do with a salesperson's success.

Assignment 1
Go to your favorite search engine and type in "sales, how to close," "sales, how to handle sales resistance," "sales, how to handle objections."

What did you find?

Write a short report to your boss that you want to lead a sales meeting and cover each of these topics. Write up some of the things you want to talk about that will help your sales force.

Assignment 2
Type in: **http://www.davekahle.com/close.htm**.
What does he mean that you have to "open" before you "close?"

Assignment 3
Type in: **www.summitconsulting.com/articles**. Next, scroll down to "overcoming objections." Click on "Overcoming Sales Resistance Areas." Read the article "Consulting Tips from the Million Dollar Consultant: Overcoming Sales Resistance Areas." Which of these four areas do you think are the most difficult to overcome? Does the article leave out any areas?

MAKING PROFESSIONAL SELLING DECISIONS

Case 8.1: Thompson Engineering

Tyler Houston sells for Thompson Engineering. He has been calling on Hudson Distributors for close to two years. Over the course of 15 calls, he has sold them nothing to date. He thinks that he is extremely close to getting an order. Houston knows that Hudson is happy with its present supplier, but he is aware that they have received some late deliveries. Tom Harris, Hudson's senior buyer, has given every indication that he likes Houston's products and Houston.

During Houston's most recent call, Harris told him that he'd have to have a couple of weeks to go over Houston's proposal. Harris really didn't have any major objections during the presentation. Houston knows his price, quality, and service are equal to or exceed Hudson's present supplier.

Questions

1. Harris told Houston that he needed a couple of weeks to think about his proposal. How should Houston handle this?
2. What should Houston have done during the sales presentation when Harris told him that he needed to think it over?
3. What techniques should Houston have used to overcome the forestalling tactic?

Situation: Read Case 8.1

Characters: Tyler Houston, sales representative; Tom Harris, senior buyer

ROLE PLAY

Scene 1:   *Location*—Harris' office.
Action—Harris has just stated that he needs a couple of weeks to go over Houston's proposal.

Role play how Houston should respond to Harris' needing two weeks to think it over.

Scene 2:   *Location*—Harris' office.
Action—Houston is summarizing his product's advantages (i.e., price, quality, service).

Role play Houston's summary and his asking for the order.

Upon completion of the role plays, address the following questions:

1. Why do buyers hesitate and ask for more time to think over proposals?

2. How hard should Houston press to get Harris to act now?

Case 8.2: Data Computers

Steve Thomas sells for Data Computers. Thomas has recently completed his training seminars and has been back in the field for three months. He has been anxious to try out the selling processes his company uses. He is equally excited about the techniques he has been taught on how to handle sales resistance and earn commitment. His trainers were very impressed with his ability to use the T-account method to earn commitment. Thomas feels this technique is very pragmatic and visually shows his prospects why they should use his products. He has been surprised at how ineffective this technique has been on recent sales calls. He is beginning to wonder if he should try some other earning commitment techniques.

Here is a copy of Thomas' notes from a prospect he has been working on.

Thomas' Notes:

Client: Anderson Printing, Bob Martin, purchasing agent

Prospect looks good—looks like a good fit

Potential to earn business—B+/A−

Present equipment—4 years old

Fact-finding call on 9/1, buyer went to local college, 2 kids

9/15 Took engineers in and looked at his present system. Basically it is ready to be replaced. Purchased in 1999.

9/22 Made major proposal to Bob Martin, couldn't get engineers to attend. They had all-day meetings. Gave proposal to Martin and made appointment to come back in two days to review proposal.

9/24 Overall good meeting, I used the T-account method with Martin, the results are shown on the following page.

Thomas is afraid he is going to lose the order. He didn't leave Martin with a good feeling.

1. Look over the notes from each one of Thomas' sales calls. Can you make any recommendations on what Thomas might have done differently?
2. Thomas and Martin came up with five reasons to buy and two reasons not to act. What is holding Martin back?

Reasons to Act	Reasons Not to Act
1. New system's faster, saves time and energy	1. Still thinks the price is high even with the cost savings
2. Can have immediate delivery, does not have to wait	2. Needs to talk over decision with engineers
3. Really likes the cost savings	
4. Can save up to $100 per month in operating cost	
5. Quality looks great	

ROLE PLAY

Situation: Read Case 8.2

Characters: Steve Thomas, sales representative; Bob Martin, purchasing agent

Scene 1:   *Location*—Martin's office.
Action—Thomas is going to review the proposal with Martin.

Role play the T-account earning commitment with Martin.

Scene 2:   *Location*—Martin's office.
Action—Thomas has just asked for the order after the T-account earning commitment technique has been used.

Role play Martin telling Thomas he needs time to think it over and Thomas' response.

Upon completion of the role plays, address the following questions:

1. Can you find any fault in Thomas' logic that there are more reasons to act than not to act?
2. What are the problems with relying on one earning commitment technique?

Enhancing Customer Relationships

Part Four concludes the book with two modules that focus on how salespeople add customer value. In Module 9, we discuss the important role of post-sale follow-up to enhance customer satisfaction and add value to the relationship. Topics include the use of technology during follow-up, how to maintain two-way communication with the customer, how to encourage critical encounters, and how to expand the collaboration between buyer and seller.

Module 10 examines how salespeople can add customer value through self-leadership and teamwork. Goal setting, territory analysis, strategy development and implementation, using technology, and evaluation are discussed as key parts of a sequential model of self-leadership. The importance of teamwork, within the salesperson's company and between the salesperson and the customer, is fully discussed in this final module.

BUILDING GOODWILL

Brett Houston (computer hardware and software salesperson) has been given the top award by his company for building goodwill with his customers. He ranks the highest of 600 sales reps for customer satisfaction with his 200 accounts. Houston has been able to blend calls on prospects with calls on existing customers, so he has been able to keep his new business growing while keeping his existing accounts as repeat purchasers. Houston has been asked what his secret to success is. He shared his secrets at a recent national sales meeting.

"I am flattered that I am here today to talk about how I balance my work load of existing customers with bringing in new business each year. First, let me say that there is not a stronger tool that a salesperson has to use than personal visits to see a new customer or call on a hot prospect. I try to make eight calls a day—that's 40 calls per week—and I generally make 20 calls on existing customers and 20 calls on prospects. This may vary depending on who will see me in any given week. I have made as many as 30 calls on existing customers in a week and as few as 10. You may remember last year when we introduced the software upgrade, I personally called all 200 of my accounts in one month. I didn't make a single call for new business. I felt my existing customers needed assurance from me that the upgrade would go smoothly—and, if they had any trouble, I was only a phone call away. I like to use personal follow-up to keep my customers informed of new developments, new products, and our new applications and upgrades. Providing this information has paved the way for additional sales.

I want to make a very important point: I have to bring value to each of these calls. I don't stay too long. I make my points, answer questions, and thank my customers for their time. We do some talking about personal things, but I do not allow these sessions to turn into chitchat sessions.

The second thing I try to do each month is touch base with all of my prospects with another form of communication. Some of my bigger clients get telephone calls once or twice per month. The cell phone is a wonderful tool. I have e-mail addresses for 175 of my customers, and I use the e-mail to provide useful information when I can. I love to send faxes to my customers—especially if I have important information to pass on. I get a sense that customers feel a fax has a certain urgency to it, and it gets read more often.

"I try also to write handwritten notes when customers place big orders. I thank them for their business. I write other notes when I notice things about my customers who have accomplished something such as a promotion. They are always glad I noticed and took the time to recognize them. I try to keep all my call report notes up to date, so I remember birthdays or special events in my customers' lives."

Objectives

After completing this module, you should be able to

1 Explain how to follow-up to assess customer satisfaction.

2 Explain how to harness technology to enhance follow-up and buyer–seller relationships.

3 Discuss how to take action to assure customer satisfaction.

4 Discuss how to maintain open, two-way communication.

5 Explain how to resolve complaints and encourage critical encounters.

6 Discuss how to expand collaborative involvement.

7 Explain how to add value and enhance mutual opportunities.

"As you can see, it is not just one thing I do to follow-up with my customers. I have to be well-organized to orchestrate all of this, but I feel it is well worth it."

"I then take all of these ideas and try to do as many as I can with my prospects to build relationships with them. This has worked for me over the past 10 years. If done properly, they can work for you. Follow-up is the key to success for any salesperson."

"Thank you for this award."

In traditional selling, salespeople too often thought that their job was over when they closed the sale. Once the order was obtained, they moved on to the next prospect. Any follow-up or customer service was minimal. The life line of an organization today is repeat business. It is important to acquire new customers, but it is critical to keep your existing customer base happy. Not following up with a new customer is a shortsighted attitude toward selling, for it fails to consider the importance of developing and maintaining a customer for your company.

Research indicates that successfully retaining customers is critical for all companies' success. Companies that set explicit targets for customer retention and make efforts to exceed these goals are 60 percent more profitable than those without such goals or those who fail to attract customer loyalty.[1]

Another study finds that it only takes a slight decline in attention from a salesperson to lead to an opportunity to consider alternative suppliers.[2]

There are several ways that a salesperson can convert new customers into highly committed lifetime customers. Examples include (1) **building goodwill** by continually **adding value** to the product, (2) handling complaints in a timely and thoughtful manner, and (3) processing requests for rush deliveries willingly and letting the customer know that the salesperson will do everything he or she can to make that request happen. However, it is just as easy for a salesperson to alienate a new customer by putting the focus on the short-term order and not the long-term activities that create a partnership. This can be done by overpromising and underdelivering, using exaggeration to get an order, and blaming everyone else for problems. Exhibit 9.1 reviews relationship enhancers and detractors that can strengthen or destroy a relationship.

Relationship-oriented salespeople are creating bonds with their customers that will partially isolate them from competitive pressures or at least minimize the importance of easily altered and matched competitive variables such as price. This module explains the importance of follow-up to assess customer satisfaction. Next, harnessing technology to enhance follow-up and buyer–seller relationships is covered. This is followed by a discussion of why it is the salesperson's job to take action (i.e., proactive) before problems arise and not wait for complaints (i.e., reactive). Within the context of resolving complaints, a procedure to handle complaints is presented. This is followed by a discussion of the importance of collaborative involvement and working to add value for the buyer. Finally, the value of customer service is reviewed.

EXHIBIT 9.1   **Relationship Enhancers and Detractors**

Enhancers	Detractors
Focus on long-term	Focus on short-term
Deliver more than salesperson promises	Overpromise—underdeliver
Call regularly	Call sporadically
Add value	Show up only for another order
Keep communication lines open	Can never reach salesperson
Take responsibility for problems	Lie, exaggerate, blame someone else

ASSESS CUSTOMER SATISFACTION

The importance of a diligent effort to maintain and enhance customer relationships is reflected in a survey of corporate buyers who were asked to identify the number one activity of salespeople that annoyed them the most. Their response? "Lack of follow through."[3] Comments such as this indicate that the emphasis on maintaining and enhancing customer relationships is definitely increasing.

John Haack, senior vice president of marketing and sales for Saint-Gobain Containers (a glass container manufacturer), knows the importance of enhancing customer relationships as opposed to focusing solely on current sales. With such customers as Anheuser-Busch, Quaker Oats, and Kraft, Haack says, "Making the sale is only the beginning. After that, you have to keep track of the process every step of the way. You have to make sure the product gets delivered on time and that everyone involved with the customer knows their customer's expectations." Haack continues, "Anybody can move product. I can go out and sell a ton of something, but if it's not right for that particular customer, it's just going to end up back on my doorstep as a major problem."[4]

Clearly, professional salespeople such as John Haack view their customer base as far too valuable an asset to risk losing it through neglect. In maintaining and enhancing customer relationships, salespeople such as Brett Houston in the opening vignette are involved in performing routine post-sale follow-up activities and in enhancing the relationship as it evolves by anticipating and adapting to changes in the customer's situation, competitive forces, and other changes in the market environment. Houston typically does field research, conducts joint brainstorming sessions, and provides sales leads he obtains through his network of business contacts. Activities like these demonstrate his service commitment.

Houston's objective in this step is to create a strong bond with his customers that will diminish the probability of his customers' terminating the relationship. In effect, he earns the business through a number of successive trials and strengthens his position as time passes through follow-up calls and by adding value.

Furthering this notion, Darrell Beaty of Ontario Systems (a collections software company) states, "We spend too much time and effort learning about our prospects to not follow through and assess satisfaction." Figure 9.1[5] demonstrates the time and commitment Beaty puts in to earn an order from a prospect. Beaty states, "We cannot be afraid to ask a customer, 'How are we doing?'" This practice should go on monthly, quarterly, and yearly. Sometimes, the salesperson will not like the answers that he or she gets from the customers. New customers generally feel special because they have received a lot of attention. Long-term customers may feel neglected because the salesperson has many new customers and cannot be as attentive as he or she was previously. Routine follow-up questions, such as, "How are we doing?" can go a long way in letting a customer know that the salesperson cares and is willing to make sure that the customer is satisfied.

HARNESS TECHNOLOGY TO ENHANCE FOLLOW-UP AND BUYER–SELLER RELATIONSHIPS

While much attention has been given to the benefits and competitive advantages resulting from enhanced buyer–seller relationships, recent research indicates that there is still much room for improvement. Consider for example:

- Most Fortune 500 companies lose 50 percent of their customers in five years.[6]
- The average company communicates only four times per year with their customers and six times a year with their prospects.[7]
- It costs 7 to 10 times more to acquire a new customer than it does to retain an existing customer.[8]
- A 5 percent increase in customer retention can increase profits from 25 to 125 percent.[9]

FIGURE 9.1   Ontario Systems Call Strategy

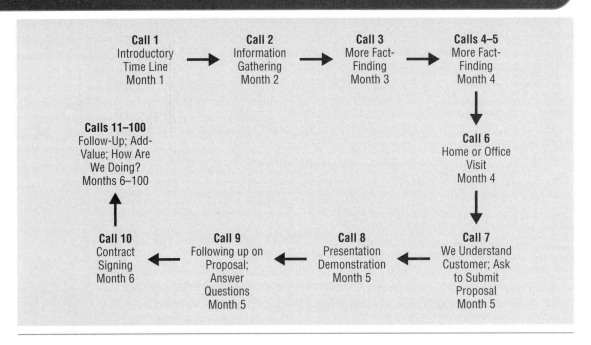

It takes many calls to earn commitment from a prospect. It can take months and even years to establish the trust needed to earn an order.

Indeed, building buyer–seller relationships is easier said than done. Building and nurturing customer relationships demands that salespeople do more than simply discover the buyer's needs and respond to them with a sales offering that resolves those needs. Relationships are formed over time through multiple buyer–seller interactions in which the seller wins the trust of the buyer. This emphasizes the importance of effective follow-up by the salesperson. As discussed in this module and illustrated in Figure 9.2, effective salesperson follow-up should include specific components designed to interact, connect, know, and relate with his or her customers.

- **Interact**—The salesperson acts to maximize the number of critical encounters with buyers in order to encourage effective dialogue and involvement between the salesperson and buyer.
- **Connect**—The salesperson maintains contact with the multiple individuals in the buying organization influencing purchase decisions and manages the various touch points the customer has in the selling organization to assure consistency in communication.
- **Know**—The salesperson coordinates and interprets the information gathered through buyer–seller contact and collaboration to develop insight regarding the buyer's changing situation, needs, and expectations.
- **Relate**—The salesperson applies relevant understanding and insight to create value-added interactions and generate relationships between the salesperson and buyer.

Salespeople have employed a variety of technology-based sales force automation tools in order to better track the increasingly complex combination of buyer–seller interactions and to manage the exchange, interpretation, and storage of diverse types of information. Among the more popular sales force automation tools are the many competing versions of PC-based software applications designed to record and manage customer contact information. Applications such as ACT!, Maximizer, and Goldmine enable salespeople to collect, file, and access comprehensive databases

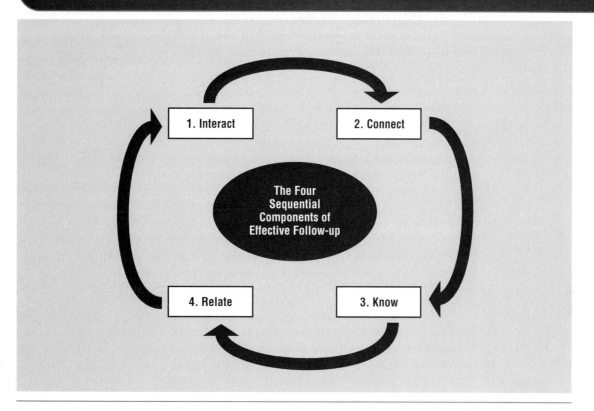

The Four Sequential Components of Effective Follow-up   **FIGURE 9.2**

Effective salesperson follow-up should include specific components designed to interact, connect, know, and relate with his or her customers.

detailing information about individual buyers and buying organizations. In addition to providing explicit details about customers and the multiple individuals influencing purchasing decisions within any given account, these databases also provide an archive of the interactions and purchasing decisions taking place over time. Salespeople using these systems have found them to be invaluable in helping them track and better service their accounts in order to assure and enhance customer satisfaction. By better understanding every transaction and buyer–seller interaction, salespeople can be more effective in communicating with each individual customer throughout the lifetime of the account.

The advent of the Internet has allowed these customer contact management tools to be used in multiorganization intranets and extranets. An intranet is an organization's dedicated and proprietary computer network offering password-controlled access to people within and outside the organization (e.g., customers and suppliers). Extranets are proprietary computer networks created by an organization for use by the organization's customers or suppliers and linked to the organization's internal systems, informational databases, and intranet.

Internet-activated and integrated with an organization's intranet and extranets, customer contact systems are transposed to full customer relationship management (CRM) systems. These systems dynamically link buyers and sellers into a rich communication network not previously possible. Salespeople and buyers have immediate, 24/7 access to one another and one another's organizations. Problems can be resolved online, routine ordering procedures can be automated, and information such as product brochures and spec sheets, inventory availability, price lists, and order status can be exchanged. Salespeople can use the Web to view everything that is relevant to any account. This can include information in the organization's databases (i.e., purchasing history, credit rating) as well as pertinent information such as news stories, stock prices, and research reports from sources outside the organization (Hoovers, Standard & Poor's, etc.).

These new customer relationship management systems enable salespeople to build and integrate multiple forms of customer information and create highly influential customer interactions that establish and reinforce long-term, profitable relationships. The benefits to salespeople learning to effectively use these advanced, integrated systems are self-evident. Every time a salesperson and buyer interact in a positive manner, the corresponding relationship is enriched. This enrichment translates to improved service levels, increased customer satisfaction, and enhanced revenues from loyal customers. For example, six months after Marriott Worldwide's salespeople began using an integrated system, sales rose by 25 percent—all of which was attributed to the use of advanced sales force automation enabling salespeople to track interactions with each customer and document each potential opportunity.[10]

ASSURE CUSTOMER SATISFACTION

Exhibit 9.2 illustrates the partnership-enhancement activities and the salesperson's responsibility that goes along with them. Specific relationship-enhancement activities vary substantially from company to company but are critical to the success of building long-term relationships. These activities include:

- Providing useful information
- Expediting orders and monitoring installation
- Training customer personnel
- Correcting billing errors
- Remembering the customer after the sale
- Resolving complaints

Traditional selling focuses on getting the order. In a sense, the sales process was over once the order was signed. The salesperson's job was to focus on getting the next order and it was left to others in the organization to deliver and install the product. However, the relational sales process shown in Figure 9.3 indicates that many activities must take place after the sale, and it is the salesperson's responsibility to oversee

---

EXHIBIT 9.2 **Relationship-Enhancement Activities**

Partnership-Enhancement Activities	Salesperson Responsibility
Provide useful information	• Relevant • Timely • High quality
Expedite orders/monitor installation	• Track orders • Inform on delays • Help with installation
Train customer personnel	• Train even when contract does not call for it
Correct billing errors	• Go over all orders • Correct problem before customer recognizes it
Remember the customer after the sale	• Set up a regular call schedule • Let customer know you'll be back
Resolve complaints	• Preferably before they happen • Ask customer how he or she wants complaint resolved

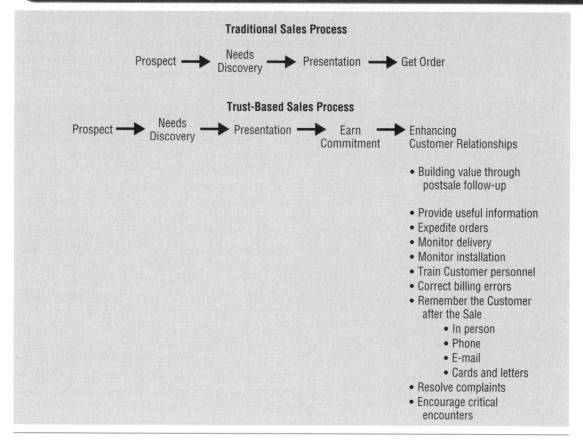

FIGURE 9.3

Traditional Versus Relational Sales Process

Traditional selling focuses on getting the order. The relational sales process indicates that many activities must take place after the sale.

and participate in all of the follow-up activities. By being actively involved during this stage, the salesperson increases the odds that a long-term relationship will develop.

Provide Useful Information

Many buyers feel neglected once they place an order with a company. They were given a lot of attention before they placed the order, but once the order had been placed, the salesperson disappeared. Once an economic relationship is established, the salesperson must continually provide timely, relevant, high-quality information to his or her customers. The job of educating the buyer never stops, and salespeople are responsible for updating customers and pointing out additional opportunities that will benefit them. By providing useful information, the salesperson is demonstrating a commitment to the buyer. The salesperson is expressing the notion that he or she is in the relationship for the long-term and that he or she values the partnership. The salesperson should not only remember to provide information to the buyer, but also to the secretaries, receptionists, department heads, and other influential members of the buyer's organization.

Several post-sale follow-up methods can be used to provide useful information. The best way to provide useful information is by a personal visit. After the sale is made, it is critical to follow-up personally and make sure that the customer is completely satisfied with all the promises that have been made (e.g., delivery, installation done properly, courteous installers). This is the only strategy that provides face-to-face communication. When a salesperson takes the time to make a well-planned personal follow-up visit, he or she indicates to the prospect that he or she really cares. A good salesperson will use the follow-up call to keep the customer informed of new developments in the industry, new products, or new applications. Providing this information may bring about future sales. When a salesperson makes a follow-up call, he or she should always have an objective for the sales call. The salesperson should be sure not to stay too long with gossip sessions or chitchat. It is the salesperson's job to add value.

An efficient option for providing useful information after a sale is by using the telephone. The telephone is a quick and efficient way to contact customers. The cell phone has provided salespeople with an opportunity to stay in touch with customers while on the road. A salesperson can easily make 7 to 10 phone calls per hour, and the cost is minimal. Although a personal note to a customer is always appropriate, the telephone has the advantage of a two-way exchange of information. The phone can be used to verify delivery, inform the customer of any changes (e.g., price, delivery schedule), and check for problems in general.

E-mail is another way to stay in touch with a customer. Most individuals and companies have e-mail addresses. The salesperson has to make this part of his or her information-gathering process. When getting pertinent company and buyer information, the salesperson should also get e-mail addresses. Some buyers will check their e-mail and respond daily; others will not check or respond for weeks. The salesperson must determine which buyers like to use e-mail and make it part of his or her follow-up process when dealing with these customers.

Finally, a handwritten thank-you card to a customer is an inexpensive and convenient form of customer follow-up. It should always be used in conjunction with the other follow-up methods. The mail can also be used to send out new promotional material, information about new products, and trade publication articles that may be of interest to customers. Periodically, a salesperson could send his or her customers a short survey that asks "How are we doing?" Exhibit 9.3 summarizes the strengths and weaknesses of follow-up methods. Checking the customers' level of satisfaction might highlight an area of customer concern for the customers that the salesperson can take care of before it becomes a major problem.

Customer preference should determine the method of communication. The salesperson should find the methods that work with individual customers and stay with them. "Professional Selling in the 21st Century: Adding Value through Follow-up" gives one salesperson's opinion on the importance of their sales process and the follow-up needed for success.

EXHIBIT 9.3   **Methods to Provide Useful Information**

Method	Strength	Weakness
1. Personal call	Best for interactive face-to-face communication; view body language	Most time-consuming Most expensive Customers won't always see salesperson
2. Telephone	Can make 7–10 calls per hour Cell phones allow call to be made from anywhere Inexpensive Immediate feedback	May interrupt your customers Can't evaluate facial expressions
3. Mail	One more touch that lets the customers know you are thinking about them	Customers get a lot of mail Customer may not see it if secretary opens mail and tosses One-way communication
4. E-mail	Easy to get many touches Inexpensive Not time-consuming	Customer may not read e-mail everyday One-way communication

PROFESSIONAL SELLING IN THE 21ST CENTURY

Adding Value through Follow-Up

Jim Micklos is an account executive with Motivation Excellence Inc. (MEI), which develops custom performance challenges. Although MEI's programs include "hard goods" (communication devices, information management and participant rewards such as brand name merchandise and deluxe group travel), what MEI has to *sell* is their ability to modify the behavior of a specific audience in a way that will benefit the client—and to do it reliably, predictably, and cost effectively. The overall product they offer is a systematic blend of strategic planning, creativity, thought leadership, operational expertise, and unparalleled responsive service, all of which must be conclusively proven before a sale is made.

A sale typically takes several months (even years) and is based on MEI's proven sales process, which includes the following definable steps: (1) Preliminary research to identify the general nature of the prospect, their industry, and their potential needs. (2) An initial presentation (always by appointment) including MEI's understanding of the client, the services and values MEI offers, and a potential fit between two companies. (3) Consultative research with the client to define their specific needs, analyze the relevant data, and identify the appropriate components for the solution. This can involve analysis of past performance data, field research, joint brainstorming sessions with the client (at the clients' offices as well as at MEI's offices), meetings with other MEI clients, and/or a variety of other processes. (4) Detailed presentations (always by appointment) of MEI's findings (for confirmation by both parties of what MEI discovered), the recommended solution, and the financial rationale, which is almost always based on measurable, predictable ROI. (5) Discussion and refinement of the recommendations until the client is comfortable with all aspects of the program.

In this process, building relationships and developing solutions go hand in hand. The resulting program recommendation is a fact-based, measurable, and collaborative solution that almost sells itself. The "close," in the usual sense, becomes nothing more than an agreement that the client's needs and concerns have been addressed and that the potential benefits (financial and other) of the program far exceed any risks.

After the sale, MEI works to further cement the relationship by exceeding the expectations created during the initial sales process. They devote considerable effort to growing the client relationship by adding value outside of immediate program needs. Examples include introducing the client's management to other compatible suppliers or clients, providing sales leads for the client organization obtained through MEI's network of business contacts, and bringing training, business process, and technology solutions that will improve the client's business in areas where MEI does not provide services.

Ultimately, establishing a joint vision with the client is the key to MEI's sales process. The creation of that vision is based on research and analysis performed before, during, and after the sales process. It is formed through a relationship nurtured by careful listening and probing to identify questions and concerns. Lastly, it is finalized and perpetuated with quick, sound responses—and follow-through to ensure the responses are sufficient and effective.

Expedite Orders and Monitor Installation

Generally, salespeople will set estimates on product delivery times. The salesperson must work to prevent a delay in delivery. The salesperson's job is to track the order status and inform the customers when there are delays. It is unpleasant to inform a buyer of a delay, but the information allows buyers to work around the inconvenience and plan accordingly. Waiting until the delivery date to announce a delay is inconsiderate and hurts the trust built between the salesperson and buyer.

Many problems with shipping and the delivery of an order are out of the salesperson's control. However, today's sophisticated tracking systems allow salespeople to track orders and find out what is causing the delay. The salesperson must keep the customer up-to-date on the delivery status and any possible delays.

Monitoring order processing and after-sale activities is critical to enhancing the relationship with a customer. Customers often have done a poor job of forecasting and may expect their salesperson to bring their emergency to a happy conclusion.

The Importance of Follow-up and Adding Value with Existing Customers

Kelly Osterling, a sales representative for R.R. Donnelly, knows that personalized service is the best way to stay in touch with her customers. She states,

I work hard at understanding how my customers want to communicate with me. Some respond well to e-mail, others in person, and some by phone. I have a few customers that only want to hear from me by fax. I have learned to use technology as a bridge to my customers and not as a wall.

I essentially have e-mail addresses and fax numbers for all of my customers. When we have

new product introductions, I attempt to see all of my customers in person. I can then follow-up with other information such as price changes and delivery dates through e-mail and voice mail.

My customers know I check my e-mails daily, and they can send me questions, requests, and complaints. I must follow-up immediately. There are times when my customers can't see me or take my phone calls; by knowing how they prefer their information delivered, I can use other forms of communication (e-mail, voice mail, and fax) to respond to them. I want my customers to know I care.

Although it is not always possible to speed up orders, the salesperson should investigate and attempt to do everything in his or her power to help the customers. If the buyer sees concern on the salesperson's part and knows that the salesperson is attempting to help the buyer, then the relationship will be strengthened, even if the order cannot be pushed through as quickly as the buyer had hoped.

Depending on the industry, salespeople generally do not help with installation. Nevertheless, some salespeople believe that it is in their best interest to supervise the installation process and to be available when customers have questions. Typically, installers do not have the same relationship with the customer and may not have the type of personality to deal with difficult situations. The salesperson can act as the buffer between the installation team and the customers. In "Professional Selling in the 21st Century: The Importance of Follow-up and Adding Value with Existing Customers," Kelly Osterling of Wallace describes how she accomplishes this.

Training Customer Personnel

Companies are always looking for ways to gain a competitive advantage. Once the order is placed, traditional salespeople are happy to get their commission or bonus and move on to their next conquest. Relationship managers understand the real work begins once the order is signed. Training customer personnel may or may not be included in the price terms of the agreement. Salespeople may use this to gain the competitive edge they need. For example, instead of only training one person as stated in the sales terms, the salesperson gladly trains three people for the same price. Adding value should always be a priority with any salesperson.

When the product is technical, customer training may require the assistance of the company trainer or engineer. The salesperson still has a key role as he or she knows the customer best and should serve as the facilitator to ensure that all of the parties have been properly introduced and started off in a positive manner. The salesperson should schedule the training sessions as conveniently as possible for the customer. Customer education is an integral part of the marketing strategy of Ontario Systems Corporation, a collections software company. What separates Ontario from its competitors is its ability to provide timely training and education for all its customers. Ontario knows service after the sale is crucial and that is why it provides an 800 telephone number for 24-hour service. Each year, Ontario strengthens its relationship with customers by providing one week of training, seminars, and goodwill at their home office. Ontario understands the importance of the team approach to providing outstanding customer service.

Correct Billing Errors

Billing errors could turn into customer complaints if not found in a timely fashion and corrected. A salesperson should go over all orders and billing records to ensure proper billing has been sent to the customer. A customer will know the salesperson has his or her best interests in mind if the salesperson corrects problems without being prompted by the customer.

Remember the Customer after the Sale

Customer follow-up methods should be used to express appreciation for the purchase and to further develop the relationship after the sale. Poor service and lack of follow-up are consistently cited by customers as the primary reasons that buyers stopped buying. In one Wallace branch office, there is a saying that hangs above the door that states "Remember the Customer between Calls." Personal visits should be the primary method to follow-up after the sale. It is the most costly but also the most effective. This method allows face-to-face, two-way communication. The customer's body language can also be observed.

The telephone can also be used to follow-up a sale. Most salespeople send a written follow-up thanking the customer for his or her business. The telephone can then be used to reinforce the written message. The customer can give verbal feedback, and the salesperson can ask questions and use probing techniques that cannot be used with written correspondence. It is important not to forget the customer after the sale.

Resolve Complaints and Encourage Critical Encounters

Complaints will never be completely eliminated by any company. Nevertheless, it is every company's hope that it can reduce the frequency of complaints. Complaints typically arise because the product did not live up to the buyer's expectations. Buyers complain for any number of reasons: (1) late delivery, (2) wrong order sent (e.g., too many, too few), (3) product performs poorly, or (4) nobody at the salesperson's company takes the buyer's problems seriously. See Exhibit 9.4 for a more comprehensive list of complaints.

Many times, the complaint is not the fault of the salesperson (e.g., late delivery, wrong order, product performs poorly). "An Ethical Dilemma" demonstrates a typically difficult complaint a salesperson has to overcome. However, this is not a concern to the buyer as they expect the salesperson to resolve it. Traditional salespeople have been known to pass the blame when complaints arise. A salesperson

---

Typical Customer Complaints   EXHIBIT 9.4

1. Late delivery
2. Damaged merchandise
3. Invoice errors
4. Out of stock—back orders
5. Shipped incorrect product
6. Shipped incorrect order size
7. Service department unresponsive
8. Product does not live up to expectations
9. Customer not informed of new developments
10. Customer's problems not taken seriously
11. Improper installation
12. Need more training
13. Price increase—no notice
14. Can't find the salesperson when needed

Sally Myers of Techno Computers has sold five personal computers to a small firm in her hometown. She secured the order by guaranteeing she could meet the delivery date of two weeks. Myers called her home office and was given the green light to sign the order with the delivery conditions. She was very excited with her order until the two-week delivery deadline had passed, and her home office needed two more weeks before the PCs could be shipped. Myers' customer was furious. What would you do if you were Myers? What else could she have done when talking to her home office about delivery dates?

would be better off to tackle the complaint by accepting responsibility and promptly fixing the problem. Salespeople get into trouble by overpromising what their product can do, being overly optimistic about delivery dates, and not being attentive to their customers when they do complain. Many complaints can be avoided by giving the customers a reasonable expectation of what the product can do for them.

If periodic meetings are taking place between the buyer and seller after the sale, then in all probability, most of the important issues are being discussed. "An Ethical Dilemma" discusses one manager's problems in getting his salespeople to follow-up after the orders are signed. Salespeople must ask their buyers to be candid with them and encourage the buyer to discuss tough issues (i.e., late deliveries, damaged products), especially in areas where the salesperson's organization is providing less than satisfactory performance. Some buyers will not complain because they feel it will not do any good. Others will not complain because they feel that the salesperson should be in tune with their problems or concerns and recognize these problems on their own. If a salesperson encourages **critical encounters** and acts accordingly to diffuse a situation where the buyer's expectations have not been met, then this will help with future meetings and sessions where critical encounters are discussed. If the salesperson does not act on these issues, then future meetings with the buyer will not uncover problem areas because the buyer is convinced nothing will be done to solve them.

Some salespeople tell the customer what he or she wants to hear to get the order and cannot deliver on promises made. Complaints can be avoided by being truthful when presenting a product's capabilities. Providing sales support can eliminate problems with late deliveries, wrong orders being sent, and the feeling that the salesperson does not care about the customer's complaints. The following section provides an outline on how to handle customer complaints.

Jim Habansky asked his sales force to set aside two to four hours per week to be out making calls on existing customers. He implemented this program because he noticed that his sales force was good at securing orders, but an unusually high number (30 percent) of their customers were not renewing their first orders. The first month of the program has gone by, and Habansky can tell his staff that has not complied with his request. He reviewed the call reports and doubted anyone has spent more than five minutes per day making follow-up calls. He suspects his company's compensation program of straight commission may have something to do with his problem. What would you do if you were Habansky? If he is correct about the compensation program being the problem, can you blame his sales force?

A Procedure to Handle Complaints

Customer complaints must be handled quickly and with great sensitivity. Customers do not care about all of the problems the company is experiencing and the reasons why the salesperson is providing less-than-stellar customer service. The reason that relationship selling is such a critical part of retaining customers is because the salesperson must have an open communication line with the customer and encourage feedback, either positive or negative. Most customers will not complain. The salesperson must have built the relationship to the point where buyers will not hesitate to speak their mind if they are unhappy with the service. If the customer does not complain, then the salesperson does not know what it is that he or she needs to fix.

One study has indicated that, if a company fails to deal with customers and prospects who complain, those customers will tell on average, up to 10 people, about their bad experience. Satisfied customers, on the other hand, tell only four or five others about their positive experiences. The research also showed that for every dissatisfied customer who complains an estimated 50 more will stop buying the product.[11]

Another study showed that a company has a 40 percent chance of winning back upset customers—which indicates that the effort to make amends is worth it.[12] A general procedure for handling customer complaints follows.

Build the Relationship to the Point That Your Customers are Comfortable Complaining

Salespeople have been overheard saying to their customers, "If I had only known that you were unhappy about our service, I could have fixed it." The buyer typically responds, "Well, I gave you enough signals, why weren't you more perceptive to the problems I was having when doing business with you?" The buyer and salesperson must work together to develop a trust so that whenever something comes up, either person feels comfortable about speaking up. Open communication channels are a must for good customer service. Companies today cannot be afraid to ask their clients, "How are we doing?"[13] Some companies are conducting 30-, 60-, and 90-day customer satisfaction follow-up visits after the sale. Beyond that, the salespeople maintain quarterly follow-ups, even if only by phone! This at least tells the customer, "We are interested in you as a company and we want to service your account well."

Listen Carefully and Get the Whole Story

The salesperson must listen carefully to what is being said and what is not being said. Good salespeople let the customer know that they are happy the complaint has been brought to their attention. Chances are that the customer will not complain again if he or she is made to feel uncomfortable with the initial complaint. The salesperson must be careful not to interrupt early in the discussion. The customer must be allowed to vent his or her frustration. Once the customer stops complaining, the salesperson may have to probe and ask follow-up questions to get the whole story. For instance, the buyer may not have told the salesperson to whom he or she talked to at the salesperson's company about the problem, and this information may be helpful to the salesperson in solving the complaint. This is a good time to show empathy. The salesperson should apologize for any inconvenience and let the buyer know that he or she is happy that the problem was brought up. The salesperson must make the buyer aware that he or she is anxious to resolve the problem and keep the buyer as a satisfied client.

Ask Customers How They Would Like Their Complaint Resolved

Many salespeople attempt to solve the complaint without understanding what the customer wants them to do. For example, a salesperson may reason that the last customer wanted a 20 percent discount to make things better. "Thus, I will offer this unhappy buyer the same thing." The salesperson may be surprised to find out the buyer wanted something totally different to resolve the problem. The salesperson cannot be afraid to ask the customer what it will take to make him or her happy. A salesperson could say something like, "Theresa, we value you and your company's business. I am sorry for the inconvenience we caused you. Can you, please, tell me what we can do to solve this problem and keep you as a satisfied customer?" Then, the salesperson must listen carefully. The buyer may simply want an apology. He or she may want a discount; still other buyers might ask for another product to be substituted until the regular shipment arrives. Salespeople typically find that the customer is not demanding as much as they thought he or she might have been, considering the circumstances of the complaint. The solution should center on what the customer wants and not what the salesperson thinks is appropriate.

Gain Agreement on a Solution

Once the salesperson hears what the customer wants, they must agree on a solution. Sometimes, the salesperson can do exactly what the customer asks. Other times, the buyer may be asking for an unrealistic solution. The salesperson's focus should always be on trying to do exactly what the customer wants. When that is not possible, the salesperson's message should concentrate on what he or she can do for the customer and then do it in a timely manner.[14] The conversation might sound like, "Jim, I'm sorry for the inconvenience we caused you. Thanks for your suggestions on what we need to do to resolve the problem. Here are a couple of things we can do—which of these will work better for you . . . ?" The salesperson is telling the buyer that he or she cannot do exactly what the buyer asked, but the salesperson can do the following. Good salespeople always focus on the positive.

Take Action—Educate the Customer

Once an agreement is reached, the salesperson must take action and solve the customer complaint in a timely fashion. The communication lines must be kept open to the customer (e.g., letting him or her know when the repair people will be arriving). When time permits, the repair work should be monitored and the customer should be kept up-to-date on the progress.

   If customers have unrealistic expectations of the services provided, then this would be a good time to educate the customers so that they have realistic expectations of the services the company will provide. Some salespeople promise the moon to secure an order, and then let the customer down when the product does not perform up to expectations. This is not the way to develop a trusting relationship.

Follow-through on All Promises—Add Value

Whatever promises are made, good salespeople must make sure that they are kept, and this is a good time to go beyond what has been promised. Those salespeople who over-deliver what is promised will truly impress their customers and build stronger relationships faster than their competitors.[15] Adding value to what the buyer expects helps ensure repeat business down the road. Exhibit 9.5 summarizes the procedures to handle complaints.

EXHIBIT 9.5   General Procedures for Handling Complaints

1. Build relationship to the point that the customer is comfortable complaining.
2. Listen carefully and get the whole story.
3. Ask the customer what he or she would like you to do.
4. Gain agreement on a solution. Tell them what you can do; don't focus on what you can't do.
5. Take action; educate the customer so he or she has realistic expectations.
6. Follow-through on all promises. Add value.

MAINTAIN OPEN, TWO-WAY COMMUNICATION

Early in the selling process, the salesperson determines the specific needs of the buyer so that a good match can be made between the product's attributes and the needs of the buyer. This is done through effective questioning and listening with the buyer. Once the sale is made, the salesperson must continue to maintain open, two-way communication with the buyer. Periodic meetings with the buyer allow for this feedback. Collaborative discussion becomes the most effective tool when dealing with customers and their problems. If the customer believes the salesperson is sincere, listens carefully, and responds accordingly to his or her concerns, then an already trusting relationship will become stronger.

EXPAND COLLABORATIVE INVOLVEMENT

A salesperson's goal is to work with customers who have entered into a strategic alliance with the salesperson's firm. This is done by building trust over a long period of time. The salesperson should always be looking for ways to take the relationship to a higher level and create a stronger bond. One way to accomplish this goal is to expand the collaborative involvement between the buyer's and salesperson's organizations. The salesperson may take a group of engineers along on a sales call and introduce them to the buyer's engineers. It may be possible for the engineers to work together to enhance the product offering. Customers often know the strengths and weaknesses of the product they use and can provide some insight into how improvements can be made.

Another example of a company's attempt to expand **collaborative involvement** is to host a week-long series of seminars, training sessions, and social engagements with its customers to expand the relationship. Brainstorming sessions with customers demonstrate a willingness to listen, show that the company cares, and often result in better ways to serve customers. Anytime the salesperson can involve additional personnel from the buyer's company during relationship building, chances are that the relationship will become stronger.

WORK TO ADD VALUE AND ENHANCE MUTUAL OPPORTUNITIES

To build mutually satisfying relationships between buyers and sellers, professional salespeople must work toward adding value and enhancing mutual opportunities for the customer. This can be done by reducing risk through repeated displays of the seller's ability to serve the customer. By demonstrating the willingness to serve the customer, the seller reduces the buyer's risk—both real and perceived. A good relationship is one that has few, if any, unpleasant surprises.

Salespeople must also establish high standards and expectations. Many relationships fail due to unmet expectations. The higher the customer's expectations, the better, provided the seller can meet or exceed those expectations. Salespeople should ensure that the customer's expectations are reasonable, and continually work to improve performance.

Finally, salespeople must monitor and take action to improve customer satisfaction. Salespeople must never let up on this. Doing so only invites competitor challenges. A good salesperson must always look for cracks in the relationship and patch them before insurmountable problems occur. All relationships require work and taking a good customer for granted is foolish. It should be remembered that the salesperson must continually add value to the relationship or he or she will run the risk of losing the customer.

Provide Quality Customer Service

Every salesperson is looking for a competitive edge to help him or her differentiate his or her products in the eyes of customers. Many of the products that a salesperson sells have essentially the same features and benefits as the competitors. Chris Crabtree of Lanier once said, "A copier is a copier, is a copier. There is just no difference between what I have to offer and my competitors. We all charge about the same price. In fact, I can match any price my competitor puts on the table. That leaves only one attribute for me to differentiate on—service."

More and more companies are turning to service quality as a strategy to acquire and maintain customers. A salesperson must be able to convince a customer that service is important, demonstrate service quality, and then maintain a high level of service over an extended period of time.

The problem is that every salesperson claims to provide outstanding service. The goal today is not to meet customer expectations but to exceed them. Salespeople will rarely be given a second chance to prove that they provide outstanding service if they do not get it right the first time. A sign in a small-town business reads,

> Service is advertised...
> Service is talked about...
> But the only time service really counts...
> Is when it is delivered...
> And we promise your experience with us will be outstanding.

Customers do not care about slogans and service claims until something happens to them. This is called a moment of truth. Each salesperson experiences daily moments of truth—brief moments that occur whenever a customer comes into contact with a salesperson, the training staff, installers, field engineers, or service personnel and has an opportunity to form an impression. These moments of truth are when the customer will determine if promises are being kept by the sales organization, and whether the salesperson truly cares about the customer or is simply an order getter!

There are four benefits of service enthusiasm that allow the sales organization to gain an advantage over its competitors.

First, reputation is an important part of any organization's ability to attract and keep new customers. Reputation allows a salesperson to distinguish himself or herself from the competition. A solid reputation tells customers that you care and will help a salesperson build a loyal relationship in his or her market. Reputations take a long time to establish and only one negative event to destroy.

Second, by providing good customer service the first time, an organization makes the profit that it needs to stay in business. Whenever mistakes are made (e.g., wrong order, short order delivered), service personnel have to sort out the problem and fix it. The result could lead to a lost customer. In any event, it does not take long to go into the red when people have to be added to fix problems. Efficient operations, cost savings, and doing things right the first time increase the chances for increased profits.

The third benefit of service enthusiasm is convenience. It is critically important to put the customer's convenience first. A salesperson must make it easy for his or her customers to discuss problems or complaints. Most customers are uncomfortable complaining. Customers generally will not complain if the salesperson does not encourage complaint behavior. The most dangerous customer to any business is a silent complainer. If a salesperson is unaware of a problem, it cannot be resolved. It is also dangerous if other customers hear this customer bad-mouthing the salesperson. It may influence other customers in how they feel about the salesperson.

Salespeople must design user-friendly feedback systems. Periodically inquiring about customer satisfaction can greatly enhance a customer's feelings toward a salesperson and his or her organization.

Ontario Systems (http://www.ontariosystems.com) provides a Client Resource Center as one of its links on its Web site. Clients can easily get up-to-date information on product support, training, industry links, and discussion lists. Ontario Systems is always looking for ways to provide more services to their clients.

Finally, service enthusiasm goes hand in hand with spirit. A customer can be turned onto an organization by meeting many caring "can-do" people. The spirit must start with an enthusiastic, service-minded corporate culture. The salesperson, sales manager, field engineer, installer, and CSR (customer service representative) must all have the same service enthusiasm to generate the benefits of service enthusiasm. That is why the salesperson must monitor and coordinate all the people who have access to the account to ensure that good customer service is taking place.

The most difficult aspect of customer service is the potential for inconsistency. For instance, field engineer A, who has a great understanding of service enthusiasm, may be called into an account early in the week. The customer is very impressed. Three weeks later, the customer calls for help again. Field engineer A is out on another account, and field engineer B, who has little or no service skills, is sent out on the next call. Field engineer B is good at fixing the problem but has a hard time relating to customers; in fact, he is downright cold! As a result of this unevenness, the customer's level of satisfaction decreases.

The inconsistency of customer service is a problem for every sales organization. By understanding the benefits of service enthusiasm and the rewards of proper spirit, the sales organization can ensure consistency and exceed customer expectations.

Customer Expectations

A salesperson must meet the needs of his or her customer. At a minimum, customers expect a warm and friendly salesperson. Buyers have enough things going on during their day that it would not be a plus to have to deal with a surly salesperson. Warmth and friendliness are the building blocks of a successful relationship.

Reliability is another attribute that buyers look for in choosing a salesperson with whom to do business. Customers must have the confidence that the expected service will be delivered accurately, consistently, and dependably. Helpfulness and assistance are two more variables that buyers expect when working with a salesperson. Will the customer be able to find his or her salesperson when he or she needs to do so? Can the salesperson provide the speed and promptness needed by the customer? The salesperson can solve this issue by developing a regular call routine so that the customer knows when to expect the salesperson. Other customer expectations include follow-through as promised; empathy; and resolution of complaints, mistakes, or defects. The customer must know that if anything goes wrong, the salesperson will move in quickly and solve the problem. Exhibit 9.6 summarizes what customers expect from their salesperson.

Develop a Service Strategy

Salespeople can calculate the lifetime value of one of their customers. Hershey Foods Corporation knows exactly how much candy it has sold at the Wal-Mart in Muncie, Indiana. It is easy for Hershey to calculate the loss if any customer decides to replace them. It is imperative for Hershey to provide the service level that each of its customers demands. Less than quality service can lead to the loss of a customer.

Developing a **service strategy** allows a salesperson to plan his or her actions for each customer. A service strategy asks a salesperson to identify his or her business

Customer Expectations of Salespeople   **EXHIBIT 9.6**

1. Warmth and friendliness
2. Reliability
3. Helpfulness/assistance
4. Speed or promptness
5. Assurance
6. Accuracy
7. Follow-through (as promised)
8. Empathy
9. Resolution of complaints, mistakes, or defects
10. Tangibles

EXHIBIT 9.7   Checklist for Developing a Service Strategy

Questions a salesperson must ask when developing a service strategy:

- What is our business?
- Who are our customers?
- What do our customers want and what is important to them?
- How are our customers' needs and perceptions changing?
- How are social, economic, and political factors affecting current and future customer needs and our ability to respond to them? How are competitors responding to these factors?
- How do customers rate us in terms of their expectations?
- What are we best known for?
- What do we do best?
- What can we do better?
- How can we position ourselves in the market to differentiate our services?

and customers and what the customers want and what is important to them. The salesperson also has to determine how his or her customers' needs and perceptions are changing. The salesperson cannot be afraid to ask how the customers rate him or her in terms of their expectations. What does the salesperson's company do best and what can the organization do better? The salesperson, ultimately, must determine how to position his or her company in the market to differentiate its products and services. All this must be done while directing efforts against the competitors. Exhibit 9.7 is an example of a checklist for developing a service strategy.

Customer Service Dimensions

The most important customer service dimension is **communication**. Most problems arise because the customer was not informed of a change in plans (e.g., late delivery, price increase). Salespeople are extremely busy and many times do not have the time to communicate with all their customers. Communication tools such as e-mail can be used to quickly do mass communication to inform customers of these changes. Over time, the telephone and personal visits can be used to confirm that the customers are aware of the changes.

Another customer service dimension is **resilience**. Resilience is the ability of a salesperson to get knocked down several times a day by a customer's verbal assault (i.e., complaint) and get right back up with a smile and ask for more. A salesperson cannot lose his or her cool just because a customer does. A tired salesperson must treat late-afternoon, difficult customers the same way that he or she would treat an early-morning dilemma while he or she was fresh. They must both be treated well.

Finally, the most important customer service dimension is the **motivation** of a salesperson to service his or her customers. Salespeople must find time each day to deal with difficult customers and problems that exist. Ignoring these activities will not make them go away. Working diligently on behalf of the customer indicates to him or her that the salesperson truly cares about the partnership. If a salesperson has a complaint from a customer and gladly fixes it, the customer becomes a more committed customer.

SUMMARY

1. **Explain how to follow-up to assess customer satisfaction.** Salespeople cannot be afraid to ask their customers, "How are we doing?" Periodic follow-up is critical to long-term sales success. New customers generally feel special because they

have received a lot of attention from the salesperson. Older customers may feel neglected because the sales rep has many new customers and cannot be as attentive as he or she was previously. Routine follow-up to assess "How are we doing?" can go a long way in letting a customer know that the salesperson cares and is willing to make sure that he or she is satisfied.

2. **Explain how to harness technology to enhance follow-up and buyer–seller relationships.** Effective salesperson follow-up should include specific components designed to interact, connect, know, and relate with their customers.

   - *Interact*—The salesperson acts to maximize the number of critical encounters with buyers in order to encourage effective dialogue and involvement between the salesperson and buyer.

   - *Connect*—The salesperson maintains contact with the multiple individuals in the buying organization influencing purchase decisions and manages the various touch points the customer has in the selling organization to assure consistency in communication.

   - *Know*—The salesperson coordinates and interprets the information gathered through buyer–seller contact and collaboration to develop insight regarding the buyer's changing situation, needs, and expectations.

   - *Relate*—The salesperson applies relevant understanding and insight to create value-added interactions and generate relationships between the salesperson and buyer.

   Salespeople have employed a variety of technology-based sales force automation tools in order to better track the increasingly complex combination of buyer–seller interactions and to manage the exchange, interpretation, and storage of diverse types of information. Among the more popular sales force automation tools are the many competing versions of PC-based software applications designed to record and manage customer contact information. Applications such as ACT!, Maximizer, and Goldmine enable salespeople to collect, file, and access comprehensive databases detailing information about individual buyers and buying organizations.

3. **Discuss how to take action to assure customer satisfaction.** Salespeople must follow up on specific relationship-enhancement activities such as:

   (a) Providing useful information to their customers
   (b) Expediting orders and monitoring a successful installation
   (c) Training customer personnel
   (d) Correcting billing errors
   (e) Remembering the customer after the sale
   (f) Resolving complaints in a timely manner

4. **Discuss how to maintain open, two-way communication.** Periodic meetings with the buyer allow for feedback. Listening becomes the most effective tool when dealing with customers and their problems. The salesperson must encourage the buyer to be candid about his or her concerns and problems and to let the salesperson know when his or her needs are not being met. If the customer believes that the salesperson is sincere, listens carefully, and responds accordingly to his or her concerns, then a trusting buyer–seller relationship can be built even stronger.

5. **Explain how to resolve complaints and encourage critical encounters.** If periodic meetings are taking place after the sale between the buyer and seller, then in all probability most of the important issues are being discussed. If an agenda is planned for a meeting, then tough issues must be placed on it and not ignored. The buyer must be encouraged to discuss service areas that are not being met periodically. Otherwise, the salesperson will not know what needs to be fixed.

6. **Discuss how to expand collaborative involvement.** The easiest way to expand collaborative involvement is to get more people involved in the relationship from both the buyer's and seller's firms.

7. **Explain how to add value and enhance mutual opportunities.** The salesperson can enhance mutual opportunities by reducing risk for the buyer by repeated displays of outstanding customer service. The salesperson can also demonstrate a willingness to serve the customer over extended periods of time. The buyer needs to experience a willingness on the seller's part to go to bat for the buyer when things get tough.

UNDERSTANDING PROFESSIONAL SELLING TERMS

building goodwill	critical encounters
adding value	collaborative involvement
interact	service strategy
connect	communication
know	resilience
relate	motivation

DEVELOPING PROFESSIONAL SELLING KNOWLEDGE

1. How can a salesperson convert new customers into highly committed customers for life?

2. Why should a salesperson follow-up to assess customer satisfaction?

3. Explain why relationship-enhancement activities are important.

4. What does a salesperson hope to accomplish by providing his or her customers with useful information after the sale?

5. Most salespeople are not trained in how to install their products. Why then should a good salesperson make it a point to oversee the installation process?

6. Why is it important for a salesperson to ask a buyer what he or she wants the salesperson to do when resolving a complaint?

7. Why should a salesperson encourage his or her customers to complain? Isn't this just asking for trouble?

8. Why is it important for a salesperson to gain agreement on a solution when dealing with a customer complaint?

9. Why do many salespeople seem to ignore after-sale activities that enhance the relationship?

10. Why is it important for a salesperson to establish expectations with a new customer?

BUILDING PROFESSIONAL SELLING SKILLS

ROLE PLAY

1. **Situation:**   Read The Ethical Dilemma on page 246.

   Characters: Sally Myers, sales representative; customer

   Scene 1:   *Location*—Customer's office.
   Action—Myers stops in to see the customer.

   Role play Myers explaining to the customer that she will be delivering the order two weeks late.

Scene 2:   *Location*—Customer's office.
                 Action—Myers stops in to monitor the installation of the two week late delivery.

Role play how Myers might go about handling this difficult situation with the customer.

Upon completion of the role plays, address the following questions:

1a. Some things are out of the control of the salesperson. How should a salesperson handle these things?

1b. Should Myers let the customer know she is not to blame? Her company did sign off on the delivery conditions.

2. **Situation:**   Read the Ethical Dilemma on page 246.

   Characters: Jim Habansky, sales manager; sales representative from his staff; sales staff

   Scene 1:   *Location*—Habansky's office.
                 Action—Habansky asks one of his salespeople to stop by for a short conference.

ROLE PLAY

Role play a conversation between Habansky and one of his representatives. Habansky starts off by saying that he is not happy with the sales representative's follow-up with existing customers.

Scene 2:   *Location*—Large conference room. *Action*—Jim has his entire sales force in the conference room (5 to 10 sales representatives).

Role play a conversation between Habansky and his salespeople. Habansky starts off by saying that he is less than happy with their follow-up calls to existing customers.

Upon completion of the role plays, address the following questions:

2a. Does Habansky have any leverage to get his sales force to make follow-up calls on existing customers if the compensation program is not changed?

2b. Even with the straight commission compensation program in place, does Habansky have any options available to get the sales force in the field to call on existing customers?

3. This exercise explores potential points of added-value differentiation by comparing various facets of the subject company's market offering with those of a principal competitor. Find a salesperson who is willing to be interviewed. After reviewing the *Customer Benefits Worksheet* and *Points for Discussion* following this introduction, interview that salesperson to determine how his or her market offering (including the activities of the salesperson) compares with that of a specific competitor. Determine where the salesperson's offering has an advantage over the competition that results in added customer value. Based on your interview, complete the following *Customer Benefits Worksheet* and *Points for Discussion* pages.

Student Name:_____   Date:_____

Name of Salesperson Interviewed:

Name of Salesperson's Company:_____

Type of Product:

Customer Benefits Worksheet

Source of Benefit	Benefits of Company's Offering	Benefits of Competitor's Offering
The Product		
Services		
The Company		
The Salesperson		

Points for Discussion

a. Describe this salesperson's relationship-marketing role in creating added customer value. What does the salesperson do that adds value for the customer?

_____
_____
_____
_____
_____
_____
_____
_____

b. What additional behaviors or activities, other than those already being performed, could the salesperson undertake that might further increase customer value?

_____
_____
_____
_____
_____
_____
_____
_____

c. Why have these behaviors or services not been implemented?

_____
_____
_____
_____
_____
_____
_____
_____

4. _Diary of Sales/Service Encounters_

Part A:

Keeping a Diary of Sales Encounters

Using the following preformatted worksheets, keep a sales/service diary for one month. Include all your encounters with salespeople, recording (1) the date, (2) where the sales encounter happened, (3) a factual description of what happened (i.e., the salesperson's attitude, behaviors, and so forth), (4) your reactions and attitudes (i.e., your perceptions, feelings, future intentions), and (5) a description of whether the salesperson provided or offered any follow-up activities to enhance the relationship.

Part B:

Written Report with Conclusion/Implications

At the end of one month, select two sales encounters from those in your diary—one encounter that you rated from good to outstanding and one that you rated from poor to terrible. Write a short report comparing the two encounters. Summarize each encounter, assess what went wrong as well as what went right, and develop conclusions and implications for salespeople relevant to relationship selling.

Part C:
Oral Presentation and Discussion

Based on your written report, prepare and deliver an oral presentation to the class. This oral presentation should be informative and emphasize your conclusions and implications for relationship selling.

Student Name: **Date:**

Diary of Sales/Service Encounters

Encounter Date	Where	What Happened/Behaviors	Your Reactions/ Attitudes
1.			
2.			
3.			
4.			
5.			
6.			
7.			
8.			
9.			
10.			
11.			
12.			

5. Go to the Internet and type in **http://www.marketingapprentice.com**. Go to Marketing Basics. On the right-hand side under "Promotion Tips" you will find "Repeat Sales with Follow-up." Click on "Repeat Sales with Follow-up." Read the article "Three Ways to Get Repeat Sales with Follow-up Marketing." Can you think of other ways a salesperson might enhance his or her follow-up activities? Write a memo to your boss discussing these activities.

6. Go to **http://www.yahoo.com** or any other search engine. Type in "sales, follow-up after the sale." What did you find? Did you find any Web sites that offer any new activities that you did not recommend in Exercise 1? Make a list of these Web sites for future reference.

MAKING PROFESSIONAL SELLING DECISIONS

Case 9.1: The Reluctant Sales Force
Background
Gary Calling, sales manager for a large engineering firm, cannot get his salespeople into the field. He summarized his problems as follows:

1. Lack of outgoing calls or e-mails to prospects and customers.
2. Lack of planning on a daily basis.
3. No use of a follow-up program to generate additional customer contacts.
4. Lack of overall planning strategy for a particular customer or group of customers.
5. Reactive sales force instead of proactive.

Current Situation
He thinks his problem is that his staff is technical in nature and wants to be thought of as experts, not salespeople. He goes on to say that his staff does great when the customers call them but do not plan for outside sales opportunities. His reps say that they are too busy with everything else to make outside calls.

Calling had the following conversation with his top salesperson, Ted (who happens to be his brother).

Calling: Ted, have you had any luck making new contacts?

Ted: Not really.

Calling: What's the problem?

Ted: What do you mean, man—what's the problem? I spend all day on the phone talking to our existing customers. They need me. I can't be out of the office all day. My customers would never be able to find me.

Calling: I'm not talking about being out of the office all day. I need you to spend one day per week following up on existing customers to build goodwill and another half-day per week looking for new business.

Ted: That sounds good, but I don't see how I can get that done. I am already overloaded.

Questions
1. What would you do if you were Calling?
2. Can you force your sales force out of the building?

Situation:	Read Case 9.1
Characters:	Calling, sales manager; Ted, salesperson
Scene 1:	*Location*—Calling's office. *Action*—Continuation of Calling

ROLE PLAY

and Ted's conversation. Ted just replied "I am already overloaded." Role play Calling's response to Ted and Ted's feedback.

Scene 2: *Location*—Conference room. *Action*—Calling and the rest of the sales force are having a meeting (3 to 5 salespeople). Role play Calling going over points 1 through 5 in the case with the sales force.

Upon completion of the role plays, address the following question:

What are the pros and cons of addressing each sales representative individually or having all of them in for a sales meeting?

Case 9.2: Whatever It Takes to Get the Order
Background
Roberta Thomas has seen the good life. Her company is paying high bonuses to bring in new customers. Thomas has earned more than $100,000 per year over the past three years. Thomas has been given increasingly higher quotas the during past two years to reach her bonus. She feels that her company is putting her in an awkward position. She wants to continue to reach her quota, but in doing so, she will spend more than 90 percent of her time trying to bring in new business. Just over two years ago, she spent half of her time keeping her present customers satisfied. Her customers have been complaining about how little attention they receive. Thomas knows that she is not spending enough time with them. She brought her dilemma to her boss, Betty Barrett, who seemed less than sympathetic.

Current Situation
Their conversation follows:

Thomas: I am really having a problem with the quota I've been assigned this year.

Barrett: Is that so? What is the problem?

Thomas: I think it is too high. I have to spend way too much time going after new business.

Barrett: That is what we pay you to do; your job is to bring in new business.

Thomas: It was not that way many years ago when I spent at least half of my time keeping my present customers happy. I enjoyed following-up with them and building a strong relationship.

Barrett: Times change, you know. We have to bring in new business or face the chance of laying some of you off.

Thomas: You can look over some of these phone messages I have received. These are some of our best customers, and they do not think we are taking very good care of them.

Barrett: Roberta, we have a big contest going on, and I do not intend to lose it. You had better bring in your share of the new business to win or you will let down your entire branch.

Thomas could see she was not getting anywhere and changed the subject.

Questions

1. What would you do if you were Thomas?
2. What would you do if you were Barrett?

ROLE PLAY

Situation:	Read Case 9.2
Characters:	Thomas; Barrett
Scene:	*Location*—Barrett's office.
	Action—Continuation of Roberta and Betty's conversation. Role play Thomas not changing the subject and pursuing her concerns.

Upon completion of the role play, address the following questions:

1. Thomas is not getting anywhere with Barrett; should she go to Barrett's boss?
2. Why can't Thomas go back to her old way of doing things and spend the time with her existing customers like she wants to?

ADDING VALUE: SELF-LEADERSHIP
AND TEAMWORK

THE 3 Ts OF SALES SUCCESS: TASK-ORIENTED PLANNING, TECHNOLOGY, AND TEAMWORK

David Waugh, software sales executive with Confio Software in Boulder, Colorado, knows the value of team selling and self-discipline in building successful relationships with high-tech customers. Waugh, a 12-year veteran of software and consulting sales as well as sales management has seen many different sales environments. With experience spanning work for a Fortune 100 corporation to managing a sales force for a start-up company, he has learned that having task-driven activity plans, utilizing automation technology, and teamwork will help pave the road to success.

At Confio, Waugh ends each day with a task-driven activity plan for the following day. He uses software products integrated with his e-mail and online calendar to lay out upcoming tasks. Automated reminders alert him when specific tasks are due and track the date and time of each event. Consequently, Waugh starts each business day knowing exactly what he must complete in order to accomplish his daily goals. Tasks are broken down into categories including telephone calls, lead management activities, strategic planning sessions, and prospecting for new clients. "No matter how you lay out your daily activity plan," he is quick to point out, "it must be straightforward and easy to follow."

When he started his career in 1994, the norm for activity plans was paper day planners and note cards. Today, Waugh utilizes a web-based sales force automation tool to manage the hundreds of e-mails, telephone calls, and business contacts in his daily activity plan. By combining his daily regimen of task-driven activity plans with an automated system, he can quickly navigate through his day and follow a sales process with each individual prospect that can be tracked for effectiveness and efficiency.

The last prerequisite for success in selling is teamwork according to Waugh. Confio has implemented a team selling environment that encourages all members of the team to assist each other in accomplishing individual and company goals. At Confio, team selling means shared revenue goals along with shared commission and bonus plans. Each salesperson's goal or quota is comprised of two components: 80 percent personal and 20 percent team, with the team portion representing the overall number that the sales team achieves. The objective is to encourage better communication and information-sharing among sales team members and their clients. For example, information gained at one customer experience may help advance a sale for a different salesperson with another customer. In addition to sharing information, lead referral programs and incentives encourage sales team members to seek out business opportunities for the overall benefit of the team. This kind of group dynamic leads to an effective team selling strategy: group account planning. Group account planning creates an environment that promotes brainstorming and idea sharing about ways to help generate more customer success. Sales team

---

Source: Interview with David Waugh, September 12, 2006.

Objectives

After completing this module, you should be able to

1 Explain the five sequential steps of self-leadership.

2 Discuss the importance of thorough and effective planning.

3 Identify the four levels of sales goals and explain their interrelationships.

4 Describe two techniques for account classification.

5 Explain the application of different territory routing techniques.

6 Interpret the usefulness of different types of selling technology and automation.

7 Delineate six skills for building internal relationships and teams.

members meet once a week to discuss various topics related to the business. Each team member presents his or her business prospects and shares the progress that has been made with the team. The entire team then discusses ways to achieve success at each of the prospects and tracks the progress of ideas to determine trends and business tactics that can be repeated and built into the company's marketing and sales methods. Such group account planning sessions may result in new enhancements to the company's products, referral introductions from current customers, and new types of marketing materials.

Waugh also emphasizes that teamwork is not limited to associates inside company walls. Networking comes in many other ways including attending trade shows and user group meetings as well as seeking out other vendors who service mutual clients. With several of his large clients, Waugh has established supplier round table meetings in which suppliers of similar interest meet to discuss issues pertaining to the mutual client and to help each other find new business opportunities. Having communications with others outside of your business circle can sometimes provide opportunities that would not otherwise be presented.

When observing the actions of a person who has truly mastered the skills of their profession, the manner of their actions seems to come naturally. However, closer consideration will most often reveal that these seemingly innate and natural abilities are actually the result of fervent and purposeful planning combined with many hours of practice over a period of years. This is true for world-class surgeons, sports stars, leading educators, top attorneys—and yes, even high-performance salespeople. As illustrated by the experiences of David Waugh in the opening vignette for this module, good salespeople are consciously developed, not born. Toward the objective of *developing* strong salespeople, this module builds on the process of self-leadership to generate a framework for developing and enhancing selling skills and abilities. First, setting effective selling goals and objectives are discussed and integrated with methods for territory analysis and account classification. This is followed by a discussion of how the objectives and information from the territory and account analysis become inputs for generating and implementing effective multilevel sales planning. The importance of assessing performance results and level of goal attainment is also reviewed. Wrapping up the module is an examination of teamwork as a vehicle for expanding the capabilities of an individual salesperson, increasing customer value, and creating sustainable competitive advantage for salespeople.

EFFECTIVE SELF-LEADERSHIP

How often have you said or thought to yourself, "I just don't have enough time to get everything done?" In reality, most people do not need more time. Rather, they need to reprioritize the time they have. There are only so many hours in a day, and highly effective salespeople know that they can never have enough quality selling time. To maximize their selling time, these high performers have developed strong self-leadership skills and treat time as a valuable, nonreplaceable resource and invest it wisely where it will accomplish the most good.

Self-leadership—a critical requirement for success in any career—has been described as doing the right things and doing them well. It is not simply the amount of effort that determines an achievement, but rather how well that effort is honed and aligned with one's goals. In selling, this is often restated as selling smarter rather than selling harder. That is, before expending valuable time and resources, salespeople must establish priorities in the form of objectives. Then, and only then, do they implement the strategic plan that has been specifically developed to achieve their objectives in the light of the available resources and market potential that exist within the territory. Self-leadership translates to a process of first deciding what is to be

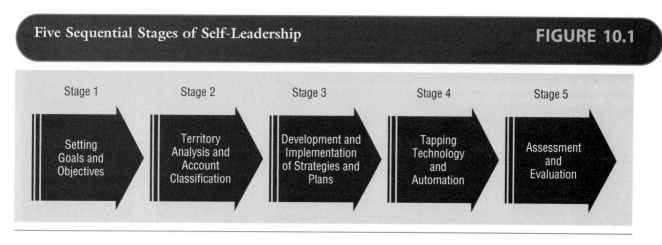

Five Sequential Stages of Self-Leadership   **FIGURE 10.1**

Stage 1 — Setting Goals and Objectives

Stage 2 — Territory Analysis and Account Classification

Stage 3 — Development and Implementation of Strategies and Plans

Stage 4 — Tapping Technology and Automation

Stage 5 — Assessment and Evaluation

Self-leadership is a process of first, deciding what is to be accomplished, and then setting into motion the proper plan to achieve the desired objectives.

accomplished and then placing into motion the proper plan designed to achieve those objectives.

The process of self-leadership is composed of five sequential stages. First, goals and objectives must be set that properly reflect what is important and what is to be accomplished. This is followed by an analysis of the territory and classification of accounts. Next, with goals in place and accounts classified, strategic plans designed to achieve the objectives through proper allocation of resources and effort are implemented. The next stage maximizes the effectiveness of allocated resources through the process of tapping technology and automation to expand resource capabilities. Finally, assessment activities are conducted to evaluate performance and goal attainment and to assess possible changes in plans and strategies. The nature of the sequential interrelationships between these five stages is illustrated in Figure 10.1.

Stage One: Setting Goals and Objectives

Establishing priorities by setting **goals and objectives** is the key to effective self-leadership. This first stage of self-leadership has been appropriately referred to as "beginning with the end in mind."[1] First of all, if a salesperson does not understand what is important, how does that salesperson know what to focus on? Further, if a salesperson does not understand what he or she is setting out to accomplish, how could that salesperson know where to begin, how to proceed, or even which plan is best for getting there? Finally, without clear goals, how could salespeople know when the objective has been achieved? Without clear goals and objectives, it is very natural to drift from task to task and typically focus on minor and less-productive tasks, as they are the easiest to complete. The end result of this natural drift is poor sales performance and frustration. The positive impact of planning ahead and establishing priorities is further evidenced by the experiences of Adam Spangler, an investment representative for Edward D. Jones & Co., in "Professional Selling in the 21st Century: Driving Sales through Setting Goals and Planning Sales Activities."

What Makes a Good Goal?

Although goals and objectives might best be described as desired outcomes, these two words carry specific meaning. *Desired* implies that it is something worthy of working toward and expending resources to reach. *Outcome* connotes that it is a

Driving Sales through Setting Goals and Planning Sales Activities

Adam Spangler is a highly successful investment representative for Edward D. Jones & Co. and knows that there is much more to building a successful business than simply pulling out the local white pages and calling faceless names on a hot stock idea. Spangler emphasizes that planning, goal setting, and time management are critical to his success in managing the financial investments of his 600 customers.

Goal setting and planning are critical for success in selling. During the last week of each calendar year, we draft our performance goals and develop business plans that set the bar for goals to be accomplished during the coming year. Setting annual goals allows us to break them down further to develop quarterly, monthly, and even daily goals that can be used to assess progress and make changes in our plans.

Time management and doing the "right" work are the keys to achieving goals. To leverage available work time better, we use a contact management system to prioritize accounts and prospects by assigning a color code of Green, Yellow, or Red based upon several criteria. Our goal is to contact Green clients and prospects over the phone at least once per month and in person three times per year. Calls to Yellow clients are made only after all of the Greens have been contacted in the month. Red clients are not proactively contacted because it is unlikely that they will ever become important clients. Having a planning system like this in place allows us to do the "right" work, staying in touch with those who have a need and have the resources to do something about their need. Also, since doing the "right" work leverages our time, we have more time to enjoy our personal life and the fruit of our labor.

specific result or effect resulting from certain activities or behaviors—something that can be described and pointed out. As illustrated in Exhibit 10.1 checklist, properly developed goals share three key characteristics: (1) realistic, yet challenging, (2) specific and quantifiable, and (3) time specific.

- *Realistic, Yet Challenging*—Goals should be realistic and reachable. When set beyond what is possible, goals cease to motivate and often become a disincentive to performance. At the same time, goals should be challenging. If goals are continually set at a level that is too easy to reach, performance tends to regress to the lower standard. Goals that are challenging tend to be more motivating than goals that are easily achieved.
- *Specific and Quantifiable*—Without specificity, goals become ambiguous and have no clear meaning. For instance, the goal of having the top territory in the district could be interpreted in many ways. Does top territory translate to having the largest increase in sales; having the fewest number of customer defections; having the highest customer satisfaction scores; having the smallest number of price discounts; or possibly having the largest reduction in travel expenses? Without specificity, the goal becomes a moving target, and it is difficult to know where to

EXHIBIT 10.1   Required Characteristics of Goals and Objectives

Effective Goals and Objectives Must Possess Three Fundamental Characteristics	
×	Goals should be realistic, yet challenging
×	Goals should be specific and quantifiable
×	Goals should be time specific

apply one's effort. In a similar fashion, goals should be quantifiable—that is, they should be measurable. The goal of increasing sales is certainly commendable, but how might it be judged as having been accomplished? Is a 1 percent increase sufficient or is 12 percent more in line with expectations? If a 12 percent increase is the expectation, then the goal should be a 12 percent increase in sales—a quantifiable and measurable outcome that can be objectively measured and assessed.

- *Time Specific*—Stating a specific time line is the third requirement of goals and objectives. A goal of achieving a 12 percent increase in sales by December 31 is much more appealing than simply stating that one's goal is to increase sales by 12 percent. Associating time lines with goals establishes a deadline for planning purposes and provides motivation by instilling a sense of urgency for taking action.

Working with Different Levels and Types of Goals

For maximum effectiveness, salespeople establish goals at four different levels: personal goals, territory goals, account goals, and sales call goals. Although each level requires different types of effort and produces different outcomes, each of the levels is interrelated and interdependent of the others. These interrelationships and dependencies are illustrated in Exhibit 10.2. A salesperson's **personal goals** might include achieving a $70,000 annual income during the current year ending December 31. If the salesperson receives a commission of 11 percent on sales, this personal goal is directly related to and dependent on achieving the **territory goal** of selling $636,364 in products across the territory in the same time period. Assuming 19 equally sized accounts comprise the territory, the territory goal is dependent on achieving the **account goal** of an average of $33,493 in products sold to each account over the course of the year. Considering that each account is called on twice every month, a **sales call goal** of $1,396 in sales per call is required to achieve the account goal. As illustrated in this example, each higher-level goal is ultimately dependent on the salesperson setting and achieving lower-level, specific goals for each and every sales call.

Although illustrative of the interdependence between different levels of goals, the previous example is admittedly simplistic in its exclusive use of goals based on sales volume. In reality, there are many different types of goals that a salesperson might effectively use. Exhibit 10.3 illustrates examples of common sales goals.

Stage Two: Territory Analysis and Account Classification

Territory analysis and classification of accounts, the second stage of self-leadership, is all about finding the customers and prospects who are most likely to buy. Who are they, and where are they located? What and why do they buy? How much and how

---

Four Interdependent Levels of Salesperson Objectives   **EXHIBIT 10.2**

Personal Goal Desired Annual Income	$ 70,000
Is dependent on Annual Territory Sales Goal (11% Commission on Sales)	$636,364
Is dependent on Annual Account Sales Goal (19 equally sized accounts)	$ 33,493
Is dependent on Sales Call Goal (each account is called on twice a month)	$ 1,396

EXHIBIT 10.3   Common Types of Sales Goals

• Financial Goals	Income, Financial Security
• Career Advancement Goals	Work in Chosen Field, Advancement
• Personal Development Goals	Education, Training, Relationships Outside Work
• Sales Volume Goals	Dollar Sales, Unit Sales, Number of Orders, Aggregates or by Groups
• Sales Call Activity Goals	Calls Made, Calls/Day, Calls/Account, Presentations Made
• Sales Expense Goals	Total Expenses, by Category, Percent of Sales
• Profitability Goals	Gross Profits, Contribution Margin, Returns and Discounts
• Market Share	Total Share of Potential Market, Peer Group Comparisons
• Share of Account	Share of Customer's Purchases
• Ancillary Activity Goals	Required Reports Turned in, Training Conducted, Service Calls Made
• Customer Retention Goals	Number of Accounts Lost, Complaints Received, Lost Account Ratios
• New Account Goals	Number of New Accounts
• Customer Service Goals	Customer Goodwill Generation, Level of Satisfaction, Receivables Collected
• Conversion Goals	Ratio of Number of Sales to Number of Calls Made

often do they purchase? Who has the authority to buy, and who can influence the purchase decision? What is the probability of selling to this account? What is the potential share of account that might be gained?

Many sources offer intelligence that will assist the salesperson in answering these questions, and the information boom on the Internet makes accessing this information easier than ever before. In addition to numerous yellow page suppliers available on the Web, commercial business information suppliers such as *OneSource Information Services, Hoovers, Standard & Poor's, Dun and Bradstreet*, and *The Thomas Register* offer easy-to-use databases that are fully searchable by company, industry, and geographic location. Salespeople can also access individual company Web sites, trade directories, professional association membership listings, and commercial mailing list providers. Personal observation, discussions with other selling professionals, and company sales records are also excellent sources for gaining valuable information.

Much of this information can be plotted to develop detailed territory maps that will begin to pinpoint pockets of existing and potential business. In addition, understanding the territory at the individual account level provides the input required for account classification.

Account Classification

Account classification places existing customers and prospects into categories based on their sales potential and assists salespeople in prioritizing accounts for call planning and time allocation purposes. During the process of account classification, it is common for salespeople to find that 80 to 90 percent of their sales potential is generated by 10 to 20 percent of the total accounts. Consequently, the results of account classification can guide salespeople in more efficient allocation of time, effort, and resources while simultaneously enabling them to be more effective in achieving sales goals. Two commonly used methods for classifying accounts are single-factor analysis and portfolio analysis.

Single-Factor Analysis

Single-factor analysis, also referred to as **ABC analysis**, is the simplest and most often used method for classifying accounts. As the name suggests, accounts are

Class of Account	Schema One: InquisLogic Inc.	Schema Two: Web Resource Associates, LLC	Schema Three: Federal Metal Products
"A" Accounts	Accounts with highest potential (the 20% that do or could account for 80% of sales)	Accounts with highest potential (the 20% that do or could account for 80% of sales)	High volume current customers (the 20% that currently account for 80% of sales volume)
	Annual number of calls = 24	Annual number of calls = 52	Annual number of calls = 48
"B" Accounts	Medium potential accounts (the 80% that account for 20% of sales volume)	Accounts with moderate sales potential, but who are regular and reliable customers	Accounts with high potential, but who are not current customers
	Annual number of calls = 12	Annual number of calls = 24	Annual number of calls = 12
"C" Accounts	Accounts with the least sales potential	Lower sales potential accounts	Medium potential accounts that are current customers
	Annual number of calls = 4	Annual number of calls = 8	Annual number of calls = 12
"D" Accounts	None. This Schema only uses 3 classes of accounts	Accounts that cost more in time and energy than they produce in sales or profits	Accounts with medium potential, but who are not current customers
		Annual number of calls = 0	Annual number of calls = 6

EXHIBIT 10.4 Different Single-Factor Account Analysis Schema Used by Different Companies

analyzed on the basis of one single factor—typically the level of sales potential. On the basis of sales potential, the accounts are placed into three or four categories denoted by letters of the alphabet, "A," "B," "C," and "D." Accounts with the highest potential are traditionally sorted into category "A," whereas those with medium potential go into "B," and so on. All accounts in the same category receive equal selling effort. For example, "A" accounts may be called on every two weeks, "B" accounts every four to six weeks, and "C" accounts might receive a personal sales call once a year and be serviced by the seller's telemarketing team during the interim. Single-factor classification schemas used by three different sales organizations are summarized in Exhibit 10.4.

The simplicity of single-factor analysis is a prime contributor to its popularity for use by field salespeople. It is straightforward and requires no statistical analysis or data manipulation. Although this lack of complexity is appealing, its ability to only use one factor for analyzing and classifying accounts is also a significant limitation. Sales potential is certainly an important input in allocating selling effort, but other factors should also be considered. Possible other factors of interest are the selling company's competitive strength in each account, the account's need for additional attention and effort, profitability of the account, and amount of competitive pressure on the account.

Portfolio Analysis

Also referred to as two-factor analysis, the **portfolio analysis** method attempts to overcome the weakness of single-factor analysis by allowing two factors to be

EXHIBIT 10.5   Portfolio/Two-Factor Account Analysis and Selling Strategies

Competitive Position

	Strong	Weak
High (Account Opportunity)	**Segment One** **Level of Attractiveness:** Accounts are very attractive because they offer high opportunity, and the seller has a strong competitive position. **Selling Effort Strategy:** Accounts should receive a heavy investment of effort and resources in order to take advantage of high opportunity and maintain/improve competitive position. **Exemplary Sales Call Strategy = 36 calls/yr.**	**Segment Two** **Level of Attractiveness:** Accounts are potentially attractive due to high opportunity, but seller currently has weak competitive position. **Selling Effort Strategy:** Where it is possible to strengthen seller's competitive position, a heavy investment of selling effort should be applied. **Exemplary Sales Call Strategy = 24 calls/yr.**
Low (Account Opportunity)	**Segment Three** **Level of Attractiveness:** Accounts are moderately attractive due to seller having a strong competitive position. However, future opportunity is low. **Selling Effort Strategy:** Accounts should receive a moderate level of selling effort that is sufficient to maintain current competitive position. **Exemplary Sales Call Strategy = 12 calls/yr.**	**Segment Four** **Level of Attractiveness:** Accounts are very unattractive. They offer low opportunity and seller has weak competitive position. **Selling Effort Strategy:** Accounts should receive minimal personal selling effort. Alternatives such as telemarketing, direct mail, and Internet should be explored. **Exemplary Sales Call Strategy = 6 calls/yr.**

considered simultaneously. Each account is examined on the basis of the two specified factors and sorted into the proper segment of a matrix. This matrix is typically divided into four cells, and accounts are placed into the proper classification cell on the basis of their individual ratings ("high" and "low" or "strong" and "weak") on each factor of interest. Cell location denotes the overall attractiveness of the different accounts and serves as a guide for the salesperson's allocation of resources and effort. Typically, each account in the same cell will receive the same amount of selling effort.

Exhibit 10.5 details the account characteristics and suggested selling effort allocations for a typical portfolio analysis incorporating the factors of (1) account opportunity and (2) seller's competitive position.[2] Account opportunity takes into consideration the buyer's level of need for and ability to purchase the seller's products, along with financial stability and growth prospects. Competitive position denotes the relationship between the account and the seller and includes variables such as seller's share of account, competitive pressure, and key decision maker's attitude toward the seller. Accounts sorted into Segment One are high on opportunity, exhibit strong competitive positions, and should receive the highest level of selling effort. Accounts falling into Segment Two are high on opportunity but weak on competitive position. These accounts should receive a high level of attention to strengthen the seller's competitive position. Segment Three contains the 80 to 90 percent of accounts doing 10 to 20 percent of the seller's volume. These accounts are loyal and regular customers (high on competitive position) but offer weak opportunity.

Strategically, these accounts should receive a lower investment of selling effort designed to maintain the seller's current competitive position. Accounts sorted into Segment Four are considered unattractive and allocated minimal selling effort as they are characterized by low opportunity and weak competitive position. Within the past several years, many sellers have been successful in servicing Segment Three and Four accounts outside the personal selling channel by using alternatives such as telemarketing, direct mail, and the Internet.

Portfolio analysis offers the advantages of enhanced flexibility and ability to incorporate multiple variables for analyzing and sorting accounts. Reflecting these strong points, the use of portfolio analysis is gaining in popularity.

Stage Three: Development and Implementation of Strategies and Plans

Stage One provides the salesperson with the guidelines of what is important and the goals to be accomplished at the levels of individual sales calls, accounts, and the overall territory. Stage Two identifies and establishes the priority and potential of each account in the territory along with the relative location of each account. Top salespeople do not stop there! They use this information to develop strategies and plans that will guide them toward achieving their goals by applying their available resources in a deliberate and organized fashion that effectively cultivates and harvests the potential sales available in the territory.

Establishing and Implementing Selling Task and Activity Plans

When properly executed, sales planning results in a schedule of activities that can be used as a map for achieving objectives. First, start with the big picture—a long-term plan spanning the next 6 to 12 months. This big picture highlights commitments and deadlines and facilitates setting up the activities required to meet those commitments and deadlines. In turn, the longer-range plans provide the basis for shorter time frame plans and selling activities. The salesperson planning program at Federal Metal Products (FMP) offers a good overview and prototype of effective salesperson planning.

> FMP, a middle market supplier of metal production components, trains its salespeople to prepare and submit annual territory plans and budgets by November 15 each year. With that recurring deadline marked on their schedules, FMP salespeople work backward on their calendars to establish key checkpoints for their planning activities. This establishes a time line to guide and assist salespeople in making the submission deadline.
>
> If the salesperson projects that it will take four weeks to assemble and draft their territory sales plan, they work back four weeks from the November 15 date and establish October 15 as the date to begin assembling their data and building their plans, how long will it take to properly collect the needed data? Six weeks? If so, their schedule should reflect beginning that activity by September 1.

Sales plans should take into consideration scheduled meetings and training sessions, holidays, trade shows, and vacation time. Plans should also contain periodic checkpoints for assessing progress toward goals. A salesperson's objective of $750,000 in sales for the year equates to a goal averaging $62,500 in sales every month. Accordingly, the long-term master plan should include monthly checkpoints to compare the schedule versus actual performance data. Is performance on course, ahead, or lagging behind? If not on schedule, the corresponding and more detailed weekly plans should be revised to reflect the salesperson's strategies for getting back on course.

Salespeople at FMP develop weekly plans from their longer-term annual plan. These shorter-term plans detail the selling-related activities to be accomplished that week. To create a weekly plan, first identify the priorities that must be accomplished to stay on schedule. Then, for each of these priorities, detail the associated activities and schedule the time that it will take for completion. What areas of the territory will be focused on? What accounts will be called on, and what is the objective for each call? What are the best times to call for appointments? Are there account preferences as to what days and times they work with salespeople? How much time must be allowed for travel, waiting, and working with each account? What products will be featured? What information and materials will be needed?

In turn, the priorities and activities identified in the weekly plan should become the points of focus for the daily plan. Days that end on a successful note begin with a thorough and written schedule detailing tasks and priorities for that day and the activities that must be carried out to achieve them. The optimum schedule emphasizes tasks and activities that will make the greatest sales impact—working with customers. As illustrated by the FMP's "Daily Sales Plan Worksheet" shown in Exhibit 10.6, daily plans should detail the amount of time projected for each scheduled task and activity. To maximize the effectiveness of daily sales plans, salespeople should adhere to two guiding principles.[3]

- *Do them, and do them in writing*. Written plans are better developed and provide more motivation and commitment for salespeople to carry them through to completion. Furthermore, written plans help to ensure that priority items do not fall through the cracks because something was forgotten.
- *Keep it current and flexible*. Make a new daily plan every day. Try as we might, things do not always go as planned. Consequently, changes may be needed, and uncompleted priorities or activities from one day may have to be carried over to the next.

Establishing Territory Routing Plans

Territory routing plans incorporate information developed in the territory analysis and account classification stage to minimize the encroachment of unproductive travel time on time that could be better spent working with customers. Good routing plans minimize the backtracking and crisscrossing that would otherwise occur and allow the salesperson to use time more efficiently.

Knowing how many calls can be made each day, the required call frequency for each account classification, and the relative geographic location of and distance between accounts, a salesperson can plot different routing strategies and decide the optimal plan. Many sales professionals continue to use the traditional colored map pins and felt-tip markers on a wall map. However, a variety of easy-to-use and affordable computer applications that plot optimal routing plans are

EXHIBIT 10.6 Example of a Typical Daily Plan

Federal Metal Products
Daily Sales Plan Worksheet

Salesperson: _Earnie Cravits_   Day: _Friday_   Date: _8/29_

Time	Task or Priority	Activity	People Involved	Time Needed	Goal/Anticipated Results	Notes & Comments
8:30 A.M.	Set appointments	Phone calls	Jill Attaway Digital Systems	10 min	Appointment for next week	Requested that I come by
	"	"	Bart Waits EnterpriseOne	10 min	"	
	"	"	Kerri Williams Flo-Forms	10 min	"	Will be placing order in 3 weeks
9:00 A.M.	"	"	Marilyn Henry InQuisLogic	10 min	Clarify service problem	Send info to engineering
10:30 A.M.	Demonstrate new bearing line	Sales call	Mike Humphreys ICOM	60 min	Info gathering	Currently buying from Gem Rollers
12 noon	Get order commitment	Sales call—Lunch	Rodney Moore MDQG	120 min	$12,000 order	Gem submitted proposal 8/20
3:00 P.M.	Take sample of proposed line	Sales call	Aimee Williams MOCO, Inc	60 min	$15,200 order	Ready to buy, wants to see pdct. sample
4:30 P.M.	Check on delivery	Service call	Ron Meier Web Resources	50 min	Delight the customer	First time to buy from us!!
6:00 P.M.	Complete paperwork	Submit call reports		45 min		
7:00 P.M.	Prepare daily schedule	Planning		45 min		

FIGURE 10.2   Straight-Line Route Pattern

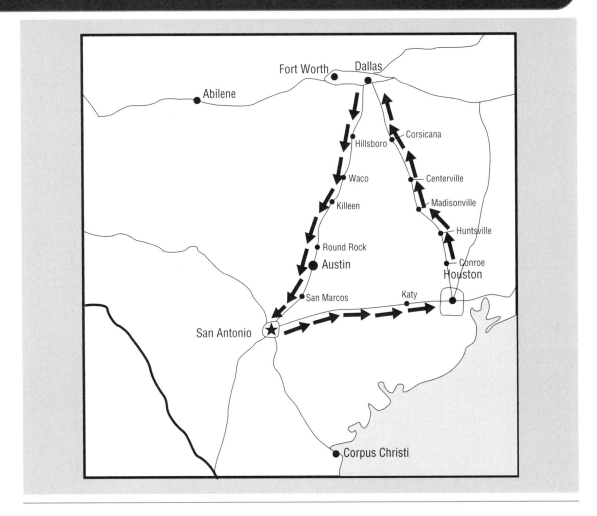

Straight-line territory routes make calls across the territory; first in one direction, and then change direction to work back to the starting point.

available and are growing in popularity.[4] Optimized routing plans correspond to one of five common patterns: straight line, cloverleaf, circular, leapfrog, and major city.

Straight Line

With a **straight-line routing plan**, salespeople start from their offices and make calls in one direction until they reach the end of the territory. As illustrated in Figure 10.2, at that point they change direction and continue to make calls on a straight line following the new vector. This continues until the salesperson returns to the office location. The straight-line pattern works best when accounts are located in clusters that are some distance from one another.

Cloverleaf

The **cloverleaf routing plan** pattern is best used when accounts are concentrated in different parts of the territory. On each trip, the salesperson works a different part of

Cloverleaf Route Pattern   **FIGURE 10.3**

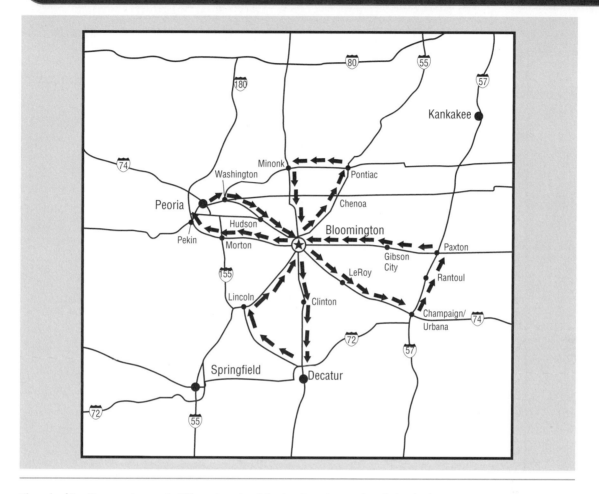

Cloverleaf territory routes work different parts of the territory in a series of circular loops.

the territory and travels in a circular loop back to the starting point. An example of the cloverleaf routing plan is depicted in Figure 10.3. Each loop could take a day, a week, or longer to complete. A new loop is covered on each trip until the entire territory has been covered.

Circular

Circular routing plans begin at the office and move in an expanding pattern of concentric circles that spiral across the territory. Figure 10.4 traces an exemplary circular routing plan working from an office in Dallas. This method works best when accounts are evenly dispersed throughout the territory.

Leapfrog

The **leapfrog routing plan** is best applied when the territory is large and accounts are clustered into several widely dispersed groups. Beginning in one cluster, the salesperson works each of the accounts at that location and then

FIGURE 10.4   **Circular Route Pattern**

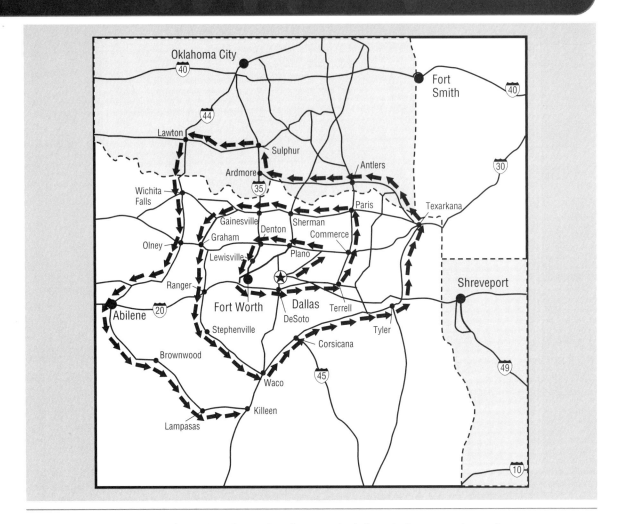

Circular territory routes cover the territory in a series of concentric circles spiraling across the territory.

jumps to the next cluster. As shown in Figure 10.5, this continues until the last cluster has been worked and the salesperson jumps back to the office or home. When the distance between clusters is great, the salesperson will typically make the jumps by flying.

Major City

When the territory is composed of a major metropolitan area, the territory is split into a series of geometric shapes reflecting each one's concentration and pattern of accounts. Figure 10.6 depicts a typical **major city routing plan**. Downtown areas are typically highly concentrated with locations controlled by a grid of city blocks and streets. Consequently, the downtown segment is typically a small square or rectangular area allowing accounts to be worked in a straight-line fashion street by street. Outlying areas are placed in evenly balanced triangles or pie-shaped quadrants, with one quadrant being covered at a time in either a straight-line or cloverleaf pattern.

Leapfrog Route Pattern   **FIGURE 10.5**

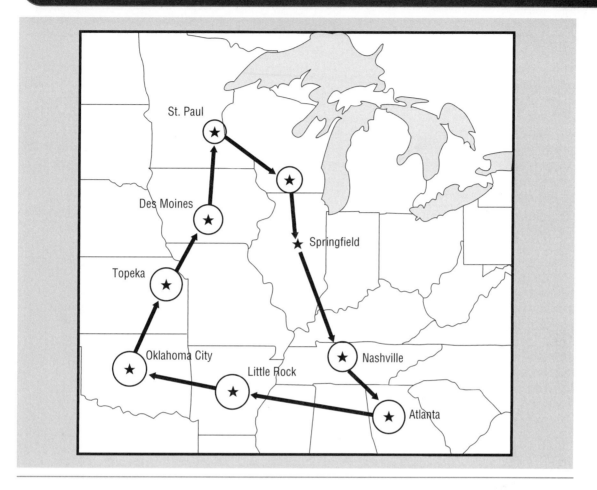

Leapfrog territory routes work accounts clustered in one location and then jump to a different cluster of accounts.

Stage Four: Tapping Technology and Automation

Selling technology and automation tools are here to stay and are being transformed from neat toys to necessary tools. Properly applied, selling technology spurs and creates creativity and innovation, streamlines all aspects of the selling process, generates new and improved selling opportunities, facilitates cross-functional teaming and intraorganizational communication, and enhances communication and follow-up with customers.[5] In summary, tapping the proper selling technologies and sales force automation tools allow salespeople to expand their available resources for enhanced selling performance and outcomes. Experiences with improved selling efficiency and customer satisfaction are illustrated in "Professional Selling in the 21st Century: Technology Impacts Sales Efficiency and Effectiveness."

Salespeople, sales managers, and customers are unanimous in their agreement that the best salespeople are those who stay up with changes in and developments of technologies with selling applications. With a multitude of rapidly changing and evolving technology choices, salespeople must not only master the technology itself, but they must also understand when and where it can be applied most effectively. Exemplary selling technologies being used by today's salespeople include the following tools.[6]

FIGURE 10.6   Major City Route Pattern

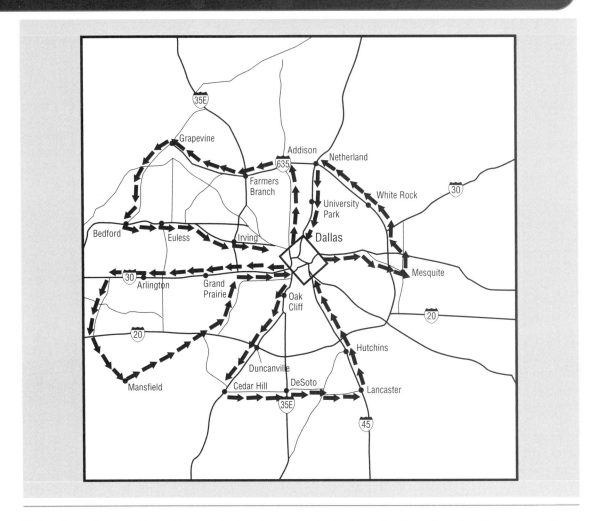

Major city territory routing patterns work downtown on a basis of street grids and work outlying areas using a cloverleaf or straight-line pattern.

Computers

At the center of virtually every selling technology is the computer. Choices include desktops, notebooks, laptops, palmtops, and personal data assistants (PDAs). For immediate immersion into the high-tech side of selling, simply walk through the waiting areas of any major airport. Salespeople can be seen generating reports and proposals by using standard word-processing packages and even customized online electronic forms. Others are analyzing customer accounts by using spreadsheet applications and query-based database programs that access and analyze a database according to the questions the user wishes to have answered. Several will be observed reviewing and updating customer files by using one of the many affordable and highly capable contact management software applications such as Siebel Systems, ACT!, Maximizer, Active-Sales, and Sales Logix. These user-friendly programs provide salespeople with a convenient option to catalogue, search, and access comprehensive information regarding individual customers. Looking closer, numerous salespeople will be revising and polishing graphics and presentations with software such as PowerPoint. Still others will be checking and responding to e-mail, submitting electronic reports, accessing online territory route maps, and using scheduling programs to set up the next day's call plans.

Technology Impacts Sales Efficiency and Effectiveness

Geoffrey James, contributing editor for *Selling Power* magazine discusses advances in sales force technology and how today's smartphones are providing a mobile technology platform that can replace the laptops, cell phones, and PDAs traditionally carried by sales reps.

The term "mobile sales technology" used to be the ultimate oxymoron. While most sales reps carried laptops, using them on the road was a royal pain. Most applications allowed data to be entered while offline, but the nightly hassle of syncing up—often in a hotel room after a hard day on the road—was not something to be looked forward to. Wireless Internet was supposed to make things better, but when you needed it the most you usually couldn't get a connection. There were times when a customer asked a question during a sales call, or when you needed to check on critical inventory to fulfill a sale, or enter an online order. And then there was the laptop itself— weighing in at some 5 to 10 pounds plus all the required cables and accessories. Most road warriors needed a separate briefcase just to haul all the stuff around.

But all that is changing with the introduction of smartphones, which make it possible for reps to have the power of their computer applications virtually anywhere. Unlike a laptop, a smartphone can be slipped into your pocket because it is the size of a standard cell phone. More important, smartphones use the cellular phone network instead of wireless hotspots to transfer information. As a result, you don't have to find your local Starbucks or friendly hotel lobby to get access to your corporate data. It used to be there were three kinds of devices sales reps had to carry on the road: laptops, cell phones, and PDAs. Smartphones offer the advantage of combining all these devices into one—plus increased mobility.

Source: James, Geoffrey, "High Wire Act: How to Make Your Team More Effective Using Wireless CRM," *Selling Power*, 26 (7) (2005): 104–110.

Internet and World Wide Web

Company networks have been used for many years; however, the advent of the Internet has made them much more affordable and easier to maintain.

Accessing the **Internet** instantly networks a salesperson with the world: customers, information sources, other salespeople, sales management, and others. More importantly, the Internet puts the salesperson into contact with his or her customer-community and support networks from anywhere in the world, 24 hours a day, seven days a week. Going beyond the convenience of e-mail, many sales organizations are setting up **intranets** and **extranets**—secure and proprietary organizational Web sites that are protected by passwords and security authorizations. Intranets are networks within the organization using the Internet or commercial channels to provide direct linkages between company units and individuals. Extranets are a special form of intranet that is still for proprietary and restricted use but links to specific suppliers and customers to allow them controlled and secure access to the organization's network to facilitate communication and exchange.

These secure Web sites become instant organizational intranets used for communication, training, videoconferencing, webconferencing and secure data interchange. Using such Web-enabled intranets, Diamond Equipment Corporation's salespeople can link to the latest product information and spec sheets, obtain updated inventory and production numbers, download company information, and print customized proposals for customer presentations from anywhere in the world. CDW provides each of their major accounts with a customized extranet that provides the customer with access to CDW on a 24-hour, seven-day-a-week basis. Buyers can track orders online, download product and technical specifications, access customer support technicians, check prices and availability of products, and even place orders for next-day delivery throughout the United States. Rather than spending time traveling to customers' offices, Diamond Equipment Corporation's salespeople deliver their

As one of the top ten multiline insurance companies in North America, National Assurance Corporation (NAC) has an extensive network of sales agents across the United States and Canada. These salespeople operate as captive agents, meaning that they are not employed by NAC, but exclusively sell NAC products and abide by NAC policies and procedures as a requirement of their agency franchise.

As part of the organization's upgrade of its sales information system to a more complete customer relationship management (CRM) system, NAC has obtained company-wide licenses for ACT! (a leading contact and customer information management application). This licensing agreement allows the sales agents to obtain the latest Web-enabled version of ACT! at extremely favorable pricing. ACT! is a sophisticated customer database application that basically makes an integrated CRM available to the agents. Basic customer profiles are enriched with detailed personal and family information along with purchase details and full tracking of contact experience histories. In addition to the richer information base, customized reports can be developed and even filed automatically—an attractive feature that can greatly reduce the time that agents had to spend every Friday to file activity reports with their district sales managers.

The roll out of the new program was going well and quickly achieved an 80 plus percent usage rate among agents. However, at last month's National Sales Meeting in Orlando, it was learned that this version of the application also allows sales supervisors and others at NAC access to their customer data files. Word quickly spread and dissension was high. Even though access to customer files is secure and requires password authentication that is controlled by NAC, sales agents are still suspicious of NAC's ability to access their customer files. They argue that these files are solely their property, and others (especially NAC) should not have access. Corporate, on the other hand, feels that it needs access to the files to properly service customers and develop new products for the agents to sell.

The question of who owns customer account files, the salesperson or the selling organization, has been a point of contention for decades. It is nothing new. However, the advent of more advanced information technologies has brought this issue back under the spotlight. How do you feel about this issue? How might this potentially divisive issue be resolved?

presentations by combining teleconferences and Web presentations. The use of Internet- and intranet-based technologies shorten the sales cycle by allowing sales meetings and presentations to be created and delivered in less time than traditional face-to-face processes would take. If a salesperson can save just ten minutes a day by using Web-based presentation libraries and online product and pricing information, he or she will gain an additional week's worth of productivity over the course of a year. However, as illustrated by the situation described in "An Ethical Dilemma," the acceptance and adoption of advanced technologies are not always an easy thing to accomplish.

Pagers and Cell Phones

Innovations in portable communication such as pagers and cell phones allow salespeople to stay in touch with customers, the home office, and even the family while traveling cross-country or just walking across the parking lot to make a customer call. Today's pagers allow customers and others to access the carrier anywhere and anytime. Much more than the simple beeper of yesterday, today's pagers are capable of receiving full-text messages and e-mail without the necessity of answering the phone. Several paging companies, such as SkyTel, have introduced pagers capable of responding to messages as well as e-mail. Cell phones have also experienced a tremendous increase in technological advances. In addition to increased coverage and smaller sizes, today's smartphones offer Internet and Web access, wireless faxing, e-mail, digital imaging, scheduling, and mobile contact management database capabilities. The ability to use two-way communication during time that would otherwise be nonproductive can significantly increase selling time, customer satisfaction, and sales productivity.

Voice Mail

Ever played the frustrating game of telephone tag? The demands on people's time are continuing to increase, and the projected result would be that it will be even more difficult to complete a telephone call on the first try. Rather than simply using voice mail to notify the other party that they called, top salespeople have become adept at using voice mail to convey and receive information to and from customers as well as sales management and support centers at the home office. Mastering the ability to use voice mail as an extension of oneself generates a significant savings in time and effort that can be redirected to provide additional time for selling.

High-Tech Sales Support Offices

Organizations having sales forces widely dispersed geographically or traveling across multiple regions of the nation or world have found it advantageous to establish **high-tech sales support offices** at multiple locations. Both resident and nonresident salespeople use these offices to access the wider range of selling technology than could be easily carried on a notebook or laptop computer. These offices also provide points of access to the various networks, intranets, and extranets maintained by the organization. IBM maintains high-tech offices such as these at its installations around the world. An IBM representative in Dallas might find himself working as part of a team on a project in Chicago. While in Chicago, the representative has access to the same technology and support as was available in Dallas. Full access is available to company networks, customer accounts, communication links, and software applications. Consequently, convenience and productive time are maximized for the benefit of all parties.

Stage Five: Assessment of Performance and Goal Attainment

A critical, and often overlooked, stage in the process of self-leadership is the periodic assessment of progress. Although certainly important, this stage should involve more than a simple check at the end of the period to determine whether goals were achieved. Assessment checkpoints should be built into plans at progressive points in time to encourage and facilitate the evaluation of one's progress. These frequent comparisons of actual performance with periodic checkpoints allow time to consider revisions or modifications before it is too late to make a difference. In addition to assessing progress, evaluation should also consider what is working well and what could be improved. This knowledge and understanding can be used to guide modifications in the various plans, tasks, and activities that populate the different stages of self-leadership to further enhance future success and performance.

INCREASING CUSTOMER VALUE THROUGH TEAMWORK

Quality customer service is taking on a key role in competitive business strategy, and as customer expectations and needs continue to grow in complexity, selling organizations are finding that they can no longer depend solely on salespeople as the exclusive arbiter of customer satisfaction. Teamwork, both inside the organization and with customers, is being emphasized as the key to customer focus and sales performance.

Internal Partnerships and Teams

The practices and experiences of top-ranked selling organizations, as well as considerable sales research, support the emphasis on teamwork as a key to long-term selling success. The results from three studies of more than 200 companies that employ some 25,000 salespeople supported the belief that cooperating as a team player was critical for success in selling.[7] Similar results have been found in other studies that examine what business-to-business buyers expect from suppliers. In two studies incorporating 6,708 customer evaluations of vendor performance and customer satisfaction in the financial services industry, the suppliers' performance in building internal and external partnerships was found to be the key driver of customer satisfaction.[8]

Building **external relationships** is the focal point of contemporary selling techniques and reflects the ongoing paradigm shift in today's sales forces. This emphasis on building *external* customer relationships could overshadow the critical role of building *internal*, close working relationships with other individuals in their own company. The importance of these **internal relationships** would seem to be logical, as a salesperson's success depends on the degree of support he or she receives from others in the various functional areas of the organization. Ultimately, the salesperson owns the responsibility for customer relationships, but the strength of those customer relationships depends on the joint efforts and resources contributed by multiple individuals across the selling organization.

Account managers at Contour Plastics Corporation have full responsibility for bringing together individuals from functional departments across the organization to work as a sales team dedicated to selling and providing pre- and post-sale services to a specific account. As needed, team members will incorporate research chemists, application specialists, production engineers, and logistics specialists. Coordinated by the salesperson, each team member contributes his or her special expertise toward maximizing the understanding of the customer's situation and needs, and then working together to create a unique, value-added solution that few, if any, competitors can equal.

Teamwork results in a synergy that produces greater outcomes and results for all parties than would be possible with multiple individuals acting independently of one another. Consequently, it is important that salespeople also develop the ability to sell internally as they represent their customers to the selling organization and give recognition to the important role others play in winning, keeping, and growing customer accounts.

James Champy, chairman of consulting for Perot Systems, notes that customers are expecting and receiving better service and product options than ever and characterizes the role of the salesperson as having been transformed to that of a trusted advisor.[9]

In this advisor role, the salesperson works with customers to develop a mutual understanding of the customer's situation, needs, possibilities, and expectations. On the basis of this information, the salesperson assembles a team of individuals, experts from across the selling organization, who work together creating a product response that will deliver more unique customer value than the competitors' offerings. In delivering this unique and added value for customers, salespeople often find themselves working with other individuals in sales, marketing, design and manufacturing, administrative support, shipping, and customer service.

Sales Partnerships

Within the sales department, salespeople often team with other salespeople to gain the strengths and expertise required for a specific selling situation or customer. Partnerships with sales managers and other sales executives are also important in winning support for developing innovative responses to customer needs. XL Capital is a global leader in alternative risk transfer products, financial risk management, and surplus lines of commercial property and casualty insurance. Selling to Fortune 500 and Fortune 1000 customers, XL Capital's salespeople (customer business unit managers) specialize along customer and industry lines. It is common for XL's salespeople to work together in teams to bring together the experience and expertise required to work with customers whose businesses span a large number of different industries.

Marketing Partnerships

Teaming with individuals in the marketing department is critical for salespeople in generating integrated solutions for customers over the long term. Marketing is responsible for developing organizational marketing strategies that serve as guidelines for the sales force. Using information gathered in the field by the sales force, marketing also assists in the generation of new market offerings in response to changing customer needs and requests. Marketing can also be a valuable partner for salespeople in accessing information and developing sales proposals.

At Pocahontas Foods, a top-10 institutional food broker with nationwide operations, account managers regularly work with members of the marketing department to communicate changes in customer needs and activities of competitors. This collaborative partnership allows Pocahontas to continue bringing innovative product offerings to the marketplace that are designed around the inputs from their salespeople.

Design and Manufacturing Partnerships

Salespeople often find themselves selling ideas for product designs and changes in manufacturing schedules to meet the needs of customers. When individuals from design, manufacturing, and sales work as a team, performance and delivery commitments are more likely to be met and customer satisfaction further enhanced. Wallace works to maintain its industry leadership in business forms and systems by aggressively nurturing a company-wide culture emphasizing customer orientation and support. As part of their training, salespeople actually work in production facilities to understand what has to be done to meet product design and delivery requirements that the salespeople might commit to in the field. By-products of this cross-training come about in the form of one-to-one personal relationships between salespeople and production staff. In the case of complex customer needs or special delivery needs, these relationships become invaluable.

Administrative Support Partnerships

Salespeople work with others from administrative support functions such as management, finance and credit, billing, and information systems. Like sales, each of these functional units has certain goals and objectives that translate to policies and procedures that govern their own activities and affect operations throughout the organization—including sales. Customer needs are served best when salespeople have worked to establish effective relationships within these units and all parties work together for the mutual good of the organization and customer. Jim Gavic, account manager for Great Lakes Trucking, manages a territory stretching from the industrial sector of south Chicago east to Gary, Indiana, and south to Indianapolis. Gavic credits his close relationships with individuals in the company's finance and credit department for making 20 percent of his annual sales. By working together, they were able to establish special billing terms for several of his larger accounts. If finance and credit had simply enforced Great Lake's standard terms, these customers would have been lost to a competitor with more flexible credit policies.

Shipping and Transportation Partnerships

Salespeople periodically find themselves facing an urgent customer need that requires special handling of an order. Perhaps it is an expedited shipment for immediate delivery or the processing and shipping of an interim order of less than economical size. Whatever the need, it will affect other shipments getting out on time and could even increase the department's operating costs. Curtis James, territory manager for General Electric Appliances, found sales going better than usual at a new store opening in Oklahoma City. To keep the customer from being caught short, he hand-carried a fill-in order to the GE district office, walked it through credit approval, hand-delivered the shipping order to the warehouse, and helped load the truck. Teamwork enabled Curtis to accomplish in less than a day what normally would have taken eight to ten days. It takes a team effort to work through exceptions such as these, and it is common to find the salesperson actually helping to make it happen by pulling orders, packing boxes, and even helping to load the truck.

Customer Service Partnerships

Teamwork between sales and customer service can create a synergy that has a broad-based impact that can translate to higher customer satisfaction, higher rates of customer retention, and increased sales performance. On the one hand, customer service personnel, such as call center operators and service technicians, often have more extensive contact with customers than the account representatives. As such, they can serve as an early warning system for salespeople and provide valuable information regarding customer complaints, problems, developing needs, and changes that they encounter through customer contacts. As a salesperson for Southwestern School Supply, Cap Williams regularly checks in and visits with the company's customer service personnel to keep abreast of contacts that they might have with any of his customers. The information he receives allows him to get ahead of any possible customer problems, provide an uncanny level of after-sale support that continues to mystify upper management, and helps to secure his consistent receipt of Top Salesperson of the Year Award year after year. When salespeople such as Williams act on the information provided by customer service to further customer relationships and increase sales, customer service personnel will also be further inclined to work together to benefit the team. On the other hand, salespeople often assist customer service personnel by working directly with customers to address problems before they become complaints and provide instruction and training to assist customers in using the products sold.

Building Teamwork Skills

As illustrated in "An Ethical Dilemma," effective teams do not form by default. Nor can a team be effective in producing synergistic benefits solely because it is called a team. Like customer relationships, internal relationships are built on reciprocal trust. The salesperson that arbitrarily and repeatedly asks for special production runs, extensions to customers' lines of credit, expedited shipments, or special

---

AN ETHICAL DILEMMA

Cliff Cody has been one of the top sales representatives for Altima Telecom for several years. Altima is one of the leading companies in outsourced-customer call center services providing both outbound and inbound customer-contact services. It is not uncommon for Cody's sales numbers to lead his region, and he has received a number of significant recognitions and promotions. However, after Cody makes the sale, the nature and quality of the actual service program delivered is totally dependent upon the service design engineers that develop the actual service program, the team of phone representatives that actually handle the calls, and the call-team supervisors that manage the phone representatives. Altima has been experiencing rapid growth over the past two years and has been adding additional personnel throughout the organization, especially phone teams. Many of these new hires have come from competitor organizations and the resulting level of delivered quality has become unpredictable, but consistently below the service levels promised by Cody and the other members of the sales force. Cody has discussed these problems with his sales supervisor, but nothing seems to change. Over the past five to six months, Cody has found himself spending more and more time trying to patch over service failures by the company's phone teams and trying to win back customers that have left Altima to go with a competitor. Cody feels that his hands are tied. The quality of services delivered continues to fall below the expectations of customers and nothing is being done to correct the problems. Not only is Cody losing sales, but he also believes his reputation will soon start to suffer. Last week one of Cody's main competitors contacted him about leaving Altima and coming to work for them. What would you do if you were Cody?

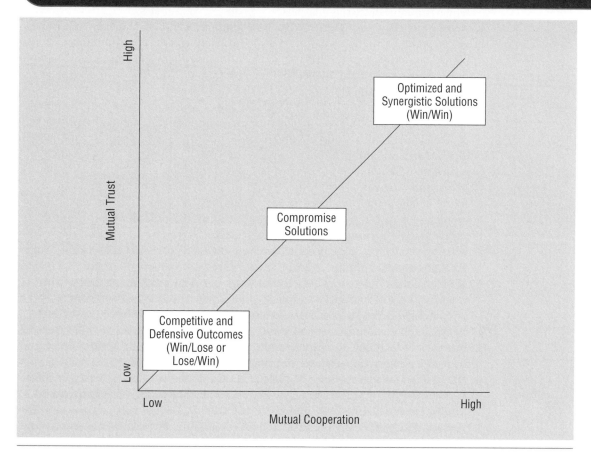

Relationship of Optimized Solutions, Trust, and Cooperation   FIGURE 10.7

Optimum buyer–seller solutions result from a team orientation and require high levels of mutual trust and mutual cooperation. (Excerpt from *The 7 Habits of Highly Effective People* © 2004 Stephen R. Covey. The Time Management Matrix phrase and model are trademarks of Franklin Covey Co., http://www.franklincovey.com. Used with permission. All rights reserved.)

attention from customer service is simply asking for quick fixes. These quick fixes serve the objectives of the customer and salesperson but often work against the objectives of the functional unit and the organization as a whole.

Synergistic teamwork requires a commitment on the part of all parties to look for and work for win/win solutions. However, in the rush to take care of a customer, it is all too easy for salespeople to fall into a win/lose orientation. It is not that they want anyone to lose, but rather that they get what they want. This win orientation is most common in everyday negotiation—in which people think and act in terms of accomplishing their own goals and leave it to others to attain theirs. As illustrated in Figure 10.7, optimum solutions develop from a team orientation based on the philosophy of win/win alternatives.[10] In turn, this can only happen when there are high levels of mutual trust and communication: "Not your way, not my way, but a better way."

In his bestseller book for personal development, Stephen Covey offers six keys to developing synergistic relationships and teams.[11] These are the six **teamwork skills** that salespeople must learn and sincerely apply in their process of building internal partnerships that translate to increased sales and organizational performance.

- *Understanding the Other Individuals*—Fully understanding and considering the other individuals in the partnership is necessary to know what is important to them. What is important to them must also be important to the salesperson if the partnership is to grow and be effective. This means that salespeople must take time to learn the objectives of other functional areas and consider how those needs and requests might affect the salesperson's goals and objectives.

- *Attending to the Little Things*—The little kindnesses and courtesies are often small in size and great in importance. In building relationships, the little things are the big things. Properly attended to and nurtured, they enhance the interrelationships. At the same time, if they are neglected or misused, they can destroy the relationship very quickly.
- *Keeping Commitments*—We all build our hopes and plans around the promises and commitments of others. When a commitment is not kept, disappointment and problems result. As a result, credibility and trust suffer major damage that is always difficult and often impossible to repair. However, consistency in keeping commitments builds and solidifies trust-based relationships.
- *Clarifying Expectations*—The root cause of most relational difficulties can be found in ambiguous expectations regarding roles and goals—exactly where are we going and who is responsible for what? Investing the time up front to clarify expectations regarding goals and roles can save even more time down the road when misunderstandings become compounded and turn into goal conflicts and breakdowns in communication.
- *Showing Personal Integrity*—Demonstrating personal integrity generates trust, whereas a lack of integrity can quickly undermine the best of teamwork orientations. People can seek to understand others, carry through on the little things, keep commitments, and clarify expectations but still fail to build trust by being inwardly duplicitous and pursuing a personal agenda. Be honest, open, and treat everyone by the same set of principles.
- *Apologizing Sincerely When a Mistake Is Made*—It is one thing to make a mistake. It is another thing not to admit it. People forgive mistakes. What is harder to forgive are the ill intentions and motives justifying any attempt to cover up. "If you are going to bow, bow low." The apology must be perceived as sincere and not simply as automated lip-service response.

SUMMARY

1. **Explain the five sequential steps of self-leadership.** As a process, self-leadership is composed of five sequential stages. First, goals and objectives must be set that properly reflect what is important and what is to be accomplished. In turn, an analysis of the territory and classification of accounts is conducted to better understand the territory potential and prioritize accounts according to revenue producing possibilities. With goals in place and accounts prioritized, the third step develops corresponding strategic plans designed to achieve sales goals through proper allocation of resources and effort. The next stage maximizes the effectiveness of allocated resources by incorporating technology and sales force automation to expand salesperson resource capabilities. Finally, assessment activities are conducted to evaluate performance and goal attainment and to assess possible changes in plans and strategies.

2. **Discuss the importance of thorough and effective planning.** Success in any career has been described as doing the right things and doing them well. It is not simply the amount of effort that determines an achievement, but rather how well that effort is honed and aligned with one's goals. In selling, this is often restated as selling smarter rather than selling harder. That is, before we expend our valuable time and resources, we must establish our priorities in the

form of objectives. Then, and only then, do we implement the strategic plan that has been specifically developed to achieve our goals in light of the available resources and market potential that exist within our territory. Self-leadership translates to a process of first deciding what is to be accomplished and then placing into motion the proper plan designed to achieve those objectives.

3. **Identify the four levels of sales goals and explain their interrelationships.** There are four different levels of goals that salespeople must establish to maximize sales effectiveness:

   (a) Personal goals—what one wants to accomplish relative to oneself.
   (b) Sales call goals—the priorities that are set out to be accomplished during a specific call.
   (c) Account goals—the objectives relative to each individual account.
   (d) Territory goals—what is to be accomplished for the overall territory.

   Each level requires different types of effort and produces different outcomes, and each of the levels is interrelated and interdependent on the others. Ultimately, each higher-level goal is dependent on the salesperson setting and achieving the specific goals for each lower level.

4. **Describe two techniques for account classification.** There are two basic methods of classifying accounts. In ascending order of complexity, these methods are: single-factor analysis and portfolio analysis (also referred to as two-factor analysis).

   - *Single-Factor Analysis*—Single-factor analysis, also referred to as ABC analysis, is the simplest and most often used method for classifying accounts. Accounts are analyzed on the basis of one single factor—typically the level of sales potential—and placed into either three or four categories denoted by letters of the alphabet, "A," "B," "C," and "D." All accounts in the same category receive equal selling effort.

   - *Portfolio Analysis (Two-Factor Analysis)*—This classification method allows two factors to be considered simultaneously. Each account is examined on the basis of the two factors selected for analysis and sorted into the proper segment of a matrix. This matrix is typically divided into four cells, with accounts placed into the proper classification cell on the basis of their individual ratings ("high" and "low" or "strong" and "weak") on each of the two factors. Accounts in the same cell share a common level of attractiveness as a customer and will receive the same amount of selling effort.

5. **Explain the application of different territory routing techniques.** Territory routing plans incorporate information developed in the territory analysis and account classification to minimize unproductive travel time that could be better spent working with customers. Good routing plans minimize the backtracking and crisscrossing that would otherwise occur. Routing plans correspond to one of five common patterns.

   - *Straight Line*—With a straight-line plan, salespeople start from their offices and make calls in one direction until they reach the end of the territory. At that point, they change direction and continue to make calls on a straight line on the new vector.

   - *Cloverleaf*—Using the cloverleaf pattern, a salesperson works a different part of the territory and travels in a circular loop back to the starting point. Each loop could take a day, a week, or longer to complete. A new loop is covered on each trip until the entire territory has been covered.

   - *Circular*—Circular patterns begin at the office and move in an expanding pattern of concentric circles that spiral across the territory. This method works best when accounts are evenly dispersed throughout the territory.

- *Leapfrog*—When the territory is exceptionally large and accounts are clustered into several widely dispersed groups, the leapfrog routing methodology is most efficient. Beginning in one cluster, the salesperson works each of the accounts at that location and then jumps (typically by flying) to the next cluster. This continues until the last cluster has been worked and the salesperson jumps back to the office or home.

- *Major City*—Downtown areas are typically highly concentrated with locations controlled by a grid of city blocks and streets. Consequently, the downtown segment is typically a small square or rectangular area allowing accounts to be worked in a straight-line fashion street by street. Outlying areas are placed in evenly balanced triangles or pie-shaped quadrants, with one quadrant being covered at a time in either a straight-line or cloverleaf pattern.

6. **Interpret the usefulness of different types of selling technology and automation.** Properly applied, selling technology spurs creativity and innovation, streamlines the selling process, generates new selling opportunities, facilitates communication, and enhances customer follow-up. Salespeople must not only master the technology itself, but they must also understand when and where it can be applied most effectively. A wide selection of different-sized computers is at the center of most selling technologies. They provide the production tools for generating reports, proposals, and graphic-enhanced presentations. Spreadsheet applications and database applications facilitate the analysis of customer accounts and searching for information needed by customers. Contact management software enables the salesperson to gather and organize account information and schedule calls. Access to the Internet and World Wide Web provide salespeople access to an assortment of public and corporate networks that enable one to communicate, research, and access company information and training from anywhere in the world. Using pagers and cell phones puts salespeople in touch with customers, the home office, and even the family while traveling cross-country or just walking across the parking lot to make a customer call. Voice mail voids the previous restrictions of time and place that accompanied the requirement to make personal contact. Messages can now be left and received 24 hours a day and seven days a week. High-tech sales support offices provide geographically dispersed salespeople with a common standard of computing technology, access to software applications, and portals to organizational networks at offices around the world. Wherever they may be working, they have the tools and capabilities identical to those available to them in their home offices.

7. **Delineate six skills for building internal relationships and teams.**

   (a) *Understanding the Other Individuals*—Fully understanding and considering the other individuals in the partnership is necessary to know what is important to them. What is important to them must also be important to the salesperson if the partnership is to grow and be effective.

   (b) *Attending to the Little Things*—The little kindnesses and courtesies are small in size, but great in importance. Properly attended to and nurtured, they enhance the interrelationships. However, when neglected or misused, they can destroy the relationship very quickly.

   (c) *Keeping Commitments*—We build hopes and plans around the promises and commitments made to us by others. When a commitment is not kept, disappointment and problems result and credibility and trust suffer major damage that will be difficult or impossible to repair.

   (d) *Clarifying Expectations*—The root cause of most relational difficulties can be found in ambiguous expectations regarding roles and goals. By clarifying goals and priorities as well as who is responsible for different activities up front, the hurt feelings, disappointments, and lost time resulting from misunderstandings and conflict can be prevented.

(e) *Showing Personal Integrity*—Demonstrating personal integrity generates trust. Be honest, open, and treat everyone by the same set of principles.

(f) *Apologizing Sincerely When a Mistake Is Made*—It is one thing to make a mistake. It is another thing to not admit it. People forgive mistakes, but ill intentions and cover-ups can destroy trust.

UNDERSTANDING PROFESSIONAL SELLING TERMS

self-leadership
goals and objectives
personal goals
territory goal
account goal
sales call goal
territory analysis
account classification
single-factor analysis
ABC analysis
portfolio analysis
sales planning
straight-line routing plan

cloverleaf routing plan
circular routing plans
leapfrog routing plan
major city routing plan
selling technology and automation
Internet
intranets
extranets
high-tech sales support offices
external relationships
internal relationships
teamwork skills

DEVELOPING PROFESSIONAL SELLING KNOWLEDGE

1. Explain why setting goals and developing formalized selling plans are represented as key requirements for success in selling.

2. Identify and discuss the three required characteristics of a goal or objective.

3. Explain the five sequential stages of self-leadership and how they affect selling success.

4. Develop an example of the four different levels of goals and how they are interrelated.

5. Using a map of your state or region, use city and town locations to establish routing plans by using the straight-line, cloverleaf, circular, leapfrog, and major city methods.

6. Explain how a salesperson might use Internet-based, online product catalogues and presentation libraries to enhance their sales productivity.

7. Explain the weaknesses and strengths of the two methods for account classification.

8. Why is a teamwork orientation important in selling?

9. Who are the individuals within the organization that salespeople are likely to team with, and how could such a team be advantageous to the salesperson?

10. What are the six teamwork skills? Explain why they are important for success in developing interpersonal relationships.

BUILDING PROFESSIONAL SELLING SKILLS

1. What are your strengths and weaknesses when it comes to managing time? Complete the worksheet on the following page by checking off the answer that

best reflects your situation and score your answers according to the instructions below.

Scoring the Time Management Skills Worksheet:

If you have fewer than three checks in the Always column—You are doing well.

If you have four to five checks in the Always column—You are well on your way to becoming overwhelmed, but not yet over the edge. Make a few changes in your habits, and you will quickly be back in control of your time.

If you have more than five checks in the Always column—Life's fast track has gotten the better of you, and you are significantly overwhelmed. It will take a significant commitment, but you can regain control. Examine your scoring pattern on the worksheet. Look for the checks in the Always column where you can begin taking control. Start there and work up through the rest over time.

Time Management Skills Worksheet

Always	Sometimes	Never	
			Do you plan your day according to the daily "emergencies" of others?
			At the end of the day, do you have a lot of tasks undone?
			Do you repeatedly run out of household necessities such as milk, juice, or ingredients for the next meal?
			Are you frequently late to appointments?
			Do you find that you are a procrastinator?
			Do you frequently have to work late or start early to meet deadlines?
			If you needed to find a specific piece of paper (bill, invitation, or note), would it take more than five minutes?
			Do you forget friends' and relatives' birthdays more often than you would like to admit?
			Is your desk frequently piled with papers?
			Are you up to date on your filing?
			Do you let mail pile up?
			Do you do tasks yourself because it is easier than teaching it to someone else?
			Do you interrupt yourself by jumping up to do something else when you are working on a project?
			Do you let other people waste your time with overly long phone calls or drop-by visits that never end?
			Do you find that you are always losing things (e.g., your keys, assignment book, or library books)?
			Add up the number of checks in each column and enter the number in the corresponding square.

2. When was the last time you said something like, "I just do not understand where all my time goes?" This exercise is designed to help you find out by actually tracking your time for one full day. Tear out or make a copy of the Time Activity Chart on pages 289–290. Carry it with you and record what activities you are involved in throughout the day. The chart is set up to be easy to use—you just need to get in the habit of using it. You will probably be surprised at how much time is really lost during a single day. Imagine what it would look like if you charted your time for a full week!

   After you complete your time chart, study it to get an idea of where your time goes.

   (a) How much time is actually spent on activities that are high priorities for you?
   (b) How much time do others take from you?
   (c) How much time is lost running errands?
   (d) How much time is lost to interruptions?
   (e) What changes could you make to reclaim some of your time?

Time Activity Chart

5:00 A.M.	5:00 P.M.
5:15	5:15
5:30	5:30
5:45	5:45
6:00	6:00
6:15	6:15
6:30	6:30
6:45	6:45
7:00	7:00
7:15	7:15
7:30	7:30
7:45	7:45
8:00	8:00
8:15	8:15
8:30	8:30
8:45	8:45
9:00	9:00
9:15	9:15
9:30	9:30
9:45	9:45
10:00	10:00
10:15	10:15
10:30	10:30
10:45	10:45
11:00	11:00
11:15	11:15
11:30	11:30
11:45	11:45
12:00 Noon	12:00 Midnight
12:15 P.M.	12:15 A.M.

(Continued)

Time Activity Chart (Continued)

12:30	12:30
12:45	12:45
1:00	1:00
1:15	1:15
1:30	1:30
1:45	1:45
2:00	2:00
2:15	2:15
2:30	2:30
2:45	2:45
3:00	3:00
3:15	3:15
3:30	3:30
3:45	3:45
4:00	4:00
4:15	4:15
4:30	4:30
4:45	4:45 A.M.

ROLE PLAY

3. **Situation:**   Read the Ethical Dilemma on page 278.

   Characters: Yourself as regional sales manager, National Assurance Corporation; other students as sales agents for National Assurance Corporation

   Scene: *Location*—A regional sales agent meeting at district headquarters. *Action*—As the regional sales manager, you are conducting the biannual meeting of all sales agents in the region. This meeting is being held three months after the National Meeting in Orlando where the ACT! program ran into significant obstacles from the sales force. One of your objectives for this meeting is to address the growing dissension between the agents and NAC regarding the ACT!-based customer information system.

Role play how you might utilize each of the "six teamwork skills" previously discussed in this module to begin the team-building process that is required if the new information system is to be successful.

Upon completion of the role play, address the following questions:

3a. What explanations might be possible for the agents' apparent suspicion regarding the new customer-information system and NAC's ability to access the information?

3b. How could the sales agents employ the "six teamwork skills" to reduce possible conflicts between agents and the company over the new information system?

ROLE PLAY

4. **Situation:**   Read the Ethical Dilemma on page 282.

   Characters: Yourself as Cliff Cody, sales representative for Altima Telecom; another student as James Well, sales manager for Altima Telecom; other students as members of phone teams

Scene: *Location*—Sales manager's office at Altima Telecom.
Action—You are meeting with your sales manager, James Well, and leaders from several of the phone teams that work on your customers' accounts hoping to resolve some of the problems.

Role play how you would approach and initiate a positive and collaborative relationship with the sales manager and phone team members that might generate positive outcomes for your customer, Altima, and everyone involved. Remember to employ the "six teamwork skills" previously discussed in this module.

Upon completion of the role play, address the following questions:

4a. What might be possible explanations for the breakdown in delivered service quality at Altima?

4b. How could collaboration and teamwork reduce and possibly minimize conflicts between Altima's salespeople and the other internal operating units of the organization?

5. As a Plano, Texas-based salesperson for American Plastics, you have responsibility for a territory that extends in a radius of 100 miles around Plano. American Plastics has introduced a line of plastisol-based materials targeted for use by accounts that mold raw plastic materials into consumer and industrial products. You are in the process of identifying leads and prospects in your territory and establishing a route-plan that will allow you to call on each of them in the most efficient manner.

Having become a regular user of the Internet and World Wide Web in digging out business-related information on prospects and accounts, you are aware that the SuperPages site has the capability to search specific geographic areas by types of business. In addition, the Web site can provide (1) a total count of the number of firms active in a specific industry and located in a specified area and (2) a detailed listing of those firms, including name, location, and phone numbers.

5a. Access the SuperPages site at http://www.superpages.com and generate a listing of firms that are active in the business/industry described as "molded plastics" within the area of your territory. Print the listing in a format suitable to hand in to your instructor.

- On the SuperPages home page, select the "Search by Distance" option to search for U.S. Businesses.
- On the "Search by Distance" page:
  - Enter the keyword category as "plastic molder."
  - Scroll down and select 100 miles in the "search within distance window."
  - In the address block, enter Plano as the city and TX as the state.
  - Click on "Find It."
  - When the screen appears and asks you to specify which type of plastic molders you are interested in, select and click on "plastic injection molding."
- How many leads did you find? Where are they located? Print the list in a format suitable for bringing to class for discussion and submitting to your instructor.

5b. Now go to the MapQuest Web site at http://www.mapquest.com.

- Use MapQuest to access a map of your territory around Plano.
- Print the map and locate the general location of each of the company leads identified in your search of the SuperPages site by placing a locator mark on the map. For cities having multiple prospects, indicate the number of leads with the corresponding number of leads located in the city next to your locator mark for that city.

5c. Considering that you work out of an office in Plano, Texas, examine the pattern of locator marks and concentrations of accounts. Based on the pattern of locator marks and concentrations, determine which territory routing method would be most efficient for you to use. Using a colored marker, trace the routing you would recommend onto the map.

5d. What routing method did you choose? Discuss your routing plan and explain why you selected the method that you chose over the other methods available to you.

MAKING PROFESSIONAL SELLING DECISIONS

Case 10.1: Emron Control Corp.

Emron Control Corp. is a leading supplier for process control systems and equipment used in a wide variety of production and distribution applications. You have taken a sales representative job with Emron, and having just completed training, you have been given a territory of your own. Your district manager has provided you with a list of accounts as well as several boxes of notes and files that had been assembled and used by your predecessor. These are the accounts currently buying your products. You are expected to build these accounts and add new accounts to the list as you increase your territory's sales performance. You have summarized the account information into the following summary (at the bottom of the page) set of account profiles.

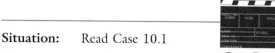

ROLE PLAY

Situation:	Read Case 10.1
Characters:	Rodney Moore, salesperson for Emron Control Corp.; Bart Waits, district sales manager and Moore's immediate supervisor
Scene:	*Location*—Bart Waits' office at Emron Control Corp.

Action—Rodney has just been assigned this territory and has completed an analysis of sales and customer files to profile the individual accounts and sales call allocation strategies utilized by the previous salesperson in the territory. Based on this information, Moore has developed information responding to each of the three questions following Case 10.1. This information includes a new sales call allocation strategy. Moore is meeting with his sales manager to explain his new sales call allocation plan.

As Moore, complete the three questions following Case 10.1. Using

Questions

1. Develop a portfolio classification of accounts and assess the allocation of sales calls made by your predecessor over the past year.
2. What problems do you find with the previous allocation of calls on these accounts?
3. Based on your account classification analysis, suggest a new sales call allocation strategy that would make better use of your time in the territory.

Account Name	Account Opportunity	Competitive Position	Annual Number of Sales Calls Last Year
Mueller Distribution	High	Low	30
Tri-State Specialties	Low	High	20
Birkey Paper Co.	Low	High	26
Normal Supply	Low	Low	12
Darnell Aggregate Products	Low	High	21
Reinhart Chemicals	High	High	26
ACCO Manufacturing	Low	High	23
Tri-State Manufacturing	High	Low	28
Ideal Engineering	Low	Low	11
Terracon	High	High	25
Lowry Foods	High	Low	26
SCS Industrial	High	High	27
Lowell Services	Low	High	18
Bowles and Sons	Low	High	21
American Foundry	High	Low	22
Hewitt & Associates	Low	Low	16
Bright Metals Inc.	High	High	22
Decatur Extrusions	Low	Low	14
King Chemicals	Low	High	22
Bear's Steel Corp.	Low	High	20
Hoffman Pharmaceuticals	High	Low	20
Barlow & Clark Systems	Low	High	18

this information, role play your interaction with your sales manager, Waits, as you discuss and explain (1) your analysis of the previous salesperson's sales call allocation and (2) your new plans and how they will increase the effectiveness and efficiency of your selling efforts in this territory.

Upon completion of the role play, address the following questions:

1. How might Moore's sales allocation plan be different if he had used single-factor analysis (ABC analysis) instead of portfolio analysis?
2. Develop a sales call allocation plan using single-factor analysis. Compare the results of Moore's portfolio analysis with the results of your single-factor analysis. Where and how are they different?
3. How might those differences translate to increased selling effectiveness and efficiency?

Case 10.2: Mark Cassidy and Milligan Adhesives Corporation

Mark Cassidy has just graduated and taken a job as a sales representative for the Milligan Adhesives Corporation, a supplier of adhesives used in the construction and manufacturing industries. Cassidy's west Dallas territory is full of opportunity, and like many new salespeople, Cassidy is finding it difficult to get everything done that needs his attention. The Daily Time and Activity Log on the following page is an actual day copied from Cassidy's records that he thinks is typical. Analyze Cassidy Time and Activity Log.

Questions

1. What problems do you find?
2. What suggestions could you make to help Cassidy make better use of his selling time?

ROLE PLAY

Situation:	Read Case 10.2
Characters:	Mark Cassidy, salesperson for Milligan Adhesives Corporation; Mitch Griffin, district sales manager for Milligan Adhesives Corporation and Cassidy's immediate supervisor
Scene:	*Location*—Mitch Griffin's office at Milligan Adhesives.

Action—As a new salesperson, Cassidy is finding it difficult to get everything done that he needs to accomplish in order to effectively fulfill his responsibilities. In response to Griffin's request, Cassidy has kept a log of his daily activities so that they might examine it for areas of ineffective time allocation.

In accordance with the questions following Case 10.2, look over the Daily Time and Activity Log that follows, then case and note any areas that might represent ineffective uses of selling time. Based on your analysis of the time log, role play the interaction with your sales manager, Griffin, as you discuss and explain (1) your analysis of effective time usage and (2) your thoughts and ideas regarding improvements that might increase the effectiveness and efficiency of your selling time allocation.

Upon completion of the role play, address the following questions:

1. What other problems do you see regarding Cassidy's time and activity allocations?
2. What other suggestions might be made for further improving Cassidy's allocation of selling time and activities?

Daily Time and Activity Log			
Salesperson Name: *Mark Cassidy*		**Date:** *Monday 8/7*	
Territory: *West Dallas*			
Time	**Activity**	**Company/People**	**Notes & Comments**
9:15–10:00	*Sales call*	*Mike Humphreys Mid West Construction Supply*	*Called on buyer to demo our 810 line of adhesives. Wrote 2 orders: $11,300 for this quarter; $12,450 following quarter.*
10:00–10:25	*Travel time*	*Jill Attaway Horner Construction job site @ 310 Maple*	*Service problem with $600 worth of wallboard adhesive. Was supposed to meet project manager this morning, but she was not at the job site yet.*
10:25–10:45	*Travel and phone call*	*"*	*Used pay phone at Walgreens to call Attaway on her cell. She is on way to job site to meet me.*
10:45–11:00	*Travel back to job site*	*"*	
11:00–11:35	*Service call*	*"*	*Met with Jill Attaway re: product problem. FedExing replacement for arrival tomorrow morning. Customer is OK with everything.*
11:35–12:05	*Travel time*	*Terrell Manufacturing Kerri Williams*	*Have appointment for 12:00 lunch.*
12:05–1:15	*Sales call and lunch*	*"*	*Follow-up call from 2 weeks ago. Closed a sale for our 2000 wood/laminate production adhesive. We will supply 50% of their needs. Should produce $12,000 per month over the year.*
1:15–1:20	*Travel time*	*TriState Cabinets Bart Waits*	*Cold call on high-potential prospect located 2 blocks down from Terrell Mfg. Already nearby—thought I would make a personal contact.*
1:20–1:45	*Waited in lobby*	*"*	*Bart Waits, head buyer, was busy but wanted to see me. Ask that I wait in lobby until he got free.*
1:45–2:10	*Sales call*	*"*	*Met with head buyer and gathered information— he wants a proposal on our 2000 line and ask that I drop back in sometime next week to present a proposal. No definite time—just drop in.*
2:10–2:55	*Travel time*	*Comanche Table Mfg. Aimee Williams*	*Drove across town to keep a 3:30 appointment with Aimee. Comanche has regularly purchased $8,000 monthly and is getting ready to open a plant expansion that will double production.*
2:55–4:00	*Sales call*	*"*	*Clarified delivery dates for added product needs. Our orders will increase to $10,000 monthly in 2 months.*
4:00–4:05	*Travel time*	*Dalco Laminates Rodney Moore*	*Cold call. Dalco is located down the street from Comanche Table. Already on this side of town and have been meaning to make a prospecting call.*
4:05–4:30	*Sales call*	*"*	*Worked with buyer to explore their needs, plans, and current suppliers. Their parent company is National Chemical, and they currently buy all adhesives from National. Low potential to sell!!*
4:30–5:55	*Return to office*	*Need to complete paperwork and orders*	*Crossing town in peak traffic. Took forever. Late getting home—family had already left for son's ball game.*

EXPERIENTIAL EXERCISES

List of Exercises

1.1

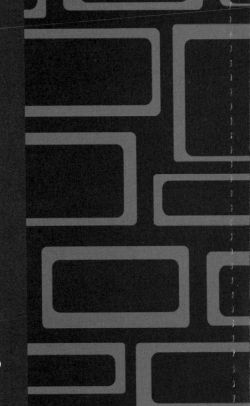

Discovering Attitudes Toward Sales Careers

Objective

You will evaluate and understand your own attitudes toward professional selling as a career and develop a sense of how and why this attitude varies from individual to individual.

THE EXERCISE ASSIGNMENT

Please complete the following survey by circling the number corresponding to your degree of agreement or disagreement for each of the statements. The meaning of the numbers is as follows:

1. Strongly Disagree
2. Disagree
3. Neither Agree or Disagree
4. Agree
5. Strongly Agree

I associate a job in professional selling with:	Strongly Disagree				Strongly Agree
Frustration	1	2	3	4	5
Insincerity and deceit	1	2	3	4	5
Low status/low prestige	1	2	3	4	5
Much traveling	1	2	3	4	5
Salespeople being "money hungry" . .	1	2	3	4	5
High pressure; forcing people to buy unwanted goods	1	2	3	4	5
Low job security	1	2	3	4	5
"Just a job," not a "career"	1	2	3	4	5
Uninteresting/no challenge	1	2	3	4	5
No need for creativity	1	2	3	4	5
Personality is crucial	1	2	3	4	5
Too little monetary reward	1	2	3	4	5
Interferes with home life	1	2	3	4	5
I prefer a nonsales position much more than a sales position	1	2	3	4	5

SCORING YOUR SURVEY

When you have completed the survey by circling a number for each and every item, **add** each of the numbers you circled and enter the **sum** here: _____

Now, **divide** the sum on the line above by 14, and enter the answer: _____

    This final number (it should be a number between 1 and 5) represents your overall attitude toward sales as a career, based on these 14 attributes. A score below 3 (disagreement with the statement) would indicate a positive attitude toward sales, while a score above 3 (agreement with the statement) would signify a negative attitude toward sales as a career.

    Experience indicates that comparing the results from this survey typically leads to a lively discussion. By all means—do join in! Among many others, some specific items you might want to examine and discuss are:

1. How does your overall score compare with those of others in the class?

_____

Can you identify any possible reasons these differences exist?_____

_____

_____

_____

2. Are your scores for any specific items significantly different (that is, more positive/negative toward sales as a career) from the scores for other statements on your survey?

_____

_____

_____

Can you identify any possible reasons for these differences?_____

_____

_____

Words That Identify Salespeople and a Sales Career

Objective

You will be able to express how you feel about salespeople and a sales career.

THE EXERCISE ASSIGNMENT

What words can you think of that describe a salesperson?

1. _____ Why? _____

   _____

2. _____ Why? _____

   _____

3. _____ Why? _____

   _____

4. _____ Why? _____

   _____

5. _____ Why? _____

   _____

6. _____ Why? _____

   _____

7. _____ Why? _____

   _____

Were your words generally positive? _____ Yes _____ No

Why?_____

_____

_____

Were your words generally negative? _____ Yes _____ No

Why?_____

_____

_____

What words can you think of that describe a sales career?

1. _____ Why?_____

_____

_____

2. _____ Why?_____

_____

_____

3. _____ Why?_____

_____

_____

4. _____ Why?_____

_____

_____

5. _____ Why?_____

_____

_____

6. _____ Why?_____

_____

_____

7. _____ Why?_____

_____

_____

Were your words generally positive? _____ Yes _____ No

Why?_____

_____

_____

Were your words generally negative? _____ Yes _____ No

Why?_____

_____

_____

Salesperson and Buyer Interviews

Objective

You will gather information from a buyer and a seller about the activities associated with their jobs.

THE EXERCISE ASSIGNMENT

This exercise will familiarize you with the day-to-day activities of a salesperson and a buyer. Ideally, the exercise will carry even more meaning if you can call on a buyer and a seller from the same industry.

To complete this exercise, you will first need to identify (a) a salesperson and (b) a buyer willing to talk with you about their job roles and activities. Use the following "Salesperson Interview Questions" and "Buyer Interview Questions" as a guide for interviewing both the salesperson and the buyer. Record the responses that you receive during these interviews and use them to complete the two discussion questions that follow the interview questions. Your survey results and responses to the discussion questions will be handed in and used as inputs for class discussions comparing your results with those of other students in the class.

Salesperson Interview Questions

1. What industry are you in?
2. What is the formal title used to designate your position in the company?
   No. of years selling with the company _____
   No. of years total selling experience _____
3. How many hours per week do you work?
4. What percent of your typical week is spent in the following activities?
   a. Prospecting
   b. Administration (that is, paperwork)
   c. Travel

   d. Face-to-face selling
   e. Internal meetings
   f. Servicing accounts

5. In a sales presentation, what percentage of your time is spent on the following activities?
   a. Information gathering
   b. Actual sales presentations
   c. Commitment (confirming, handling objections, closing)
   d. Follow through (servicing the account after the sale)

6. What preparations do you make before meeting with a prospective buyer?

7. On average, how many sales calls do you make to the same prospect in order to successfully make the sale?

8. What percentage of your sales calls result in a sale?

9. How often do you talk with the buyer between sales?

10. On a scale of 1 = no stress to 10 = a great deal of stress, how stressful do you perceive your job to be? What do you find most stressful about your job?

11. On a scale of 1 = very negative to 10 = very positive, what do you believe are the customers' perceptions of the salespeople associated with your industry?

12. Do you eventually develop an opinion or attitude about a buyer and adjust your presentation accordingly or is it typical in your industry to use a fairly standard sales presentation?

13. What percent of your total compensation is salary and bonus? Does this compensation plan provide adequate incentive for you? How could the compensation plan be improved to enhance your motivation?

14. What abilities (characteristics) do you believe are crucial for success in your industry?

15. As you carry out your roles as a salesperson, how important are each of the following? Why do you think they are perceived in this manner?
   a. Trust
   b. Communication
   c. Relationships
   d. Ethics

16. What college courses prepared you the most for your career in sales?

17. How often do you set goals for your sales calls? Are these formalized (that is, written)? Give me an example of a prospecting goal you would set. Give me an example of a selling goal you would set.

18. Do you keep formal records of sales calls? May I have a blank copy of your sales call report?

19. How much formal sales training does your organization provide? Is there a continuous sales training program in place? At what intervals do you participate in this training?

20. What aspects of your job do you enjoy most? What aspects do you enjoy least?

21. What is your most memorable sales call?

Buyer Interview Questions

1. What business or industry are you in?

2. What is the formal title used to designate your position in the company?
   No. of years in purchasing with this company _____
   No. of years total purchasing experience _____

3. How many hours per week do you work?

4. What percent of your typical week is spent in the following activities?
   a. Researching, identifying, and clarifying needs
   b. Specifying product requirements (quality, features, volume, and so on)
   c. Researching and identifying potential suppliers
   d. Requesting and acquiring sales proposals
   e. Evaluating proposals and selecting suppliers

    f. Evaluation of satisfaction with purchase

    g. Problem resolution

    h. Administration (that is, record keeping and paperwork)

5. As a buyer in a sales presentation, what percentage of your time is spent on the following activities?
   a. Giving information
   b. Information gathering
   c. Negotiating details

6. As a buyer, what preparations do you make before meeting with a salesperson? How do these preparations differ between salespeople that you currently buy from and salespeople from whom you are not already buying?

7. On average, how many sales meetings are required *with the same salesperson* before you make a purchase?

8. On average, how often do you talk with a salesperson between purchases from that salesperson or his or her company?

9. On a scale from 1 = no stress to 10 = a great deal of stress, how stressful do you perceive your job to be? What do you find most stressful about your job?

10. On a scale from 1 = very negative to 10 = very positive, what do you believe is the typical customer's perception of the salespeople associated with your industry?

11. What percent of your total compensation is salary, commission, and bonus? Does this compensation plan provide adequate incentive for you? How could the compensation plan be improved to enhance your motivation?

12. What abilities (characteristics) do you believe are crucial for success as a buyer?

13. What college courses prepared you the most for your career as a buyer?

14. Considering your experience as a buyer, what characteristics do you perceive as important in salespeople? Please rank the following items in order of importance (1 = most important, 2 = next most important, 8 = least important).

    Aggressive   _____

    Creative   _____

    Disciplined   _____

    Likable   _____

    Knowledgeable   _____

    Professional   _____

    Verbally skilled   _____

    Well-groomed   _____

15. What percentage of your company's purchases requires the input of more than one person in the purchase decision?

16. What aspects of your job do you enjoy most? What aspects do you enjoy least?

17. As you carry out your role as a buyer dealing with different suppliers and salespeople, how important are each of the following? Why do you think they are perceived in this manner?
    a. Trust
    b. Communication
    c. Relationships
    d. Ethics

18. What is your most memorable sales interaction with a salesperson?

19. What time of day do you find best to work with salespeople?

Discussion Questions

1. After you have interviewed your buyer and seller, describe what characteristics appear to be essential to be successful in each of these professions.

   a. Sales _____

      _____

      _____

      _____

      _____

      _____

   b. Buyer _____

      _____

      _____

      _____

      _____

      _____

2. If your salesperson or buyer perceived their job to be stressful, what made it so?

   _____

   _____

   _____

   _____

   _____

   _____

   _____

3. If your salesperson or buyer perceived their job not to be stressful, what made it so?

   _____

   _____

   _____

   _____

   _____

   _____

   _____

A.1

What Are the Options?

Objective

You will narrow down sales career options. This exercise provides you with a framework for and experience in setting up your "focus set" of firms in which to explore job possibilities and opportunities.

WHAT TYPE OF SELLING DO YOU PREFER?

As your first step toward identifying companies that you might like to work for, you need to make a basic decision as to what type of selling activities you prefer. There are a multitude of career options available in selling. As the role of the professional salesperson continues to evolve and organizations actively increase the career opportunities available through the selling track, the term salesperson loses more and more meaning as a unique descriptor. Prior to beginning this exercise, review pages 23–25 to refresh your memory of the six basic classifications of selling: Sales Support, New Business Sales, Existing Business Sales, Inside Sales (Nonretail), Direct-to-Consumer Sales, and Combination Sales Jobs.

THE EXERCISE ASSIGNMENT

Using the preceding six basic classifications of selling as a guide, **circle the column heading** in the following table that corresponds to the type of selling activity that you prefer. Next, consider the different industries (far left column) that might be open to you within that specific type of selling. As you consider the possible industries that are attractive to you, rank your five most preferred choices by placing the corresponding ranking number in the proper cell of the column (1 indicating your top choice and 5 indicating your fifth choice).

Considering your choices, use your own base of experience, input from other knowledgeable people (parents, relatives, friends and acquaintances, faculty, and library/career placement resources) to identify ten companies that are active in each of the five cells that you have chosen on the matrix. These 50 companies should become your "career focus companies"—companies on which you are going to place a priority focus for your job search. Now that you have identified your priority companies, you should (a) learn all you can about each of them, (b) identify an effective point of contact that can get you into the companies' recruiting processes, and (c) make the necessary contacts to get your cover letter and résumé placed for consideration.

Industry Classification	Sales Support	New Business Sales	Existing Sales	Inside Sales (Nonretail)	Direct-to-Consumer Sales	Combination Sales Jobs
Business Services						
Communications						
Electronics						
Fabricated Metals						
Health Services						
Drugs						
Insurance						
Machinery						
Manufacturing						
Paper and Allied Products						
Printing/Publishing						

Industry Classification	Sales Support	New Business Sales	Existing Sales	Inside Sales (Nonretail)	Direct-to-Consumer Sales	Combination Sales Jobs
Hotels/Lodging						
Other						
Other						
Other						
Other						
Other						
Other						
Other						

A.2

How Salespeople Spend Their Time

Objective

You will be able to determine the scope of a salesperson's job and how salespeople spend their time.

THE EXERCISE ASSIGNMENT

Based on your knowledge of a sales career, how do you think a salesperson spends his or her time? What sales activities will a typical salesperson be responsible for?

1. Activity: _____

    _____

2. Activity: _____

    _____

3. Activity: _____

    _____

4. Activity: _____

    _____

5. Activity: _____

    _____

6. Activity: _____

    _____

7. Activity: _____

_____

8. Activity: _____

_____

9. Activity: _____

_____

10. Activity: _____

_____

11. Activity: _____

_____

12. Activity: _____

_____

13. Activity: _____

_____

14. Activity: _____

_____

15. Activity: _____

_____

EXPERIENTIAL EXERCISE

A.3

What Attributes Are Essential to a Successful Sales Career?

Objective

You will be able to determine what characteristics are essential for a successful salesperson.

THE EXERCISE ASSIGNMENT

Based on your knowledge of salespeople that you have been around, what characteristics do you believe are essential for success in selling? Why?

1. Characteristic _____ Why? _____

    _____

    _____

2. Characteristic _____ Why? _____

    _____

    _____

3. Characteristic _____ Why? _____

    _____

    _____

4. Characteristic _____ Why? _____

    _____

    _____

5. Characteristic _____ Why? _____

_____

_____

6. Characteristic _____ Why? _____

_____

_____

7. Characteristic _____ Why? _____

_____

_____

8. Characteristic _____ Why? _____

_____

_____

9. Characteristic _____ Why? _____

_____

_____

10. Characteristic _____ Why? _____

_____

_____

11. Characteristic _____ Why? _____

_____

_____

12. Characteristic _____ Why? _____

_____

_____

EXPERIENTIAL EXERCISE

A.4

Résumé Writing I: Identifying Your Accomplishments and Skills

Objective

You will increase your understanding of the résumé writing process while developing your own résumé in preparation for graduation.

IDENTIFYING MEANINGFUL ACCOMPLISHMENTS AND SKILLS

The Foundation for Your Job Search

An effective self-analysis provides the foundation for your job search campaign. It directs you by identifying what you have to "sell." If you can think of yourself as "being on the market," then your first need is to define clearly what your product qualities are, or the skills and strengths that you have to offer in the job market.

To describe your qualities, you need to go beyond the title or task description of your last job and become aware of your general experience, background, knowledge, skills, and abilities. You should be able to break down your jobs into their component parts. This preciseness will help you visualize and plan how those very same strengths might be *transferable* to a new type of job that, on the surface, appears to be quite different from your recent work.

Accomplishments

As you look back over your last few years on the job or in school, you can recollect special things you have done that made you very proud. These were the times when you went beyond the call of duty—meeting an emergency, solving a problem, or seizing a red-hot opportunity. Usually these accomplishments were of great benefit to your employer, to your fellow workers, to your peers in school, or to yourself. The accomplishment may or may not have received recognition or praise from someone higher up. More important, these achievements illustrate your skills and capabilities—your future potential for solving problems.

THE EXERCISE ASSIGNMENT

Your first assignment is to discover and write down 12 lifetime accomplishments. Aim for completeness rather than conciseness. You may discover that you have a lot more to be proud of than you thought. However, the purpose in writing the accomplishments is not merely to boost your self-esteem (although that is a worthwhile by-product). Writing down your accomplishments will:

- Supply you with material for creating or enhancing your résumé.
- Give you a foundation for deriving your skills and strengths.
- Make you more comfortable about recounting your strengths—in a letter or in an interview.

To get started writing your first accomplishments:

- Identify a problem, opportunity, or situation you faced at work or at school that required you to take some sort of action.
- Explain the action or approach that you took in solving the problem or taking advantage of the opportunity. Your explanation should focus on how you analyzed and prepared to solve the problem and on the resources (people, equipment, and so on) that you used in your solution or plan.
- Identify the results you obtained. Results may be quantified in terms of savings, days, sales volume, and so on or qualified in terms of usefulness to yourself or others. Or you might explain how the plan was implemented and who utilized the information.

Where to Look

In digging up your accomplishments, do not feel obliged to look for something cosmic. Some of your accomplishments may be so noteworthy that you will want to use them later in your résumé or in an interview. But other, less spectacular accomplishments may be equally useful in uncovering your true talents, skills, knowledge, and strengths. In fact, you may find key accomplishments performed off the job. For example, you may have accomplished great things in community activities or in your church; if so, do not hesitate to list these as valid accomplishments. Accomplishments in school are valid indicators of what you have to "sell." Remember, an accomplishment is not dictated by the rewards you receive from the outside world, but by your own sense of satisfaction for having done the job.

Use the following to "jog your memory":

- Did you take the initiative to solve a problem or address an issue that no one else was tackling?
- Did you see an opportunity for great improvement, develop a plan to seize the opportunity, and help carry it through to success?
- Did you develop a new gadget or new approach that improved daily output?
- Did you conceive of or create a new organization, function, service, department, or product that filled an important niche?
- Did you devise and carry through a complex plan or procedure, perhaps for the first time?
- Did you participate with your peers or superiors at work or school on an important project where your input was part of the key to its success?
- Have you dealt with customers? Were some of them irate? How did you deal with them? What skills did you use in this type of situation?
- Did you have responsibility for scheduling employees for work or an ongoing project that needed to be completed on a timely basis?

- Were you ever left to supervise yourself and/or others? What kinds of things were you responsible for?
- Did you support yourself while you were in school?
- Did you "close" at your place of work?
- Were you involved in clubs at school? Were you an officer? Did you start or help start any new activities? Have you been in charge of any projects?
- Do you have any specific computer hardware or software knowledge?
- Did you complete any major projects in classes that relate to your desired job?
- Did you ever train other employees?
- Were you ever in charge of inventory or buying for inventory?
- Do you have any academic honors?
- Did you participate in an internship program?

How You Say It Is Important Too!

When writing your accomplishments, *begin by using action words* where possible. Examples of these clear-cut, punchy words follow:

Action Words

Administer	Determine	Investigate	Reduce
Advise	Develop	Lead	Relate
Affect	Devise	Maintain	Renew
Analyze	Direct	Manage	Report
Anticipate	Distribute	Manipulate	Represent
Apply	Draft	Market	Reorganize
Approach	Edit	Mediate	Research
Approve	Educate	Merchandise	Resolve
Arrange	Encourage	Moderate	Responsible
Assemble	Enlarge	Modify	Review
Assess	Enlist	Monitor	Revise
Assign	Establish	Motivate	Scan
Assist	Estimate	Negotiate	Schedule
Attain	Evaluate	Obtain	Screen
Author	Examine	Operate	Select
Build	Execute	Order	Serve
Calculate	Expand	Organize	Speak
Catalog	Expedite	Originate	Staff
Chair	Facilitate	Participate	Standardize
Collaborate	Forecast	Perform	Stimulate
Communicate	Formulate	Persuade	Successful
Compare	Generate	Placate	Summarize
Conceive	Guide	Plan	Supervise
Conceptualize	Handle	Prepare	Support
Consult	Identify	Present	Survey
Contract	Implement	Preside	Synthesize
Control	Improve	Problem-solve	Systemize
Cooperate	Increase	Process	Teach
Coordinate	Influence	Produce	Team
Counsel	Inform	Promote	Team-build
Create	Initiate	Provide	Technical
Decide	Innovate	Recommend	Train
Define	Install	Reconcile	Transmit
Delegate	Institute	Record	Update
Demonstrate	Instruct	Recruit	Utilize
Design	Integrate	Rectify	Versatile
Detail	Invent	Redesign	Write

Résumés should clearly accent those accomplishments that transfer as work related skills. How you phrase these is also important. Translate accomplishments so that they represent benefits to your target companies. Sample accomplishments follow. Notice that several of these accomplishments are quantified as to *results*. When the accomplishments are used in your résumé, they should be condensed (usually to two or three lines) without losing their impact.

Work Related Accomplishments

- Managed warehouse and accounted for $300,000 inventory.
- Received Salesperson of the Month Award four times.
- Achieved 2nd Place in Salesperson of the Year Competition.
- Averaged 137 percent of quota over three years.

Career Related Achievements

- National Sales Hall of Fame Winner—4th out of 200 salespeople.
- Headed Marketing Committee for Pi Sigma Epsilon, a Professional Fraternity in Sales and Marketing.
- Headed Student Program at Illinois Central College.
- Organized and Directed the 2005 Illinois State University Follies.

Now, think about what you have been doing over the past three or four years. What are your accomplishments and achievements? How are they career related? After you have identified and recalled 12 accomplishments, write them out in the space provided. Do not forget to use the action verbs that were listed earlier. After you have filled in all 12 accomplishments, compare them and rank each one in describing your value in the job market. You may decide to use the top-ranked ones to produce an accomplishment-oriented résumé, rather than a list of job descriptions.

Name: _____

MY ACCOMPLISHMENTS AND ACHIEVEMENTS

Description of Accomplishment	Rank
• _____	
_____	_____
• _____	
_____	_____
• _____	
_____	_____
• _____	
_____	_____
• _____	
_____	_____
• _____	
_____	_____
• _____	
_____	_____
• _____	
_____	_____
• _____	
_____	_____
• _____	
_____	_____
• _____	
_____	_____

Résumé Writing II: Preparing Your Résumé

Objective

You will develop your own résumé in preparation for graduation.

PREPARING YOUR RÉSUMÉ

Purposes of a Résumé

To prepare the most effective résumé, you need to consider your target employer. An ideal résumé will reveal your most saleable skills and attributes as they relate to a specific position within a certain company. The résumé should be designed to *arouse* a prospective employer's interest and *inspire* the employer to call you for an interview. The résumé should provide enough information to show the employer that you are qualified for the job, but at the same time create compelling questions in the mind of the recruiter.

This means that you *should not* tell the employer "everything there is to know" about yourself. If you provide too much detail, a recruiter might notice an item that excludes you, or the recruiter might not be inspired to find out more about you.

To arouse interest, a résumé should be like a good advertisement—a deliberately crafted picture that beckons the reader to learn more through personal contact. Rather than tell all, you tell what is interesting and relevant for the reader's needs.

Different Résumé Formats

The two most commonly used formats are *chronological* and *functional*.

- The *chronological résumé* emphasizes your employment record—your job titles, where you worked, how long, and what responsibilities you held. Your jobs are listed in reverse order, beginning with the most recent.
- The *functional résumé* emphasizes the kinds of work you have done and what you accomplished in various aspects of business.

Actually, each type incorporates a bit of the other. The chronological résumé becomes more meaningful when you list accomplishments under each job. Likewise, a functional résumé will usually have a condensed employment history (showing company, date, and job title).

The functional résumé organizes work experience by functions, such as general marketing, management, production, finance, or any of their subfunctions. It usually incorporates a range of accomplishments to illustrate the job seeker's expertise in each area.

In addition to these two main types of résumés, others exist to fit special situations. For example, in the academic world the emphasis may be on educational background and published papers. In publishing or public relations, a résumé might have a narrative style or show a certain creative flair in the writing. A law firm or a public accounting firm might expect a very formal or conservative résumé.

If you are about to graduate from college and do not have a substantial work history, you may want to emphasize your education. Include *special* classes that you feel have a bearing on your marketability, any awards or honors you received, and any special responsibilities and involvements in organizations. Provide more than just a listing of names or titles. Think in terms of skills and knowledge gained to illustrate how and why this item of experience is important to the position that you are trying to obtain. If you supported yourself while in school, mention this. The best format for students is the functional résumé—it allows you to present your accomplishments without emphasizing the types of jobs that you held. Examples of two formats that may be useful for student résumés follow.

Résumé Format #1

YOUR NAME
ADDRESS AND PHONE

Objective

Summary

Education

| UNIVERSITY | DEGREE | DATE |

Educational and Work-Related Accomplishments

-

-

-

-

Work History

| JOB TITLE | DATES OF EMPLOYMENT |
| COMPANY | |

| JOB TITLE | DATES OF EMPLOYMENT |
| COMPANY | |

Résumé Format #2

YOUR NAME
ADDRESS AND PHONE

Objective

Summary

Academic Accomplishments

University	Degree	Date

-
-
-

Work History and Accomplishments

JOB TITLE   DATES OF EMPLOYMENT
COMPANY

-
-

JOB TITLE   DATES OF EMPLOYMENT
COMPANY

-

Writing the Objective

Almost every reader wants to know right away what you are looking for. Therefore, many authorities recommend that you begin with a clearly stated Job Objective that defines the kind of job that you want. This objective can be very broad or very specific. Several examples of objectives follow.

A position in marketing that would utilize my technical communications experience and capitalize on my ability to communicate effectively with customers.

A position that utilizes my business training and broad experience in oil industry operations.

An internship opportunity with a dynamic, growth-oriented public relations firm or department which would utilize my project development experience and enhance my ongoing MBA program.

If you are pursuing several different types of positions, *do not* include two objectives on the same résumé. Instead, develop two résumés with different objectives at the top, or even completely different résumés, with different objectives and accomplishments. When possible, a relevant and company-specific objective should be utilized.

Always include an objective. Otherwise, you force the recruiter or selection specialist to "figure out" where you belong in the company. If I have 500 résumés to evaluate, I am not going to take the time to "figure out" where you belong.

Also, do not use the term *entry level* in your objective. What if I do not have any entry level jobs? I wll immediately eliminate you from a secondary level position—even if you might be qualified. Do not overly restrict yourself. A final point on writing your objective: Do not copy it from this exercise or from a résumé writing book. If you do, it will sound just like all the rest.

Writing a Summary

The summary explains in a few lines who you are and why you deserve the job mentioned in your objective. In other words, it summarizes your credentials, skills, and qualifications—as they relate to your job objective. One paragraph of four to eight lines is usually enough. If the summary gets too long, you can break it down into subsections with bullets. Several examples of summaries follow.

Five years experience in project development, cost forecasting, and economic analysis. Areas of expertise include:

- Project planning
- Program implementation
- Computer skills
- Report writing
- Oral presentation skills

Over 15 years production experience at various domestic locations with direct responsibility for a broad range of technical functions, including equipment installations, water floods, steam operations, work overs, and recompletions. Extensive field experience in conjunction with this work.

Fourteen years experience, including nine years in the telecommunications industry and four years in a supervisory capacity. Skills include:

- Problem solving
- Communication and systems analysis
- Customer relations
- Project development

For individuals possessing little or no experience, such as a new college graduate, you might consider using a profile or highlight in place of the paragraph format. Examples of three different student profiles follow.

Professional Profile

- Well-developed oral and written communication skills
- Dependable and willing to accept responsibilities
- Proven organizational and leadership skills
- Goal-oriented, confident, professional

Professional Profile

- Outstanding academic achievement (3.88/4.00)
- Well-developed written and oral communication skills
- Proven organizational and problem solving skills
- Responsible, friendly, and thorough

Highlights of Qualifications

- 100% self-financed my college education
- Excelled at balancing work and academic responsibilities
- Functional with Microsoft Office and database software
- Self-motivated, responsible, and hard-working

Highlighting Academic and Work Accomplishments

You may want to use two separate categories if you have a rather impressive work history or many academic accomplishments. List several accomplishments. Try to use accomplishments that support your objective and summary. Your accomplishments should come from those identified in the preceding exercise. They should be concise and begin with an action verb.

Employment History—or Working Experience—or Career Background

For recent jobs it is usually worthwhile to list each job assignment within each company. A good framework begins with the job title followed by the approximate dates, the company name, and your accomplishment(s). The amount of detail for each job should taper down as you move farther back in your career.

Work History and Accomplishments

JOB TITLE   DATES OF EMPLOYMENT
COMPANY

- ░░░░░░░░░░░░░░░░░░░░░░░░░░░░░░░░░░░░░░░

If you are highlighting your accomplishments and simply including a work history, group your accomplishments under a functional heading and use the framework described earlier to list your jobs.

Educational and Work-Related Accomplishments

- ░░░░░░░░░░░░░░░░░░░░░░░░░░░░░░░░░░░░░░░

- ░░░░░░░░░░░░░░░░░░░░░░░░░░░░░░░░░░░░░░░

- ░░░░░░░░░░░░░░░░░░░░░░░░░░░░░░░░░░░░░░░

Work History

JOB TITLE   DATES OF EMPLOYMENT
COMPANY

JOB TITLE   DATES OF EMPLOYMENT
COMPANY

Summarizing Your Education

If you are just graduating and have very little work experience, education might be right near the top of your résumé. But for most commercial or industrial jobs, it can come at the end. This is also a good place to list supplementary training that you have received, such as workshops, conferences, seminars, special courses, etc. For example:

2005   B.S./Applied Computer Science at Illinois State University
2004   Harvard University—Thirteen-week general management course

If you are emphasizing your education (placing it at the beginning of the résumé), you may want to use a slightly different format. For example:

B.B.A.   Illinois State University—May, 2005
            Area of Concentration: Human Resource Management

Illinois State University   B.B.A.—May, 2005
                              Magna Cum Laude
                              Major: Marketing

You may decide to include a special section related to academic awards or honors and accomplishments (as discussed earlier). You may also want to include member-ships in organizations, especially if they are related to the type of work that you are seeking.

A Few More Helpful Hints

- Present yourself accurately and positively.
- Include enough information to get the "buyer's" interest.
- DO NOT include salary required. It may end negotiations prematurely. Have a range in mind for face-to-face discussion after you have the lay of the land.
- DO NOT include references. That comes later when parties both agree that there is strong interest.
- AVOID long, complicated sentences or paragraphs.
- DO NOT "overstuff" your résumé. Save some good items for the interview.
- Use capital letters, bullets, underlining, and so forth, to dress up your résumé. Use underlining with care as it can sometimes be difficult to read on copies.
- Have several people proofread your résumé before printing.
- Smaller type will permit more on a page without looking crowded. Play with fonts and margins to get the best layout. RÉSUMÉS SHOULD BE NO LONGER THAN ONE PAGE.

The following are the most common faults observed by professional résumé readers:

- Failure to state a clear objective early on the résumé.
- Failure to describe any accomplishments.
- Using an objective for which the applicant is obviously unqualified.
- Wordiness, incorrect spelling, and bad grammar.
- Incomplete employment history.
- Poor layout, paper, and general appearance.

THE EXERCISE ASSIGNMENT

Write an accomplishments-oriented résumé for yourself. Decide on a general format. Pull together a draft and get someone to help you critique and revise it. You should expect to go through several revisions.

The final résumé that you hand in for this assignment must be typed on a single sheet of paper. We suggest that you use a computer and save a final copy on disk in order to facilitate future revisions. Remember, your résumé is an evolving reflection of you. As you continue your job search it may need to be improved, or the objective may need to be changed. These types of changes are natural as your job search continues.

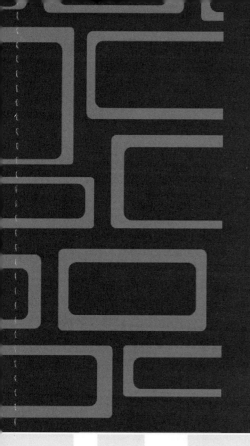

Résumé Writing III: Developing a Marketing Letter

Objective

You will write a cover letter to accompany your personal résumé.

The Role of Marketing Letters in Your Job Search

Good marketing letters can supplement and work in tandem with your networking and other search techniques. In your letter approach to any company, the ultimate purpose is to get an interview. The first response to your letter may be a phone or written request for more information. Make the letter interesting enough to provoke a request for more information.

There are several different types of letters that you can use in your job search process:

- The *search letter* tends to be more of a cover letter briefly summarizing your objective and background and referring to the attached résumé.
- The *company broadcast letter* will give you more room for creative writing since it usually tells your story without a résumé.
- The *customized* or *personalized letter* is aimed at a particular company and individual, usually someone that you have selected as a target. It is a rifle letter, not a shotgun. Often it is designed to stand on its own without an attached résumé.
- The *follow-up letter* is usually just an informal note. For example, it may convey your thanks and your enjoyment of an interview. It may attempt to get closure regarding the next step. Or it may simply be a reminder that you are still interested.

Your marketing letter should always include a résumé unless you are sending a follow-up letter.

Reach the Right Person

Finding the correct person to write to is an important part of your task. Companies and top executives are flooded with letters and résumés, so they each develop their own way of handling them. Most commonly, an executive who receives this flood of mail will ask his or her secretary (or some other gatekeeper) to screen it. Gate-keepers may:

- Throw your letter in the trash.
- Send it to Personnel or Human Resources.
- Pass it down the ladder or to another department or division.
- Put it in the boss' mail pile.
- Call it to the boss' attention because it looks interesting.

Your real challenge is to address your letter to a person who takes a keen interest in hiring your type of talent. If you have experience and are seeking a job in a specific function, your best bet is to address the letter to the executive in charge of that function. Otherwise, you should probably address your letter to the human resources manager (make sure that you confirm the name).

In searching for marketing and sales positions, many students have been successful in identifying the proper contact person within a specific target company by first finding that company's products in the marketplace. With this as a starting point, they begin working backward through the various intermediaries until they find the information that they are seeking. The following is an example of the backward process that was used successfully by one student:

> In preparing for her job search, Jamie Smith identified Flexall Industries as one of her primary target companies. Smith did not have any networks into Flexall and the company had never recruited at her university. Nevertheless, the information that Smith had been acquiring about the company did identify several of its products by name. Knowing these products were sold to hospitals and pharmacies, Smith called on several hospital purchasing offices and local pharmacies. It took perseverance, but she walked out with the name and address of Jim Burnett, the salesperson responsible for that region. After several calls, she finally made contact with Burnett.
>
> Naturally, he was guarded at first, but Smith was careful to establish up front that she just wanted to talk about Flexall and was not asking for an employment interview with him. After several minutes of small talk, Smith offered to buy Burnett coffee the next time that he was in town calling on his accounts. He not only accepted but also paid for the coffee. During their meeting, Smith got a lot of information that she could never have found in the career resources library or in the Flexall Annual Report. Included with this information was the name and address of the national sales director who had the primary responsibility for recruiting and hiring as well as the name and address of a district manager who was actively recruiting to fill a vacancy.
>
> Smith responded by sending a marketing letter and résumé to both individuals (different letters, by the way). You might be interested in a couple of points. First, Smith is working for Flexall—and has been ranked as one of their top performing rookies! Second, about two weeks into the training program, the national sales director let her know that her ingenuity in finding a way to make contact with the company was one of the chief reasons that she got the job offer. It had something to do with "…that's what we are looking for in our salespeople."

Once you identify who to contact, make sure that the information is current and correct. The directories that you read can easily be one or two year old, and companies tend to move people around. Your chances of getting through are greatly improved if your letter is correctly addressed to a responsible person, with the correct spelling and title. There is only one way to be sure of this: Call the headquarters, saying, "I would like to write a letter to _____. Is he or she still V.P. of _____? Can you help me with the exact spelling of his or her name and initials? Is he or she still located at this address?" If the telephone operator or receptionist does not sound well informed, try the Personnel Department. Admittedly, this double-checking is all very time consuming, but it will increase your yield of inquiries or interviews.

Writing the Marketing Letter

The opening paragraph counts most. It must hook the executive's attention with something that he or she wants to hear about—something that touches on his or her needs.

- Note that this paragraph is *not* about what *you* need.
- Most often it will describe an accomplishment that relates to the sort of job you are seeking.
- Or it may be one of the other attention-getting devices described below.

Typical strategies include the corporate needs and accomplishments approach, the direct approach, the narrative approach, the current events approach, and the provocative approach. Examples of each approach follow:

The Corporate Needs and Accomplishments Approach. Here you describe a problem that is common to your industry, how you tackled it, and what results you got. This approach gets right to the meat of why people might want to hire you.

The Direct Approach. You tell briefly in the first paragraph who you are and what you seek. This may be very similar to the first half-page of your resumé. This approach works well if you are just naturally marketable—you are the right age, you are a high achiever, you have a great track record, and you come from well-known companies.

The Tell a Story or Narrative Approach. Here you tell about yourself in narrative fashion, incorporating something unusual or very interesting that has happened to you recently.

The Current Events Approach. You relate your recent experience to something going on in the industry that is of wide interest.

The Provocative Approach. The first paragraph must contain something startling. Example: "I've just been fired and realize it was a good thing," or "I'd be willing to work for no salary if you would give me half of the utility costs I can save you." This approach is a bit risky unless it is carried off well.

Guidelines

In writing your marketing letter, there are several general guidelines you should incorporate. Some of these guidelines follow:

- Sell your accomplishments and your relevant experience.
- Don't go back too far.
- Omit personal data, such as age, hobbies, marital status, or children (unless they relate directly to the job).
- Omit salary, past or desired.
- Omit employment dates—in fact, all dates.
- Omit the common resumé references. Use a reference in the marketing letter only if it is a person who suggested you write this letter.
- Plan on sweating through several drafts. Polish them!!!! Mistakes—spelling or grammar—will kill your chances!!

THE EXERCISE ASSIGNMENT

Develop and craft a marketing letter to accompany your resumé. Use one of the approaches discussed earlier. Your final drafts must be typed as if they were to be mailed. Again, using a computer and saving copies of files on disk are highly recommended.

EXPERIENTIAL EXERCISE

2.1

Ethics Scale

Objective

You will develop an understanding of the multitude of ethical situations that exist.

THE EXERCISE ASSIGNMENT

How ethical is each of the following situations? Be prepared to defend your answer. Please circle your response for each situation.

1. The salesperson seeks confidential information about competitors by questioning suppliers.

   very ethical   **ethical**   **neither**   **unethical**   **very unethical**

2. The salesperson seeks information from the purchaser on competitors' quotations for the purpose of submitting another quotation.

   very ethical   **ethical**   **neither**   **unethical**   **very unethical**

3. The buyer gives the salesperson information on competitors' quotations, then allows him or her to requote.

   very ethical   **ethical**   **neither**   **unethical**   **very unethical**

4. The buyer exaggerates the seriousness of a problem to a salesperson in order to get a better price or some other concession.

   very ethical   **ethical**   **neither**   **unethical**   **very unethical**

Sources: Adapted from I. F. Trawick, J. E. Swan, G. W. McGee, and D. R. Rink, *Journal of The Academy of Marketing Science*, 19 (1) (1991): 17–23; A. J. Dubinsky, and T. N. Ingram, "Correlates of Salespeople Ethical Conflict: An Exploratory Investigation," *Journal of Business Ethics*, 3 (1984): 343–353; A. J. Dubinsky, and I. M. Gwin, "Business Ethics: Buyers and Sellers," *Journal of Purchasing and Materials Management*, 17 (Winter, 1981): 9–16.

5. To obtain a lower price or other concession, the buyer *falsely* informs an existing supplier that the company may use another source.

very ethical   ethical   neither   unethical   very unethical

6. The buyer solicits quotations from new sources, when a marked preference for existing suppliers is the norm, merely to fill a quota for bids.

very ethical   ethical   neither   unethical   very unethical

7. The salesperson attempts to get the buyer to divulge competitors' bids in low-bid buying situations.

very ethical   ethical   neither   unethical   very unethical

8. The salesperson exaggerates how quickly orders will be delivered to get a sale.

very ethical   ethical   neither   unethical   very unethical

9. The salesperson lets it be known that he or she has information about a competitor if the purchasing agent is interested.

very ethical   ethical   neither   unethical   very unethical

10. The salesperson hints that, if the order is placed, the price might be lower on the next order, when it is not so.

very ethical   ethical   neither   unethical   very unethical

11. The salesperson stresses only positive aspects of the product, omitting possible problems that the purchasing firm might have with it.

very ethical   ethical   neither   unethical   very unethical

12. The buyer allows factors such as race, sex, ethnic group affiliation, and religious persuasion to affect his or her salesperson selection.

very ethical   ethical   neither   unethical   very unethical

13. The buyer discriminates against a vendor whose salespeople use "backdoor" selling instead of going through the purchasing department.

very ethical   ethical   neither   unethical   very unethical

14. The buyer discriminates on the basis of nepotism. (Nepotism is used here in a broad sense to cover all preferential treatment extended to suppliers who are relatives or friends, or who are recommended by higher management.)

very ethical   ethical   neither   unethical   very unethical

15. In a shortage situation, the salesperson allocates product shipments to purchasing agents that the seller personally likes.

very ethical   ethical   neither   unethical   very unethical

16. In order to obtain a lower price or other concession, the buyer informs an existing supplier that the company may use a second source.

very ethical   ethical   neither   unethical   very unethical

17. In a reciprocal buying situation, the salesperson hints that unless an order is forthcoming, the prospect's sales to the selling firm might suffer.

very ethical   ethical   neither   unethical   very unethical

18. The salesperson attempts to use the economic power of the firm to obtain concessions from the buyer.

very ethical   ethical   neither   unethical   very unethical

19. The salesperson has less competitive prices or other terms for buyers who depend on the firm as the sole source of supply.

very ethical   ethical   neither   unethical   very unethical

20. The buyer accepts from a supplier gifts such as sales promotion prizes and "purchase volume incentives."

very ethical   ethical   neither   unethical   very unethical

21. The buyer accepts trips, meals, or other free entertainment.

very ethical   ethical   neither   unethical   very unethical

22. The salesperson gives a purchaser who was one of the best customers a gift worth $50 or more at Christmas or other occasions.

very ethical   ethical   neither   unethical   very unethical

23. The salesperson gives a potential customer a gift worth $50 or more at Christmas or other occasions.

very ethical   ethical   neither   unethical   very unethical

24. The salesperson grants price concessions to purchasing agents of companies in which the salesperson owns stock.

very ethical   ethical   neither   unethical   very unethical

25. The salesperson attempts to sell to a purchasing agent a product that has little or no value to buyer's company.

very ethical   ethical   neither   unethical   very unethical

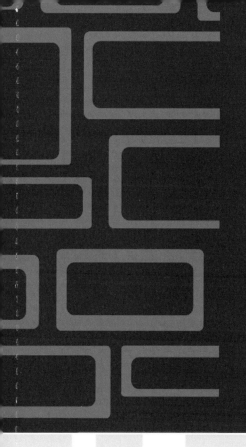

Building Relationships after the Sale

Objective

You will discover the importance of follow-up activities in building relationships.

THE EXERCISE ASSIGNMENT

Not many years ago, salespeople often thought that their jobs were complete once the order was signed. Today, for a business to survive, repeat business is critical. A greater emphasis has been placed on the follow-up stage of the selling process. Continued building of the relationship should be your goal well after the sale.

1. Show appreciation after the sale. How might you accomplish this?

_____

_____

_____

2. Monitor delivery and installation. Why is this important?

_____

_____

_____

3. Learn the names of the switchboard operator, receptionists, office manager, users of the product, etc. How might you accomplish this and why is it important?

_____

_____

_____

4. Keep all of your promises. How might you accomplish this and why is this important?

_____

_____

_____

5. Find ways to add value to your product or service. How might you accomplish this and why is it important?

_____

_____

_____

6. What should you try to accomplish during follow-up calls?

_____

_____

_____

Comparing the Traditional Selling Process with the Process of Trust-Based Relationship Selling

Objective

To assist the student in acquiring a richer understanding of the differences between the traditional process of selling and the process inherent to trust-based relationship selling.

THE EXERCISE ASSIGNMENT

Study and discuss the activities comprising the traditional task-focused selling process and the trust-based relationship selling process (See Exhibit 1.2 on page 9). As you study these two processes, compare and contrast their component activities, their emphasis, and focus. Then complete the following study questions:

1. Compare and contrast these two processes of selling. How are they similar? How do they differ?

_____

_____

_____

_____

_____

_____

_____

_____

2. What is the primary focus of each of the two processes?

_____

_____

_____

_____

_____

_____

_____

_____

_____

3. Why has the evolution toward trust-based relationship selling taken place? What has caused (is causing) this shift from one process to another?

_____

_____

_____

_____

_____

_____

_____

_____

_____

4. What advantages are offered to the seller by trust-based relationship selling?

_____

_____

_____

_____

_____

_____

_____

To the buyer?

_____

_____

_____

_____

_____

5. What inherent disadvantages to the seller result from trust-based relationship selling?

_____

_____

_____

_____

_____

_____

_____

To the buyer?

_____

_____

_____

_____

_____

_____

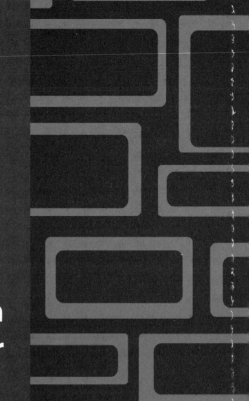

EXPERIENTIAL EXERCISE

3.1

Gathering Information about the Buyer

Objective

You will understand why collecting information about your prospect is important.

THE EXERCISE ASSIGNMENT

The more that you know about your buyer, the better chance you have to sell. Over time you should be able to accumulate knowledge about your prospect. The information that you will need varies with the kind of product you are selling. As a rule, you should definitely know a few basic things about your customers. A salesperson can learn a great deal about a customer over time by collecting bits and pieces of information, sorting them out, and developing a personalized, custom presentation for the customer.

The following information is helpful in preparing this personalized presentation.

1. The prospect's name, with correct spelling and correct pronunciation. Why is it important to know the correct spelling and pronunciation of your prospect's name?

   _____

   _____

   _____

2. The prospect's correct title. Why is it important to know the correct title of your prospect?

   _____

   _____

   _____

3. The prospect's hobbies. Why is it important to know your prospect's hobbies?

_____

_____

_____

4. The prospect's friends. Why is it important to know the names of your prospect's friends?

_____

_____

_____

5. The prospect's status in the community. Why is it important to know the prospect's status in the community?

_____

_____

_____

6. Things not to talk about with the prospect. Why is it important to know certain topics not to talk about with the prospect?

_____

_____

_____

7. The prospect's children. Why is it important to know the names and ages of your prospect's children?

_____

_____

_____

8. The prospect's favorite teams. Why is it important to know your prospect's favorite sports teams?

_____

_____

_____

9. Harvey Mackay in _Swim with the Sharks without Being Eaten Alive_ has his sales force collect information on 66 items that profile their customers. Some of these include:

(1) Does the customer smoke?
(2) What is the spouse's education?
(3) Graduated from what university?
(4) Members of which clubs or service clubs?
(5) Their vacation habits?
(6) The make and model of car they drive?

Why is this type of information important to the salesperson?

_____

_____

_____

_____

_____

POINTS FOR DISCUSSION

1. How can this information improve the communication process with the buyer?

_____

_____

_____

_____

2. How do you collect this information?

_____

_____

_____

_____

3. How long should it take you to collect this information?

_____

_____

_____

_____

4. What other types of information would be valuable to have?

_____

_____

_____

_____

Key Questions during the Buying Process

Objective

You will be able to understand the importance of good, effective questioning.

THE EXERCISE ASSIGNMENT

During the buying process, the salesperson must always be gathering pertinent information. Answers to the following questions will help the salesperson identify the key individuals in a buying center and devise a strategy to penetrate the buying process. These questions should be asked of the various individuals that the salesperson meets within a company.

1. Who, besides you, will be making the decision to buy? Explain why this question is important. _____

   _____

   _____

2. What problems do you foresee in changing suppliers? Explain why this question is important. _____

   _____

   _____

3. What will you need to do to win the support of the others? Explain why this question is important. _____

   _____

   _____

4. When do you plan to make the purchase decision? Explain why this question is important. _____

_____

_____

5. What sense of urgency do you feel about this buying decision? Explain why this question is important._____

_____

_____

6. Other important questions?_____

_____

_____

_____

_____

_____

_____

_____

Why?_____

_____

_____

_____

_____

_____

_____

_____

Triggering the Buying Process— Needs Awareness

Objective

You will be able to determine both external and internal stimuli of the buying process needs recognition stage.

THE EXERCISE ASSIGNMENT

One of the most simple, yet far-reaching insights into buying behavior is that it is actually a *process*. There is a logical sequence of stages that collectively result in product and vendor choices. The salesperson is most concerned with *who* triggers stage one and *how* it becomes activated. As described earlier in Module 3, the eight sequential stages comprising the organizational buyer's decision process are as follows:

Stage 1. Anticipation or recognition of a problem (need) and a general solution.

Stage 2. Determination of characteristics and quantity of needed item.

Stage 3. Description of characteristics and quantity of needed item.

Stage 4. Search for and qualification of potential source.

Stage 5. Acquisition and analysis of proposal.

Stage 6. Evaluation of proposals and selection of supplier(s).

Stage 7. Selection of order routine.

Stage 8. Performance feedback and evaluation.

The buying process begins when someone realizes that a problem can be solved or an opportunity can be met by purchasing a product or service. This needs recognition can be initiated by either internal or external stimuli.

Assume that you are a salesperson for Sharp Business Equipment. An existing account, Performance Services International, has expressed interest in updating its office and communications equipment. With the understanding that needs can be initiated by internal as well as external cues and stimuli, you have been working with the central purchasing office to develop better recognition and understanding of the company's needs and potential solutions.

Use the following worksheet to identify internal and external stimuli or cues that might arouse anticipation or recognition of a problem or need and initiate the buying process.

Internal Stimuli:

E
X   *Accounting department requests FAX machine.* How might this source be triggered?
A   *Salesperson meets with and works with different members of the accounting department*
M
P   *and demonstrates the usefulness and benefits of a FAX.*
L
E   _____

1. _____. How might this source be triggered?

   _____

   _____

   _____

2. _____. How might this source be triggered?

   _____

   _____

   _____

3. _____. How might this source be triggered?

   _____

   _____

   _____

4. _____. How might this source be triggered?

   _____

   _____

   _____

External Stimuli:

E
X
A
M
P
L
E

Data processing department sees ad in trade publication. How might this source be triggered? _Understanding that members of the data processing department are_ _exploring the benefits of using a FAX machine, salesperson leaves several trade_ _publications in the office for them to read._

1. _____. How might this source be triggered?

   _____

   _____

   _____

2. _____. How might this source be triggered?

   _____

   _____

   _____

3. _____. How might this source be triggered?

   _____

   _____

   _____

4. _____. How might this source be triggered?

   _____

   _____

   _____

Activating the ADAPT Process for Developing and Confirming Customer Needs

Objective

You will further develop your understanding and ability to apply the ADAPT process of needs development.

THE EXERCISE ASSIGNMENT

Congratulations!! You have recently joined Addvance Frozen Foods as their salesperson in the Midwestern Territory. A food processor specializing in providing the meat entrees for large institutions such as prisons and hospitals, Addvance is recognized as one of the industry leaders. This reputation not only includes market share, but also extends to leadership in innovative products and customer relations.

You have been working for several weeks to gain access to Jane Cummings, the foods buyer for the State of Illinois Prison System. With several other major food processors (including Kraft and General Foods) located in Chicago, the competition in this region has been great. As a result, Addvance has never been able to get any of its product line into the Illinois system. Nevertheless, Addvance has recently introduced and started shipping an innovative turkey-based line of products that averages 18 percent higher protein and 23 percent lower fat content than anything marketed by the competition. The higher protein level per serving is extremely important to such institutions as prisons, as it allows them to meet nutrition requirements with smaller servings of meat entrees and thus creates an opportunity for cost reduction. In addition to these tangible benefits, the product line's average selling price of $2.10 per pound is $0.22 a pound lower than Kraft's competing products and $0.20 under those of General Foods. Documenting the higher protein level and lower fat content certainly got Cummings' attention. However, it was the combination of increased protein and lower price that got you the appointment to talk with Cummings and members of her buying group in person.

As part of preparing for your sales call, you are compiling a set of anticipated questions that might assist you in better understanding Cummings' current situation and confirming her needs. Information gained through this sort of effective questioning has proven valuable to you in the past as it helps you to better respond to the customer's needs. Following the ADAPT model of questioning, develop a series of effective Assessment, Discovery, Activation, Projection, and Transition questions that you might use in the sales call with Cummings.

Please use the following workbook pages to develop your questions:

Assessment Questions

1. _____
2. _____
3. _____
4. _____
5. _____
6. _____

Discovery Questions

1. _____
2. _____
3. _____
4. _____
5. _____
6. _____

Activation Questions

1. _____
2. _____
3. _____
4. _____
5. _____
6. _____

Projection Questions

1. _____
2. _____
3. _____
4. _____
5. _____
6. _____

Transition Questions

1. _____

2. _____

3. _____

4. _____

5. _____

6. _____

Role Plays for ADAPTive Questioning

Objective

You will continue building your listening skills and self-confidence in ADAPTive questioning through the use of in-class, minirole plays.

INTRODUCTION

In this role play exercise, the instructor will be the prospect and students will take turns asking each type of question. As the role play progresses, it should become easier for you to understand the ADAPT process and what is required to make it effective.

THE COMPANY YOU REPRESENT

Students will assume the role of salesperson for Sonoco. Founded in 1899 as the Southern Novelty Company, Sonoco Products Corporation is headquartered in Hartsville, South Carolina. This past year, it employed 17,000 people in 24 countries and ranked 22nd on the *Fortune* 500 list. For that same year, the company earned $117.5 million on nearly $2 billion in sales. The company specializes in producing many different types of packaging, from composite cans that hold orange juice, noodles, and tennis balls to labels that cover dozens of products in the health care and medical industries. Textile companies worldwide use the company's paper and plastic cones and tubes. The company also produces industrial containers, caulking tubes, recyclable plastic grocery bags, and even paper lids on the glasses that travelers find at hotels.

YOUR PRODUCT

Sonoco produces both chipboard and corrugated partitions that are custom designed to fit the customer's packaging needs. The partitions are designed so that all cells within the box have the same size, which means that the product fits snugly throughout the box, minimizing chances for breakage and scratching. The company also manufactures machinery for inserting products into boxes. The following chart summarizes the features and advantages of Sonoco's packaging products:

Feature	Advantage
Custom designed and manufactured	Packaging will fit snugly around any size or shape product.
Broad range of surface finishes, including water and starch finished, wax impregnated, and polyethylene coated	Allows versatility in shipping; not necessary to shop from several manufacturers to meet different packaging requirements.
Automatic product insertion machinery available	Provides smooth product insertion without damage to glass or labeling.
Easy-grip edges	Keeps partitions from falling out of cartons during manual or automatic decasing.
Uses recyclable cardboard	Meets demand for environmental awareness.
Durable, solid fibers	Helps withstand abrupt shocks.
Clean, uniform edges and surfaces	Product arrives clean, dust-free, and looking its best.
Custom-designed graphics available for outside of package	Can enhance company image and make product easier to sell in self-service stores.
Frequent delivery available	Reduces need for large inventory of empty packaging.
Design of flutes provides stronger boxes with less weight	Provides maximum protection while reducing shipping costs.

THE EXERCISE ASSIGNMENT

In this role play, it is assumed that the Lilly Fields Glass Co. has called Sonoco and expressed an interest in Sonoco's packaging. This lead has been turned over to you, and today you will make the initial call on the purchasing manager of the Lilly Fields Glass Co., a manufacturer of water glasses, water pitchers, cocktail glasses, and glass beer steins. Its products are all currently sold to bars and restaurants.

Your task in this call is to first use **Assessment** questions to find out more about the Lilly Fields Glass Co. For example, are they considering any changes in their target market? Then, using **Discovery** questions, **Activation** questions, **Projection** questions, and **Transition** questions, explore (a) the prospect's problems, (b) the consequences of these problems, and (c) what solving these problems might mean to the purchasing manager. However, *you will not present solutions during this role play.*

To assist you in preparing for this call, here are examples of the kinds of problems your prospect might be having:

- Lilly Fields may need equipment to automatically insert glass products into shipping containers.
- Lilly Fields may need packaging with nonstandard specifications.
- Lilly Fields may need different materials incorporated into the same package.
- Lilly Fields may not know how to go about designing packaging.
- Lilly Fields may have been having a large amount of damage in shipping.
- Lilly Fields may be spending a lot for extra warehouse space to store packaging.
- The purchasing manager may also have personal needs beyond those of the firm.

Based on the features and advantages explained earlier, you should be able to think of other problems that might be solved by using your product.

Prepare for the call by listing the potential consequences that you might want to explore during the call. Use the **Salesperson's Preparation Form** provided for your use on the following pages to list questions that you could use during the role play. At this point, do not be too concerned about the quality of the questions; it is more important that you focus on getting practice asking each kind of question. As you go through the next several role plays, you will learn more about what provides quality to each kind of question.

Remember that the purpose of the role play is to practice ADAPT questioning. Do not "pitch" to the prospect. Focus instead on getting information about his or her problems, needs, and concerns.

You will also be asked to summarize what you have heard and check that the prospect agrees with your summary. If you were going to propose a solution, you would want to be certain that you had properly interpreted the prospect's concerns.

SALESPERSON'S PREPARATION FORM

Assessment Questions

1. _____

2. _____

3. _____

4. _____

5. _____

6. _____

Discovery Questions

1. _____

2. _____

3. _____

4. _____

5. _____

6. _____

Activation Questions

1. _____

2. _____

3. _____

4. _____

5. _____

6. _____

Projection Questions

1. _____
2. _____
3. _____
4. _____
5. _____
6. _____

Transition Questions

1. _____
2. _____
3. _____
4. _____
5. _____
6. _____

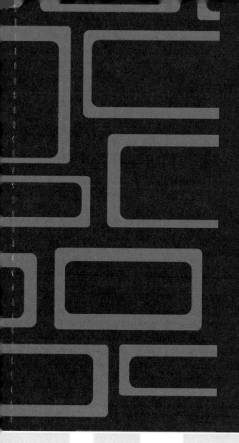

Effective Questioning

Objective

You will understand the importance of asking effective questions.

INTRODUCTION

There are two ways to dominate or control a sales conversation. A salesperson can talk all the time, or the salesperson can be in control by asking good, effective questions. Effective questioning offers the salesperson the following advantages:

1. Questions establish an atmosphere of control.
2. Questions help you determine how cooperative your customer will be.
3. Questions get you valuable information about your customer's needs, desires, and problems.
4. Questions help you identify your customer's style and opinions as well as his or her current understanding and awareness of needs and of your product or service.
5. Questions help you avoid rejection.
6. Questions build trust and rapport.
7. Questions save you time.
8. Questions keep you from talking too much.
9. Questions get the customer involved.
10. Questions get and maintain the customer's attention.
11. Questions make your customer think.
12. Questions and subsequent answers, if you listen attentively, create a willingness on the part of the customer to listen to you when it is your turn to talk.
13. Intelligent questions make you look competent and knowledgeable.

A salesperson can use open-ended and closed-ended questions for effective questioning.

Open-Ended and Closed-Ended Questions

Open-Ended Questions—Open-ended questions, also called nondirective questions, are designed to let the customer respond freely. That is, the customer is not limited to one- or two-word answers, and is encouraged to disclose personal and/or business information. These questions are typically used to probe the customer for descriptive information that allows the salesperson to better understand the specific needs of the customer.

Closed-Ended Questions—Closed-ended questions, also called directive questions, are designed to limit the customer's response to one or two words. Although the most common form is the yes/no question; closed-ended questions can come in many forms—provided the response is limited to one or two words. For instance, "How many . . ." and "How often . . ." are examples of closed-ended questions. These questions are typically used to confirm or clarify information gleaned from responses to open-ended questions.

THE EXERCISE ASSIGNMENT

Used in combination, open- and closed-ended questions help the salesperson uncover and confirm customer needs, dissatisfactions, and opportunities. Let's now look at how these questions are used in the ADAPT process.

1. Observe a salesperson during an introductory call with a new prospect. What open-ended questions did the salesperson use?

   a. _____

   b. _____

   c. _____

   d. _____

   e. _____

   What types of information were gathered using open-ended questions? After the sales call, ask the salesperson how he or she will use this information.

   _____

   _____

   _____

   _____

   _____

   _____

2. What closed-ended questions did the salesperson use?

   a. _____

   b. _____

   c. _____

   d. _____

   e. _____

What types of information were gathered using closed-ended questions? After the sales call, ask the salesperson how he or she will use this information.

_____

_____

_____

_____

_____

_____

EXPERIENTIAL EXERCISE

4.4

Thank-You Letters

Objective

You will increase your awareness of the important, effective, and efficient role played by thank-you letters in customer follow-up while gaining practice in writing thank-you letters.

THE EXERCISE ASSIGNMENT

Visualize yourself as a salesperson for Montgomery Paper Products, one of the top three firms in business supplies, paper, and paper products. Today has been a very hectic day, but one that you feel has been productive nevertheless. You have just returned to your office from calling on John Tracy, the head buyer for Worldwide Systems, Inc.

Worldwide currently sources all their paper needs from Acme Office Products. However, Acme has failed to keep Worldwide current on several technological advances. The fact that Montgomery Paper Products is the innovator and pioneer for several of these technological advances gives you an advantage in the marketplace. You have been using the potential benefits this new technology would produce for Worldwide as leverage to gain access to a portion of Worldwide's business.

Although Tracy recognizes the benefits of changing to your line of products, he still has some reservations regarding your products being compatible with his existing equipment. You have been chipping away at this account for several months now. In fact, today's call is the sixth time that you have met with Tracy and other interested parties at Worldwide. Even though they continue to express interest and ask that you keep them informed, they still have not committed to a purchase. Nevertheless, you sense that they are moving closer.

Part One:

Using the following worksheet, compose a thank-you letter to John Tracy for his consideration in visiting with you today. You never know—a small act of professionalism might just be the one event that gets you the sale. Besides, the letter gives you an opportunity to get your name and product benefits in front of him one more time.

MONTGOMERY PAPER PRODUCTS

1800 Eastport Road   Chicago, IL 63984   (715) 756-8333

Part Two:

Visualize the same scenario, except that you did get the order that you were after. Not only that, Tracy indicated that if you and Montgomery Paper Products carry through and do what you say you will do, there is strong potential for added business. How would your thank-you letter differ from that in the earlier scenario? Compose this new letter in the space below:

MONTGOMERY PAPER PRODUCTS
1800 Eastport Road   Chicago, IL 63984   (715) 756-8333

Part Three:

Now for the hard one. Suppose that the scenario is changed and Montgomery Paper is the primary supplier for Worldwide. You still service the account and Tracy is the buyer. You still call on Tracy, but you also spend a lot of time working with the people in the office and shop who actually use your products. In fact, relations are so good that most of the ordering is automatic. How would this letter look? Compose it in the space below:

MONTGOMERY PAPER PRODUCTS
1800 Eastport Road   Chicago, IL 63984   (715) 756-8333

EXPERIENTIAL EXERCISE

5.1

Assessing the Effectiveness of Different Customer Contact Methods

Objective

You will develop your understanding of the various methods for making customer contact and how each method's effectiveness varies according to the desired outcomes.

THE EXERCISE ASSIGNMENT

The effectiveness of the various methods available for salespeople to make contact with prospects and customers will vary according to what the salesperson hopes to accomplish. This exercise requires that you consider certain outcomes that a salesperson might desire and designate which contact method(s) might be the most effective. To encourage your thoughtful consideration of each method's strengths and weaknesses, the exercise also requires you to explain why you made your selections.

EVALUATING THE EFFECTIVENESS OF CUSTOMER CONTACT METHODS

For each of the following desired outcomes, indicate which customer contact method would be the best to use. Indicate your choice by entering the letter(s) corresponding to the chosen contact method(s):

In-Person (P)
Form Letter (F)
Telephone (T)

E-mail (E)
Personalized Letter (L)
World Wide Web (W)

After you have made your selection, briefly explain why you believe this to be the optimal choice. This information will be used for class discussion.

Method

Creating awareness of product or company.   _____

Why: _____

_____

_____

_____

Introducing yourself.   _____

Why? _____

_____

_____

_____

Getting an initial appointment.   _____

Why? _____

_____

_____

_____

Confirming an appointment.   _____

Why? _____

_____

_____

_____

Getting acquainted.   _____

Why? _____

_____

_____

_____

Discovering customer needs.   _____

Why? _____

_____

_____

_____

Method

Determining customer buying motives.   _____

Why? _____

_____

_____

_____

Determining influencers and decision makers in the   _____
buying organization.

Why? _____

_____

_____

_____

Assessing the Lifetime Value of a Customer

Objective

The life line of an organization is repeat business, obtained by keeping present customers happy. In this exercise you will calculate the value of a customer over a five-year period.

THE LIFETIME VALUE OF A CUSTOMER

Identify a salesperson with whom you can establish a rapport and working relationship that allows you to accompany or shadow the salesperson for a day. Note the various behaviors and activities the salesperson performs that have some relationship (good and bad) to the development and maintenance of buyer–seller relationships.

With the assistance of the salesperson, select one customer and calculate the lifetime value of that customer.

In a short report, present the relationship activities (good and bad) that you observed during the shadowing opportunity, along with the lifetime value calculation. The report must contain an explanation and support the determined value.

As noted earlier, the life line of organizations today is repeat business. Present customers have already developed trust with their salesperson and, with proper nurturing, should be easier to sell to over time.

In the grocery industry, the average customer spends $100 per week for 50 weeks each year. The value of this customer each year is $5,000 and over five years, $25,000.

In the consumer goods industry, an average order from a small grocery store (independent grocer) is $1,000 per week. The value of this customer per year is $50,000 and over five years, $250,000.

THE EXERCISE ASSIGNMENT

1. Contact a salesperson and ask what an average customer would order per month. Calculate the value over five years for this customer.

   _____

   _____

   _____

   _____

   _____

   _____

   _____

2. Discuss with the salesperson how much time it takes to develop this type of customer.

   _____

   _____

   _____

   _____

   _____

   _____

   _____

3. Discuss the implications of losing an active customer and how much time and effort it takes to replace a lost customer.

   _____

   _____

   _____

   _____

   _____

   _____

4. Ask your salesperson the amount of effort it takes to get business from an existing account versus generating new business.

   _____

   _____

   _____

   _____

   _____

   _____

Prospecting Effectiveness

Objective

You will be able to identify several popular prospecting techniques and determine the effectiveness of the techniques.

THE EXERCISE ASSIGNMENT

Review the discussion of prospecting sources and methods on pages 142–147. Select two methods from each category of external sources, internal sources, and personal contact sources and complete the following section.

List prospecting methods and record your opinion of their effectiveness.

External Sources

1. Prospecting method _____

    In your opinion, what is the strength or weakness of this prospecting method?

_____

_____

_____

2. Prospecting method _____

    In your opinion, what is the strength or weakness of this prospecting method?

_____

_____

Internal Sources

1. Prospecting method _____

In your opinion, what is the strength or weakness of this prospecting method?

_____

_____

_____

2. Prospecting method _____

In your opinion, what is the strength or weakness of this prospecting method?

_____

_____

_____

Personal Contact Sources

1. Prospecting method _____

In your opinion, what is the strength or weakness of this prospecting method?

_____

_____

_____

2. Prospecting method _____

In your opinion, what is the strength or weakness of this prospecting method?

_____

_____

_____

Source: Adapted from T. N. Ingram, SMEI *Certification Study Guide,* The University of Memphis: SMEI Accreditation Institute, 1994.

Developing Feature and Benefit Statements for Your School

Objective

You will be able to develop feature and benefit statements for your school and apply them to relevant markets.

INTRODUCTION

Benefit statements describe a feature from a specific customer's point of view. They answer such customer questions as "How is this going to help *me* solve *my* problems?"

Any given feature may produce different benefits for different customers and no benefits for others. Therefore, it is important to develop benefit statements for specific markets. The more precisely you can express the benefit *in the language of the customer*, the more effective your statements will be. The following example will help you get started on this assignment.

Example

First, choose three groups that represent target markets at your school (examples could be: Greeks, athletes, students with disabilities, faculty, staff, graduate students, general student population, freshmen, and so on).

1. Target Market (*for example, athletes*)
2. Target Market (*for example, students with disabilities*)
3. Target Market (*for example, graduate students*)

Next, select a feature of your school (an example might be a tutoring program that is available at your school).

1. Feature: *Tutoring program available to our students.*

Finally, develop a benefit statement for each of your target markets. Remember, any given feature may produce different benefits for one target group and no benefit for the others.

Target Market 1. *Athletes* Benefit Statement: *Athletes spend time at practice and away games. The benefit of the tutoring program to athletes is that they can use the program to catch up on their work and not fall behind.*

Target Market 2. *Students with disabilities* Benefit Statement: *Students who are blind have readers available to read lessons to them. The benefit to the students is that they do not have to pay for a reader.*

Target Market 3. *Graduate students* Benefit Statement: *Graduate students are used as the tutors. The benefit to graduate students is that they can supplement their income and feel good about helping others.*

THE EXERCISE ASSIGNMENT

Based on the examples provided, develop additional features and benefit statements for your three target markets.

1. Feature: _____
   Target Market 1: _____ Benefit Statement: _____
   _____

   Target Market 2: _____ Benefit Statement: _____
   _____

   Target Market 3: _____ Benefit Statement: _____
   _____

2. Feature: _____
   Target Market 1: _____ Benefit Statement: _____
   _____

   Target Market 2: _____ Benefit Statement: _____
   _____

   Target Market 3: _____ Benefit Statement: _____
   _____

3. Feature: _____
   Target Market 1: _____ Benefit Statement: _____
   _____

   Target Market 2: _____ Benefit Statement: _____
   _____

   Target Market 3: _____ Benefit Statement: _____
   _____

4. Feature: _____
   Target Market 1: _____ Benefit Statement: _____
   _____

Target Market 2: _____ Benefit Statement: _____
_____
_____

Target Market 3: _____ Benefit Statement: _____
_____
_____

5. Feature: _____
   Target Market 1: _____ Benefit Statement: _____
   _____
   _____

   Target Market 2: _____ Benefit Statement: _____
   _____
   _____

   Target Market 3: _____ Benefit Statement: _____
   _____
   _____

6. Feature: _____
   Target Market 1: _____ Benefit Statement: _____
   _____
   _____

   Target Market 2: _____ Benefit Statement: _____
   _____
   _____

   Target Market 3: _____ Benefit Statement: _____
   _____
   _____

7. Feature: _____
   Target Market 1: _____ Benefit Statement: _____
   _____
   _____

   Target Market 2: _____ Benefit Statement: _____
   _____
   _____

   Target Market 3: _____ Benefit Statement: _____
   _____
   _____

8. Feature: _____
   Target Market 1: _____ Benefit Statement: _____
   _____
   _____

   Target Market 2: _____ Benefit Statement: _____
   _____
   _____

   Target Market 3: _____ Benefit Statement: _____
   _____
   _____

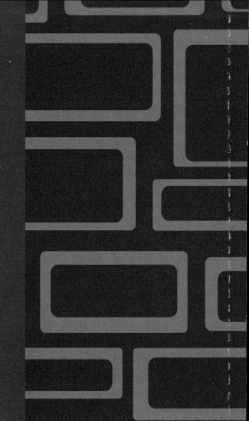

EXPERIENTIAL EXERCISE

6.2

Presentation Effectiveness—Discussion Questions

Objective

You will be able to think through the presentation and understand its key components.

THE EXERCISE ASSIGNMENT

Please respond to the following statements:

1. What is the main objective of a good presentation? _____
   _____
   _____

2. How long should a good presentation be? _____
   _____
   _____

3. Why are questions an important part of a presentation? _____
   _____
   _____

4. When should you terminate a presentation? _____
   _____
   _____

5. How should you terminate a sales call? _____
   _____
   _____

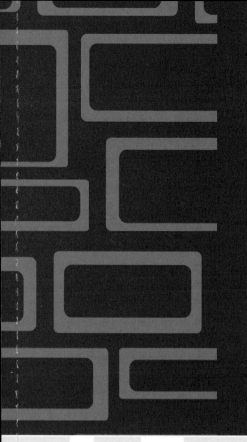

Sales Call Planning Report

Objective

You will build your understanding of the importance of thorough strategic planning prior to calling on the customer by illustrating the integration of sales call objectives, features and benefits (FAB), and the ADAPT questioning process.

INTRODUCTION

Successful selling is based on thorough planning and preparation *before* the sales call and presentation. One of the most important areas of preparation pertains to understanding a product's features and how they might solve buyer needs. The link between product features and buyer needs is accomplished by converting a product's *FEATURES (what it is)* to *ADVANTAGES (what it does)*, and then translating these advantages into *BENEFITS that are relevant and meaningful to your buyer.*

Benefits are solutions to needs. It is important to realize that specific features may yield different benefits to different buyers. Thus, preparation includes imagining the variety of buyer needs that a feature might address and how to uncover potential benefits through questioning. Such preparation forces the salesperson to cognitively examine prospects in terms of:

1. Product features that might give rise to buyer benefits.
2. ADAPT questions to use in assessing the prospect's needs in relation to available product benefits.
3. Potential resistance in accepting and committing to the benefits as solutions to the prospect's problems and needs.

THE EXERCISE ASSIGNMENT

Unlike the other experiential exercises in this workbook in which the scenario was already set out for you, this exercise requires that you develop your own selling scenario, including (a) the product being sold, (b) the company that you sell for, and (c) the prospect to whom you are selling. These product, company, and prospect profiles will then be used to anticipate the events and responses within a sales call in order to develop a detailed, strategic plan for making that call. All this will come together in a formal written report consisting of certain specific components.

We recommend that this assignment be done in groups of two students. You may exchange ideas, work through the various parts of the report together, and turn in one report. The assignment will be evaluated in terms of its preparation as well as its content. The report must be typed, be professional in appearance, and double spaced with one-inch margins. Headings, subheadings, and page numbers should be used to organize the report. A comb binder (available at Kinko's or PIP's) should be used rather than a plastic slip-on cover. The front cover should creatively, professionally, and neatly identify the specific product that the report addresses, the members of the sales team, and the project due date. Inside, the report should consist of the following major sections:

Letter of Transmittal. Assuming that your sales manager has requested a copy of your sales call plan, the first component of your report should be a letter of transmittal addressed to your sales manager (your instructor). Similar to an executive summary, this letter of transmittal references the manager's request, identifies your subject prospect along with the time and place of the sales call appointment, establishes the specific objectives you have set for this sales call, and provides a synopsis of the report's contents. This letter should be single-spaced and limited to one page.

Identification of Your Company. This section profiles the company for which you sell. Actual companies may be used if you desire. This portion of the report develops detailed information, such as the name of the company, its size, and a brief history. Other information should also be included that might be relevant to a buyer. This information will facilitate the profile's use should it be used in a subsequent buyer–seller role play.

Identification of Your Product. Choose a good or service that you would like to sell. (You might consider using a product from a company that you might want to go to work for, as this project can be quite beneficial to you in your job interviews.) All products are to be sold to another business or institution. Sales of products to individuals for their own use is not allowed. Experience indicates that the closer a product is to the retail marketplace, the harder it is to use, and the closer the product is to being industrial in nature, the better it seems to work. Your product choice should be in good taste and legal, and must not be in conflict with any school rules or policies.

The last portion of this section should be a chart of the product's general features, advantages, and benefits. To assist you in developing this information, an example of an FAB chart is included at the end of this exercise.

Profile of Competition. Who are the major competitors? What are their strengths and weaknesses? How do competitive products compare to the FABs of your product? This section must develop and describe at least two competitors.

Profile of Prospect. This section profiles both the buyer and the buyer's company. What is the name of the person you are calling on? What is his or her position and history with the firm? What is the company name and type of business? Where are they located? What information do we know before actually making a sales call? How is our product relevant to them? Is the use for resale or manufacture? What brands and suppliers are currently being used?

Expected Problems and Needs. What types of customer problems might be discovered in working with this prospect? What advance information or intelligence do you have regarding problems or needs? In this section you should develop four potential problems relevant to both your prospect and your type of product. In the following section you will use these four potential problems as a guide to develop a series of ADAPT questions that would address these problems and ascertain corresponding needs.

Develop ADAPT Questioning Sequence. As a major part of this section, you should develop and include a series of product and customer relevant questions that can be used to assess the needs of your prospects. These questions should follow the ADAPT questioning sequence (explained in Module 4, Questioning Skills). Workbook pages for developing ADAPT questions are included on pages 379–380. Keep in mind that the ADAPT sequence of questions is intended to help your prospect discover and solve a problem, as opposed to "pitching" a product.

Expected Objections and Resistance. What forms of resistance are expected? This section should detail ten specific objections that you expect in making your presentation to this account. Classify each of these objections by type. For each objection, describe how you would respond. Classify each response by type. Note that you will need to read Module 8 in the text before completing this section.

Gaining Customer Commitment. Describe and illustrate how you will gain customer commitment and finalize the sale. Your description should include a statement classifying the type of commitment-gaining method being used. Note that you will need to read Module 8 in the text before completing this section.

Customer Follow-Up. This section discusses the follow-up activities that will be undertaken and provides a timetable for their implementation. Follow-up activities should be developed for both contingencies: (a) that you are successful in achieving the objectives set out for this sales call and (b) that you are not successful in achieving the sales call objectives.

PROSPECT NEEDS	FEATURES	ADVANTAGES	BENEFITS

Your Name: _____

SALESPERSON'S PREPARATION FORM

Assessment Questions:

_____

_____

_____

_____

Discovery Questions:

_____

_____

_____

_____

Activation Questions:

_____

_____

_____

_____

Projection Questions:

_____

_____

_____

_____

Transition Questions:

_____

_____

_____

_____

_____

Helpful Hints for Sales Presentations

Objective

You will be able to understand some key issues that can make the sales presentation more effective.

THE EXERCISE ASSIGNMENT

Please respond to the following statements:

1. Use short, simple, uncomplicated words. Why? _____
   _____
   _____

2. Use words that create a visual image. Why? _____
   _____
   _____

3. Get the customers involved. Why? _____
   _____
   _____

4. Never argue with your customers. Why? _____
   _____
   _____

5. Work from appointments—this is the mark of a professional. Why?_____

_____

_____

_____

6. Plan each presentation. Have a specific objective. Why? _____

_____

_____

_____

7. Terminate the presentation as soon as you discover the prospect does not qualify. Why? _____

_____

_____

_____

8. Use *questions* to control the presentation. Why? _____

_____

_____

_____

9. Increase your effectiveness—practice, practice, practice! Why? _____

_____

_____

_____

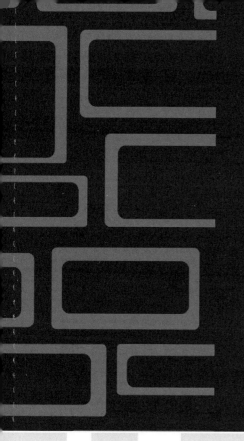

Generating Buyer Involvement

Objective

You will increase your skills in generating the active involvement of the prospect in the presentation.

INTRODUCTION

Communication research suggests that both educational and persuasive communications are more effective when the buyer is actively involved in the presentation rather than being a passive observer. However, creating opportunities for buyer involvement often takes some thought and encouragement on the part of the salesperson.

THE EXERCISE ASSIGNMENT

Working in groups of three, consider yourselves in each of the four following selling situations. Brainstorm different techniques you could use to involve the customer for each selling situation. Using the space provided, identify five techniques you feel would be the most effective along with a brief discussion explaining why.

SITUATION 1: A retail salesperson for Mike's Bike Shop selling a new style, ultra-light racing bike to a racing fanatic.

Technique 1 _____

_____

Why? _____

_____

Technique 2 _____

_____

Why? _____

_____

Technique 3 _____

_____

Why? _____

_____

Technique 4 _____

_____

Why? _____

_____

Technique 5 _____

_____

Why? _____

_____

SITUATION 2: A manufacturer's representative selling a new line of ultra-light racing bicycles to the buyer for Mike's Bike Shop.

Technique 1 _____

_____

Why? _____

_____

Technique 2 _____

_____

Why? _____

_____

Technique 3 _____

_____

Why? _____

_____

Technique 4 _____

_____

Why? _____

_____

Technique 5 _____

_____

Why? _____

_____

SITUATION 3: An industrial–chemical salesperson selling corrosion and acid-proof polymer coatings to a manufacturer of acid dispensing equipment that is used in medical research labs.

Technique 1 _____

_____

Why? _____

_____

Technique 2 _____

_____

Why? _____

_____

Technique 3 _____

_____

Why? _____

_____

Technique 4 _____

_____

Why? _____

_____

Technique 5 _____

_____

Why? _____

_____

SITUATION 4: A salesperson for General Electric Jet Engine Division presenting a high-thrust, low-noise, fuel-efficient jet engine to the buying team at American Airlines to retrofit 150 of their 727-model aircraft.

Technique 1 _____

_____

Why? _____

_____

Technique 2 _____

_____

Why? _____

_____

Technique 3 _____

_____

Why? _____

_____

Technique 4 _____

_____

Why? _____

_____

Technique 5 _____

_____

Why? _____

_____

Why Salespeople Fail
to Gain Commitment

Objective

You will be able to understand the issue of failure in gaining commitment.

THE EXERCISE ASSIGNMENT

One reason why sales are not completed is the salesperson makes no attempt to close the sale. Why, after investing all the time and effort in prospecting, qualifying, and making the presentation, would a salesperson not attempt to gain commitment? What are some other reasons why salespeople fail to gain commitment? Record your responses on the following lines.

1. _____

_____

2. _____

_____

3. _____

_____

4. _____

_____

5. _____

_____

6. _____

_____

Gaining Commitment— Caution Signals

Objective

You will be able to recognize gaining commitment caution signals.

INTRODUCTION

There are situations that do not warrant the salesperson attempting to gain customer commitment. It is risky to ask for the order when you are getting negative signals or when there is an indication that the prospect is uncomfortable about something. Trying to gain commitment following a negative indication without resolving the problem is being unresponsive to the prospect's need. Here are some situations where the salesperson should do something else before attempting to gain commitment.

THE EXERCISE ASSIGNMENT

Here are some situations where the salesperson should do something else before attempting to gain commitment. Examine each of the situations and explain why they should be viewed as a caution signal.

1. The prospect requests additional information on a technical product. Why would this be a buying caution signal?

   _____

   _____

   _____

2. A rushed or inadequate presentation has been made. Why would this be a buying caution signal?

_____

_____

_____

3. The prospect is hostile or defensive and is not making an attempt to bargain. Why would this be a buying caution signal?

_____

_____

_____

4. The prospect raises an objection or asks for more information. Why would this be a buying caution signal?

_____

_____

_____

5. A significant interruption has disturbed the buying mood. Why would this be a buying caution signal?

_____

_____

_____

6. Gaining commitment on a minor point failed to reveal positive signs of interest. Why would this be a buying caution signal?

_____

_____

_____

8.3

Reasons for Sales Resistance

Objective

You will be able to understand the different reasons for sales resistance and how to overcome these barriers.

INTRODUCTION

There are two types of sales resistance: psychological and logical. Psychological resistance refers to an unwillingness to buy based on attitude, emotion, or prejudice. Such resistance is very subjective and varies from one prospect to another. Logical resistance or objections to the sales presentation refers to unwillingness to buy based on tangible considerations related to some aspect of the product.

THE EXERCISE ASSIGNMENT

The following are brief descriptions of the most common types of psychological and logical sales resistance. Write your suggestions for addressing these barriers in the space provided.

Psychological Barriers

1. Resistance to interference: Salesperson's call or visit is viewed as an interruption of what the prospect is doing.

   Suggestions for salespeople to overcome this type of resistance:

   _____

   _____

   _____

2. Preference for established habits: Prospect finds comfort in present habits. A purchase usually involves a change in habits.

   Suggestions for salespeople to overcome this type of resistance:

   _____

   _____

   _____

3. Apathy toward product: Prospect feels no need for product, so is unwilling to spend money for it.

   Suggestions for salespeople to overcome this type of resistance:

   _____

   _____

   _____

4. Resistance to giving up something: Prospect views purchase as giving up money in exchange for product.

   Suggestions for salespeople to overcome this type of resistance:

   _____

   _____

   _____

5. Negative stereotype of salesperson: Prospect has feeling of contempt and suspicion toward all salespeople.

   Suggestions for salespeople to overcome this type of resistance:

   _____

   _____

   _____

6. Resistance to domination: Prospect has a need to feel in control of the situation.

   Suggestions for salespeople to overcome this type of resistance:

   _____

   _____

   _____

7. Preconceived ideas about product: Prospect's ideas and feelings, accurate or not, may close his or her mind to the purchase.

   Suggestions for salespeople to overcome this type of resistance:

   _____

   _____

   _____

8. Dislike of making decisions: Prospect may fear consequences of deciding and dread disturbing the status quo. May be due to lack of self-confidence.

Suggestions for salespeople to overcome this type of resistance:

_____

_____

_____

Logical Barriers

When a prospect raises an objection, he or she is signaling the feeling of conflict between buying and not buying the product. A pessimistic salesperson will feel discouraged by objections. The optimistic salesperson will welcome logical objections, realizing that they indicate at least some desire to buy.

The specific causes of logical resistance vary from industry to industry, so only the broadest categories will be included here. Later in the session you will develop a list of the specific resistance you encounter in your interactions with prospects.

1. Price: Probably the most frequently cited objection.

Suggestions for salespeople to overcome this type of resistance:

_____

_____

_____

2. Delivery schedule: The importance of delivery time varies with the time-related priorities of the prospect.

Suggestions for salespeople to overcome this type of resistance:

_____

_____

_____

3. Specifications: Drawn up with input from the end user or by the technical experts.

Suggestions for salespeople to overcome this type of resistance:

_____

_____

_____

4. Inadequate warranty.

Suggestions for salespeople to overcome this type of resistance:

_____

_____

_____

5. Does not have feature a competitor has.

Suggestions for salespeople to overcome this type of resistance:

_____

_____

_____

6. Performance does not measure up to the competition.

Suggestions for salespeople to overcome this type of resistance:

_____

_____

_____

7. Other?

Suggestions for salespeople to overcome this type of resistance:

_____

_____

_____

Negotiating Buyer Resistance

Objective

You will develop your skills in recognizing and dealing with different forms of buyer resistance.

THE EXERCISE ASSIGNMENT

At the beginning of this exercise, your instructor will pass out cards to all members of the class. Each card contains a statement or comment that is commonly made by buyers to salespeople. These buyer statements illustrate a wide variety of the different forms of resistance. After reviewing the resistance statement appearing on the card, each member of the class will role play the part of a salesperson and demonstrate how he or she would handle the situation while negotiating the specific buyer resistance. Your role play should:

1. Be conducted within the LAARC framework for working through buyer resistance (as discussed in the introduction to Exercise 8.3).
2. Incorporate a variety of the strategies for responding to buyer resistance that have been discussed in class. Some of the more common strategies are listed below.

COMMONLY USED METHODS
FOR NEGOTIATING SALES RESISTANCE

   I. Put-Off Strategies

  II. Switching Focus Strategies
     a. Alternative Product
     b. Feel, Felt, Found
     c. Comparison and Contrast

III. Offsetting Strategies
   a. Compensation and Counter-Balance
   b. Boomerang

IV. Denial Strategies
   a. Indirect
   b. Direct

V. Handling Price Strategies
   a. Build Perceived Value
   b. Break Into Smaller Units
   c. Price-Value Comparisons
   d. Emphasize Uniqueness

VI. Proof Providing Strategies
   a. Case Histories
   b. Demonstrations
   c. Trial Usage

Source: Adapted from an exercise submitted by Jill S. Attaway, Michael A. Humphreys, Timothy A. Longfellow, and Michael R. Williams; Department of Marketing, Illinois State University, (1995).

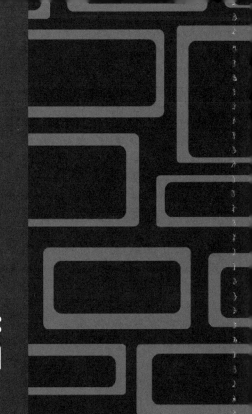

EXPERIENTIAL EXERCISE

9.1

Post-Presentation Follow-up: Analyzing a Sales Call

Objective

You will be able to analyze the sales call of a salesperson during a shadow call.

THE EXERCISE ASSIGNMENT

After you have shadowed a salesperson on a sales call, you will be able to evaluate the strengths and weaknesses of the call by responding to the following questions.

1. What might the salesperson have done better? _____
_____
_____

2. What did the salesperson say or do that he or she wish he are she had not?_____
_____
_____

3. Did the salesperson discuss topics that were not relevant to the sale?_____
_____
_____
_____

4. Did the salesperson venture into subjects that could have led to an argument?
_____
_____
_____

5. Did the salesperson's talk stray from the purpose at hand? _____

   _____

   _____

6. Did the salesperson talk too much? _____

   _____

   _____

7. Did the salesperson detect the prospect becoming weary when points were
   belabored?

   _____

   _____

   _____

8. Did the salesperson interrupt or cut the customer off during the discussion?

   _____

   _____

   _____

9. Was the presentation too one-sided? _____

   _____

   _____

10. How could the sale have been increased? _____

    _____

    _____

11. Could the salesperson's presentation have been more persuasive and the sales
    results better?

    _____

    _____

    _____

12. Did the salesperson listen to what the customer had to say? _____

    _____

    _____

13. Did the salesperson present the product in terms of customer needs?

    _____

    _____

    _____

14. As the salesperson talked, was he or she thinking of the customer?

_____

_____

_____

15. Were the suggested applications interesting to the customer? _____

_____

_____

_____

16. Whose real interest did the salesperson have in mind? _____

_____

_____

17. Will the salesperson be welcome on the next call to this customer?

_____

_____

_____

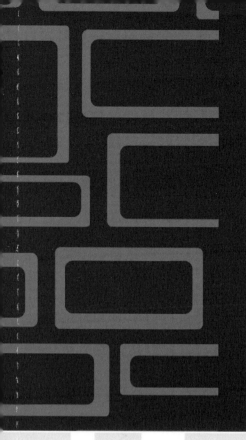

What to Do after Gaining Commitment

Objective

The salesperson has to complete a number of activities once the order has been signed. You will understand what activities must be completed after earning commitment.

THE EXERCISE ASSIGNMENT

You are a salesperson calling on your school's purchasing department and the buyer has just informed you that they have made the buying decision in your favor. What do you do now? Please respond to the following questions.

1. Confirm the customer's decision. How do you accomplish this?

_____

_____

_____

2. Show appreciation. How do you accomplish this?

_____

_____

_____

3. Cement the relationship. How do you accomplish this?

_____

_____

_____

4. Monitor delivery. How do you accomplish this?

_____

_____

_____

5. Monitor installation. How do you accomplish this?

_____

_____

_____

6. Keep your promises. How do you accomplish this?

_____

_____

_____

7. Handle complaints with sensitivity. How do you accomplish this?

_____

_____

_____

8. Respect the customer's time. How do you accomplish this?

_____

_____

_____

9. Provide information on the care and use of products. How do you accomplish this?

_____

_____

_____

10. List some specific follow-up actions that will cement the relationship between you and your customer.

_____

_____

_____

Enhancing Customer Relationships

Objective

You will be able to understand that building mutually satisfying relationships between buyers and sellers is essential for success in sales.

THE EXERCISE ASSIGNMENT

To build mutually satisfying relationships between buyers and sellers, professional salespeople must be competent in accomplishing five ongoing tasks:

1. Provide information. What does this mean and why is it important to building a relationship?

_____

_____

_____

_____

2. Reduce risk. What does this mean and why is it important to building a relationship?

_____

_____

_____

3. Establish high standards and expectations. What does this mean and why is it important to building a relationship?

_____

_____

_____

_____

4. Anticipate and respond to customer problems and concerns. What does this mean and why is it important to building a relationship?

_____

_____

_____

_____

5. Monitor and improve customer satisfaction. What does this mean and why is it important to building a relationship?

_____

_____

_____

_____

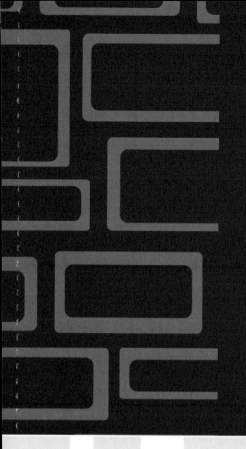

Written Sales Proposals— Summarizing Quantitative Data

Objective

You will master the skills of working in teams and present numbers and related data in clear, summarized formats for maximum clarity and persuasive impact.

INTRODUCTION

In this exercise, you will work in groups of two or three to develop a written sales proposal including quantitative product costs and client benefits, a clear synopsis of a timetable for installation, and a summary of the terms of a contract. This proposal has been requested by the client following four sales calls in which needs and expectations have been fully explored. The formal written proposal is to be mailed to the client along with a cover letter.

THE EXERCISE ASSIGNMENT

You are a salesperson for PRE-SELECT, Inc. (PSI). Headquartered in Chicago, PSI is the industry leader in pre-interview assessment and testing for the insurance industry. Focusing primarily on sales-related recruiting and selection, PSI's Interactive Employee Assessment System (IEAS) has been quite successful in lowering payroll costs by reducing sales agent turnover rates. Because of its highly recognized rate of success, PSI's customers include 13 of the top 20 insurance companies in the United States.

Although the system is continuously revised and updated, the basic program has been operating for six years. Using a personal computer in the field—usually at the branch office or agent's location—the IEAS consists of three computer-based components:

1. Pre-interview attitude and aptitude testing.
2. Interactive simulations of critical work situations for use as part of the interview process.
3. Periodic, post-hiring assessment for training focus.

Salesperson Instructions

Ron Lovell, National Agency Director for Secure Future Insurance Company (SFIC), is interested in improving his company's recruiting and selection process for sales agents. SFIC is a national company with 150 agents across the United States. Although not ranked among the top 20 insurers, SFIC is a large and successful firm listed in the *Fortune* 1000. You have met with Lovell on four previous occasions exploring problems, opportunities, and needs. During these meetings you discovered that SFIC's turnover rate among its sales agents approaches 42 percent. Compared to industry averages, that is not bad, but it does require hiring 375 new salespeople every year. SFIC's own estimate of hiring, training, and licensing costs is $7,500, for a total annual cost exceeding $2.8 million. Field experience indicates that, using PSI's computer-based system, turnover would fall to an average ranging from 15 to 20 percent, which offers considerable savings to SFIC.

You have been working up the figures for implementing the system at headquarters and in each of the 150 general offices. One-time hardware costs total $610,000. Although minimal training is required, installation and training would be priced out at $75,000 plus another $5,500 for chargeable travel expenses. Software licensing fees would total $135,000 per year. Sales tax on the hardware and software license would be computed at 6.5 percent. Finally, software maintenance fees run 15 percent of the annual licensing cost. According to the technical support department, this installation could be completed, with the full system operating in just over four months from the date of the order.

During your last call, you detailed the basics of the Interactive Employee Assessment System scaled to meet the needs of SFIC. Lovell, along with the other officers attending the presentation, liked what they saw and requested that you put together a formal proposal. On your way out of the building, Lovell mentioned that the proposal would have to be detailed enough to allow him to pass it through the capital budgeting department. This means detailing costs, projected savings, the payback period, and the installation-implementation schedule. As another positive indicator, Lovell also asked that you arrange a follow-up meeting approximately two weeks after the proposal is received. Your task is to develop a follow-up letter and written sales proposal for his immediate attention.

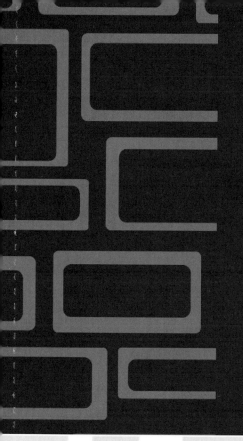

Gaining Commitment with Buying Teams

Objective

You will master the skills of working in teams and develop skills in gaining customer commitment.

INTRODUCTION

You will work in groups of three and brainstorm different methods for gaining the buyer's commitment in the following selling scenario. After reading the scenario, work in your groups to develop closes that could be applied. Use the worksheets to develop and illustrate each technique listed. Notice that the worksheets also call for you to explain why you feel this is a good technique. The examples that each group develops will form the basis for a class discussion.

National Payroll Corporation (NPC) is the leading provider of electronic payroll processing. Their services include a full menu of payroll services, including accounting and record keeping, check writing, and the calculation and filing of all city, state, and federal payroll taxes. Their benefits offered to clients include not only lower costs than companies incur doing it all in-house, but also higher levels of accuracy and on-time filings of the ever-increasing number of tax forms.

As a salesperson for National Payroll Corporation, you have been calling on Acme Mechanical for about seven months now. Tony Fiona, the chief financial officer at Acme, likes what you have to offer and states that he is in favor of outsourcing the full payroll function to NPC. In fact, they have been close to signing several times, but it seems like some crisis always pops up at the last minute and diverts everyone's attention away from your proposition.

Fiona has just called you at the office and requested that you come over to Acme this next week. He indicated that things looked pretty good right now. In fact, as a result of the crisis that left you sitting in the board room alone with an unsigned contract, the company has begun a major acquisition of one of its primary competitors. To handle all the auditing and accounting that the merger requires, Fiona needs his full staff. At the same time, annual payroll tax reports are due in about three months and will require a large percentage of his staff's time.

Fiona has presented the situation and available options to the various financial officers who would have to sign-off on the outsourcing decision. The response seemed favorable toward NPC's proposal. The only exceptions were two or three individuals who are reluctant to have an outsider handling delicate payroll information. Fiona has set the meeting up so that all these individuals can be present. As Fiona said right before he ended the phone conversation with you, "I've done everything I can to set it up for you. Now the ball is in your court. Get over here and see what you can do to tie this thing together. I have other fish to fry!"

THE EXERCISE ASSIGNMENT

With this scenario as the basis for your assumptions, use the following worksheet space to develop, explain, and illustrate with examples just how you would use different techniques to gain the commitment of the financial services buying team at Acme.

Method One:

_____

_____

_____

Method Two:

_____

_____

_____

Method Three:

_____

_____

_____

Method Four:

_____

_____

_____

Method Five:

_____

_____

_____

Method Six:

_____

_____

_____

Method Seven:

_____

_____

_____

A

ABC analysis *See* single-factor analysis.

acceleration principle Demand for goods and services in the business market that is more volatile than that of the consumer market; when demand increases (or decreases) in the consumer market, the business market reacts by accelerating the buildup (or reduction) of inventories and increasing (or decreasing) plant capacity.

account classification The process of placing existing customers and prospects into categories based on their sales potential.

account goal A salesperson's desire of selling a certain amount of product to one customer, or account.

activation questions One of the five stages of questions in the ADAPT questioning system used to "activate" the customer's interest in solving discovered problems by helping him or her gain insight into the true ramifications of the problem and to realize that what may initially seem to be of little consequence is, in fact, of significant consequence.

active listening The cognitive process of actively sensing, interpreting, evaluating, and responding to the verbal and nonverbal messages of present or potential customers.

actual states A buyer's actual state of being.

ADAPT A questioning system that uses a logic-based funneling sequence of questions, beginning with broad and generalized inquiries designed to identify and assess the buyer's situation; it is an acronym for the five stages of strategic questioning: assessment questions, discovery questions, activation questions, projection questions, and transition questions.

adaptive selling The ability of a salesperson to alter their sales messages and behaviors during a sales presentation or as they encounter different sales situations and different customers.

adding value The process of improving a product for the customer.

advertising inquiries Responses from sales leads to company advertising efforts.

AIDA An acronym for the various mental states the salesperson must lead their customers through when using mental states selling: attention, interest, desire, and action.

amiables Individuals who are high on responsiveness and low on assertiveness; they have a preference for belonging to groups and their sincere interest in other people.

analyticals Individuals who are low on responsiveness and assertiveness; they prefer gathering and analyzing facts and details before making a decision and are meticulous and disciplined in everything they do.

anecdotes and examples Verbal presentation tools; examples are brief descriptions of a specific instance used to illustrate features and benefits of a product; anecdotes are a type of example that is provided in the form of a story describing a specific incident or occurrence.

approaching the customer An act in the sales process that involves (1) securing an appointment for the sales interview and (2) covering the first few minutes of the sales call.

assertiveness The degree to which a person holds opinions about issues and attempts to dominate or control situations by directing the thoughts and actions of others.

assessment questions One of the five stages of questions in the ADAPT questioning system that do not seek conclusions but rather should address the buyer's company and operations, goals and objectives, market trends and customers, current suppliers, and even the buyer as an individual.

assessment questions Questions designed to elicit factual information about the customer's current situation to help identify problems and needs.

assumptive close A sales closing technique in which the salesperson assumes that an agreement has been reached and places the order form in front of the buyer and hands him or her a pen.

B

balance sheet or T-account commitment A selling technique in which a salesperson asks the prospect to brainstorm reasons on paper of why to buy and why not to buy.

basis of the bargain A term used when a buyer relied on the seller's statements in making a purchase decision.

benefit approach A sales approach that begins with a strong statement about a benefit that the product brings to the customer.

benefit selling A form of selling that focuses on the features and benefits of a product.

boomerang or translation A response to buyer objections in which the salesperson converts the objection into a reason the prospect should buy.

building goodwill The process of converting new customers into lifetime customers by continually adding value to the product.

business buyers' purchase process The process business buyers go through when making purchasing decisions.

business consultant A role the salesperson plays in consultative selling where he or she uses internal and external (outside the sales organization) sources to become an expert on the customer's business. This role also involves educating customers on the sales firm's products and how these products compare with competitive offerings.

business markets A market composed of firms, institutions, and governments; members of a business market acquire goods and services to use as inputs into their own manufacturing process, for use in their day-to-day operations, or for resale to their own customers.

buying centers *See* buying teams.

buying motives A need-activated drive to search for and acquire a solution to resolve a need or problem.

buying teams Teams of individuals in organizations that incorporate the expertise and multiple buying influences of people from different departments throughout the organization.

C

candor Term used by buyers to define trust; honesty of the spoken word.

canned sales presentation Sales presentations that include scripted sales calls, memorized presentations, and automated presentations.

case histories A testimonial in story or anecdotal form.

center of influence A well-known and influential person who can help a salesperson prospect and gain leads.

charts and graphs Visual aids used during sales presentations that are useful in showing trends and illustrating relationships.

check-backs *See* trial closes.

circular routing plan A territory routing plan in which the salesperson begins at the office and moves in an expanding pattern of concentric circles that spiral across the territory.

closed-end questions Questions designed to limit the customer's responses to one or two words.

cloverleaf routing plan A territory routing plan in which the salesperson works a different part of the territory and travels in a circular loop back to the starting point.

cold calling Contacting a sales lead unannounced and with little or no information about the lead.

cold canvassing Unannounced call on prospects.

collaborative involvement A way to build on buyer–salesperson relationships in which the buyer's organization and the salesperson's organization join together to improve a product.

combination sales job A sales job in which the salesperson performs multiple types of sales jobs within the framework of a single position.

commercial lead lists Lists designed to focus on virtually any type of business and/or individual; they range from simple listings of names, addresses, and phone numbers to more detailed listings with a full profile of the different entities included in the list.

commitment signals Favorable statements a buyer makes during a sales presentation that signal buyer commitment.

communication A two-way flow of information between salesperson and customer.

communication styles The verbal and nonverbal messages used by individuals when communicating with others.

company knowledge Knowledge salespeople must have about their own company's operation and policies.

company records Information about customers in a company database.

company or source objection Resistance to a product/service that results when a buyer has never heard or is not familiar with the product's company.

comparisons and analogies A comparison is a statement that points out and illustrates the similarities between two points; an analogy is a special and useful form of comparison that explains one thing in terms of another.

compatibility/likeability A salesperson's commonalities with other individuals.

compensation A response to buyer objections in which the salesperson counterbalances the objection with an offsetting benefit.

competitive depositioning A strategy of the evaluation procedures used by buyers that alters a buyer's beliefs about a competitor's offering in which a salesperson provides information to evidence a more accurate picture of the competitor's attributes.

competitor knowledge Knowledge of a competitor's strengths and weaknesses in the market.

compliment approach A sales approach that begins with complimenting a prospect.

computer-based presentations Powerful multimedia sales presentations that use a combination of computers such as laptops and hand-held computers and presentation software such as PowerPoint.

confidentiality Term used by buyers to define trust.

confirmed benefits A form of value that has been acknowledged and considered important to the buyer's situation.

connect A way to enhance follow-up with a customer in which the salesperson maintains contact with the multiple individuals in the buying organization influencing purchase decisions and manages the various touch points the customer has in the selling organization to assure consistency in communication.

consultative selling The process of helping customers reach their strategic goals by using the products, services, and expertise of the sales organization.

consumer markets A market in which consumers purchase

goods and services for their use or consumption that is highly influenced by peer group behavior, aesthetics, and personal taste.

continued affirmation An example of stimulus response selling in which a series of questions or statements furnished by the salesperson is designed to condition the prospective buyer to answering "yes" time after time, until, it is hoped, he or she will be inclined to say "yes" to the entire sales proposition.

continuous yes close A sales closing technique that uses the principle that saying yes gets to be a habit; the salesperson asks a number of questions formulated so that the prospect answers yes.

contributions Something given to better a situation or state for a buyer.

critical encounters Meetings in which the salesperson encourages the buyer to discuss tough issues especially in areas where the salesperson's organization is providing less than satisfactory performance.

customer knowledge Information about customers that is gathered over time and from very different sources that helps the salesperson determine what needs those customers have to better serve them.

customer orientation The act of salespeople placing as much emphasis on the customer's interests as their own.

customer value The customer's perception of what they get for what they have to give, for example, benefits from buying a product in exchange for money paid.

customer value proposition A statement of how the sales offering will add value to the prospect's business by meeting a need or providing an opportunity.

D

deciders Individuals within an organization who have the ultimate responsibility of determining which product or service will be purchased.

delighter attributes *See* psychological attributes.

dependability Term used by buyers to define trust; predictability of a person's actions.

depth of inquiry The extent to which the salesperson goes to ascertain the prospect's needs and decision process.

derived demand Demand in business markets that is closely associated with the demand for consumer goods.

desired states A state of being based on what the buyer desires.

detailer A salesperson in the pharmaceutical industry working at the physician level to furnish valuable information regarding the capabilities and limitations of medications in an attempt to get the physician to prescribe their product.

dichotomous questions A directive form of questioning; they ask the customer to choose from two or more options.

diffusion of innovation The process whereby new products, services, and ideas are distributed to the members of society.

direct commitment A selling technique in which the salesperson asks the customer directly to buy.

direct denial A response to buyer objections in which the salesperson tells the customer that he or she is wrong.

directories and lists Sources of locating prospects that list all the community's businesses.

discovery questions One of the five stages of questions in the ADAPT questioning system that follow up on the assessment questions; they should drill down and probe for further details needed to fully develop, clarify, and understand the nature of the buyer's problems.

disruptions Interruptions that distract the buyer's attention away from the presentation.

drivers Individuals who are low on responsiveness and high on assertiveness; they are hard and detached from relationships with others.

E

economic stimuli Something that stimulates or incites activity in the economy.

ego drive An indication of the degree of determination a person has to achieve goals and overcome obstacles in striving for success.

ego strength The degree to which a person is able to achieve an approximation of inner drives.

electronic media Computer- and technology-based tools such as laptops and hand-held computers, VCRs and DVDs, and slide and overhead projectors that help salespeople customize graphical presentations.

emotional motives A purchase situation in which there is a sense of urgency and a solution is needed quickly.

enthusiasm A strong excitement of feeling. Salespeople should have an enthusiastic attitude in a general sense and a special enthusiasm for selling.

ethics The right and wrong conduct of individuals and institutions of which they are a part.

evaluating A step in active listening in which the receiver sorts results of the interpretation stage into facts or opinions and emotions.

evaluative questions Questions that use the open- and closed-end question formats to gain confirmation and to uncover attitudes, opinions, and preferences held by the prospect.

examples and anecdotes Verbal presentation tools; examples are brief descriptions of a specific instance used to illustrate features and benefits of a product; anecdotes are a type of example that is provided in the form of a story describing a specific incident or occurrence.

expertise The ability, knowledge, and resources to meet customer expectations.

express warranty A way a salesperson can create product liabilities by giving a product warranty or guarantee that obligates the selling organization even if the salesperson does not intend to give the warranty.

expressives Individuals who are high on both responsiveness and assertiveness; they are animated and highly communicative and value building close relationships with others.

external relationships Relationships salespeople build with customers outside the working environment.

extranets A special form of intranet that is still for proprietary and restricted use but links to specific suppliers and customers to allow them controlled and secure access to the organization's network to facilitate communication and exchange.

F

FAB *See* benefit selling.

fairness Term used by buyers to define trust.

fear or emotional close A sales closing technique in which the salesperson tells a story of something bad happening if the purchase is not made.

features A quality or characteristic of a product or service that is designed to provide value to a buyer.

feel-felt-found A technique used to answer a concern a prospect or buyer might have with the sales proposal.

forestalling A response to buyer objections in which the salesperson answers the objection during the presentation before the buyer has a chance to ask it.

functional attributes The features and characteristics that are related to what the product actually does or is expected to do; its functional characteristics.

functional needs The need for a specific core task or function to be performed; the functional purpose of a specific product or service.

G

gatekeepers Members of an organization who are in the position to control the flow of information to and between vendors and other buying center members.

goals and objectives Something a salesperson sets out to accomplish.

H

high-tech sales support offices Offices set up at multiple locations where salespeople can go to access the wider range of selling technology than could be easily carried on a notebook or laptop computer.

honesty Term used by buyers to define trust.

I

ideal customer profile The characteristics of a firm's best customers or the perfect customer.

implication questions One of the four types of questions in the SPIN questioning system that follow and relate to the information flowing from problem questions; they are used to assist the buyer in thinking about the potential consequences of the problem and understanding the urgency of resolving the problem in a way that motivates him or her to seek a solution.

inbound telemarketing A source of locating prospects where the prospect calls the company using a telephone number (usually an 800 number) to get information.

indirect denial A response to buyer objections in which the salesperson takes a softer more tactful approach when correcting a prospect or customer's information.

industry knowledge Knowledge a salesperson must have about their industry's history and current situation.

influencers Individuals within an organization who guide the decision process by making recommendations and expressing preferences.

initiators Individuals within an organization who identify a need or perhaps realize that the acquisition of a product might solve a need or problem.

inside sales Nonretail salespeople who remain in their employer's place of business while dealing with customers.

interact A way to enhance follow-up with a customer in which the salesperson acts to minimize the number of critical encounters with buyers in order to encourage effective dialogue and involvement between the salesperson and buyer.

internal relationships Relationships salespeople have with other individuals in their own company.

Internet A technology tool that instantly networks the salesperson with customers, information sources, other salespeople, sales management, and others.

interpersonal communication skills Skills that include listening and questioning.

interpreting A step in active listening that addresses the question of "What meaning does the sender intend?"

intranets Networks within the organization using the Internet or commercial channels to provide direct linkages between company units and individuals.

introduction A variation of a referral where, in addition to requesting the names of prospects, the salesperson asks the prospect or customer to prepare a note or letter of introduction that can be sent to the potential customer.

introductory approach A sales approach that involves only stating your name and company name when first meeting a customer; the weakest type of sales approach.

K

know A way to enhance follow-up with a customer in which the salesperson coordinates and interprets the information gathered through buyer–seller contact and collaboration to develop insight regarding the buyer's changing situation, needs, and expectations.

knowledge needs The desire for personal development, information, and knowledge to increase thought and understanding as to how and why things happen.

L

LAARC An acronym for listen, acknowledge, assess, respond, and confirm that describes an effective process for salespeople to follow to overcome sales resistance.

leads A potential candidate that may or may not prove to be a valid prospect.

leapfrog routing plan A territory routing plan in which, beginning in one cluster, the salesperson works each of the accounts at that location and then jumps to the next cluster.

legitimate choice A selling technique in which the salesperson asks the prospect to select from two or more choices during a sales presentation.

lists and directories Sources of locating prospects that list all the community's businesses.

location The place where the sales presentation takes place.

long-term ally A role the salesperson plays in consultative selling where he or she supports the customer, even when an immediate sale is not expected.

M

major buying motives A prospect's most important concerns that have the most influence on the ultimate purchase decision.

major city routing plan A territory routing plan used when the territory is composed of a major metropolitan area and the territory is split into a series of geometric shapes reflecting each one's concentration and pattern of accounts.

market knowledge Knowledge tools salespeople must have if larger companies break their customers into distinct markets; salespeople must be familiar with these markets to specialize their sales presentations.

marketing An organizational function that creates, communicates, and delivers value to customers and manages customer relationships in ways that benefit both the organization and its stockholders.

mental states selling An approach to personal selling that assumes that the buying process for most buyers is essentially identical and that buyers can be led through certain mental states, or steps, in the buying process; also called the formula approach.

minor buying motives A prospect's least important concerns and thus secondary to major buying motives.

minor-points close A sales closing technique in which the salesperson seeks agreement on relatively minor issues associated with the full order.

misrepresentation A way a salesperson can create product liabilities by making a false claim about a product thinking it is true.

missionary salespeople Salespeople who usually work for a manufacturer but may also be found working for brokers and manufacturing representatives. Sales missionaries are expected to "spread the word" to convert noncustomers to customers.

modified rebuy decision A purchase decision that occurs when a buyer has experience in purchasing a product in the past but is interested in acquiring additional information regarding alternative products and/or suppliers.

motivation The desire to service of a salesperson to service customers each day.

multiattribute model A procedure for evaluating suppliers and products that incorporates weighted averages across desired characteristics.

must-have attributes *See* functional attributes.

N

need objection Resistance to a product/service in which a buyer says that he or she does not need the product/service.

need-payoff questions One of the four types of questions in the SPIN questioning system that are based on the implications of a problem; they are used to propose a solution and develop commitment from the buyer.

need satisfaction selling An approach to selling based on the notion that the customer is buying to satisfy a particular need or set of needs.

needs The result of a gap between buyers' desired states and their actual states.

needs gap A perceived difference between a buyer's desired state of being and his or her actual state of being.

negligence A way a salesperson can create product liability by making a claim about a product without exercising reasonable care to see that this claim is accurate.

new task decision A purchase decision that occurs when a buyer is purchasing a product or service for the first time.

noncompeting salesperson A salesperson for noncompeting products.

nonverbal clusters Groups of related expressions, gestures, and movements.

nonverbal communication The conscious and unconscious reactions, movements, and utterances that people use in addition to the words and symbols associated with language.

O

objections Anything the prospect or customer says or does to interfere with the likelihood of a sale.

observation The act of monitoring territories for potential sales.

open-end questions Questions designed to let the customer respond freely; the customer is not limited to one- or two-word answers but is encouraged to disclose personal and/or business information.

openness Term used by buyers to define trust.

order-getters Salespeople who actively seek orders, usually in a highly competitive environment.

order-takers Salespeople who specialize in maintaining existing business.

organized sales dialogue Also known as the organized sales presentation. Unlike a canned sales presentation, an organized sales dialogue has a high level of customer involvement.

organized sales presentation A sales presentation that allows a salesperson to implement appropriate sales strategies and tactics by outlining them from information gathered during previous sales calls.

outbound telemarketing A source of locating prospects where the salesperson contacts the prospect through direct mail pieces and advertising campaigns.

outsourcing The process of giving to a supplier certain activities that were previously performed by the buying organization.

overhead transparencies Still pictures copied onto acetates that are projected onto a screen with an overhead projector.

P

personal goals A salesperson's individual desired accomplishment, such as achieving a desired annual income.

personal selling Personal communication with an audience through paid personnel of an organization or its agents in such a way that the audience perceives the communicator's organization as being the source of the message.

photographs and illustrations Visual aids used during sales presentations that provide the buyer with a realistic portrayal of the product or service.

pioneers Salespeople who are constantly involved with either new products, new customers, or both. Their task requires creative selling and the ability to counter the resistance to change that will likely be present in prospective customers.

portfolio analysis A method for analyzing accounts that allows two factors to be considered simultaneously.

positioning and seating arrangements The placement, whether sitting or standing, of the salesperson(s) and prospective buyer(s) during a sales presentation.

potential benefits A general form of value that is assumed to be of importance by the salesperson but not yet acknowledged as such by the buyer.

predictability Term used by buyers to define trust.

presell A selling process in which salespeople present their product/service to individual buyers or sub-groups of buyers before a major sales presentation to the entire group.

presentation A process in which the salesperson expands on the rapport, knowledge, and understanding established in the preceding portions of the sales process and during previous sales calls; the salesperson presents a solution to the buyer's needs, nurtures the buyer's perceived value of the sales offering as a unique solution for the individual buyer, and confirms the buyer's understanding of and interest in obtaining the benefits offered by the salesperson's solution.

presentation pace The speed with which the salesperson intends to move through the sales presentation.

presentation scope The selection of benefits and terms of sale to be included in the sales presentation.

price knowledge Knowledge tools salespeople must have about pricing policies in order to quote prices and offer discounts on products.

price objection Resistance to a product/service based on the price of the product being too high for the buyer.

printed materials Visual aids used during sales presentations that include brochures, pamphlets, catalogs, articles, reprints, reports, testimonial letters, and guarantees.

probing questions Questions designed to penetrate below generalized or superficial information to elicit more articulate and precise details for use in needs discovery and solution identification.

problem questions One of the four types of questions in the SPIN questioning system that follow the more general situation questions to further probe for specific difficulties, developing problems and areas of

dissatisfaction that might be positively addressed by the salesperson's proposed sales offering.

problem-solving selling An extension of need satisfaction selling that goes beyond identifying needs to developing alternative solutions for satisfying these needs.

product approach A sales approach that involves bringing the actual product or literature about the product to the sales meeting, maximizing the use of a prospect's senses.

product demonstrations and models A visual aid that uses the actual product or model of the product during a sales presentation to show how the product works or how the product can benefit a buyer.

product knowledge Detailed information on the manufacture of a product and knowing whether the company has up-to-date production methods.

product or service objection Resistance to a product/service in which a buyer does not like the way the product/service looks or feels.

projection questions One of the five stages of questions in the ADAPT questioning system used to encourage and facilitate the buyer in "projecting" what it would be like without the problems that have been previously "discovered" and "activated."

promotion knowledge Knowledge tools salespeople must have to explain promotional programs their firms have.

proof providers Claims of benefits and value produced and provided to the buyer during a sales presentation that have been backed up with evidence to highlight their believability.

prospecting The first step in the selling process; a series of sequential activities designed to identify, qualify, and prioritize organizations and individuals that have the need for and potential to purchase the salesperson's market offering of products and services.

prospects Qualified strong candidates for making a sale.

proxemics The personal distance that individuals prefer to keep between themselves and other individuals; an important element of nonverbal communication.

psychological attributes The features and characteristics that are related to how things are carried out and done between the buyer and seller; the augmented features and characteristics included in the total market offering that go beyond buyer expectations and have a significant positive impact on customer satisfaction.

psychological needs The desire for feelings of assurance and risk reduction, as well as positive emotions and feelings such as success, joy, excitement, and stimulation.

purchasers Individuals within an organization who have the responsibility of negotiating final terms of purchase with suppliers and executing the actual purchase or acquisition.

Q

qualifying a lead The act performed by salespeople of searching out, collecting, and analyzing information to determine the likelihood of the lead being a good candidate for making a sale.

question approach A sales approach that begins by describing an interesting characteristic about the product and then following it up with a question.

questioning or assessing A response to buyer objections in which the salesperson asks the buyer assessment questions to gain a better understanding of what they are objecting to.

R

rational buying motives Typically relate to the economics of the situation, including cost, profitability, quality, services offered, and the total value of the seller's offering as perceived by the customer.

reactive questions Questions that refer to or directly result from information previously provided by the other party.

referral A name of a company or person given to the salesperson as a lead by customer or even a prospect who did not buy at this time.

referral approach A sales approach that begins by citing the name of a satisfied customer or friend of the prospect.

relate A way to enhance follow-up with a customer in which the salesperson applies relevant understanding and insight to create value-added interactions and generate relationships between the salesperson and buyer.

relational sales communication A two-way and naturally collaborative interaction that allows buyers and sellers alike to develop a better understanding of the need situation and work together to generate the best response for solving the customer's needs.

reliability Term used by buyers to define trust.

requests for proposals (RFPs) A form developed by firms and distributed to qualified potential suppliers that helps suppliers develop and submit proposals to provide products as specified by the firm.

resilience The ability of a salesperson to get knocked down several times a day by a customer's verbal assault and get right back up with a smile and ask for more.

resistance Anything the prospect or customer says or does to interfere with the likelihood of a sale.

responding A step in active listening that is expected and required and that provides feedback to the other party, emphasizes understanding, encourages further elaboration, and can serve as a beginning point for the receiver to transition into the role of sender for the next message set.

response-checks *See* trial closes.

responsiveness The level of feelings and sociability an individual openly displays.

revenue producers Something that brings in revenue or income to a firm or company.

S

sales call goal A salesperson's desire of selling a certain amount of product per each sales call.

sales call objective The outcome of a single sales call that is sought by the salesperson. Each sales call should be guided by at least one sales call objective that requires customer action such as making a purchase or agreeing to a next step in the buying process.

sales call setting The time and place in which a sales call takes place.

sales dialogue business conversations between buyers and sellers that occur as salespeople attempt to initiate, develop, and enhance customer relationships. Sales dialogue should be customer-focused and have a clear purpose.

sales funnel or pipeline A representation of the trust-based sales process vertically in the form of a funnel.

sales lead Organizations or individuals who might possibly purchase the product or service offered by a salesperson.

sales planning The process of scheduling activities that can be used as a map for achieving objectives.

sales presentation checklist A checklist sales forces can use to be sure that all pertinent content areas are covered with each prospect.

sales presentation planning A plan that guides the salesperson through the sales presentation.

sales process A series of interrelated steps beginning with locating qualified prospective customers. From there, the salesperson plans the sales presentation, makes an appointment to see the customer, completes the sale, and performs postsale activities.

sales professionalism A customer-oriented approach that uses truthful, nonmanipulative tactics to satisfy the long-term needs of both the customer and the selling firm.

sales resistance Buyer's objections to a product or service during a sales presentation.

sales support personnel A firm's personnel whose primary responsibility is dissemination of information and performance of other activities designed to stimulate sales.

security Term used by buyers to define trust.

self-efficacy The strong belief that success will occur in the job.

self-leadership The process of doing the right things and doing them well.

SELL Sequence A presentation model that guides salespeople through the successive presentation of features and benefits in gaining the prospective buyer's confirmation of the benefits.

selling automation and technology The use of technology to perform any sales related activity.

selling point A combination of a specific feature and its meaningful benefit statement.

selling technology and automation Necessary tools that spur and create creativity and innovation, streamline all aspects of the selling process, generate new and improved selling opportunities, facilitate cross-functional teaming and intraorganizational communication, and enhance communication and follow-up with customers.

seminars A presentation given by salespeople to generate leads and provide information to prospective customers who are invited to the seminar by direct mail, word of mouth, or advertising on local television or radio.

sensing A step in active listening that involves hearing and seeing the verbal and nonverbal components of the message being sent.

serious listening A form of listening that is associated with events or topics in which it is important to sort through, interpret, understand, and respond to received messages.

service issues Concerns of the buyer that should be addressed by the salesperson.

service motivation A strong desire to provide service to the customer. Service motivation comes from desiring the approval of others.

service strategy A plan in which a salesperson identifies his or her business and customers and what the customers want and what is important to them.

SIER A model that depicts active listening as a hierarchical, four-step sequence of sensing, interpreting, evaluating, and responding.

single-factor analysis A method for analyzing accounts that is based on one single factor, typically the level of sales potential.

situation questions One of the four types of questions in the SPIN questioning system used early in the sales call that provides salespeople with leads to fully develop the buyer's needs and expectations.

situational needs The specific needs that are contingent on, and often a result of, conditions related to the specific environment, time, and place.

slides Still pictures that are projected onto a screen to illustrate a product's benefits during a sales presentation.

social listening An informal mode of listening that can be associated with day-to-day conversation and entertainment.

social needs The need for acceptance from and association with others; a desire to belong to some reference group.

SPES Sequence An acronym salespeople can follow during a sales presentation to remind them of what features are relevant and what benefits are meaningful to the prospective buyer in terms of value to be realized.

SPIN A questioning system that sequences four types of questions designed to uncover a buyer's current situation and inherent problems, enhance the buyer's understanding of the consequences and implications of those problems, and lead to

the proposed solution; it is an acronym for the four types of questions making up the multiple choice sequence: situation questions, problem questions, implication questions, and need-payoff questions.

standing-room only close A sales closing technique in which the salesperson puts a time limit on the client in an attempt to hurry the decision to close.

statistics Facts that lend believability to claims of value and benefit.

stimulus response selling An approach to selling where the key idea is that various stimuli can elicit predictable responses from customers. Salespeople furnish the stimuli from a repertoire of words and actions designed to produce the desired response.

straight-line routing plan A territory routing plan in which salespeople start from their offices and make calls in one direction until they reach the end of the territory.

straight rebuy decision A purchase decision resulting from a long-term purchase agreement in which needs have been predetermined with the corresponding specifications, pricing, and shipping requirements already established by a blanket purchase order or annual purchase agreement.

strategic orchestrator A role the salesperson plays in consultative selling where he or she arranges the use of the sales organization's resources in an effort to satisfy the customer.

strategic prospecting plan A salesperson's plan for generating qualified prospects.

style flexing A process in which a salesperson adjusts his or her communication style to minimize possible negative effects stemming from mismatched communication styles and to better match that of the buyer's style.

success story commitment A selling technique in which a salesperson relates how one of his or her customers had a problem similar to the prospect's and solved it by using the salesperson's product.

summary commitment A selling technique in which the salesperson summarizes all the major benefits the buyer has confirmed over the course of the sales calls.

supply chain management The strategic coordination and integration of purchasing with other functions within the buying organization as well as external organizations including customers, customers' customers, suppliers, and suppliers' suppliers.

survey approach A sales approach that uses gathering information as an attention-getting statement.

T

T-account or balance sheet commitment A selling technique in which a salesperson asks the prospect to brainstorm reasons on paper of why to buy and why not to buy.

tactical questions Questions used to shift or redirect the topic of discussion when the discussion gets off course or when a line of questioning proves to be of little interest or value.

target price The price buyers determine for their final products through information gathered from researching the marketplace.

teamwork skills Skills salespeople must learn to build internal partnerships that translate into increased sales and organizational performance.

technical support salespeople Technical specialist who may assist in design and specification processes, installation of equipment, training of the customer's employees, and follow-up service of a technical nature.

technology knowledge Knowledge tools salespeople must have about the latest technology.

territory analysis The process of surveying an area to determine customers and prospects who are most likely to buy.

territory goal A salesperson's desire of selling a certain amount of product within an area, or territory.

testimonials Proof providers that are in the form of statements from satisfied users of the selling organization's products and services.

third-party reinforcement A response to buyer objections in which the salesperson uses the opinion or data from a third-party source to help overcome the objection and reinforce the salesperson's points.

time objection Resistance to a product/service in which a buyer puts off the decision to buy until a later date.

tracking system Part of the prospecting plan that records comprehensive information about the prospect, traces the prospecting methods used, and chronologically archives outcomes from any contacts with the prospect.

trade shows Events where companies purchase booth space and set up stands that clearly identify each company and its offerings and that are staffed with salespeople who demonstrate the products and answer questions.

transition questions One of the five stages of questions in the ADAPT questioning system used to smooth the transition from needs discovery into the presentation and demonstration of the proposed solution's features, advantages, and benefits.

translation or boomerang A response to buyer objections in which the salesperson converts the objection into a reason the prospect should buy.

trial closes Confirmatory questions in search of simple "yes" or "no" responses from the buyer.

trust The extent of the buyer's confidence that he or she can rely on the salesperson's integrity.

trust-based professional selling A form of personal selling that focuses primarily on interpersonal communication between buyers and sellers with the goal of establishing relationships.

two-factor model of evaluation A postpurchase evaluation process used by buyers that evaluates a product purchase using two characteristics of the product: functional attributes and psychological attributes.

two-way communication Interactive communication between salesperson and customer.

U

users Individuals within an organization who will actually use the product being purchased.

V

value proposition A confirmed benefit that is provided by the proposed solution.

verbal support A presentation tool based on the voice that holds the prospective buyer's attention, builds interest, and increases both understanding and retention of information.

video Media such as VHS tapes and DVD disks used during sales presentations.

visual aids Tools such as flip charts and video demonstrations that supplement the spoken word during a sales presentation.

voice characteristics A verbal presentation tool involving the salesperson's voice quality that can bring excitement and drama to the sales presentation.

W

Web World Wide Web

written sales proposals A complete self-contained sales presentation on paper, often accompanied by other verbal sales presentations before or after the proposal is delivered.

Module 1

[1]Adapted from the American Marketing Association definition of marketing or shown at www.marketing power.com/content4620.php, October 5, 2006.

[2]Marjorie J. Caballero, Roger A. Dickinson, and Dabney Townsend, "Aristotle and Personal Selling," *Journal of Personal Selling & Sales Management* 4 (May 1984): 13.

[3]William T. Kelley, "The Development of Early Thought in Marketing," in *Salesmanship: Selected Readings,* ed. John M. Rathmell (Homewood, IL: Irwin, 1969): 3.

[4]Thomas L. Powers, Warren S. Martin, Hugh Rushing, and Scott Daniels, "Selling before 1900: A Historical Perspective," *Journal of Personal Selling & Sales Management* 7 (November 1987): 5. For additional review of personal selling from 1600 to the present era, see Robert Desman and Terry E. Powell, "Personal Selling: Chicken or Egg," in *Proceedings,* 13th Annual Conference of the Academy of Marketing Science, ed. Jon M. Hawes (Orlando, FL: 1989).

[5]Michael Bell, *The Salesman in the Field* (Geneva: International Labour Office, 1980): 1.

[6]Stanley C. Hollander, "Anti-Salesman Ordinances of the Mid-19th Century," in *Salesmanship: Selected Readings,* ed. John M. Rathmell (Homewood, IL: Irwin, 1969): 9.

[7]Ibid., 10.

[8]Jon M. Hawes, "Leaders in Selling and Sales Management," *Journal of Personal Selling & Sales Management* 5 (November 1985): 60.

[9]Charles W. Hoyt, *Scientific Sales Management* (New Haven, CT: George W. Woolson and Co., 1913): 3.

[10]Ibid., 4.

[11]Edward C. Bursk, "Low-Pressure Selling," *Harvard Business Review* 25 (Winter 1947): 227.

[12]Jon M. Hawes, Anne K. Rich, and Scott Widmier, "Assessing the Development of the Sales Profession," *Journal of Personal Selling & Sales Management* 24 (Winter 2004): 27–38.

[13]Synthesized from Thomas N. Ingram, "Relationship Selling: Moving from Rhetoric to Reality," *Mid-American Journal of Business* 11 (Spring 1996): 5; David W. Cravens, Emin Babakus, Ken Grant, Thomas N. Ingram, and Raymond W. LaForge, "Removing Salesforce Performance Hurdles," *Journal of Business and Industrial Marketing* 9, no. 3 (1994): 19; Eli Jones, Steven P. Brown, Andris A. Zoltners, and Barton A. Weitz, "The Changing Environment of Selling and Sales Management," *Journal of Personal Selling & Sales Management* 25 (Spring 2005): 105–111.

[14]"America's 500 Largest Sales Forces," *Selling Power* (October 2005): 57–82.

[15]Laura Heller, "Customer-Centric Model Future Focus at Best Buy," *DSN Retailing Today* (April 25, 2005): 22.

[16]To learn more about what customers expect from salespeople, see Tom Atkinson and Ron Koprowski, "Sales Reps' Biggest Mistakes," *Harvard Business Review* 84 (July–August 2006): 20; Philip Kreindler and Gopal Rajguru, "What B2B Customers Really Expect," *Harvard Business Review* 84 (July–August 2006): 22–24.

[17]Robert F. Gwinner, "Base Theory in the Formulation of Sales Strategy," *MSU Business Topics* (Autumn 1968): 37.

[18]Adapted from D. Forbes Ley, *The Best Seller* (Newport Beach, CA: Sales Success Press, 1986).

[19]Gina Rollins, "This Thing Will Sell Itself!" *Selling Power* (June 2004): 69–71.

[20]This section on consultative selling is based on Kevin J. Corcoran, Laura K. Petersen, Daniel B. Baitch, and Mark F. Barrett, *High Performance Sales Organizations* (Chicago: Irwin, 1995): 44.

[21]Mark Marone and Seleste Lunsford, *Strategies that Win Sales* (Chicago, IL: Dearborn Trade Publishing, 2005): 83.

[22]Jon M. Hawes, Kenneth E. Mast, and John E. Swan, "Trust Earning Perceptions of Sellers and Buyers," *Journal of Personal Selling & Sales Management* 9 (Spring 1989): 1.

[23]Interview by the authors with Blake Conrad, sales representative with Centurion Specialty Care.

Appendix 1

[1]"Numeric Change in Employment, 2004–2014," (Washington, D.C.: U.S. Department of Labor, Bureau of Labor Statistics), http://www.data.bls.gov.

[2]*Occupational Outlook Handbook, 2006–07, Bulletin 2600* (Washington, D.C.: U.S. Department of Labor, Bureau of Labor Statistics), http://www.bls.gov.

[3]*Occupational Outlook Handbook, 2006–07, Bulletin 2000* (Washington, D.C.: U.S. Department of Labor, Bureau of Labor Statistics), http://www.bls.gov.

[4]Thomas N. Ingram and Charles H. Schwepker Jr., "Perceptions of Salespeople: Implications for Sales Managers and Sales Trainers," *Journal of Marketing Management* 2 (Fall/Winter 1992–1993): 1.

[5]Katherine B. Hartman, "Television and Movie Representations of Salespeople: Beyond Willie Loman," *Journal of Personal Selling & Sales Management* 26 (Summer 2006): 283–292.

[6]Thomas N. Ingram, "Relationship Selling: Moving from Rhetoric to Reality," *Mid-American Journal of Business* 11 (Spring 1996): 5.

[7]"Here's to the Winners," *Sales & Marketing Management* (July 1999): 66.

[8]Michael J. Swenson, William R. Swinyard, Frederick W. Langrehr, and Scott M. Smith, "The Appeal of Personal Selling as a Career: A Decade Later," *Journal of Personal Selling & Sales Management* 13 (Winter 1993): 51.

[9]Emin Babakus, David W. Cravens, Ken Grant, Thomas N. Ingram, and Raymond W. LaForge, "Removing Salesforce Performance Hurdles," *Journal of Business and Industrial Marketing* 9, no. 3 (1994): 19.

[10]See Herbert M. Greenberg and Jeanne Greenberg, *What It Takes to Succeed in Sales* (Homewood, IL: Dow-Jones Irwin, 1990).

[11]James M. Comer and Alan J. Dubinsky, *Managing the Successful Sales Force* (Lexington, MA: D.C. Heath and Co., 1985): 5; Steven P. Brown, Thomas W. Leigh, and J. Martin Haygood, "Salesperson Performance and Job Attitudes," in *The Marketing Manager's Handbook,* 3rd ed., eds. Sidney J. Levy, George R. Frerichs, and Howard L. Gordon (Chicago: The Dartnell Corporation, 1994): 107.

[12]Babakus et al., "Removing Salesforce Performance Hurdles," 19; Greg W. Marshall, Daniel J. Goebel, and William C. Moncrief, "Hiring for Success at the Buyer-Seller Interface," *Journal of Business Research* 56 (April 2003): 247–255.

[13]Rosann L. Spiro and Barton A. Weitz, "Adaptive Selling: Conceptualization, Measurement, and Nomological Validity," *Journal of Marketing Research* 27 (February 1990): 61.

[14]Marshall et al., "Hiring for Success," 251.

[15]Kevin J. Corcoran, Laura K. Petersen, Daniel B. Baitch, and Mark F. Barrett, *High Performance Sales Organizations* (Chicago: Irwin Professional Publishing, 1995): 77.

[16]Marshall et al., "Hiring for Success," 251.

[17]Arun Sharma and Rajnandini Pillai, "Customers' Decision-Making Styles and Their Preference for Sales Strategies: Conceptual Examination and an Empirical Study," *Journal of Personal Selling & Sales Management* 16 (Winter 1996): 21.

[18]Victoria D. Bush, Gregory M. Rose, Faye Gilbert, and Thomas N. Ingram, "Managing Culturally Diverse Buyer–Seller Relationships: The Role of Intercultural Disposition and Adaptive Selling Behavior in Developing Intercultural Communication Competence," *Journal of the Academy of Marketing Science* 29, 4 (Fall 2001): 391–404.

[19]Gabriel R. Gonzalez, K. Douglas Hoffman, and Thomas N. Ingram, "Improving Relationship Selling Through Failure Analysis and Recovery Efforts: A Framework and Call to Action," *Journal of Personal Selling & Sales Management* 25 (Winter 2005): 57–66.

Module 2

[1]Sherry Kilgus, "Building Trust into High Level Alliances," *NAMA Journal* 34 (Winter 1998).

[2]*Ibid.*

[3]John E. Swan and Johannah Jones Nolan, "Gaining Customer Trust: A Conceptual Guide for the Salesperson," *Journal of Personal Selling & Sales Management* V, 2 (November 1985): 39.

[4]Robert F. Dwyer, Paul H. Schurr, and Sejo Oh, "Developing Buyer–Seller Relationships," *Journal of Marketing* 51 (April 1987): 11.

[5]This was the concluding point of the symposium on trust held by the National Account Management Association at Wake Forest University, September 24–26, 1997.

[6]Interview with Missy Rust, GlaxoSmithKline, February 13, 2000.

[7]Robert Petersen, "Consultative Selling: A Qualitative Look at the Salesperson Credibility Requirements," *AMA Educator Proceeding Enhancing Knowledge Development in Marketing* 8 (1997): 224.

[8]*Ibid.*

[9]From "Balancing Act: By Learning How to Balance Two Basic Drives—The Need to Close with the Need to Develop Relationships—Every Salesperson Can Become a Star" by L. B. Gschwandtner and Gerhard Gschwandtner from *Selling Power* (June 1996): 24. Reprinted with permission from *Selling Power* magazine.

[10]Interview with Doug Lingo, Hoechst Marion Roussel Pharmaceutical, May 23, 1997.

[11]Interview with Darrell Beaty, Ontario Systems Corporation, February 29, 2000.

[12]American Marketing Association's Code of Ethics. Reprinted by permission of American Marketing Association.

[13]Reprinted by permission of Sales & Marketing Executives International, Inc. (http://www.smei.org). "SMEI Certified Professional Salesperson" and "SCPS" are registered trademarks of Sales & Marketing Executives International, Inc.

[14]*Ibid.*

[15]Thomas Ingram, Scott Inks, and Lee Mabie, *Sales and Marketing Executive Certification Study Guide* (1994).

[16]Interview with John Huff, Shering-Plough, November 15, 2004.

[17]SMEI Accreditation Institute, The University of Memphis.

Module 3

[1]Thull, Jeff, *Mastering the Complex Sale* (Hoboken, NJ: John Wiley & Sons, Inc.)

[2]Adapted from Jagdish N. Sheth, Bahwari Mittal, and Bruce I. Newman, *Customer Behavior: Consumer Behavior and Beyond* (Fort Worth, TX: The Dryden Press, 1999); Jagdish N. Sheth, Bruce I. Newman, and Barbara L. Gross, *Consumption Values and Market Choice: Theory and Application* (Cincinnati, OH: South-Western Publishing Co., 1991).

[3]Bixby Cooper, Cornelia Drodge, and Patricia Daughtery, "How Buyers and Operations Personnel Evaluate Service," *Industrial Marketing Management* (February 1991): 81–85.

[4]Adapted from Michael A. Humphreys and Michael R. Williams, "Exploring the Relative Effects of Salesperson Interpersonal Process Attributes and Technical Product Attributes on Customer Satisfaction," *Journal of Personal Selling & Sales Management* 16 (Summer 1996): 47–58; Michael A. Humphreys, Michael R. Williams, and Ronald L. Meier, "Leveraging the Total Market Offering in the Agile Enterprise," *ASQ Quality Management Journal* 5 (1997): 60–74.

[5]D. W. Merrill and R. H. Reid, *Personal Styles and Effective Performance* (Radnor, PA: Chilton Book Company, 1981).

[6]Reprinted by permission of Growmark, Inc.

[7]Wesley J. Johnston and Thomas V. Bonoma, "The Buying Center: Structure and Interaction Patterns," *Journal of Marketing* (Summer 1981): 143–156.

[8]Jakki Mohr and John R. Nevin, "Communication Strategies in Marketing Channels: A Theoretical Perspective," *Journal of Marketing* (October 1990): 36–51.

[9]Rivchin, Jessica, "Staying Productive in a Mobile World," *Mobile Enterprise,* July 19, 2006. http://www.mobileenterprisemag.com/mobilizer/071906 leadsfory.shtml (accessed July 19, 2006).

[10]Merrill and Reid, *Personal Styles and Effective Performance;* and G. L. Manning and B. L. Reece, *Selling Today: Building Quality Partnerships* (Upper Saddle River, NJ: Prentice Hall, 2001).

Module 4

[1]Mark Shonka and Dan Kosch, *Beyond Selling Value* (Chicago IL: Dearborn Trade Publishing, 2002).

[2]S. D. Morgan, *Selling with Integrity: Reinventing Sales Through Collaboration, Respect, and Serving* (San Francisco, CA: Berrett-Koehler Publishers, Inc., 1997).

[3]R. L. Jolles, *Customer Centered Selling* (New York: The Free Press, 1998).

[4]Ibid.

[5]Neil Rackham, *Spin Selling* (New York: McGraw Hill, 1998).

[6]Thomas Ingram, Tubs Scott, and Lee Mabie, *Certification Study Guide* (New York: Sales and Marketing Executives International, 1994): 44–46.

[7]Jerry Acuff and Wally Wood, *The Relationship Edge in Business* (Hoboker NJ: John Wiley & Sons, Inc., 2004): 149–150; Geoffrey James, "How to Build Customer Relationships—An Interview with Jerry Acuff," *Selling Power* (March 2006): 43–46.

[8]T. N. Ingram, C. Schwepker Jr., and D. Huston, "Why Salespeople Fail," *Industrial Marketing Management* 21 (1992): 225–230.

[9]R. P. Ramsey and R. S. Sohi, "Listening to Your Customers: The Impact of Perceived Salesperson Listening Behavior on Relationship Outcomes," *Journal of the Academy of Marketing Science* 25 (Spring 1997): 127–137.

[10]L. Barker, *Listening Behavior* (Englewood Cliffs, NJ: Prentice Hall, 1971): 30–32.

[11]Castleberry and Shepherd, "Effective Interpersonal Listening and Personal Selling."

[12]From *Effective Listening: Key to Your Success* by L. K. Steil, L. L. Barker, and K. W. Watson: 21. Reprinted by permission of The McGraw-Hill Companies.

[13]*Ibid.*; Ramsey and Sohi, "Listening to Your Customers."

[14]*Ibid.*, 72–73.

[15]J. C. Mowen and M. Minor, *Consumer Behavior* (New York: Macmillan Publishing Co., 1997).

[16]G. P. Thomas, "The Influence of Processing Conversational Information on Inference, Argument Elaboration, and Memory," *Journal of Consumer Research* 19 (June 1992): 83–92.

[17]R. A. Avila, T. N. Ingram, R. W. LaForge, and M. R. Williams, *The Professional Selling Skills Workbook* (Fort Worth, TX: The Dryden Press, 1996): 83.

[18]R. A. Peterson, M. P. Cannito, and S. P. Brown, "An Exploratory Investigation of Voice Characteristics and Selling Effectiveness," *Journal of Personal Selling & Sales Management* 15 (Winter 1995): 1–15.

[19]Ibid.

[20]Adapted from R. M. Rozelle, D. Druckman, and J. C. Baxter, "Nonverbal Communication," in *A Handbook of Communication Skills*, ed. O. Hargie (London: Croom and Helm, 1986): 59–94; T. Alessandra and R. Barrera, *Collaborative Selling* (New York: John Wiley & Sons, Inc., 1993): 121–122.

[21]D. Bonet, *The Business of Listening: A Practical Guide to Effective Listening* (Menlo Park, CA: Crisp Publications, 1988): 30–31.

Module 5

[1]Author: Interview with Gwen Tranguillo, Hershey Chocolate, U.S.A.

[2]Author: Interview with Thomas Avila, Davis and Davis.

[3]Author: Interview with Mark Thomas, United Insurance Agency.

[4]Author: Interview with Kristen Solik, Walker Group.

Module 6

[1]Geoffrey James, "Tom Sant Demystifies the Mystery of Effective Proposals", *Selling Power* (June, 2004): 27–30.

[2]J. Conlin, "The Write Stuff, "*Sales & Marketing Management* (January 1998): 71–75.

[3]From "Quality Selling through Quality Proposals, A Guide to Writing Winning Sales Proposals," le by R. F. Kantin and M. W. Hardwick. Copyright © 1994. Reprinted with permission of South-Western, a division of Thomson Learning: http://www.thomsonrights.com. Fax 800-730-2215.

[4]Adapted from A. C. Lowander, "How to Write Good (Uh, We Mean Well)," in "The Write Stuff," *Sales & Marketing Management* (January 1998): 73.

[5]For more discussion of customer value propositions, see James C. Anderson, James A. Narus, and Wouter van Rossum, "Customer Value Propositions in Business Markets," *Harvard Business Review* (March 2006): 91–99.

[6]Thomas N. Ingram, Michael D. Hartline, and Charles H. Schwepker Jr., "Gatekeeper Perceptions: Implications for Improving Sales Ethics and Professionalism," *Proceedings of the Academy of Marketing Science* (1992): 328.

Module 7

[1]Adapted from Brian Tracy, *Advanced Selling Strategies* (New York: Simon & Schuster, 1995): 302.

[2]Author: Interview with Jamie Howard, August 1, 2004.

[3]Author: Interview with David Jacoby.

[4]Jeffrey Jacobi, "Voice Power," *Selling Power* (October 2000): 66.

[5]From "Missing the Point" by Mark McMaster from *Sales & Marketing Management* (September 2002): 23–24. Reprinted by permission of Reprint Management Services.

[6]Adapted from Mary Ann Oberhaus, Sharon Ratliffe, and Vernon Stauble, *Professional Selling: A Relationship Approach* (Fort Worth, TX: The Dryden Press, 1995): 410–412.

Module 8

[1]Marc Deiner, "Don't Know When to Cut Your Losses and Leave the Negotiating Table? Look for these Telltale Signs," *Entrepreneur Magazine* (August 2003).

[2]Brad Huisken, "Saving the Sale: Objections, Rejections and Getting to Yes," *JCK*, (January 2003): 62–63.

[3]Tom Reilly, "Why Do You Cut Prices?" *Industrial Distribution* (June 2003): 72.

[4]Robert Menard, "'Cost' Is About More Than the Price," *Selling* (July 2003): 9.

[5]Salespeople can forestall known concerns, but shouldn't bring up issues that aren't even a problem with a particular prospect. Thus, the need for good precall information gathering becomes obvious. See "Think Like a Consumer to Make Buying From a Cinch," *Selling* (November 2004): 8.

[6]Mark Borkowski, "How to Succeed in Closing Deals, without Closing," *Canadian Electronics* 19 (May 2004): 6.

[7]Neil Rackham, *Spin Selling* (New York: McGraw-Hill, 1988): 19–51.

[8]Joan Leotta, "Effortless Closing," *Selling Power* (October 2001): 28–31.

[9]Susan Del Vecchio, James Zemanek, Roger McIntyre, and Reid Claxton, "Updating the Adaptive Selling Behaviors: Tactics to Keep and Tactics to Discard," *Journal of Marketing Management* 20 (2004): 859–875.

Module 9

[1]Deloitte & Touche Survey, *Selling Power* (October 2001): 17.

[2]John Tashek, "How to Avoid a CRM Failure," *eWeek* 18:40 (October 15, 2001): 31.

[3]*Purchasing* (November 27, 1997): 65.

[4]Interview with John Haack, Saint-Gobain Containers, April 19, 2000.

[5]Ontario Systems.

[6]Marketing, Inc., in *Customer Relationship Management: Transforming Transactions into Relationships* (2000), NCR.

[7]NCDM, in *Customer Relationship Management: Transforming Transactions into Relationships* (2000), NCR.

[8]Yankee Research, in *Customer Relationships Management: Transforming into Relationships* (2000), NCR.

[9]Frederick F. Reichheld, *The Loyalty Effect* (Boston: Harvard Business School Press, 1998).

[10]Denise D. Jackson, Director of Marketing Operations, Marriott Worldwide, "All-time SalesLogix Sales Leaders," *Sales & Marketing Managemets* (March 2000): 29.

[11]The Forum Corporation, "Why Do Customers Stop Buying?" *Sales & Marketing Management,* (January 1998): 14.

[12]Chris Taylor, "The Art of the Winback," *Sales & Marketing Management* 157 (April 2005): 30–34.

[13]"The Best Offense Is a Great Defense," *Personal Selling Power* (September 1994): 56.

[14]"Consistent Success in an Inconsistent World: Solid Customer Relationships Are the Key," *Selling Power* (May 1996): 28.

[15]"At Your Customer's Service: The True Test of a Salesperson's Value Comes after the Sale," *Selling Power* (May 1996): 58.

Module 10

[1]S. R. Covey, *The 7 Habits of Highly Effective People,* (New York: Simon & Schuster, 2004).

[2]T. Ingram, R. W. LaForge, R. Avila, C. H. Schwepker Jr., and M. Williams, *Sales Management: Analysis and Decision Making*, 4th ed. (Fort Worth, TX: The Dryden Press, 2001). Copyright © 2001. Reprinted with permission of South-Western, a division of Thomson Learning: http://www.thomsonrights.com. Fax 800-730-2215.

[3]B. Kimball, *AMA Handbook for Professional Selling* (Chicago: American Marketing Association; Lincolnwood, IL: NTC Business Books, 1994).

[4]W. Ferguson, "A New Method for Routing Salespersons," *Industrial Marketing Management* (April 1980): 171–178; "Planning a Road Trip?" *An Executive Guide to Sales and Marketing Technology,* a supplement to *Sales & Marketing Management* (June 1996): 39; E. Strout, "Charting a Course," *Sales & Marketing Management* (August 1999): 46–53.

[5]For a good discussion of selling technology, see D. Peppers and M. Rogers, "Marketing's New Direction: How Campaigns Are Becoming Faster and More Precise through Automation," *Sales & Marketing Management* (March 1999): 48–54.

[6]For a comprehensive and comparative guide to sales and marketing automation systems, technology, and software, see http://www.salesandmarketing.com/more.

[7]E. Babakus, D. W. Cravens, K. Grant, T. N. Ingram, and R. W. LaForge, "Removing Salesforce Performance Hurdles," *Journal of Business and Industrial Marketing* 9, 3 (1994): 19–29.

[8]J. Attaway, M. Williams, and M. Griffin, *The Rims-QIC Quality Scorecard* (Nashville, TN: The Quality Insurance Congress, 1998, 1999).

[9]James Champy, "Selling to Tomorrow's Customer," *Sales & Marketing Management* (March 1999): 28.

[10]Excerpt from *The 7 Habits of Highly Effective People,* © 2004 Stephen R. Covey. The Time Management Matrix phrase and model are trademarks of Franklin Covey Co., http://www.franklincovey.com. Used with permission. All rights reserved.

[11]Covey, *The 7 Habits of Highly Effective People.*